SOVIET POLICY
IN AFRICA

SOVIET POLICY IN AFRICA

From Lenin to Brezhnev

O. IGHO NATUFE

iUniverse, Inc.
Bloomington

Soviet Policy in Africa
From Lenin to Brezhnev

iUniverse books may be ordered through booksellers or by contacting:

iUniverse
1663 Liberty Drive
Bloomington, IN 47403
www.iuniverse.com
1-800-Authors (1-800-288-4677)

ISBN: 978-1-4620-1649-5 (sc)
ISBN: 978-1-4620-1647-1 (hc)
ISBN: 978-1-4620-1648-8 (ebk)

Library of Congress Control Number: 2011919781

Printed in the United States of America

iUniverse rev. date: 11/02/2011

CONTENTS

Dedicated to my sons,
Eyituoyo and Onome, for they will understand

ACKNOWLEDGMENTS

Many people have helped me in this book in so many ways. My teachers and mentors, colleagues and postgraduate students have all helped to sharpen my critical and analytical skills. It is not possible to mention all of them here. However, I must recognize the invaluable assistance and guidance I received from my professors of two conflicting ideological backgrounds during the turbulent years of the cold war:—German L. Rozanov and Nikolai Nikolaivich Malchanov of Moscow, and Teresa Rakowska-Harmstone of Ottawa, Ontario, Canada. They, in their own ways, encouraged and advised me to pursue my interests in International Relations and Sovietology, respectively. The results of that encouragement and advice are contained in this study.

Over the years, several of my colleagues in academia have offered critical advice to me as the central themes of this study were developed. I thank my colleagues at the University of Benin, Benin City, Nigeria; Wang Metuge, Andrew O. Igbineweka, Ugbana Okpu, and Stanley Orobator for their scholarly advice during our numerous debates and discussions on the various subjects related to this study. I also thank my postgraduate students, especially Felix Idigbe and Mark Amachere for their scholarly inquisitiveness that propelled me to broaden the frontiers of knowledge in this field.

Many of the ideas in this book benefit from the analyses of scholars whose works I have cited in this study. I thank them for instigating the debate on such a key subject in global politics.

Undertaking a research leading to the publication of any work usually involves many people who may have contributed in the formative stages of the research. The research for this study took place at the Institute for the Study of the USSR, Munich, Germany, the Soviet Academy's Institutes of Africa, and International Relations & World Economy in Moscow, and at the Royal Institute of International Affairs, London, England. The selfless help I received from the librarians of these world-renowned research centers cannot be underestimated. I owe them a world of gratitude for their painstaking research of Western and Soviet newspapers, which provided me with invaluable sources on Soviet politics and foreign policy.

While I benefitted tremendously from the advice of my colleagues, the errors or omissions in this study are entirely mine.

O. Igho Natufe
Ottawa, Ontario, Canada

INTRODUCTION

World civilization has witnessed the rise and fall of a series of empires across the globe. When many of these empires were at their zenith, very few people believed they would ever fall. For example, during the Roman Empire it was said that all roads lead to Rome. But when most roads began to lead away from Rome, the Romans knew that their empire was doomed. The British had believed that "the sun never sets on the British Empire" as most of the colonies in Africa, Asia and the Western Hemisphere were under the rule of Pax Britannica. But when the sun did actually set on the British Empire, Britain found itself on a downward trend as a subordinate player in a global movement dominated by one of its erstwhile colonies—the United States of America (USA).

Arguably the most significant event in the 20th century was the rise and fall of the Soviet Empire. The 1917 October socialist revolution in Russia that gave birth to the first socialist state in history ushered in a new era in the study of inter-state relations. It was a major turning point in the history of international relations. The Union of Soviet Socialist Republics (USSR; or the Soviet Union), which was formally established in 1922 as a federation of independent socialist states that had been colonized by Imperial Russia, played a major role in defining the conduct of international politics and diplomacy from its inception until its demise in 1991. The Soviet state, which had inherited the spoils of imperial Russia, now condemned the economic policies of imperial powers as it immediately assumed leadership of the global anti-colonial struggle, proclaiming itself a true friend of the oppressed and colonized peoples.

The Soviet Union based its policies on the social and political thought of a 19th century German philosopher, Karl Marx, and viewed itself as the champion of the oppressed and colonized peoples. Prior to 1917 bourgeois ideology had defined the contents of politics and international relations. Imperial powers had challenged and fought each other over a series of questions, for military and strategic supremacy, colonial aggrandizement, but strictly within the ethos of capitalism. By allying itself with the oppressed and colonized peoples of the world, the Soviet Union sought to weaken both the power and influence of the capitalist states in global politics. It sponsored the establishment of an International Communist Movement (Comintern) as an instrument of its foreign policy to combat Western powers' colonial and imperial designs in the international community. If prior to 1917 the main focus of inter-state struggle for power was defined by the capitalist ethos, the emergence of a socialist state radically transformed the form and content of that struggle by injecting into the system a revolutionary ideological orientation diametrically opposed to capitalism. The new socialist state declared as its objective the overthrow of the capitalist system. This led to ideological confrontation in the international political system as the Soviet Union began to internationalize the class struggle concept for the victory of world Communism. Regarding the existence of Soviet Russia as a threat to their imperial interests, the Western powers organized to crush the new socialist state immediately following the 1917 revolution. Thus began phase one of the so-called cold war which became a hot war in 1918-1921 during the imperialist armed intervention.

The Soviet state survived the intervention as well as the attempt by the West to isolate it in the inter-war years. Its position was dramatically strengthened immediately following the war of 1939-1945 with the emergence of Moscow-led socialist states in Eastern Europe and Asia. Moscow was no longer encircled by capitalism as it had succeeded in extending its socialist borders into the heart of Europe. The emergence of these states, following the defeat of Nazi Germany, coupled with the political disarray in Western Europe, further encouraged the Soviet Union to propagate its ideology, in light of its belief that the demise of world capitalism was at hand. Soviet Union emerged from the war as the undisputed power in Europe, and shared the international stage with the US as a contending power in a hostile bi-power world.

The Soviet perception of its ideological mandate significantly transformed the conduct of international politics as it polarized political discourse along class lines. Each congress of the Communist Party of the Soviet Union (CPSU) defined and re-defined the form and content of this struggle as the Soviets projected themselves as the *saviour* of mankind from class oppression. Thus, in their view, the borders of the Soviet Marxist State included the territories of the oppressed and colonized peoples. They believed in the victory of world communism, the subsequent collapse of capitalism, and the re-arrangement of international relations based on the principles of scientific socialism. This self-anointed role posed a major challenge to capitalism as a system.

Global anti-colonial struggle was intensified after 1945 as the colonial powers could no longer maintain their grip in the colonies. The cost of domestic reconstruction coupled with the strong aspiration toward independence in the colonies tremendously affected the position of world capitalism. The independence of India and Burma, the defeat of the Netherlands in Indonesia, and the capitulation of France in Vietnam were events of great political significance which the Soviet Union welcomed and sought to utilize in order to maximize its ideological confrontation with the international capitalist system. The de-colonization of Africa, especially in the 1957-1960 period, and the anti-colonial movements on the continent were regarded by the Kremlin as indications of the gradual collapse of world capitalism. The Soviet Union hoped to ally with the emerging independent states in the struggle against Western imperialism. It was this hope that brought the Soviet Union into contact with independent Africa.

The present study traces the evolution and growth of Soviet foreign policy toward Africa from the reign of V.I. Lenin to the era of Leonid Brezhnev. Soviet contact with Africa throughout this period was a case study of revolving contradictions as the Soviet Union sought to first understand Africa's political reality and subsequently incorporate it into its ideology. For example, in expressing Soviet bewilderment over Africa's stance in international relations, a seasoned Soviet diplomat, D.D. Degtiar, Soviet Ambassador to Guinea (in 1962) declared: "Anyone can understand neutralism. But what on earth do these people mean by positive neutrality?"[1] But, soon after this, the Soviets became Africa's defenders of positive neutrality.

The theoretical argumentation enunciated by Lenin did not seem to provide tangible results as the Soviet Union experimented with these theories in its relations with Africa. For instance, the concepts of national democracy, revolutionary democracy, and the non-capitalist path of development were designed to enhance class consciousness leading to the establishment of a socialist political system. As Moscow was in a hurry to win over African countries to its camp during the cold war, it bestowed on some of these countries revolutionary and socialist status which did not reflect the reality of their respective political development.

A key element in the study of Soviet foreign policy is the role ideology played in the process. This issue is grappled with in chapter one, where I reviewed the contending theories of ideology and national interest vis-a-vis their functions in foreign policy analysis. During the course of its existence, the Soviet Union compelled its foreign policy analysts to take a more serious look at the role of ideology in shaping the behaviour of states in the international political system. The analysis in chapter one is a critical review of the contending views as I evaluated the intricate blending of ideology and national interest as a guide toward an understanding of Soviet foreign policy. This set the stage for the analysis in chapter two where I examined the challenges posed to the international system by Soviet Marxist-Leninist world outlook.

---

[1] As cited in Aidan Crawley, "The Russian Gamble for Africa", *Sunday Times*, London, April 15, 1962.

Given that Soviet actions were based on the theoretical assumptions inherent in Marxist philosophy, as well as in the works of Lenin and his successors in the Kremlin, it is imperative that an evolutionary analysis of the theoretical constructs of Soviet policy be undertaken. Between 1917 and 1980, for example, which is the scope of this study, the international community had undergone tremendous changes. Irrespective of these changes, the theoretical assumptions of Marxism-Leninism, especially the writings of Lenin, remained constant as the Soviets dealt with global issues. Over these years, post Lenin Soviet leaders professed their adherence to the teachings of Lenin as they interpreted these teachings in their respective articulations of Soviet ideology and foreign policy. Joseph Stalin's interpretations differed from those of Nikita Khrushchev, just as Khrushchev's differed from those of Brezhnev. Each succeeding interpretation was informed by the changing nature of international politics it had to deal with. The twists and turns of these seemingly contradictory variants of Leninism posed significant problems for Soviet foreign policy. This issue is the task of chapter three.

In the Soviet view, the immediate post-1945 re-alignment of forces in Europe created favourable revolutionary situations in the world, particularly in the colonies. European colonial powers, having been exhausted and devastated by the war of 1939-1945 found themselves engaged in three wars simultaneously: 1) on the home front: they were concerned with how to re-build their ruined economies and avoid an internal revolt by an organized labour force, 2) in Europe: they were concerned with how to deal with the Soviet threat as the frontiers of Soviet socialism had moved right into the heart of Europe, and 3) beyond Europe they were concerned with how the emerging alliance of Moscow's socialist internationalism and the independence movements in the colonies posed a serious challenge to European colonial powers as they sought for strategies to either delay de-colonization or establish close ideological alliance with the emergent states. Phase two of the cold war was brewing, and Africa became a testing ground for East-West ideological rivalry. The opportunities and threats this phenomenon posed to Africa and the continent's independence movements, the Soviet Union, China, and the West are reviewed in chapters four and five. Chapters six and seven are case studies of Soviet foreign policy under Nikita Khrushchev and Leonid Brezhnev, respectively.

CHAPTER ONE

UNDERSTANDING SOVIET FOREIGN POLICY

A theoretical discussion of the content of policy constitutes a vital aspect of an analysis of the foreign policy of any country. This is particularly true with regards to the study of Soviet foreign policy. The USSR was perhaps the only state whose foreign policy was subjected to a detailed analysis by scholars in their quest to clarify the problematic of its foreign policy. Such an analysis usually seeks to answer the question: What determines Soviet foreign policy; ideology or national interest? This either-or position vis-à-vis ideology and national interest in our analysis of Soviet foreign policy suggests the negation of either the existence of ideology or the significance of national interest in Soviet Marxist-Leninist world outlook. While this approach may be fashionable, it also has its problem: a distortion of reality. We shall return to this question later in the present study. But first, it is imperative that we seek clarification regarding the concepts of ideology and national interest. The concept of ideology and its role in foreign policy has led to a considerable controversy among scholars of international politics. This conceptual problem is, arguably justified, a manifestation of the competing class interest in politics.

Arthur Schlesinger defines ideology as a "body of systematic and rigid dogma by which people seek to understand the world—and to preserve or transform it."[1] According to Schlesinger, ideology is a set of "systematic and rigid" dogmatic theory applied by people in their quest to either "preserve or transform" the world. Thus, ideology has to be a "rigid dogma" if it is "systematic." This conception of ideology was formulated at a time when prominent western scholars, mainly American, had decreed the "death" or "end of ideology" in their anti-Marxist expositions.[2] This systematic-rigid component of ideology as posited by Schlesinger is meant to challenge the rationale of Marxist ideology whose premise is the overthrow of capitalism as a socio-economic and political system. Daniel Bell perceives ideology as a manipulative system of ideas employed to maintain and reinforce a given socio-economic and political system.[3] Exponents of the "end of ideology" school view Marxism as a "rigid dogma" and have been influenced by this position to relegate ideology to the background in their analysis of Soviet politics.

On the other hand, a Soviet analyst, M. V. Yakovlev perceives ideology as "first and foremost a class consciousness which reflects the social condition of defined classes in a society and assists them in the realization of their vital interests and tasks."[4] Thus, ideology is viewed as a set of philosophical ideas which influence and define the world outlook of each class in its relationship with an opposing class. Therefore, as a theory, it defines the tactics and strategies of

---

[1] A. Schlesinger and M. White, eds., Paths of American Thought, Boston, Mass., 1963, p.532.

[2] See, for example, D. Bell, The End of Ideology. On the Exhaustion of Political Ideas in the Fifties, New York, 1967 (first published in 1960); S.M. Lipset, Political Man. The Social Bases of Politics, Baltimore, Maryland, 1981 (first published in 1959) Note chapters 13 and 15; C.I. Waxman, ed., The End of Ideology Debate, New York, 1968. For a Soviet critique of the "end of ideology" school of thought, see L.N. Moskvichov, The End of Ideology Theory: Illusions and Reality, Moscow, 1974.

[3] See Bell, The End of Ideology, passim.

[4] M. V. Yakovlev, Ideologiia, Moscow, 1979, p.24.

attaining the declared objectives of a class. For it to be meaningful, such a theory must be flexible without compromising its *vital* aspects, and neither rigid nor dogmatic. According to Marxist scholars, Marxism is a guide to action, and not a dogma. Not being a dogma, it is logical to expect, and arguably so, that its applicability would be influenced by the peculiarities of individual countries. Thus, it would be considered anti-Marxist for a country to impose or dictate its application and interpretation of Marxist ideology on other countries.

National interest as a foreign policy determinant is universally recognized as the aggregate interest of a state in its relation towards other actors and phenomena in the international political system. We frequently hear a president or prime minister of a state declaring that his government's action is dictated by "national interest." Such a statement naturally beclouds the concept and content of national interest as applied in international politics. National interest thus defined demonstrates a lack of conceptual clarity. The objective of this chapter is to attempt to clarify the issues of conceptualization of ideology and national interest as a guide towards an understanding of Soviet foreign policy.

In the view of W.W. Kulski, national interest *and not* ideology determines the form and content of a state's (foreign) policy. Illustrating a situation whereby ideology "becomes a subordinate consideration" to national interest he opined:

> If necessary, Western governments consolidate their external position and security by supporting non-democratic foreign regimes for fear that the alternative would be the emergence of unfriendly governments. The phrase "free world", which has become a part of the Western lexicon, includes all non-Communist regimes, especially if they are not unfriendly to the West. Thus Fascist regimes or military dictatorships are considered members of the Free World,

and democratic ideology fades away for the sake of national interest.[5]

Relating the above to the role of national interest in Soviet foreign policy, Kulski concluded:

> The Soviet government indulges in the same practice. If a non-Communist or even anti-Communist foreign regime follows a policy friendly to the USSR and quarrels with the West, that regime is considered a welcome ally in international competition.[6]

The above citations from Kulski's analysis represent the trend in most western scholarship on this subject. Two key phrases emerge from the above:

(a) ". . . ideology fades away for the sake of national interest" and
(b) a hostile regime "is considered a welcome ally in international competition."

An in-depth analysis of these propositions reveals an inability to understand the concept of ideology. We pose the questions: Why would any country consider a hostile foreign regime "a welcome ally in international competition"? Is it not obvious that the dialectics of political relations dictate such an alliance which usually serves a defined purpose? What is ideology? What is national interest? Who determines a state's national interest, and how?

The divergent postulate of national interests among socialist states is viewed by Kulski as a demonstration of the primacy of national interest in the foreign policies of these states.[7] This position

---

[5]   W.W. Kulski, The Soviet Union in World Affairs. A Documented Analysis, 1964-1972, Syracuse, New York, 1973, p.20.

[6]   Ibid.

[7]   Ibid., pp.22-27.

is faulty on the following grounds. First, it implies that ideological tenets must be rigid. Second, it ignores the applicability of Marxism to suit the objective and subjective peculiarities of individual states. For example, the phrase "capitalism is capitalism" is true in as much as the recognizable basic properties of capitalism are concerned, notwithstanding the variations found in different capitalist states. The modification of ideology to suit particular national environments does not obliterate the primacy of ideological constructs in the formulation of a state's policies. Goran Therborn posits:

> But "interests" by themselves do not explain anything . . .
> The problem to be explained, however, is how members
> of different classes come to define the world and their
> situation and possibilities in it in a particular way.[8]

It is a fruitless attempt to claim the primacy of national interest in foreign policy analysis[9], because, in the final analysis, *national interest* is determined by the specific *ideological orientation* of the *particular class* in power. National interest as a category cannot be defined or conceptualized outside the parameters of ideology. Within the broad framework of ideology, therefore, a government projects its national interests which are a direct product of the blending of ideological considerations and various domestic environmental constrains, with ideology at the apex. Georgi Arbatov (1923-2010), founding Director and subsequent Director Emeritus of the Institute of the USA and Canada in Moscow, and a foreign policy adviser to the Soviet Government, argues that western scholars interpret "ideological struggle in foreign (and, as a matter of fact, domestic)

---

8   Goran Therborn, <u>The Ideology of Power and the Power of Ideology</u>, London, 1980, p.10.

9   See, for example, F.S. Northedge, <u>The Foreign Policies of the Powers</u>, London, 1965, p.15; Joseph Frankel, <u>The Making of Foreign Policy</u>, London, 1968, p.3; Joseph Frankel, <u>National Interest</u>, London, 1970, <u>passim</u>.

5

policy . . . outside the genuinely ideological, class concepts and categories." He concludes:

> A favourable and customary method of this interpretation
> is to supplant the concept of ideology with the concept
> of "public opinion."[10]

Samuel L. Sharp rejects the ideological approach, arguing that Soviet foreign policy should be seen purely as national interest motivation.[11] When it is posited that a particular foreign policy action is motivated by national interest, as Sharp argues, it does not imply that the given action is devoid of ideological content. What it does mean is that the particular foreign policy action is less doctrinaire. When we recognize specific issues that can be related to national interest, i.e., the survival of the state which is supposed to be "non-ideological", it is interesting to note that its strategic articulation emanates from reasoned ideological argumentation. Thus, it is reasonable to postulate that ideology and national interest are strongly blended as variables in the decision-making process. A communist state is perhaps the only state capable of consistently relating its political actions to the ideas of a defined ideological construct, no matter how inept these actions may seem to critics. This intricate blending of national interest and ideology in the conduct of Soviet foreign policy afforded the USSR a greater level of manoeuvrability not heartily appreciated by non-Soviets. For example, after being encouraged to join the anti-imperialist struggle, local communists felt disillusioned by Soviet action in reaching a rapprochement with western colonial powers who were supposed to be enslaving Moscow's fellow comrades. The Baku communist

10   Georgi Arbatov, The War of Ideas in Contemporary International Relations, Moscow, 1973, p.37.
11   See Samuel L. Sharp, "National Interest: Key to Soviet Politics", in Erik P. Hoffman and Federic J. Fleron, Jr., eds., The conduct of Soviet Foreign Policy, New York, 1971, pp.114-116.

congress of 1920 was organized by Moscow to stir up revolutionary, anti-colonial revolts in the Near East and Asia. However, when the British Government agreed to endorse a bilateral trade agreement with the USSR, the latter advised local communists in the areas to "cool their anti-British" demonstrations.[12]

Abdurakhman Avtorkhanov, a former Soviet citizen who defected to (west) Germany and later became a leading western analyst of Soviet policies, dichotomized the determinants of Soviet foreign policy into two categories: the "substantive" and "functional" factors. According to him, the "substantive" properties are manifested in the "political and ideological, the strategic and military, and the economic factors", while the "functional" factors are embodied in the propagation of "peace, the right of people to self-determination, respect for national sovereignty, coexistence."[13] While such a dichotomy is useful, the intermediary factor—"national factor"—which Avtorkhanov defined as the "'national state interest of the country" is in fact embodied in the other two categories. In Avtorkhanov's view, the interest of the "system" is alien to that of the "country."

It should be recognized that when a sovereign state negotiates an international agreement it is at the same time fulfilling a dual role by blending its national and ideological interests; it is assumed that the state's action is in consonant with its *national_interest* as determined and defined by its *ideological* postulates. This is the case with every sovereign state. The series of treaties signed between the USSR and neighbouring countries in the 1920s and 1930s were designed to guarantee the former's existence *as a state*, while, in the Soviet view, the survival of the state would serve as a model

---

[12] See Stephen White, "Communism and the East: The Baku Congress of 1920", Slavic Review, 33, 3, September 1974, pp.492-514. Note pp.503-504.

[13] Abdurakhman Avtorkhanov, "Factors Determining Soviet Foreign Policy", in Oliver J. Frederiksen, ed., Problems of Soviet Foreign Policy. A Symposium of the Institute for the Study of the USSR, Munich, Germany, 1959, p.1.

for the victory of world communism.[14] Thus, we therefore have a situation whereby, according to the Soviets, the goals of world socialist revolution were inseparable from the ideological interests of the USSR. It is instructive that we should grasp the essence of this logic; if we desire to understand Soviet foreign policy.

Carew Hunt argued that ". . . the current Soviet ideology is intended to strengthen the party and reinforce its claims to rule." To achieve this objective the party "is assigned the duty of fertilizing the masses with its ideas."[15] In support of Hunt's assertion, R.V. Daniels posits that ideological arguments are employed *primarily* to maintain the party's rule and to manipulate the masses into believing in the inviolability of the Soviet communist state.[16] Both Hunt and Daniels would agree that the *function of ideology* they ascribed to the USSR is not different from the *function of ideology* in any other polity, irrespective of the colour of its ideological strips. Ideology serves a defined *function*. An American analyst, P. Fliess, argues:

> Ideology has not only played a negative role in the bipolar world by confusing political thinking; it has also played a positive role as a political tool . . . In as much as the struggle for power has largely been a struggle for the control of the minds of men, ideology has become a weapon of primary importance.[17]

One of Moscow's leading foreign policy analysts, N. Kapchenko, opines that any attempt to separate politics from ideology, in the

---

[14] See John A. Armstrong, "Domestic Roots of Soviet Foreign Policy", in Hoffman and Fleron, Jr., op.cit., p.51.

[15] R.N. Carew Hunt, "The Importance of Doctrine", in ibid., p.102.

[16] See Robert V. Daniels, "Doctrine and Foreign Policy", in ibid., p.157.

[17] P. Fliess, International Relations in the Bipolar World, New York, 1963, pp.168-169.

sphere of foreign policy, renders "the idea of a foreign policy that does not reflect the ideology of the ruling class."[18]

It would be unrealistic to discard ideology in any analysis of a state's foreign policy; rather it should be employed as a yardstick to measure its behaviour in international politics. For example, it is not enough to dismiss a given foreign policy action with the terms "pragmatism" or "political realism", neither is it a display of analytical sophistication to hide under the unexplained concept of national interest. A leading U.S. Sovietologist, Vernon V. Aspaturian, cautioned:

> The abstraction of a Soviet national interest outside the context of Soviet ideology, no matter how superficially attractive it may appear to be as a useful analytical tool, ruptures the image of Soviet reality and results in the calculation of Soviet foreign policy on the basis of false assumptions. Soviet foreign policy is based on the image of reality provided by the Marxist-Leninist ideological prism.[19]

The Soviets always justified their foreign policy actions from the perspective of Marxist-Leninist ideology. Every Soviet foreign policy action, from the treaty of Brest-Litovsk to SALT II, is justified on this basis. The Soviet perception of its ideological mandate radically altered the conduct of international politics as it polarized political discourse along class lines. The Soviets assumed the role of the "saviour" of mankind from class oppression. Such a role projection, explained in Marxist-Leninist ideological terms, had an in-built expansionist tendency "since the Soviet state was conceived as an

---

18 N. Kapchenko, "Foreign Policy and Ideology", International Affairs, Moscow, No. 11, November 1979, p.80.

19 Vernon V. Aspaturian, "Soviet Foreign Policy", in Roy C. Macridis, ed., Foreign Policy in World Politics, Englewood Cliffs, New Jersey, 1976, p.167. See also Aspaturian, Process and Power in Soviet Foreign Policy, Boston, Mass., 1971, 9.333.

ideological state without fixed geographical frontiers."[20] Upholding the basic tenet of this argument, Arbatov opined:

> The fact that the pivot of the struggle in international relations has become the contradiction between the two world systems representing the two principal antagonistic classes of contemporary society also determines the content of that struggle.[21]

He predicted that the struggle will lead "to the victory of the most advanced system, socialism, and to the subsequent reorganization of all international relations in accordance with the laws of life and the development of the new society."[22] The withering away of socialism in both the Soviet Union and other east European socialist countries, and the demise of the Soviet Union in late 1991 may have put Arbatov's optimism to rest. However, one of the recently revealed Kennedy-Khrushchev secret letters seems to suggest a ray of hope for socialism. In his letter of December 13, 1961 to U.S. President John Kennedy, Soviet leader Nikita Khrushchev noted: "But socialism is a progressive vital system, it has no time limit, it will constantly develop and strengthen."[23]

The Soviets maintained that the principles of Marxism, which were "further developed" by V. I. Lenin, "in a new situation of the revolutionary struggle of the working class in the epoch of imperialism and proletarian revolutions",[24] constituted the ideological basis of Soviet foreign policy. They argued that the emergence of socialist Russia would create "new international relations based on equality

---

[20]   Aspaturian, in Macridis, ed., op.cit., p.169.

[21]   Arbatov, The War of Idea . . . , p.35.

[22]   Ibid

[23]   See "The Kennedy-Khrushchev Letters", The Ottawa Citizen, July 31, 1993, p.H9.

[24]   M. Airapetian and P. Kabanov, Leninskie printsipy vneshnei politiki sovetskogo gosudarstva, Moscow, 1957, p.9.

and justice" among nations.[25] However, the communists reasoned that equality and justice among nations "can be attained only by the forcible overthrow of all existing social" structure, since the "proletarians have nothing to lose but their chains. They have a world to win."[26] As the first socialist state the Soviet Union found itself struggling to fulfil the ideological prescription of Marxism. Even long before the October 1917 revolution, Russian communists had started to assume the leading role in world revolutionary movement. In 1901 Lenin wrote:

> The implementation of this task, the destruction of the most mighty stronghold of reaction, not only European but also (we can now say) Asian, would have made the Russian proletariat the avant-garde of the international revolutionary proletariat. And we have a right to expect that we would achieve this honorary title.[27]

Moscow's foreign policy goals and objectives were geared toward the realization of this "honorary title." The ideological struggle between the opposing socio-economic and political systems represented by Moscow and Washington, respectively, was a battle of ideas to conquer the minds of men, especially in the international political scene. As Marx and Engels put it:

> The ideas of a ruling class are in every epoch the ruling ideas: i.e., the class, which is the ruling material force of society, is at the same time its ruling intellectual force.

Marx and Engels further postulated that: "The class which has the means of material production at its disposal has control at the

---

25   Ibid., p.12.

26   K. Marx and F. Engels, <u>The Manifesto of the Communist Party</u>, New York, 1964, p.44.

27   V.I. Lenin, <u>Sochineniia</u>, 4th edition, Moscow, 1949, vol.5, p.345.

same time over the means of mental production . . . "[28] Simply put, the political class in power in any society determines the form and content of political and economic behaviour. Its ideas become the dominant ideas of society. Marx and Engels explained:

> For each new class which puts itself in the place of one ruling before it, is compelled, merely in order to carry through its aims, to represent its interest as the common interest of all members of society, put in an ideal form; it will give its ideas the form of universality, and represent them as the only rationale, universally valid ones. The class making a revolution appears from the very start, merely because it is opposed to a *class*, not as a class but as the representative of the whole society; it appears as the whole mass of society confronting the one ruling class. It can do this because, to start with, its interest really is more connected with the common interest of all other non-ruling classes . . . Every new class, therefore, achieves its hegemony only on a broader basis than that of the class ruling previously, in return for which the opposition of the non-ruling class against the new ruling class later develops all the more sharply and profoundly.[29]

If, prior to October 1917, the seizure of political power and the establishment of communist rule in Russia constituted a *particular* class interest for the Bolshevik party, it is pertinent to note that, after the Bolsheviks had consolidated their power and Russia became a force in international politics, this particular class interest began to be articulated by the Soviets as the *universal* class interest of the world revolutionary movement represented by the Soviet state. As

---

[28] Marx and Engels, The German Ideology, New York, 1968, p.39. See also Marx and Engels, Manifesto, p.39.

[29] Marx and Engels, The German Ideology, pp.40-41.

Marx and Engels postulated, the "workingmen have no country" and it is impossible to "take from them what they have not got." The proletariat "must first of all acquire political hegemony, must rise to be the ruling class of the nation, must constitute the nation . . ."[30] In conformity with this ideological prescription, the Soviets regarded themselves as the legitimate apostles to transform the world.

Following the October 1917 revolution the young socialist state withdrew Russia from the war of 1914-1918. The Peace Decree adopted by the Second All-Russian Congress of Soviets on November 8, 1917, called on "all warring peoples and their governments to start an immediate negotiation for a just and democratic peace."[31] The dual appeal to "people" and "governments" became a constant phenomenon in Soviet foreign policy. To underscore the significance of this duality, Lenin argued that the Soviets "cannot ignore the states, as this would delay the possibility of concluding" the required peace negotiations, but at the same time the Soviets "have no right, simultaneously, not to appeal to the peoples."[32] Thus, the Soviet government appealed to the "creative workers" of England, France and Germany to assist it to "liberate mankind from the horrors of war and its consequences" and help to successfully bring to an end the issue of peace along with it the issue of liberating the workers and the exploited masses of the population from all forms of slavery and all forms of exploitation.[33]

It is very important for us to note the ideological linkage established by the Soviet Government between itself and the "workers and exploited masses" of the capitalist states immediately after the October 1917 revolution. The young Soviet state, in its Peace Decree, also called for peace "without annexation and indemnities" and declared that territories conquered by the great powers, notwithstanding the time of conquest, should be granted

30   Marx and Engels, <u>Manifesto</u>, p.28.
31   <u>MID. Dokumenty</u>, Moscow, 1957, vol.1, p.11.
32   Lenin, <u>Sochineniia</u>, vol.26, p.220.
33   <u>MID. Dokumenty</u>, vol.1, pp.13-14; 58-59.

freedom since such conquests were forcibly carried out. The Soviets were obviously trying to link themselves with the plight of the colonized peoples and territories whose faith was to be discussed at the Paris Peace Conference. As a point of departure from the European concept of self-determination, which prior to 1917 was applied to Europe and the so-called "civilised" nations, Lenin, according to Arno J. Mayer, "established the inextricable connexion between the national movements and the class struggle" and also "posited the right of national self-determination as a universal principle",[34] to be championed by the Soviet Union.

The Soviet Government called for "open diplomacy" and condemned the signing of secret agreements. The first act towards this was the publication of all secret agreements contracted by the Imperial Russian Government "from February to October 25, 1917."[35] The publication of these selective agreements indicated that the Soviet regime condoned other agreements entered into by the Tsars before February 1917. This gave the credence to the view that Soviet foreign policy was essentially a continuation of Russian (Tsarist) foreign policy. The Soviet government had inherited both the prestige and power aspirations of the Tsarist regime in its bid to acquire its own spheres of influence globally. It became imperative to view Soviet foreign policy as a process in motion for the division of the world into permanent spheres of influence.[36] This was a valid thesis; but it implied that the Soviet Union would be satisfied with the division of the world into communist and capitalist spheres of influence. Marxists do not appreciate this position. According to

---

[34] Arno J. Mayer, Political Origins of the New Diplomacy, 1917-1918, New Haven, Conn., 1959, p.299.

[35] MID. Dokumenty, vol.1, pp.13-22. See also Mayer, passim.

[36] See Frederick L. Schuman, Soviet Politics at Home and Abroad, New York, 1953; Charles O. Lerche, Snr., Principles of International Politics, New York, 1956; Hans J. Morgenthau, Politics Among Nations. The Struggle for Power and Peace, Fifth Edition, revised, New York, 1978.

Lenin, there cannot be any permanent division of the world into spheres of influence between communism and capitalism. He explained:

> While capitalism and socialism exist, they cannot live in peace; either one or the other, in the final analysis, will be victorious; either a requiem will be sung over the Soviet Republic, or over world capitalism.[37]

The above citation from Lenin describes international relations as a continuous process of struggle epitomized by the dialectical law of the unity and struggle of opposites. The realization of this enhances our understanding of the *state* interests of the Soviet Union, viewed as an expression of the *class* interests of the Soviet Union. Thus, ideology is regarded as the only rational determinant with national interest subsumed under it. However, it was natural to expect the primary interest of the USSR to be the survival of the Soviet State—the "socialist motherland", followed by the promotion of and support for the cause of world revolution. In analytical terms, it may seem logical to posit that there is a syntactical relation between "national interest" as a category and the "survival of the Soviet state", while the promotion of world revolution is the "ideological" interest of the USSR.

Immediately following the October 1917 revolution the Bolsheviks sought ways to withdraw Soviet Russia from the war. In the turbulent days preceding the revolution they had promised the impoverished peoples of Russia *peace, land* and *bread.* To attain peace, the most important priority of the new regime which had yet to establish a firm power base, the Bolsheviks proposed the halting of hostilities on all fronts and the concluding of a general peace treaty. When this was not forthcoming the Bolsheviks decided to negotiate a separate peace with Germany. In early 1918 Soviet Russia

---

[37]   Lenin, <u>Sochineniia</u>, vol.31, pp.426-427.

and Germany signed the Brest-Litovsk Peace Treaty.[38] The peace negotiations with Germany opened at Brest-Litovsk on November 20, 1917. Lenin's slogan preceding the negotiations had been a "just and democratic peace", "without annexation and indemnities." Initially the Soviets maintained this position at the peace talks. Realizing that Soviet Russia had no power to back its peace terms, the Germans ignored Lenin's peace slogans. They wanted Soviet Russia to purchase peace with its lands and populations.

The German peace terms generated a political crisis within the Bolshevik leadership. Leon Trotsky, who had led Soviet delegation to one of the peace negotiations, called the German terms imperialistic and argued for its rejection. He proposed instead a policy of "no war, no peace." He wanted both Germany and Soviet Russia to halt military hostilities without signing a peace treaty. Trotsky was formulating his concept of "permanent revolution" postulating that Soviet Russia's firm position would encourage European communists, especially in Germany, to intensify their struggle against west European governments amidst the internal dissent caused by the war in those countries. Nikolai Bukharin, Soviet Russia's foremost theorist, endorsed Trotsky's basic concept. He, like Trotsky, was against a peace treaty with Germany on such humiliating terms. Instead, he called for a "revolutionary war", and that the Soviets should take the revolution into German soil where local communists would join with them in a peoples' war against the German state. Lenin disagreed with both Trotsky and Bukharin. His immediate concern was the survival of a Socialist Russia. While Trotsky and Bukharin were urging Russia to export the revolution into central Europe, Lenin was preoccupied with the thoughts of preserving the revolutionary gains in Soviet Russia. He opined that Soviet Russia needed peace not war; bread for the poor and hungry not bullets. The Bolsheviks must preserve the revolution, he maintained. Thus, he was prepared to sign a peace treaty with

---

[38]   See Adam B. Ulam, Expansion and Coexistence: The History of Soviet Foreign Policy, 1917-67, New York, 1968; Mayer, passim.

Germany even if the latter had demanded more territories as long as the Germans left the Bolsheviks a piece of territory called Soviet Socialist Russia. According to the terms of the peace treaty signed at Brest-Litovsk on March 3, 1918, Soviet Russia gave up a substantial part of its European territory, in regard to both human and natural resources. The Germans got about one quarter the territory of European Russia which constituted its most viable land, and about one-third its population. The treaty was a humiliating experience for Soviet Russia. Lenin's slogan of peace "without annexation and indemnities" was shattered. The socialist revolution needed and got a costly breathing spell. Lenin's position formed the ideological basis of Joseph Stalin's "socialism in one country", a concept which the latter formulated in his power struggle with Trotsky following Lenin's death.

The Nazi-Soviet Non-Aggression Pact of 1939[39] is another interesting case for an analysis of Soviet foreign policy vis-à-vis ideology and national interest. The inter-war years in Europe were marked with tensions. European governments did not conceal their ideological hostility toward Soviet communism. This enmity was best articulated by Adolf Hitler who emerged as leader of the German state in 1932. Hitler and Stalin represented the opposite poles of European politics. By the mid-1930s it was obvious to most political observers that both Italy and Germany were preparing to wage a major military conflict in Europe. With the assistance of Britain and France, Austria had fallen victim to German aggression while Czechoslovakia was dismembered in 1938 as a result of the Munich conspiracy.

There *appeared* to be a desire in London, Paris and Moscow to form a tripartite military accord to halt German aggression. However, the Anglo-French military mission in Moscow could not reach a definitive agreement with Moscow regarding the logistics of Soviet military involvement in the design to combat German war machine. The protracted negotiation technique of Britain

---

[39]   See Ulam, <u>Expansion and Coexistence.</u>

and France is alleged to have compelled the Soviet Union to enter into a non-aggression pact with Germany.[40] The Nazi-Soviet Non-Aggression Pact was signed on August 23, 1939, and both parties formed an alliance on terms that surprised the international community.[41] The Soviet Union aided German policy by providing a corridor through which some strategic materials were shipped to Germany.[42]

The Pact was an embarrassment to members of the Comintern. All visible opposition parties, including the Communist party had been outlawed in Germany. The Comintern, in all its deliberations in Moscow, had condemned Hitler and regarded his state as the most vicious enemy of communism. It was in reaction to the Pact that George Padmore, a prominent West Indian member of the Comintern, resigned his advisory position in the Kremlin. If judged singularly, the Pact, particularly its secret protocols, compelled other states, especially the smaller ones, to view the Soviet Union as *any other state* in the international political scene. But such a position will fail to address itself to the rationale for signing the Pact. The contradictions in European international politics in the inter-war years were further compounded by the emergence of Hitler.

The ideological conflict between the Soviet Union and the capitalist states was an established fact. When the western alliance failed in its military intervention to strangulate the young Soviet state (1918-1921), it did not however abandon its design to obliterate socialism as both an idea and a state. The rise of Hitler and his National Socialist Movement in Germany undoubtedly afforded the

[40] See, ibid., pp.267-279; A.J.P. Taylor, The Origins of the Second World War, New York, 1961; William L. Shirer, The Rise and Fall of the Third Reich: A History of Nazi Germany, New York, 1960, pp.521, 533-538.

[41] See Shirer, op.cit., pp.513-514.

[42] See Vladimir Petrov, "The Nazi-Soviet Pact: A Missing Page in Soviet Historiography", Problems of Communism, XVII, 1, January-February, 1968, pp.42-50; Shirer, op.cit.

West an opportunity to experiment with its anti-communist policy, a policy which Hitler, in his book[43], endorsed and articulated. In Mein Kampf, published in 1927, Hitler outlined Germany's plan to destroy (Soviet) communism, first by entering into a tactical alliance with the USSR, since, in his views, the USSR would not observe the terms of such an alliance. [44]Hitler, on the other hand, was convinced that Britain and Italy were "the only two states in Europe with which a closer relationship would be desirable and promising for" Germany. Commenting on the military significance of an Anglo-Italo-German alliance, he opined:

> The military consequences of concluding this alliance would in every respect be the opposite of the consequences of an alliance with Russia.[45]

The strategy of the West, as articulated by Hitler's Germany was clear and straightforward: Consolidate the western front and attack the USSR. It would be simplistic to dismiss this as a "mere hindsight", particularly since the developments of international politics between 1932 and 1941 demonstrated the implementation of this strategy.

The Munich Agreement on the dismemberment of Czechoslovakia, signed by Germany, Italy, Britain and France on September 30, 1938, was not only designed to mollify Germany, but was intended to concretize the foundation of the West's strategy.[46] Though Adam Ulam agreed that the Munich Agreement represented an alliance against the USSR he, however, maintained that the Agreement did not signify "a total loss" of Moscow's "policy of collective security so indefatigably followed by Litvinov between 1934 and 1938", because, he argued, "there was no fascist

---

43 Adolf Hitler, Mein Kampf, Boston, Mass., 1971.
44 Ibid., pp.660-661.
45 Ibid., pp.664-665.
46 Diplomaticheskii slovar, Moscow, 1961, vol.2, pp.357-364. See also Ulam, op.cit., pp.255-258.

government in Paris."[47] This position distorts the political climate in Europe between 1934 and 1938. It is true that the USSR had consistently called for a European collective security arrangement to combat Hitler and Benito Mussolini of Italy[48], but, in response, Britain and France joined Hitler and Mussolini to produce the notorious Munich Agreement. Furthermore, the strategic consensus reached in Munich also influenced the Anglo-French military mission to stale in its negotiations with the USSR in Moscow. The dialectics of political relations explains *why* a state allies with "a hostile regime" in international politics. We encountered this in Kulski's analysis. It is in this context that we should view Moscow's decision to sign the Non-Aggression Pact with Berlin. Though the Pact did not neutralize the USSR from German invasion on June 22, 1941, it did however create a respite for Moscow.

While the above cases (the Brest-Litovsk Treaty and the Non-Aggression pact) were relations with a *bourgeois* state, frictions in Sino-Soviet relations were not. Both the People's Republic of China (PRC) and the USSR were communist states, and thus by definition fraternal allies against the West. In pursuance of the framework for fraternal bilateral relations already established in 1949, China and the USSR in 1959 signed an agreement by which the latter was to provide China the atomic bomb. This accord was entered into at the time when China proposed that the USSR distribute its atomic weapons among communist states for a final bloodbath with colonialism and imperialism.[49] Later that year the Soviet Government unilaterally abrogated the agreement amidst its desire to attain peaceful coexistence with the U.S. government over disarmament. This was on the eve of Nikita Khrushchev's visit to

47 Ulam, ibid., p.257.
48 See SSSR v borbe za mir nakanune vtoroi mirovoi voiny (sentiabr 1938g - avgust 1939g). Dokumenty i materialy, Moscow, 1971.
49 See Donald S. Zagoria, The Sino-Soviet Conflict 1956-1961, Princeton, New Jersey, 1962; and O.B. Borisov and B.T. Koloskov, Sino-Soviet Relations, Moscow, 1975

Washington in September 1959. Irrespective of the frictions that had started to crystallize, Khrushchev rushed to Beijing (Peking) after his Camp David summit with U.S. president Dwight Eisenhower. Why did Moscow abrogate its atomic agreement with Beijing? It was apparent that the Kremlin was concerned on how to mollify the White House on the eve of Khrushchev's visit.

At the Moscow meeting of world communist and workers' parties in 1957, China had challenged Soviet claim to leadership of the international communist movement. Since the Soviet Union adopted its policy of de-Stalinisation at the 20th Congress of the Communist Party of the Soviet Union (CPSU) in 1956, China began to lay claim to the leadership of the international communist movement. Differences in ideological interpretation and Moscow's desire to bring the Chinese leaders to adopt a "general party line" may have compelled the Soviet government to abrogate the atomic agreement as a move to curb China's claim to lead the communist movement.

The question of interpreting Marxism remained the source of Sino-Soviet schism. Moscow claimed to be the authoritative interpreter[50], while Beijing strongly rejected Moscow's claim.[51] About two decades before the October 1917 revolution in Russia, Lenin had recommended that each country apply Marxism to suit its own domestics requirements, since, according to him, Marxism was neither a dogma nor a theology but a theoretical guide to action.[52] Herbert Marcuse, a renowned U.S. Marxologist, captured the essence of Lenin's position when he conceptualized Soviet Marxism as "the attempt to reconcile the inherited body of Marxian theory with a historical situation which seemed to vitiate the central

---

[50]   Borisov and Koloskov, op.cit., pp.94-126; G.V. Astafyev and A.M. Dubinsky, eds., From Anti-Imperialism to Anti-Sovietism: The Evolution of Peking's Foreign Policy, Moscow, 1974, pp.34-41.

[51]   Long Live Leninism, Peking, 1960; "The Origins and Development of the Differences Between the Leadership of the CPSU and Ourselves", Peking Review, VI, 37, September 13, 1963, pp.6-20.

[52]   See, Lenin, Collected Works, Moscow, 1960, vol.IV, pp.211-212.

conception of the theory itself, namely the Marxian conception of the transition from capitalism to socialism."[53]

This leads us to an examination of two key interpretative variables of Soviet foreign policy: proletarian socialist internationalism and peaceful coexistence. The USSR maintained that its policies—domestic and foreign—were based on these variables. Proletarian internationalism, which embodies socialist internationalism is, in the words of Airapetian and Kabanov, the "ideology of the international working class solidarity of the proletarians . . . in their struggle for the victory of Communism", which constitutes an indivisible part of the CPSU's programme as it is "one of the most important principles of Lenin's foreign policy of the Soviet State."[54] It is therefore the *principle* which defines the fraternal bilateral relations among socialist states on one hand, and also defines the fraternal relations between socialist states and the revolutionary working class movement in non-socialist states. It presupposes the "unity and indivisibility of the national and international tasks of the proletariat."[55] As a principle, it implies the commitment and readiness of a socialist state or groups of socialist states to aid other socialist states in their struggle to strengthen the gains of socialism in their respective countries. As articulated by Pravda, the CPSU maintained that the national interest of any given communist state "cannot contradict its international socialist interests."[56] Thus, as a matter of principle, a Communist is expected to maintain an inimical attitude toward his own state because his primary loyalty is for international communism, a policy which calls for the negation of national interest where the international interest

[53] Herbert Marcuse, Soviet Marxism: A Critical Analysis, London, 1958, pp.12-13.

[54] Airapetian and Kabanov, op.cit., p.110. See also, Sh. P. Sanakoev and N.I. Kapchenko, O teorii vneshnei politiki sotsializma, Moscow, 1977, passim.

[55] Airapetian and Kabanov, p.112.

[56] Pravda, July 16, 1956.

of communism is threatened.[57] The Soviet Union always indicated the ideological path of proletarian socialist internationalism irrespective of the views of other socialist states and movements.[58]

Peaceful coexistence, on the other hand, is the principle of peaceful *cohabitation* between states of conflicting socio-economic and political systems. The concept was formulated by Lenin on November 8, 1917 when he issued the Peace Decree. According to G.L. Rozanov, a leading Soviet foreign policy analyst, Lenin formulated such a policy at a time when the young Soviet socialist state was faced with the "question of life and death for the revolution."[59] In Razanov's view, the "life and death" issue compelled the Soviet state to propose peaceful coexistence as a mechanism for resolving international conflicts between socialism and capitalism, not at the battle field, but through peaceful competition in the "political and ideological" spheres, in "economic competition and competition in the improvement of the standard of living" of the respective political systems.[60] Rozanov was echoing the official strategic position of the Soviet Government on the concept of peaceful coexistence when he stated:

> Only the policy of peaceful coexistence can create the maximum conducive conditions for the successful implementation of the grandiose tasks of socialist construction and the development of the world revolutionary process.[61]

---

57   See Charles T. Baroch, "The Soviet Doctrine of Sovereignty", <u>Bulletin</u>, Institute for the Study of the USSR, Munich, August 1971, XVIII, 8, pp.7-25.

58   See Donald S. Carlise, "The Sino-Soviet Schism", <u>Orbis</u>, Winter 1965, XIII, 4, pp.790-815.

59   G.L. Rozanov, <u>Politika sotrudnichestva - velenie vremeni. SSSR i kapitalisticheskie strany 70-e gody</u>, Moscow, 1977, p.8.

60   <u>Ibid.</u>, p.10.

61   <u>Ibid.</u>, p.11.

As I have argued elsewhere[62] every Sovietologist should grasp the essence of the dialectics of peaceful coexistence as it is a significant concept in the study of contemporary international politics. It propagates peaceful cohabitation between conflicting socio-economic and political systems on a government-to-government basis, but it *does not* apply to relations between opposing class forces in a non-socialist polity. The basic idea of the concept is to eradicate war, and promote peaceful economic competition between states with different political systems without, however, jeopardizing the class struggle of the working class against the bourgeoisie.[63] Joseph Stalin, who had reasons to doubt the efficacy of the concept immediately after 1945, argued that the essence of the concept was to exploit the contradictions among capitalist states with the primary objective of "disintegrating imperialism."[64] As Michael P. Gehlen observed, Soviet interpretation of the concept "applies only to relations between states with different social systems" while "states within the system of party-states are excluded by definition."[65]

Articulating the dialectical-materialist contents of peaceful coexistence vis-à-vis the ideological struggle for world hegemony between Moscow and Washington, N. Lebedev posited:

> Struggle between them is inevitable in all spheres of mutual relations, international politics included. For this reason elements of co-operation dialectically intertwine here with elements of confrontation. Co-operation and

---

[62] O. Igho Natufe, "Detente and Disarmament: An Analysis of Moscow's Strategy", A Paper Presented at the <u>International Conference on Disarmament, Development and Regional Security in Africa</u>, Nigerian Institute of International Affairs, Lagos, July 15-17, 1981, p. 3.

[63] See <u>Diplomaticheskii slovar</u>, vol.2, pp.297-300; <u>A Dictionary of Philosophy</u>, Moscow, 1967, pp.334-335.

[64] J. Stalin, <u>Sochineniia</u>, Moscow, 1953, vol.5, p.113.

[65] Michael P. Gehlen, <u>The Politics of Coexistence: Soviet Methods and Motives</u>, London, 1967, p.259.

confrontation are the most important facets of peaceful coexistence, as components of a single process. Their unity is of a dialectical character; they cannot be isolated from one another, nor can one of them be discarded and the other retained.[66]

Proletarian socialist internationalism and peaceful coexistence are organically linked in Soviet foreign policy. The former expresses the "class content and class direction of the socialist revolution" while peaceful coexistence "implies a stable and consistent strategy of the policy and diplomacy of the socialist countries' relations toward the capitalist states regarding the question of war and peace."[67]

To ensure that the West did not obstruct the course of peaceful coexistence beneficial to the Soviet Union and the world revolutionary process, Soviet strategists sought to utilize, encourage and exploit the objective and subjective factors inherent in the capitalist camp. The dialectics of political relations manifested in the unified anti-communist policies of the capitalist states, and the economic and political contradictions inherent in their struggle to acquire and retain market opportunities in the less developed countries, significantly increased the potentialities for the Soviet Union to exploit. Similarly, the emergence of disarray in the socialist camp afforded the West opportunities to counter Moscow's calculations. In his analysis of the significance of ideology in Soviet stratagem, John Keep stated:

---

[66] N. Lebedev, "The Dialectics of the Development of International Relations", International Affairs, Moscow, no.9, September 1980, p.70. See also G. Arbatov, "Detente and the Problem of Conflict", Social Sciences, X, 3, Moscow, 1979, p.45; and Nikolai Inozemtsev, "Policy of Peaceful Coexistence: Underlying Principles", in ibid., pp.56-71.

[67] Sanakoev and Kapchenko, O teorii vneshnei politiki sotsializma, pp.89 and 106. See also Rozanov, op.cit., p.15.

> The zealous Communist makes no compromise except
> as a tactical manoeuvre to outwit the class enemy;
> he relates all his actions, however trivial they may be
> in themselves, to the ultimate goal . . . In this way he
> translates abstract theory into concrete revolutionary
> actions.[68]

In the view of Zbigniew Brzezinski, Soviet peaceful coexistence policy is but an ideological offensive, translated into the encouragement of radical nationalist revolutions made possible by the peaceful and paralyzing mutual nuclear blackmail of the USSR and the United States.[69]

A decade before Brzezinski published his Ideology and Power in Soviet Politics, E.A. Korovin (1892-1964), a Soviet international politics specialist, underlined the basic concept inherent in Brzezinski's analysis but from a different ideological perspective. He wrote that the Soviet Union stood "for peace also because, armed with the scientific Marxist-Leninist insight and the building of Communism, we know that time is working for us" and predicted that "the fall of capitalism as a system is inescapable, and that all roads lead to Communism."[70] In his analysis of Communist policy Brzezinski observed that the notion:

---

[68] John Keep, "Soviet Foreign Policy: Doctrine and Realities", Survey, no.4, January 1962, p.11.

[69] Zbigniew Brzezinski, Ideology and Power in Soviet Politics, New York, 1962, p.93. See also Marcuse, Soviet Marxism, pp.7 and 39.

[70] E.A. Korovin, Osnovnye printsipy vneshnei politiki SSSR, Moscow, 1951, p.28. See also S.Iu. Vygodskii, U istokov sovetskoi diplomatii, Moscow, 1965, p.97: Peaceful coexistence will "stimulate the development of the socialist society, and defines the cause of its foreign policy activity to a defined historical frontier - the establishment of socialism in all parts of the globe."

that ultimate peace depends on the total victory of a particular social system led by a particular political party injects into international affairs an element of a fundamental struggle for survival that may not be conducive to conflict resolution.[71]

The Soviets succeeded in making ideological (class) struggle the central theme in post 1917 international politics. They publicly stated that peaceful coexistence did not apply to relations between "antagonistic classes within each country or to the relations between foreign oppressors and the people oppressed"[72], and that ideological struggle, which Brzezinski referred to as "a fundamental struggle for survival," "does not allow any peaceful coexistence since there can be no class peace between the proletariat and the bourgeoisie."[73]

The concept of peaceful coexistence served two basic functions in Soviet foreign policy. First, it helped the Kremlin to maintain Soviet leadership in the international communist movement. Second, it facilitated the process for Soviet economic and technological advancement as witnessed in Soviet co-operation with the industrially advanced capitalist countries. In his address to the delegates at the 23rd CPSU Congress in 1966, Leonid Brezhnev declared:

> Comrades, while exposing the aggressive policy of imperialism we are consistently and unswervingly pursuing a policy of peaceful coexistence of states with different social systems. This means that while regarding

---

[71] Brzezinski, op.cit., p.113.

[72] Pravda, September 14, 1963. This was the definition contained in the Statement prepared by the Soviet Solidarity Committee and distributed by Soviet delegates to members of the Afro-Asian Solidarity during the Executive Council's meeting in Nicosia, September 1963.

[73] S. Vishnevskii, "The Ideological Struggle and Current International Relations", International Affairs, Moscow, February-March, 1970, Nos.2-3, p.38.

> the coexistence of states with different social systems
> as a form of the class struggle between socialism and
> capitalism the Soviet Union consistently advocates
> normal, peaceful relations with capitalist countries
> and a settlement of controversial inter-state issues by
> negotiations, not by war.[74]

The twin policy of proletarian internationalism and peaceful coexistence afforded the Soviet Union a dual approach to maximize its ideological interests and maintain its leadership role in the socialist Commonwealth of Nations, a phenomenon which John Armstrong defined as "a delicate mixture of dynamic expansionism and caution."[75]

This "delicate mixture of dynamic expansionism and caution" was most manifest in Soviet interpretation of the concept of proletarian socialist internationalism. A basic assumption of Sovietism was the equation of Soviet ideological interests with those of other socialist states and the international communist movement. Soviet interpretation was considered immutable until cracks began to emerge in what was once known as the Soviet "monolithic bloc." The Tito-Stalin quarrel and the subsequent excommunication of Yugoslavia from the bloc (1948); Moscow's military therapy in Hungary (1956) and in Czechoslovakia (1968); and the Sino-Soviet schism fatally ruptured the basis of this assumption. Prior to these cracks the institution of Marxist-Leninist political structures in a number of Asian and East European countries was a sufficient ground for pursuing Moscow's dictated "common" policy by socialist states. As some socialist states began to demonstrate their independence of Moscow internationally, the principle of proletarian socialist

---

[74] Leonid Brezhnev, "Report of the Central Committee of the Communist Party of the Soviet Union to the 23rd Congress of the CPSU", 23rd Congress of the Communist Party of the Soviet Union (March 29 - April 8, 1966), Moscow, 1966, p.50.

[75] Armstrong, "The Domestic Roots of Soviet Foreign Policy", p.57.

internationalism gradually became irrelevant to these states. The concept *on* its own could no longer guarantee Moscow its claim as the sole interpreter of Marxism. In its bid to reclaim this role, the Soviets formulated the Brezhnev Doctrine which sought to limit the independence of East European member-states of the Warsaw Treaty Organization (WTO) vis-à-vis the Soviet Union. It was used, *post facto*, to rationalize Soviet military invasion of Czechoslovakia in 1968, which Georgi Arbatov claimed was a "fraternal internationalist assistance to the Czechoslovakian people."[76] It is interesting to note that, a leading Soviet political analyst, A. Bovin, did not agree with Arbatov. He argued that the expectation that the establishment of socialism in East European countries was "a guarantee that national and international interests would somehow be harmonized" had proved futile. He concluded:

> Life has proved to be more complicated and contradictory than this formula. The actual practice of contact among the countries of socialism has shown that this homogeneity of socio-economic, political, and ideological structures is a necessary but insufficient prerequisite for the real establishment of the principles of fraternity and co-operation, complete trust, and mutual understanding in the relations among socialist states.[77]

Irrespective of the divergence in interpreting Marxism, Seweryn Bialer was of the view that the Soviet experience of socialist construction was an "emulative revolutionary model" for other socialist states.[78] From the perspective of the colonies,

---

[76]   Arbatov, The War of Ideas . . . , p.262. See also ibid., pp.274-282.

[77]   A. Bovin, "The International Principles of Socialism", Izvestia, September 21, 1966.

[78]   Seweryn Bialer, "Ideology and Soviet Foreign Policy', in George Schwab, ed., Ideology and Foreign Policy. A Global Perspective, New York, 1978, p.84. See also Donald S. Zagoria, "ideology and Chinese

the emergent states of Africa, Asia, and Latin America, the Soviet Union was considered a formidable ally to counter the U.S. and her allies in international politics. The anti-colonial movements of these countries gained tremendously from Soviet assistance in their struggle for independence. The polarization of global politics represented by Moscow and Washington afforded these countries the opportunities to maximize their policies in the international arena. For most of them, and especially the anti-colonial revolutionary movements, the question of allying with the Soviet Union was a foregone conclusion. In his address at the 25th CPSU Congress in 1976, Leonid Brezhnev elaborated on the relationship between peaceful coexistence and proletarian internationalism vis-à-vis Moscow's support for anti-colonial movements:

> This means, first of all, that quarrels and conflicts between countries must not be resolved by war through the use of force or by the threat of force. Detente does not in any way abolish and cannot abolish or change the laws of class struggle. No one can expect that in the condition of detente Communist will make peace with capitalist exploitation or that monopolies will become supporters of revolution.[79]

Foreign Policy", in ibid., pp.103-116; Seweryn Bialer and Sophia Sluzar, eds., Radicalism in the Contemporary Age, 3 vols., Boulder, Colorado, 1977; William E. Griffith, ed., The Soviet Empire: Expansion and Detente, Lexington, Mass., 1976; Peter van Ness, Revolution and Chines Foreign Policy, Berkeley, California, 1971; Bernard E. Brown, ed., Eurocommunism and Eurosocialism: The Left Confronts Modernity, New York, 1978; and Wolfgang Leohard, Eurocommunism: Challenge for East and West, translated by Mark Vecchio, New York, 1978.

[79] L.I. Brezhnev, XXV sesd kommunisticheskoi partii sovetskogo soiuza. Stenograficheskii otchet, Moscow, 1976, vol.1, p.57.

CHAPTER TWO

THE CHALLENGES OF SOVIET POLICY

Even though The Soviet Union actively sought cooperation with the capitalist states, particularly with the U.S. in resolving global conflicts, its approach to international politics posed a challenge to Western interests. This cooperation-confrontational basis of Soviet-U.S. relations constituted the most significant issue that shaped the contour of post 1945 contemporary international politics. This chapter shall briefly analyse the nature of Soviet-U.S. relations as a conceptual base for our analysis of Soviet interests in Africa.

When in 1835 the French social scientist, Alexis de Tocqueville, wrote about the United Sates and Tsarist Russia stating that "their starting point is different and their courses are not the same; yet each of them seems marked out by the will of Heaven to sway the destinies of half the globe"[1], little did he know that a completely new social order would emerge in the demise of Tsarist Russia that would radically transform the alignment of forces in world politics. He had no means of predicting the socialist revolution that overthrew Tsarism. His speculation on the future role of Russia in global politics was based on the immense size of the Russian empire that

---

[1]   Alexis de Tocqueville, <u>Democracy in America</u>, New York, 1945, vol.1, p.434.

engulfed two continents, and the close similarity between American and Tsarist Russia's empire building. Unlike Britain, France and other European colonial powers the U.S. and Russian colonial acquisitions were contiguous and subsequently incorporated into the respective nation-states. Besides the size of the Russian empire, the defeat of Napoleon Bonaparte at Barodino in 1812 must have impressed de Tocqueville as it also frightened Europe. The Soviet Union, as the successor state to Tsarist Russia, was prepared to fulfil de Tocqueville's prophecy.

While France, Britain and Germany had attained a higher level of industrialization, Russia remained a feudal and agrarian society. Tsarist Russia's alliance with Britain and France against Germany and her allies in the war of 1914-1918 posed a puzzle for U.S. president Woodrow Wilson. De Tocqueville's prediction that the U.S. and Russia seemed marked by Heaven "to sway the destinies of half the globe", obviously bothered Wilson's adviser, Colonel Edward House as he pondered over the prospects of the U.S. having to confront either a victorious Russia or a victorious Germany. According to Colonel House, either prospect would place America in a no-win situation: "If the Allies win, it means the domination of Russia on the continent of Europe; and if Germany wins, it means the unspeakable tyranny of militarism for generations to come."[2] The Russia whose domination of Europe Colonel House was concerned about was not the Russia that emerged in October 1917. The allies won the war, but without Russia as the Socialist Russia that emerged on October 25, 1917 had withdrawn from the war. In fact, the choices that confronted the U.S. in 1914 were mild by comparison with the threat which socialist Russia posed for the U.S.

The emergence of a socialist government in Russia injected a profoundly new dimension to the conduct of international politics. Lenin and his associates radically transformed the conduct of politics. Post 1917 international politics became more complex;

---

[2]   As cited in Arthur S. Link, <u>Wilson: The Struggle for Neutrality, 1914-1915</u>, Princeton, New Jersey, 1960, p.48.

as the contradictions became more sharpen and the alliances more structured ideologically. The structured nature of the alliances emanated from the internationalization of the class struggle concept which pitted Moscow and Washington on a diametrically opposed path. Socialist Russia posited itself as the leader of the international socialist movement with a mission to overthrow capitalism, irrespective of its professed policy of peaceful coexistence with the capitalist states. It is interesting to note that, notwithstanding the fact that the Soviet Union remained militarily inferior to the U.S. for decades, it did not conceal its ideological interest vis-à-vis the question of the demise of capitalism. The intensity with which the Soviets propagated this notion caused grave concerns for the West. As recent as 1980, i.e., eleven years before the demise of communism and the disintegration of the Soviet Union, Nikolai Lebedev, a prominent Soviet foreign policy scholar, could still say that: "The disintegration of the capitalist system and the formation of a world socialist system is a gradual process." Maintaining that "countries with different social systems must coexist for a period" Lebedev warned that "this does not mean that in the period of peaceful coexistence the process of revolutionary transformation stops. The foreign policy of socialism, having adopted the principle of peaceful coexistence, does not cease to be the instrument of class struggle in the international arena."[3] This dialectical relationship was undoubtedly the most profound theoretical problem in contemporary international politics. Its resolution could not be peaceful as the consequences of defeat haunted policy planners and decision makers in both the Kremlin and the White House.

The immediate reaction of the West to Soviet challenge was its multi-national military intervention against Soviet Russia in 1918. Having failed in this enterprise the western alliance sought to ostracize the Soviets in international politics. However, the dynamics

---

[3]   Nikolai Lebedev, <u>The USSR in World Politics</u>, Moscow, 1980, p.11. See also Sanakoev and Kapchenko, <u>O teorii vneshnei politiki sotsializma</u>, p.109.

of intra-capitalist contradictions rendered ineffective the policy of ostracization as the system of Versailles put excessive strain in the immediate post 1919 European politics. The Soviets broke the chains of isolation in 1922 by signing the Russo-German Treaty in Rapallo on April 12 while the Geneva Conference was in session.

Soviet preparation for the Genoa Conference revealed a high level strategic thinking as the Soviets mapped out a plan to confront the West. Soviet Foreign Minister, G.V. Chicherin proposed "a broad pacifist programme" that would introduce a new international system. Chicherin, who was a researcher in Tsarist Russia's foreign ministry before enlisting in Russia's revolutionary movement in 1905, was the son of a retired diplomat. He replaced Leon Trotsky in the foreign ministry in early 1918, and eventually signed the Brest-Litovsk Treaty with Germany. The Cannes Conference, convened in January 1922 without Soviet Russia's participation, was reconvened in Genoa with Soviet participation. The decision to invite the Soviets to Genoa was considered a victory for Soviet diplomacy. Genoa would offer Soviet Russia an opportunity to articulate its communist agenda before other European countries. In his letter to Lenin outlining Soviet Russia's basis strategies for the Genoa Conference, Chicherin wrote:

> The chief difficulty is that the present international political and economic forms serve as permanent fig-leaves covering the predatory acts of the imperialists; . . . The League of Nations is simply a tool of the Entente, which has already used it against us.

In order to effectively confront the Entente, Chicherin proposed:

> We have to introduce something new into the customary modern international forms to prevent those forms from being turned into a tool of imperialism. This new something is provided by our experience and our creative activity as well as by the creative activity of life itself in the process of the growing ruin and break-up

of the imperialist world. The world war has resulted in the intensification of the liberation movement of all oppressed and colonial peoples . . . Our international programme must bring all oppressed colonial peoples into the international scheme. The rights of all peoples to secession or to home rule must be recognized. The African Conference of 1885 resulted in the horrors of the Belgian Congo, because the European powers at that conference indulged in philanthropy towards the Negroes and that philanthropy turned out to be a fig-leaf covering the most barbaric exploitation. The novelty of our international scheme must be that the Negro and other colonial peoples participate on equal footing with the European peoples in conferences and commissions and have the right to prevent interference in their internal affairs. Another novelty is the obligatory participation of working-class organisations.

As he attempted to give meaning to the liberation of the colonies from imperialist rule, Chicherin further argued:

These two novelties, however, are not sufficient to protect the oppressed countries and downtrodden countries from the domination of the imperialists, because the upper stratum of the colonial peoples may well be puppets in the same way as treacherous labour leaders are. Working-class organisations will be confronted with the task of struggling for the liberation of the colonial peoples, for aid to the Soviet power and against imperialist depredation. The leaders, however, will try to betray them. Therefore, another novelty to be established is the principle of non-intervention on the part of international conferences or congress in the internal affairs of various peoples. Voluntary co-operation and aid for the weak on the part of the strong must be applied without subordinating the former to the latter.[4]

As the reader can see from the above quotations, Chicherin had established the foundation of much of the Soviet Union's strategic considerations in formulating its foreign policy. Lenin considered the points raised by Chicherin to be "excellent" and, referring to the other participants of the Genoa Conference, Lenin opined: "If they prevent us from making it public, we shall print it with our protest." This, in Lenin's views, "will help to demoralize the enemy." He concluded: "If we adopt such tactics we shall win out, <u>even</u> if Genoa is a failure. We shall <u>not accept</u> any unprofitable deal."[5]

The lengthy quotation from Chicherin's proposal constituted a vital contribution to the evolution of the theories of contemporary international relations. Specifically, the Chicherin proposal on the recognition of the rights of "all peoples to home rule"—independence—was meant to serve dual function: first, to confront European colonial powers, and secondly, to assure the colonized peoples of Soviet support. This proposal grew from the Leninist concept of the rights of nations to self-determination, a concept which, according to Arno J. Mayer, "posited the right of national self-determination as a universal principle"[6] in sharp contrast to the Eurocentric Wilsonian variant. Chicherin's proposals, coming as they did in 1922 when the Soviets had just survived a U.S. inspired military intervention, constituted a challenge to the West to readjust its conduct to correspond with the demands of the <u>new</u> international political system. The consistency with which the Soviets approached the question of a <u>new</u> international order, even in the embryonic stages of 1917-1922, put the West on the defensive over the issues of decolonization and anti-imperialism.

---

4 V.I. Lenin, <u>Completed Works</u>, Moscow, 1976, vol.45, pp.508-509.
5 <u>Ibid</u>., p.507.
6 Arno J. Mayer, <u>Political Origins of the New Diplomacy, 1917-1918</u>, p.299.

An ideological basis for an anti-West quadripartite alliance began to crystallize in Soviet foreign policy. Members of the alliance included the Soviet Union, the colonies, the international working class movement, and the new states of Africa, Asia, the Caribbean and Latin America (the so-called "third world"). A key role in this alliance was to be played by workers and communists in both the capitalist states and the new states. These constituted the fifth columnists in the global anti-imperialist strategy of the Soviet Union. Lenin's Peace Decree addresses itself to this fundamental stratagem.[7] When Lenin, in his endorsement of Chicherin's proposals, insisted that the Soviets "shall win out, <u>even</u> if Genoa is a failure" he was underlining the universal ideological propaganda value of Soviet foreign policy, a mechanism which contributed to the enhancement of Soviet international status in the anti-imperialist struggle.

This anti-West ideological thrust of the Kremlin, wrapped in the overcoat of peaceful coexistence, "has a beneficial influence on the development of the struggle against imperialism both in particular countries and on a world scale."[8] The hitherto dominant value system of the structure of international politics had been altered by the Soviet Union. Operating from a defensive posture, the West sought to isolate the Soviet Union internationally. Since Soviet policies were considered detrimental to the interests of colonialism and imperialism, the centres of international capitalism formulated the concept of a Soviet "threat." The ideologues of a Soviet "threat" had three basic objectives. "Firstly, it is essentially an anti-Soviet stratagem. Secondly, it creates an ideological platform for launching imperialist aggression against anti-colonial and national liberation movements. Thirdly, it forms the basis of integrating emergent nations of Africa, Asia and Latin America into the international capitalist market."[9] The reluctance of the West to endorse Soviet

---

7   See Lenin, <u>Sochineniia</u>, Moscow, 1949, 4th. edition, vol.26, p.220.

8   Lebedev, <u>op.cit.</u>, p.11.

9   O. Igho Natufe, "West, South Africa and Soviet 'threat' ", <u>The Nigerian Observer</u>, Benin City, Nigeria, July 31, 1986.

proposals for peace, collective security and the strengthening of the Covenant of the League of Nations in the inter-war years was influenced by its perception of a Soviet "threat." The League of Nations, ably manipulated by the Western powers, went to sleep as Italy launched its aggression against Ethiopia, a member-state of the League; the Soviet Union was alone in the League to condemn the Italian aggression. F.P. Walters, who was a Deputy Secretary General of the League, paid tribute to Moscow's peace policy which he described as "more consistent with the Covenant than that of any other great power."[10]

The policies of Italy and Germany posed severe threat to world peace and security, and called for a concerted effort of the international community to halt fascism and Nazism. Cut in the web of anti-Sovietism and anti-Nazism, Anglo-French diplomacy oscillated between an alliance with Moscow and/or to mollify Berlin. Eduard Daladier and Neville Chamberlain considered both Hitler and Stalin obstacles to French and British imperial policies. But the logic of politics compelled France and Britain to appease German aggression as was exemplified by the Munich Agreement of September 30, 1938 that dismembered Czechoslovakia and encouraged Hitler to fuel his war machines. As a result of the Munich Agreement further Anglo-Franco-Soviet negotiations on an anti-German alliance became meaningless. Inter-war diplomacy in Europe witnessed a series of security agreements as states sought to maximize their respective security potentials. The Soviet Union also entered into a series of such agreements with a number of central and east European states.

When the Anglo-Franco-Soviet negotiations broke down and the Munich Agreement had been signed, the Soviets decided to enter into a pact with Germany. The guarantee which London and Paris failed to give to Moscow was readily agreed to by Berlin, particularly in Eastern Europe and the Baltic region. The

[10] F.P. Walters, <u>A History of the League of Nations</u>, London, 1952, vol.2, p.585.

Nazi-Soviet Non-Aggression Pact was signed on August 23, 1939. The Soviets argued that they had no other alternative but to enter into an alliance with Germany. The Pact generated misgivings about Soviet global strategy. According to A.J.P. Taylor: "It was no doubt disgraceful that Soviet Russia should make any agreement with the leading Fascist state; . . ."[11] Taylor was convinced that the Pact was the only viable option left for the Soviets as "the British policy of drawing out negotiations in Moscow without seriously striving for a conclusion" increased "Soviet apprehensions of a European alliance against Russia." These apprehensions, Taylor argued, "were exaggerated, though not groundless." He further opined that Soviet decision to sign the Pact "was right according to the textbooks of diplomacy. It contained all the same a grave blunder: by concluding a written agreement, the Soviet statesmen, like Western statesmen before them, slipped into the delusion that Hitler would keep his word."[12]

The Pact is one of the sore points in Soviet diplomacy that Soviet scholars prefer to ignore. Their standard explanation was that the Pact afforded Moscow a breathing space, just as Brest-Litovsk had done. They believed that the West was encouraging Germany to march eastward, thus enclosing the Soviet Union between Germany and Japan. They also maintained that the Pact was an off-shoot of the Soviet-German Treaty on Nonaggression and Neutrality signed in Berlin on April 24, 1926.[13] Notwithstanding the Anglo-French connection in Soviet rationalization of the Pact, it should be stressed that the enthusiasm with which the Soviets promoted pro-Nazi policies between August 23, 1939 and June 22, 1941 raised serious doubts about Soviet policies. The Soviet Government considered it "senseless" and "criminal" for anyone, including Soviet citizens to

---

[11]   A.J.P. Taylor, <u>The Origins of the Second World War</u>, p.252.

[12]   <u>Ibid.</u>, p.253.

[13]   See <u>Diplomaticheskii slovar.</u>, Moscow, 1973, vol.3, p.259; I.M. Maiski, <u>Kto pomogal Gitleru</u>, Moscow, 1962.

agitate for "the destruction of Hitlerism."[14] Taylor's view that the Pact "was in the last resort anti-German"[15] contradicts the conclusions of an American scholar who argued that Germany gained substantially from the Pact.[16]

The quadripartite (Anglo-Franco-Soviet-US) alliance that was established against Germany and its allies began to crumble immediately after the war ended in 1945. An ideologically structured international alliance system—capitalism versus communism—was considered more appropriate to the resolution of post 1945 global conflicts. The rationale for the quadripartite alliance quickly dissipated. Richard J. Barnet aptly described this process:

> When old enemies disappear, mellow, or turn into allies, as frequently happens in international relations, new enemies must be found and new threats must be discovered.[17]

If in the inter-war years Moscow was considered a threat to world peace, this tag was worn by the Berlin-Rome-Tokyo axis during 1939-1945, a period when Soviet war machines proved crucial in the defeat of the axis powers and thus facilitated the process for the restoration of world peace. The division of Germany and the emergence of communist regimes in Eastern Europe and Asia further sharpen the contradictions between the West and the Soviet Union. Washington's acquisition of the atomic bomb injected a new dimension to American strategy. Both Bernard Baruch and Clark M.

---

[14]   See <u>Stenograficheskii otchet vneocherednoi piatoi sessii verkhovnogo soveta SSSR</u>, Moscow, 1939, pp.8-10.

[15]   Taylor, <u>op.cit.</u>, p.253.

[16]   See Vladimir Petrov, "The Nazi-Soviet Pact: A Missing Page in Soviet Historiography", <u>Problems of Communism</u>, Washington, DC, XVII, 1, 1968, pp.42-50. Note p.45n.

[17]   Richard J. Barnet, <u>Roots of War. The Men and Institutions Behind U.S. Foreign Policy</u>, New York, 1976, p.97.

Clifford emphasized the use of force to compel Soviet compliance with the West's conception of international relations. While Baruch advocated for a policy that would empower the U.S. to monitor, control and inspect "the industrial uses of nuclear energy <u>within</u> the Soviet Union"[18], Clifford advised President Harry Truman that in order for the U.S. to maintain its strength

> at a level which will be effective in restraining the Soviet Union, the United States must be prepared to wage atomic and biological warfare . . . The United States, with a military potential composed primarily of highly effective technical weapons, should entertain no proposal for disarmament or limitation of armament as long as the possibility of Soviet aggression exists.[19]

Clifford's view, in varied forms, found expression in subsequent U.S. policies as the U.S. State Department came to believe that "Soviet aggression exists" everywhere in the world.

The formation of the North Atlantic Treaty Organization (NATO) in 1949 was informed by the desire of the U.S. and its European allies to check Soviet moves as exemplified by the numerous NATO military bases within striking distance from the Soviet Union. The idea of <u>liberating</u> the citizens of socialist countries from communism by encouraging internal strife and also to curb the spread of communism by outlawing "communist activities" in non-communist countries, particularly in the colonies, gained currency in U.S. strategic thinking.[20] Dean Acheson, U.S. Secretary

---

[18] As cited in Walter LaFeber, <u>America, Russia, and the Cold War, 1945-1980</u>, New York, 1980, p.43. Italics in the original.

[19] As cited in Barnet, <u>op. cit.</u>, p.100.

[20] See J. Burnham, <u>Containment or Liberation: An Inquiry in the Aims of United States Foreign Policy</u>, New York, 1953, pp.31-14; 130-140.

of State, postulated the use of force to halt Soviet and communist advances.[21]

In response to NATO, the Soviet Union engineered the establishment of the Warsaw Treaty Organization (WTO), incorporating East European communist states excluding Yugoslavia and Albania, in 1955. These competing military alliances concretized the ideological struggle between capitalism and socialism in the international system. As the main representatives of these competing military alliances, the U.S. and the Soviet Union became engulfed in an international struggle for peace, power and influence around the globe. The struggle was most pronounced in Asia, Africa and in Latin America. Like its Western competitors, the Soviet Union began to employ the military as a political tool to advance its policy objectives outside the boundaries of East European socialist countries. According to a Soviet analyst, V.M. Kulish, "In some situations, the very knowledge of a Soviet military presence in an area in which a conflict situation is developing may serve to restrain the imperialists and local reaction."[22]

While Moscow and Washington did manage to avoid direct military confrontation, they however actively financed and armed competing forces in conflicts outside the boundaries of NATO and the WTO. This process advanced the development of the cold war as well as it enhanced the power prospects of Moscow and Washington globally. With reference to Africa, Soviet-U.S. rivalry injected a new dimension resulting in what can be called A New Scramble for

---

21 See D. Acheson, "Total Diplomacy to Strengthen U.S. Leadership for Human Freedom", Department of State Bulletin, March 20, 1950, pp.427-430; and his "Tension between the United States and the Soviet Union", in ibid., March 27, 1950, pp.473-478.

22 V.M. Kulish, Military force and International Relations, Moscow, 1972. Joint Publications Research Service 58947, May 8, 1973, p.103. As cited in Carol R. Saivetz and Sylvia Woodby, Soviet-Third World Relations, Boulder, Colorado, 1985, p.177.

Africa, the title of a book by a Soviet Africanist, E.A. Tarabrin.[23] Though Tarabrin excluded the Soviet Union from this "new scramble for Africa", it is obvious that any objective analyst would not exclude the Soviet Union from this "new scramble." Soviet-U.S. confrontation in Africa was a re-creation of the environment that led to the infamous Berlin Conference of 1884-1885, as both parties were engulfed in a continuous struggle to court favourable African allies for the protection and projection of their respective ideological positions. Referring to the effects of Soviet policy of detente on Africa, N.D. Kosukhin, a Soviet Africanist, declared:

> The atmosphere created by international detente intensifies the ideological scrambles which reflect the domestic and international class antagonisms in African countries.[24]

By employing the phrase, "ideological scrambles", Kosukhin, unlike Tarabrin, was able to include the Soviet Union in the "new scramble for Africa."

The U.S. monopoly of the atomic bomb in the immediate post 1945 period undoubtedly influenced Washington's disinclination in discussing disarmament issues with the Soviet Union as evidenced in Clifford's proposal. However, the Soviets continued to demand for a universal disarmament as the main thrust of Moscow's foreign policy strategy. This position was not discarded even after the Soviet Union acquired the atomic bomb and attained "parity" with the U.S. Nevertheless, mutual distrust arising from mutual hostility prevented the attainment of a bilateral agreement on disarmament during this period. Soviet policy of peaceful coexistence created a theoretical

---

23   See E.A. Tarabrin, Novaia skhavatka za Afriku, Moscow, 1972.

24   N.D. Kosukhin, "K voprosu o stanovlenii revoliutsionno-demokraticheskikh vzgliadov v stranakh sotsialisticheskoi orientatsii tropicheskoi Afriki", XXV sezd KPSS i promlemy ideologicheskoi borby v stranakh Azii i Afriki, Moscow, 1979, p.112. Italics mine.

barrier in Soviet-U.S. discussions of universal disarmament. The Soviets perceived peaceful coexistence as a continuous ideological struggle to weaken the West in the international system. This created a problem for U.S. policy makers as it posits the eventual victory of socialism over capitalism. In his criticism of this policy, Richard Allen called upon the U.S. to formulate counter-policies to halt Moscow's "long-range goal of world domination."[25] A U.S. Sovietologist, Zbigniew Brzezinski, viewed Soviet policy of peaceful coexistence as

> an ideological offensive, translated into the encouragement of radical nationalist revolutions made possible by the peaceful and paralyzing mutual nuclear blackmail of the USSR and the United States.

He further argued that Soviet policy

> that ultimate peace depends on the total victory of a particular social system led by a particular party injects into international affairs an element of a fundamental struggle for survival that may not be conducive to conflict resolution.[26]

Georgi Arbatov, Moscow's leading U.S. expert, agreed with Brzezinski's analysis. He acknowledged that Moscow and Washington represented opposing ideological classes whose policies determined "the content of that struggle." He defined this as "an antagonistic struggle which leads not to any reciprocal drawing together or even fusion of the two systems . . . but to the victory of the most advanced system, socialism, and to the subsequent reorganisation of

[25] Richard V. Allen, <u>Peace or Peaceful Coexistence?</u>, Chicago, Ill., 1966, p.174.

[26] Zbigniew Brzezinski, <u>Ideology and Power in Soviet Politics</u>, pp.93 and 113.

all international relations in accordance with the laws of life and the development of the new society."[27] Like Soviet leaders before him, Leonid Brezhnev, in his report to the 25th Congress of the CPSU, underlined the general policy direction which was later reflected in Arbatov's analysis. Regarding the nature of detente in contemporary international politics Brezhnev declared:

> Detente does not in the slightest abolish, nor can it abolish or alter, the laws of the class struggle. No one should expect that because of detente Communists will reconcile themselves with capitalist exploitation or that monopolists will become followers of the revolution . . . We make no secret of the fact that we see detente as the way to create favourable conditions for peaceful socialist and communist construction.[28]

The above Soviet position raised a vital question regarding the seriousness of the Kremlin to coexist peacefully with the capitalist nations. Washington's suspicion of Moscow's detente must be understood within the context of the tactical manoeuvring role detente was designed to play in Soviet global policy. The Soviets never renounced their claim to achieve global socialism. It was argued that:

> Whether or not this goal is realizable seems irrelevant as long as its consistent pursuance serves the fundamental interests of the Soviet state. Domestically, it rallies the population together in constant preparation against the

---

[27]   Georgi Arbatov, The War of Ideas . . . , p.35.

[28]   L. Brezhnev, "Report of the CPSU Central Committee and the Immediate Tasks of the Party in Home and Foreign Policy", XXVth Congress of the CPSU: Documents and Resolutions, Moscow, 1976, p.39.

agents of anti-socialism, while it helps to consolidate Moscow's allies in the international scene.[29]

It is this challenge posed by the concept of detente that informed Soviet-U.S. controversy over disarmament and the non-proliferation of destructive weapons systems. It could be argued that the Soviet Union knew it could not achieve its objective of obliterating capitalism as a global socio-economic and political system, and that its insistence on this issue was a mere propaganda. Raised to the level of state policy, however, this propaganda acquired a scientific character as it posited itself vis-à-vis capitalism on a philosophical plane. Just like anti-communism influences the course of U.S. foreign policy so too did anti-capitalism dictate the direction of Soviet foreign policy. In as much as the U.S. remains the centre of international capitalism, an ally of West European nations that colonized, enslaved and plundered the peoples of Africa, it will always bear the historical guilt of colonialism. Soviet anti neo-colonialism was targeted against U.S. interests in Africa. According to I. William Zartman:

> The focussing of discontent on Western scapegoats is the most unpalatable aspect of Communist control from the American point of view, for it provides a permanent bias against cooperation with the West on common concerns.[30]

---

29   O. Igho Natufe, "Detente and Disarmament: An Analysis of Moscow's Strategy", A Paper Presented at the International Conference on Disarmament, Development and Regional Security in Africa, Nigerian Institute of International Affairs, Lagos, July 15-17, 1981, p.6.

30   I. William Zartman, "Coming Political Problems in Black Africa", in Jennifer Seymour Whitaker, ed., Africa and the United States: Vital Interests, New York, 1978, p.89.

What Zartman referred to as "a permanent bias against cooperation with the West" was dialectically explained in Nikolai Lebedev's analysis of Soviet-U.S. ideological struggle for world hegemony:

> Struggle between them is inevitable in all spheres of
> mutual relations, international politics included. For this
> reason elements of cooperation dialectically intertwine
> here with elements of confrontation. Cooperation and
> confrontation are the most important facets of peaceful
> coexistence, as components of a single process. Their
> unity is of a dialectical character; they cannot be isolated
> from one another, nor can one of them be discarded and
> the other retained.[31]

Soviet perception of the role of cooperation-confrontation in political intercourse placed the agenda of global social development squarely on the deterministic interpretation of history, thus demonstrating a profound sense of strategy and vision to the chagrin of the U.S. and its allies whose main concern since post 1945 has been much of strategic planning devoid of vision.[32] Irrespective of our criticism of Soviet foreign policy, it should be stressed, however, that the Soviet Union successfully placed the U.S. and its allies on the defensive ideologically, as Moscow posited itself as the historically logical ally of global anti-colonialism. For most African states, for example, Moscow's alliance with anti-colonialism served a defined historical function just as any other alliance. In defence of their independence and suspicious of foreign powers, including the Soviet Union and the United States, these states pursued policies designed to keep both Moscow and Washington at bay. Even though

---

[31]   N. Lebedev, "The Dialectics of the Development of International Relations", p.109.

[32]   For a detailed discussion of this dilemma in U.S. foreign policy, see Zbigniew Brzezinski, <u>Game Plan: A Geostrategic Framework for the Conduct of the U.S.-Soviet Contest</u>, Boston, Mass., 1986, passim.

the Soviets denied the linkage, African leaders were aware of Soviet basic political interest wrapped in Moscow's anti-colonialism and economic cooperation with respective African governments who feared that the Soviet Union would exploit such a cooperation to facilitate the "penetration of Communism into their countries."[33] Thus, Soviet "cooperation" with African countries was viewed with suspicion by African political leaders

---

[33] See my "Diplomatiia i vneshniaia politika Afrikanskikh gosudarstv 1963-1968gg", Master's thesis, Friendship University, Moscow, 1969, p.108.

CHAPTER THREE

ISSUES IN SOVIET AFRICAN POLICY

In international politics, a state's conception of a phenomenon constitutes an important index of its foreign policy. The articulation of this conception is normally influenced by a combination of endogenous and exogenous factors. A fairly balanced admixture of these factors, objectively analysed and evaluated, is expected from foreign policy analysts. In discussing the issues in Soviet African policy one is confronted with the problematics of explaining the changes in Soviet foreign policy and their ideological legitimization, beginning from the reign of Joseph Stalin through N. S. Khrushchev to L. I. Brezhnev, with the brief period of V. I. Lenin's leadership as a vital background for ideological stimulation and guidance. Soviet scholars, in their analyses of Soviet foreign policy, had to walk a very tight rope. Even though the Khrushchevian and the Brezhnevian regimes witnessed an appreciable level of academic liberalization, Soviet scholars, as a rule, refrained from an in-depth analysis of Soviet foreign policy. Any semblance of an in-depth analysis surfaced in Soviet scholarship only after the exit of a political leader whose rule was being analyzed. Either their explanations are muddled up or they deliberately ignore external linkages to Soviet policy actions. I shall expatiate on this phenomenon in the following pages.

The issues to be discussed in this chapter are:

- ■ bourgeois nationalism and revolutionary democracy;
- ■ neutralism; and
- ■ the non-capitalist path of development.

These three concepts significantly influenced the formulation and implementation of Soviet African policy during the period under study. Soviet positions on these issues formed the basis of its policy towards Africa since the days of Lenin. This chapter seeks, therefore, to critically analyse the evolution of Soviet policies relating to these concepts. The historical-analytical approach shall be utilized to enhance our understanding of the ideological shifts made and their legitimization by respective Soviet leaders. Thus, these issues will be analyzed within the leadership period of Lenin, Stalin, Khrushchev, and Brezhnev with each of the last three legitimizing his policies with references to the writings of Marx, Engels and Lenin. As a rule, Soviet analysts working under a particular leadership eulogize the leader, only to condemn him and his policies in a succeeding leadership. Non Soviet Marxists who disagree with a eulogized Soviet leader are criticized as "left" or "right" wing deviationists by Soviet scholars, but, ironically, are praised by these same scholars in a succeeding Soviet leadership. For example, the well-known Italian Marxist and a leading member of the Comintern, Palmiro Togliatti, was vilified by the Soviets for his polycentric views in the immediate post-Stalinist era. He was however later rehabilitated and even had a Soviet town named after him—TOGLIATTI—where Soviet Lada (Fiat) is being produced. The same twist is observed in Soviet policies toward Bros Tito, Pandit Nehru, Kwame Nkrumah, etc. The rationale for these shifts is well summarized by Marcuse:

> The class interests of the Western proletariat (and for
> that matter of the entire proletariat) are sustained only

<u>to the degree to which they do not conflict with the</u> <u>political interests</u> of the USSR.[1]

A state's interest cannot be defined outside the realms of ideology. Thus, it is imperative that foreign policy analysts take into consideration the ideological rationalization of a state's foreign policy no matter how inept such a policy might seem. Such an ideological rationalization is never static, but dynamic and evolving in time and space. It is within the confines of this phenomenon that I undertake to study the evolution of Soviet policies toward the issues enumerated above.

The Source: Lenin

A discussion of Soviet policy towards bourgeois nationalism and the concept of revolution in Africa must be linked with the activities of the Comintern. This is so for the following reasons. First, the Comintern was established by the Soviet Government as its external organ of global socialist revolution. Second, it was through the Comintern that Moscow initially intended to affect a socialist revolution in the colonies and "backward countries" of Africa and Asia. Third, some of Lenin's most significant theoretical pronouncements on Soviet foreign policy were made at the congresses of the Comintern. Finally, Soviet policies toward bourgeois nationalism emanated from Lenin's formulations at the 2nd and 3rd congresses of the Comintern. Thus, before we dwell on the separate periods of analysis—the Stalinist, Khrushchevian, and the Brezhnevian—it is instructive that we analyse the proceedings and decisions of the Comintern congresses, especially from the 1st to the 4th congresses that Lenin attended.

The Comintern, or III International as it is otherwise known, was conceived as a follow-up to, or a replacement of the Socialist II International. During the war of 1914-1918 Lenin had called upon

---

[1]   Marcuse, <u>op. cit</u>. p.97. Italics mine.

respective parties in the socialist II International to attack the war effort of their home governments and, where possible, to engineer a civil war as a catalyst for a socialist revolution. However, this call was ignored by a gross majority of socialist parties who remained patriotic toward their respective governments' war effort. Lenin's attempt to reverse this trend failed at a conference of the socialist II International held in Zimmerwald, Switzerland, in 1915. He condemned the "Zimmerwaldists":

> The Zimmerwald bog can no longer be tolerated. We must not, for the sake of the Zimmerwald "Kautskyites", continue the semi-alliance with the Chauvinist International of the Plekhanovs and Scheidemanns. We must break with this International immediately. We must remain in Zimmerwald only for purposes of information.[2]

For Lenin and the Russian Social Democratic Labour Party (B)—(RSDLP (B))—the break with the socialist II international was final. Soon after the October 1917 socialist revolution in Russia the young Soviet government, in its Decree of December 26, 1917, invited foreign socialist parties to establish an international alliance. The Decree, which was signed by Lenin as Head of Government and Leon Trotsky as the Commissar (Minister) of Foreign Affairs, made available "two million rubles for the needs of the revolutionary international movement." Furthermore, the Decree added, realizing that "the struggle against war and imperialism can lead toward complete victory only if waged on an international scale, the Soviet of People's Commissar (Council of Ministers—OIN) considers it necessary to offer assistance by all possible means, including money, to the left international wing of the labour movement of all

---

[2]   V. I. Lenin, Selected Works, Moscow, 1967, vol. 2, p.44. Italics in the original.

countries . . ."[3] In early 1918 the responsibility of dealing with foreign socialist/communist parties was transferred from Trotsky's ministry to the Commissariat (Ministry) of Nationalities headed by Stalin. There was no question about Soviet Government membership in the Comintern, and the latter's role in the global strategy of Soviet foreign policy. However, V. G. Trukhanovskii, a prominent Soviet foreign policy expert, did not appreciate the constant reference to the Comintern as an instrument of Soviet foreign policy. He argued, but rather lamely, that the CPSU, "and not the Soviet government", was a member of the Comintern.[4] This type of argument, which was common among Soviet scholars writing on Soviet policies, was a reflection of the timidity in Soviet scholarship

The 1ˢᵗ Comintern Congress

The 1ˢᵗ Comintern Congress was held in Petrograde (named Leningrad following Lenin's death, but now known as St. Petersburg following the demise of the Soviet Union in later 1991) on March 2-6, 1919, with G. Y. Zinoviev as Chairman. He was also elected Chairman of the Executive Committee of the Communist International (ECCI). Though most of the foreign delegates at the inaugural congress were residents of the Soviet Union, Soviet authorities nevertheless described them as representing their respective countries. The intention was obvious.

Lenin's speech at the congress, "Theses and Report on Bourgeois Democracy and the Dictatorship of the Proletariat", outlined the global strategy of the Comintern and its linkage with Soviet foreign policy. He attacked the apologists of "democracy in general" and "dictatorship in general" and those who supported "bourgeois

---

3   Sobranie uzakonenii i rasporiazhenii rabocheego i krestianskogo pravitelstva, No. 8, Petrograde, 1917, p.119.

4   V. G. Trukhanovskii, Mirnoe sosushchestvovanie - norma otnoshenii gosudarstv razlichnym obshchestvennym stroem, Moscow, 1975, p.34.

democracy and the bourgeois parliamentary system", calling them the class enemies of Marxism. Employing the Marxist analysis of class and politics he criticized the class basis of bourgeois democracy as an instrument of suppressing the working class "by a handful of capitalists." Dictatorship of the proletariat, continued Lenin, represents the only authentic form of dictatorship and as such delegates at the Comintern Congress were enjoined to intensify the class struggle in their respective countries in alliance with the Soviet Union.[5]

TABLE 1. COMINTERN CONGRESSES

Congress	Date	Venue	Delegates	Countries	Chair	Leader
1st	March 2-6, 1919	Petrograde (now St. Petersburg)	52	30	Zinoviev	Lenin
2nd	1920 July 19-22 July 23 -Aug.7	Petrograde Moscow	217	37	Zinoviev	Lenin
3rd	June 22- July 12,1921	Moscow	608	52	Zinoviev	Lenin
4th*	Nov. 5- Dec. 5, 1922	Petrograde/ Moscow	408	58	Zinoviev	Lenin
5th	June 17 -July 8, 1924	Moscow	475	49	Zinoviev	Stalin
6th	July 17-Sept.1, 1928	Moscow	515	57	Bukharin	Stalin
7th	July 25- Aug.21, 1935	Moscow	510	57	Molotov	Stalin

---

[5]   For a full text of the speech, see Lenin, <u>Selected Works</u>, 3, 128-142.

Sources: <u>Sovetskaia istoricheskaia entsiklopediia</u>, vol. 7, Moscow, 1961, cc. 746-770.

*The 4th was Lenin's last congress. He died on January 21, 1924, five months before the sitting of the 5th Congress.

The Congress ended its deliberations with a call to "workers of all countries to unite under the Communist banner which has become the banner of great victories" for the international class struggle against imperialism.[6]

The role of the Comintern in Soviet global strategy was clear and precise. Respective members of the Comintern, particularly the West European parties whose countries had colonies in Africa, Asia, and the Western Hemisphere were required to stir anti-colonial revolts in those colonies, in order to divert the attention of the imperialist powers from organizing a frontal attack against the Soviet Union. This was particularly vital in the first decades of the October 1917 revolution. While most Soviet political analysts deliberately dismissed any linkage between Comintern political agenda and the goals of Soviet foreign policy, K. N. Brutents, a leading Soviet theorist of national liberation, admitted that:

> After the October Revolution, the national liberation movement helped the Soviet Republic to win time to consolidate its positions by diverting the imperialist forces.[7]

This position was forcefully underlined by Lenin at the 2nd Comintern Congress.

---

6   <u>Kommunisticheskii international v dokumentakh</u>, Moscow, 1933, p.60.
7   K. N. Brutents, <u>National Liberation Revolutions Today</u>, Moscow, 1977, vol. 1, p. 65.

The 2ⁿᵈ Comintern Congress

The 2ⁿᵈ Comintern Congress (July 19-August 7, 1920) was the most crucial gathering of the movement as far as the concept of an alliance between Communism and bourgeois nationalism is concerned. It laid the foundation for subsequent Soviet policies vis-à-vis bourgeois nationalism and revolutionary democracy. Soviet policy on the subject, as articulated by Lenin at the 2ⁿᵈ Comintern Congress, remains an embodiment of flexible policy options which can be implemented differently without distorting the spirit of Leninism. Subsequent Soviet leaders' conceptions of bourgeois nationalism and revolutionary democracy were guided by the policy formulated by Lenin at this congress. Differences in policy options pursued by Soviet leaders in their relations with bourgeois nationalists and revolutionary democrats <u>did not</u> contradict the basic tenets of Leninism. The obvious exception, of course, was Stalin who, after the 7ᵗʰ Comintern Congress of 1935, systematically destroyed the fabric of an alliance between Soviet Marxism and bourgeois nationalism. Such diverse applications can only be understood by the dictates of time and space, i.e., the exigencies of dealing with concrete historical and political situations. Thus, Lenin's policy outlined at the 2ⁿᵈ Comintern congress formed the basis for understanding Soviet foreign policy actions towards bourgeois nationalism and revolutionary democracy in general.

In his "Preliminary Draft Theses on the National and the Colonial Questions" Lenin recognized the vital role of the colonies in a world socialist revolution. He perceived a revolutionary upheaval in the colonies as a catalyst for West European communist revolutions. He emphasized that the Comintern's policy on the national and the colonial questions should be based "on a closer union of the proletarians and the working masses of all nations and countries for a joint revolutionary struggle to overthrow the land-owners and the bourgeoisie. This union", he continued, "will guarantee victory over capitalism, without which the abolition of national oppression and inequality is impossible."[8] Viewing the international polity as a battle ground between the forces of imperialism and those of socialism, Lenin argued that "all the national liberation movements in the colonies and among the oppressed nationalities", through their own "bitter experience" must realize that *their only salvation lies in the Soviet system's victory over world imperialism.*"[9] Thus, Lenin established a linkage between the "salvation" of the colonies and the survival of the Soviet Union as a key element in Soviet foreign policy. The underlining stratagem of this linkage is the primacy of the survival of the Soviet Union as it is only through this process that the "salvation" of the "colonies and oppressed nationalities" can be guaranteed. Lenin further opined that the alliance between the colonies/oppressed nationalities and the Soviet Union "should be determined by the degree of development of the Communist movement in the proletariat of each country, or *of the bourgeois-democratic liberation movement* of the workers and peasants in backward countries or among backward nationalities."[10] The basis of such an alliance, Lenin maintained, is proletarian internationalism. He criticized "petty-bourgeois nationalism" which "preserves national self-interest intact, whereas":

> Proletarian internationalism demands, first, that the interests of the proletarian struggle in any one country should be subordinated to the interests of that struggle on world-wide scale, and, second, that a nation which is achieving victory over the bourgeoisie should be able and willing to make the greatest national sacrifices for the overthrow of international capital.[11]

---

8   Lenin, <u>Selected Works</u>, 3, 423.
9   <u>Ibid</u>., 424. Italics mine.
10   <u>Ibid</u>. Italics mine.
11   <u>Ibid</u>., 425-426.

The major problem with proletarian internationalism is the non-identification of whose determination of "a world-wide" interest of the proletariat is supreme. Neither is there anywhere in the literature a set of criteria indicating the priority scale of global proletarian interest to which "a country should be subordinated to." However, it was obvious to non-Soviet Sovietologists that the Soviet Union perceived itself as the sole authority to determine when and how the interests of a "country should be subordinated" to proletarian internationalism. Lenin made this clear in 1901 when he stated that "the Russian proletariat" had "a right" to lead "the international revolutionary proletariat."

With particular reference to the "backward states and nations" where "feudal or patriarchal and patriarchal-peasant relations predominate", Lenin, in his "Preliminary Draft Theses" discussed at the 2nd Comintern congress, tabled six proposals to enhance communism in the colonies. The significance of these proposals as a theoretical construct for understanding Soviet foreign policy demands that they be quoted in full. Lenin postulated:

> first, that all Communist parties must assist the bourgeois-democratic liberation movement in these countries, and that the duty of rendering the most active assistance rests primarily with the workers of the country the backward nation is colonially or financially dependent on; second, the need for a struggle against the clergy and other influential reactionary and medieval elements in backward countries; third, the need to combat Pan-Islamism and similar trends which strive to combine the liberation movement against European and American imperialism with an attempt to strengthen the positions of the Khans, landowners, mullahs, etc.: fourth, the need, in backward countries, to give special support to the peasant movement against the landowners, against landed proprietorship, and against all manifestations or survival of feudalism, and to strive

to lend the peasant movement the most revolutionary character by establishing the closest possible alliance between the West-European Communist proletariat and the revolutionary peasant movement in the East, in the colonies, and in the backward countries generally. It is particularly necessary to exert every effort to apply the basic principles of the Soviet system in countries where pre-capitalist relations predominate—by setting up "working people's Soviets", etc.; fifth, the need for a determined struggle against attempts to give a communist colouring to bourgeois-democratic liberation trends in the backward countries; the Communist International should support bourgeois-democratic national movements in colonies and backward countries only on condition that, in these countries, the elements of future proletarian parties, which will be Communist not only in name, are brought together and trained to understand their special tasks i.e. those of the struggle against the bourgeois-democratic movements with their own nations. The Communist International must enter into a temporary alliance with bourgeois democracy in the colonies and backward countries, but should not merge with it, and should under all circumstances uphold the independence of the proletariat movement even if it is in its most embryonic form; sixth, the need constantly to explain and expose among the broadest working masses of all countries, and particularly of the backward countries, the deception systematically practised by the imperialist powers, which, under the guise of politically independent states, set up states that are wholly dependent upon them economically, financially and militarily. Under present international

conditions there is no salvation for dependent and weak
nations except in a union of Soviet Republics.[12]

Soviet views as articulated by Lenin at the 2d Comintern
Congress were never altered. They formed the basis of Soviet strategic
thinking on the questions of an alliance with bourgeois nationalism
and the tactical exploitation of such an alliance to enhance the
revolutionary potentialities of the communist class enemies of
bourgeois nationalism of the given country. Diagram 1 illustrates
this position. This is a dialectical approach to politics. Any concept
of political relations that ignores the dialectical categories of class
conflict and class harmony, as

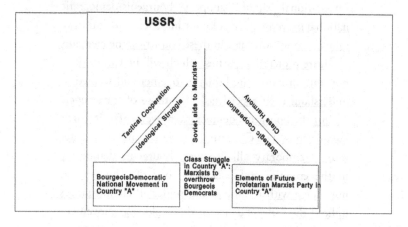

outlined in the unity and struggle of opposites, is not likely to yield
tangible result. Diagram 1 illustrates this position:

The 2nd Comintern Congress set up a Commission on the
National and Colonial Questions to synthesize the views of delegates.
Lenin's "Report of the Commission on the National and the Colonial
Questions" which was presented to the Congress on July 26, 1920,
contained amendments to certain issues of tactics suggested in his
"Preliminary Draft Theses." M. N. Roy and some members of

---

[12]   Ibid., 426-427. Italics in original.

the Commission rejected Lenin's proposed alliance between the Comintern and "the bourgeois-democratic movement in backward countries." In presenting the "Report of the Commission . . ." Lenin stated:

> As a result of our discussion, we have arrived at the unanimous decision to speak of the national-revolutionary movement rather than the "bourgeois-democratic" movement.[13]

In its report, the 2nd Comintern Congress described bourgeois-democratic as "reformist" while it considered national-revolutionary to be "revolutionist." According to Lenin, the "significance of this change is that we, as Communists, should and will support bourgeois-liberation movements in the colonies only when they are genuinely revolutionary, and when their exponents do not hinder our work of educating and organising in a revolutionary spirit the peasantry and the masses of the exploited."[14] This clarification, as contained in the Comintern's Report of the Commission, succinctly spelt out the conditions for an alliance between Marxists and bourgeois nationalists. Stalin, Khrushchev and Brezhnev contracted such an alliance based on their respective perceptions of the given political situations. Lenin had always described the first stage of a revolution as a bourgeois democratic revolution after which Marxists, in alliance with the peasantry and the proletariat, should push aside the bourgeois nationalists, assume the leadership of the movement and pilot the revolutionary struggle toward a successful socialist revolution. This Leninist position remained central in the strategic calculation of Soviet policy.

However, opposition to Lenin's proposals did emerge at the 2nd Comintern congress. The Indian delegate, M. N. Roy, expressed his scepticism on the question of collaborating with the

---

[13] Lenin, III, 457. Italics mine.
[14] Ibid., 458.

61

national bourgeoisie. His supplementary theses challenged Lenin's proposals, and the decision reached at the congress did not reflect a unanimous view of the delegates. Three fundamental questions faced the Comintern in 1920. First, should the Communists ally with bourgeois nationalism in the initial stage of the revolutionary struggle? Second, should the Communists seize political power of the anti-colonial movement at the initial stage of the struggle? Finally, is it expedient for the Communists to cede political control of the anti-colonial movement to bourgeois nationalists? A unanimous policy toward these vital questions of tactics and strategies has not been reached among Marxists ideologues. However, the fact that unanimity on these issues eluded the Comintern delegates in 1920 should not be regarded as a failure on the part of Lenin, as argued by Allen Whiting.[15] Such a position obviously ignores the dialectics of the universal and particular elements of revolutionary situations. The correlation of forces in a particular revolutionary situation of a country determines the <u>necessity</u> and <u>timing</u> of a tactical alliance between contending forces.

The 3rd and 4th Comintern Congresses:

The 3rd Comintern Congress (June 22-July 12, 1921) enunciated a tactical policy on <u>how</u> to ally with elements of bourgeois nationalism in a revolutionary situation. Lenin's proposal that Communists should go directly to the masses of bourgeois democratic parties and forge an alliance with them, bypassing their bourgeois Democratic Party leadership, became known as a policy of the "United Front From Below." This policy did not call for an alliance per se with bourgeois democratic parties, but was rather intended as a stratagem of Marxists' infiltration and subsequent subversion of these bourgeois democratic parties. The 4th Comintern

---

[15] See Allen S. Whiting, <u>Soviet Policies in China, 1917-1924</u>, New York, 1954. Note Chapter 3, "The Second Comintern Congress."

Congress (November 5-December 5, 1992), Lenin's last, reiterated the United Front From Below policy.

Lenin's death (January 21, 1924) and the ensuing power struggle had a profound impact on Soviet policy formulation as the contending alliances for power in the Kremlin began to perceive the question of Communist alliance with bourgeois nationalism differently. Divergent perceptions had their respective choices which obviously led to different expectations on the vital issue of Marxism's alliance with bourgeois nationalism. The Stalin-Zinoviev-Kamenev triumvirate that emerged after Lenin's death, proved to be a temporary alliance of forces. N. I. Bukharin and Leon Trotsky opposed the triumvirate. Zinoviev, a member of the triumvirate still enjoyed Stalin's support and thus was able to retain his chairmanship of the ECCI.

Policy in Disarray: Stalin

The 5ᵗʰ Comintern Congress:

Following Lenin's death Stalin immediately began to exert his position as the leader of the Comintern. This marked the beginning of the Stalinist era in Soviet policy. The Stalin-Trotsky power tussle tremendously influenced Stalin's perception of the revolutionary situation, as Communists became either pro or anti Stalin or Trotsky.

The 5ᵗʰ Comintern Congress (June 17-July 8, 1924) met in Moscow with Zinoviev as the chairman. As a result of the emerging disarray in the rank and file of international communism, which was a consequence of the Trotsky-Stalin controversy, the 5ᵗʰ Comintern Congress, on Moscow's prompting, took decisions to further enhance the leading position of the Soviet Union as the leader of the Comintern. The 5ᵗʰ Comintern Congress became known in "history as the Congress of the struggle for the bolshevization of the world communist parties."[16] At the 5th Plenum of the ECCI, the Comintern defined bolshevization thus:

> Bolshevization is the capability to apply the general principles of Leninism to a given concrete situation in a particular country. Bolshevization is the capability to seize the main "link" with whose assistance it would be possible to take off the "chains". And a "link" cannot be the same in each country hence the diverse socio-political situations we are observing.[17]

Stalin's anti Trotskyism became a key element in Comintern's policy. The "United Front From Below" policy gradually began to give way to a "United Front From Above" policy in Comintern's stratagem on the alliance with bourgeois nationalism. Stalin, in his speech at the 7th Plenum of the ECCI defined Trotskyism as "a petty-bourgeois social democratic deviation in the international working class movement."[18] Soviet analysts concluded:

> The decisive ideological and political struggle against Trotskyism within the Communist International where an active role was played by the representatives of the All-Union Communist Party (B), I. V. Stalin, D. Z. Manuilskii, V. G. Knorin, I. A. Piatnitskii, E. M. Yaroslavskii and others . . . aided the strengthening of the Communist parties along the positions of Leninism.[19]

---

[16]   Sovetskaia istoricheskaia entsiklopedia, Moscow, 1961, vol. VII, col.757.

[17]   Kommunisticheskii international v dokumentakh, p.478.

[18]   Sovetskaia istoricheskaia entsiklopediia, VII, c.758.

[19]   Ibid., c.759. See also Borba partii bolshevikov protiv trotskizma v posleoktiabrskii period, Moscow, 1969, p.160.

The intra party ideological conflict over the interpretation of Leninism affected the Comintern as member parties were divided between supporting either Stalin or Trotsky. The Chinese communists were victims to this ideological schism on the application of Lenin's flexible alliance tactics with bourgeois nationalists. Stalin proposed the "United Front From Above" policy, and Chinese communists were advised to ally with Chiang Kai-Shek's Kuomintang, an action which Trotsky opposed. The Communist-Kuomintang alliance was short lived. In 1927 Chiang Kai-Shek expelled communists from the Kuomintang and executed many communists, an action which necessitated a dramatic *volte face* in Soviet policy. Henceforth, Moscow viewed communism's alliance with bourgeois nationalism as detrimental to the cause of a socialist revolution. George Padmore was very critical of Soviet policy on this question:

> This orientation toward Asia and Africa was a violent departure from Orthodox Marxist strategy, which affirmed that the proletarian revolution which was to usher in communism would first occur in the highly developed countries of Europe and America . . . [20]

Padmore's criticism could also be seen as a negation of the October 1917 Russian socialist revolution. It however underlined the inability to apply Marxism to concrete historical situations based on an assessment of both the subjective and objective factors within a given country. A Russian social democrat, N. Mikhailovsky, who shared similar views with Padmore, was criticized by Lenin in 1894. Lenin responded to Mikhailovsky:

> No Marxist has ever argued anywhere that there "must be" capitalism in Russia "because" there was capitalism in

---

[20] George Padmore, "A Guide to Pan-Africanism", in William H. Friedland and Carl G. Rosberg, Jr., eds, <u>African Socialism</u>, Stanford, California, 1964, p.225.

the West, and so on. No Marxist has ever regarded Marx's theory as some universally compulsory philosophical scheme of history, as anything more than an explanation of a particular socio-economic formation.[21]

As a result of the Chinese fiasco bourgeois nationalists were excluded from the revolutionary movement and regarded as the mainstay of Western imperialism in the colonies. In this revised policy only revolutionary proletariat in alliance with the working class and the peasantry were considered sufficiently ideologically conscious to carry through a socialist revolution.

The 6th Comintern Congress:

The disaster of the "United Front From Above" policy in China had its casualties also in the Kremlin. The result of the Chinese episode affected the alignment of forces in the Soviet political leadership. Zinoviev was now expendable, and in his place Stalin's former opponent, Bukharin, was appointed Chairman of the ECCI. Stalin revised Soviet policy and returned to Lenin's "United Front From Below" policy. The 6th Comintern Congress (July 17-September 1, 1928) adopted the tactical policy of class against class, which meant an intensification of the class struggle against social democracy and bourgeois nationalism. Accordingly, social democrats and bourgeois nationalists were classified as communism's principal class "enemies" while Italian and German fascists were regarded as "lesser" enemies. This policy inflicted profound damage to international communism <u>and</u> the anti-colonial movements in the colonies. It aided the easy emergence of fascist dictatorships in both Italy and Germany as the communist parties of these countries, in accordance with Moscow's diktat, declined to join the broad anti-fascist fronts in their respective countries. Writing in 1961

[21] Lenin, <u>What the "Friends of the People" are and How They Fight the Social-Democrats</u>, Moscow, 1973, p.93.

Soviet scholars condemned the "class-against-class" policy. They conceded that: "The policy did not adequately assess the dangers of fascism, . . ."[22] This post Stalinist analysis by Soviet scholars was typical of the de-Stalinization process and represented the general dilemma we witnessed throughout in Soviet scholarship.

The Soviet Union had always linked its survival as a state with the fortunes and activities of the international communist and working class movements. Stalin insisted that this linkage was reflected in the programme adopted at the 6th Comintern Congress:

> In case of attack on the USSR by imperialist powers, it is imperative that in the colonies—especially in the colonies of imperialist countries attacking Russia—Communists seek to use the distraction of the military forces of imperialism with a view to exerting maximum efforts to develop anti-imperialist struggles and to organize revolutionary demonstrations which will have the purpose of overthrowing the yoke of imperialism and winning the battle for full independence.[23]

The basis for implementing such a grand alliance had been shattered by Stalin's class-against-class policy which the 6th Comintern Congress had also adopted. The alliance constructs capable of challenging fascism and Nazism had been rendered impotent by Stalin. Roy A. Medvedev, in the first major study on Stalinism by a Soviet scholar, summarized:

> Whatever may be said for Comintern policy toward the social Democratic parties in the early and middle twenties, it is impossible to approve the policy of 1929-1934. In this period fascist movements developed

---

[22] Sovetskaia istoricheskaia entsiklopediia, VII, c.759.
[23] Stenograficheskii otchet VI kongressa kominterna, III, Moscow, 1929, p.186.

rapidly in many European countries. The Social Democrats, excluded from power almost everywhere, went into opposition. Many of them took a clear if not always consistent anti-fascist stand. But Stalin, instead of changing Comintern policy, continued to insist on fighting social Democracy[24]

The 7ᵗʰ Comintern Congress:

A new twist in the domestic power struggle in the Kremlin left Bukharin in the cold. He was dropped as chairman of the Comintern and replaced with V. M. Molotov. The Moscow gathering of July 25-August 21, 1935 was the last congress of the Comintern, while the ECCI had its last meeting on November 6, 1939. Between August 1935 and 1939 Soviet policy as articulated by Stalin seemed to be in complete disarray. Stalin's perception of the correlation of forces in international politics militated against the emergence of an anti-fascist alliance at the crucial stages.

The paralyzing effect of the decisions of the 6ᵗʰ Comintern congress on the issues of tactics and strategies of individual communist parties vis-à-vis the twin questions of an alliance with bourgeois nationalism and the anti-fascist front necessitated another change in Comintern policy. Delegates at the 7ᵗʰ congress demanded greater independence in their domestic affairs. In order to escape from Moscow's intervention and to enhance the effectiveness of their respective strategies, delegates resolved "to avoid direct intervention in internal organizational matters of the Communist parties" and agreed to be guided by "the concrete situation and specific conditions obtaining in each particular country" before arriving at a unanimous decision.[25] This polycentric policy had greater significance than the

---

24   Roy A. Medvedev, Let History Judge. The Origins and Consequences of Stalinism, New York, 1972, p.438.

25   Seventh Congress of the Communist International: Abridged Stenographic Report, Moscow, 1939, p.566. See also Sovetskaia

popular front policy against fascism which was also endorsed at the 7th Comintern congress. The "United Front From Above" tactics reversed the earlier position. It implied an alliance construct of communist parties with the hitherto condemned social democratic and bourgeois nationalist parties against fascism. Both the polycentric and the "United Front From Above" (Popular Front) policies were not implemented because of "the Stalinist sectarian attitude" which ignored the resolutions of the 7th Comintern congress.[26]

Without any doubt Soviet dogmatic approach to Comintern policies between 1928 and 1935 seriously hampered the development of establishing a viable anti-fascist alliance. The deteriorating internal political process manifested in the various arrests and executions of Soviet leaders who were bold enough to disagree with Stalin did not only deplete the quality of political, academic and military personnel needed for national integration[27], but, more importantly, encouraged the perpetuation of the atrocities committed by both Hitler and Mussolini during this period. The "capitalist encirclement" bogey and the concept of "socialism in one country" undoubtedly clouded the perceptive lenses of Stalin and his followers.

Moscow's call for an alliance of all progressive forces in Europe, including the national bourgeoisie, to stop fascist aggression came too late and seemed to have no credibility when viewed against the background of the class-against-class policy which had already had its toll among Europe's social democrats. With the international class solidarity gradually withering away, and the domestic front in disarray due to Stalin's purge, the Soviet Union found itself gravitating toward a rapprochement with Hitler's Germany. The Nazi-Soviet Non-Aggression Pact, as we analyzed in the preceding chapters, was

---

istoricheskaia entsiklopediia, VII, c.766.

[26]   Medvedev, Let History Judge . . . , p.440.

[27]   For a detailed account of Stalin's crimes against his country, see Robert Conquest, The Great Terror. Stalin's Purge of the Thirties, New York, 1968; Robert C. Tucker, The Soviet Political Mind. Stalinism and Post-Stalin Change, London, 1972, pp.49-86.

an embarrassment to both the Comintern and the anti-colonial movement in the colonies. Irrespective of any attempt to rationalize it within the context of the dialectics of politics, its ramifications completely derailed Soviet credibility in the colonies as well as in the international revolutionary movement. The fact that the Pact's secret protocols compromised the independence aspirations of the African peoples[28] further lend credence to the accusation that the Soviet Union was also an imperialist power. The signing of the Pact led some prominent communists, including George Padmore who had played an important role in the Comintern, to consider the Soviet Union an imperialist country. They argued that the Hitler-Stalin alliance jeopardized the anti-colonial struggle in the colonies. Both contracting parties agreed to suppress any hostile demonstration or publication against each other in their respective countries. It was within this context that V. M. Molotov, the chairman of the Comintern and Soviet Foreign Minister, in late 1939 in a speech before the Supreme Soviet, underlined Soviet-German friendship. He declared:

> During the past few months such concepts as "aggression" and "aggressor" have acquired a new concrete context, have taken on another meaning... Now... it is Germany that is striving for a quick end to the war, for peace, while England and France, who only yesterday were campaigning against aggression, are for continuation of the war and against concluding a peace. Roles, as you see, change... The ideology of Hitlerism, like any other ideological system, can be accepted or rejected—that is a

---

28   See Secret Protocol No. 1 (Draft) of "Agreement Between the States of the Three Power Pact, Germany, Italy and Japan, on the One side, and the Soviet Union, on the Other Side", in Raymond J. Sontag and James S. Biddie, eds., Nazi-Soviet Relations, 1939-1941: Documents from the Archives of the German Foreign Office, Washington, DC, 1948, p.257,

matter of one's political views. But everyone can see that an ideology cannot be destroyed by force . . . Thus, it is not only senseless; it is criminal to wage such a war for "the destruction of Hitlerism", under the false flag of a struggle for democracy.[29]

The alliance between Soviet Marxism and German Nazism created revulsion in the rank and file of international communism. This was reinforced by the Soviet position that it was both "senseless" and "criminal" to wage a war for "the destruction of Hitlerism." Thus, anti-fascists were arrested as criminals in the Soviet Union. The zeal with which the Soviet Government articulated pro fascist policies between August 23, 1939 and June 22, 1941 remained a permanent scar in Soviet politics. It was anti-Marxist. Non Soviet Marxists, particularly in Africa, Asia and Latin America trace their schism with Moscow to this event. Subsequent attempts by the Soviet Union to re-establish its leadership of the international communist and working class movement were resisted and viewed with suspect. The gulf in ideological interpretation between Soviet and non-Soviet Marxists became widened. If prior to August 23, 1939, it was considered sacrilegious for a non-Soviet Marxist to disagree with, or mildly criticize Soviet policy, the desire for independent Marxist analysis gained currency in post 1939 and had become an established fact universally since the mid-1960s. Marxism was therefore freed from the ideological rigidity imposed by Stalinism, a freedom which Tito's Yugoslavia took advantage of in 1948 and which the CPSU at its 20th Congress in 1956 universalized.

Between 1917 and 1939 we witnessed periodic changes in Soviet policy vis-à-vis bourgeois nationalism from Lenin's flexible tactics of Marxist/bourgeois nationalist cooperation to Stalin's class against class policy. Stalin's policy reversal and his call for a progressive popular front composed of Marxists and social democrats against fascism

---

[29]   Stenograficheskii otchet vneocherednoi piatoi sessii verkhovnogo soveta SSSR, Moscow, 1939, pp.8-10.

71

came too late. Neither did the Nazi-Soviet Non-Aggression Pact of 1939 contribute to foster an anti-fascist popular front. Germany's invasion of the Soviet Union on June 22, 1941 compelled Moscow to seek an alliance with the main imperialist powers—Britain and the United States of America—for "the destruction of Hitlerism", an action which the Soviet Government had declared both "senseless" and "criminal."

Immediately following the war of 1939-1945 the Stalinist stance in politics became a dominant factor in Soviet foreign policy. The Soviet Union promulgated the "two camps" doctrine which was pursued rather vigorously. The outcome of the war influenced Soviet initiation of this doctrine. First, the emergence of Communist regimes in Eastern Europe and in Asia with Moscow as the undisputed leader compelled the Kremlin policy makers to talk of the "socialist camp." Second, the Soviet Government contended that the socialist camp, inspired by revolutionary Marxism as witnessed by the presence of Soviet Red Army troops in East European socialist countries, could now wage a successful ideological battle with western imperialism. Thus, Moscow viewed the world in a clear-cut, two camps, and East-West ideological confrontation. According to the Soviet definition of this doctrine the international system had no room for neutral states that preferred to remain equidistant in the ensuing East-West ideological struggle. Neutralism was considered highly untenable as Moscow was not impressed by Turkey's neutralism during the war. Soviet policy then negated the role of leaders of African liberation movements as a result of Stalin's conception of international communism and international politics.

Although a slight shift was perceptible in this period of Soviet African policy, it was not based on any sustained framework that would have radicalized Soviet thinking on the role of Africa's "bourgeois nationalists." In a 1953 article devoted to the national liberation movement in the Middle East, G. Akopian's views on the subject coincided with those of V. Vasileva on Africa which was written in 1952.[30] Akopian argued that in the "colonial and dependent countries the national <u>bourgeoisie</u> at a particular stage and at a particular time can support the revolutionary movement of its country against imperialist oppression", because "in colonial and dependent countries foreign monopolies not only exploit and oppress the workers of these countries, but also jeopardize the interests of the national <u>bourgeoisie</u>. He concluded: "The colonial and national oppression of imperialism in this situation plays a revolutionizing role."[31] While these views of Vasileva and Akopian, expressed in 1952 and 1953 respectively, revealed a subtle positive assessment of the national bourgeoisie, they did not find expression in official Soviet policy until 1956.

As argued by David Morrison, this delay in policy "was an impediment to Soviet appreciation and effective exploitation of political realities in Africa".[32] The anti-colonial liberation movements of Africa and Asia exemplified by the independence of India, Burma and Indonesia, and which the Soviet Union failed to recognize in the immediate post 1945 years, constituted a vital aspect of Soviet strategy at the time. Writing in 1977, Brutents, a leading Soviet scholar on the national liberation movement, acknowledged that:

> In the post war period, especially in the early years, the tide of national liberation revolutions dealt heavy blows at the imperialist policy of aggression, <u>helped substantially</u> to thin out the forces of imperialism and <u>to create more favourable international conditions for the</u>

---

[30]   See G. Akopian, "O natsionalno-osvoboditelnom dvizhenii narodov blizhnego i srednego vostoka", <u>Voprosy ekonomiki</u>, Moscow, No. 1, 1953, pp.58-75; V. Vasileva, "Narody Afriki v borbe za mir i svobodu", <u>ibid.</u>, No. 1, 1952, pp.90-103.

[31]   Akopian, <u>loc.cit.</u>, p.61.

[32]   David L. Morrison, "Communism in Africa: Moscow's First Steps", <u>Problems of Communism</u>, vol.X, November - December, 1961, p.6.

effort to rehabilitate the USSR's economy and build up
the emerging socialist community.[33]

Unfortunately, such an objective analysis by a Soviet scholar was
a ticket to concentration camps under Stalin. At the time he wrote
this piece, Brutents was a Secretary in the Secretariat of the CPSU.
While he represented a school of objective post Stalinist analysts
in the Soviet Union, it must be pointed out that a strong group
of historical falsifiers did exist in post Stalinist Soviet scholarship.
A representative of this group, R. A. Tuzmukhamedov, a Soviet
specialist on African and Asian affairs, stated that the non-aligned
movement "is a product of the general crisis of capitalism,"[34] and
not as a response to the "two camps" ideological polarization of
world politics which the Soviet Union initiated immediately after
1945. Referring to Pandit Nehru's conception of nonalignment
as formulated in 1947, Tuzmukhamedov claimed that the Soviet
Union had always applauded India's nonalignment as a factor in "the
development of new international relations" in the immediate post
1945 global politics.[35] This is historical falsification par excellence.
Let us go back to 1949, to E. Zhukov, a major exponent of Stalinist
politics on this subject.

When Nehru spoke of neutralism and nonalignment as
guidelines of India's foreign policy in the late 1940s, there was
grave concern in the Kremlin. He was branded the "Kerensky of
the Indian Revolution", while Sukarno of Indonesia was regarded
as an agent of imperialism. In his address to the USSR Academy of
Sciences on June 8, 1949, Zhukov underlined Soviet policy on this
subject:

---

[33] Brutents, 1, 65-66. Italics mine.
[34] R.A. Tuzmukhamedov, Nepresoedinenie i razriadka mezhdunarodnoi naprizhennosti, Moscow, 1976, p.22.
[35] Ibid., p.27.

Bourgeois nationalism is especially directed against the unification of the national liberation movements in the colonial and dependent countries with the anti-imperialist, democratic camp. Bourgeois nationalism is the most important ideological weapon used by the Anglo-American aggressive bloc for the goal of strengthening the shaky system of imperialism . . . Similar to the situation in the developed capitalist countries where the right socialist betrayers of the working class have attempted to spread the rotten notions of the possibility of some sort of "third", middle path between Communism and capitalism, but actively serves the forces of imperialist reaction plotting a war against the USSR, the countries are deceitfully chanting about their desire to "stand aside" from the struggle of the two camps, about their "neutrality" towards what they call the "ideological conflict" between the USSR and the USA. Actually they are allied with the reactionary bourgeoisie and slander the USSR and actively help the imperialists.[36]

Soviet distrust of neutralism and bourgeois nationalism did not change until the mid-1950s, after the death of Stalin, when the dynamics of international politics necessitated a reappraisal and remodelling of Soviet policy. Prior to 1954, Stalinist dogmatic approach to politics dominated Soviet foreign policy and academic assessment of African political development. Ivan Potekhin, the Doyen of Soviet Africanist, wrote in 1950 that the

Stalinist theory of colonial revolution proceeds from the premise that the solution of the colonial problem and

---

[36] E. Zhukov, "Voprosy natsionalno-kolonialnoi borby posle vtoroi mirovoi voiny", <u>Voprosy ekonomiki</u>, Moscow, no. 9, 1949, pp.57-58.

the liberation of the oppressed peoples from colonial slavery are impossible without a proletarian revolutions and the overthrow of imperialism.[37]

Potekhin was agitating for a "proletarian revolution" in tropical and southern Africa in 1950, arguing that the bourgeois nationalist leaders could not liberate their countries from colonial rule. The need for a tactical alliance between the Soviet Union and Africa's "bourgeois nationalist" leaders, as articulated by Lenin at the 2nd Comintern Congress, was brushed aside.

In the then Gold Coast (now Ghana) Kwame Nkrumah's Convention People's Party (CPP) won a decisive election in 1951, and he emerged from behind the prison walls to head the government. This election victory set the stage for Ghana's "peaceful, parliamentary transition" from a colonial status to independence. The Soviet Union, under Stalin, would not recognize any peaceful transition headed by a "bourgeois nationalist." Writing in 1953 Potekhin condemned Nkrumah's CPP:

> The government of the People's Party is basically a screen concealing the actual rule of English imperialism . . .
> The People's Party, representing the interests of the big national bourgeoisie of the Gold Coast, deceived the confidence of the people; the leaders of the party made a shape turn to the right, to the side of collaboration with English imperialism . . .[38]

Potekhin's evaluation of the CPP as a party "representing the interests of the big national bourgeoisie" was a reflection of the poverty of

---

[37] I.I. Potekhin, "Stalinskaia teoriia o kolonialnoi revoliutsii i natsionalno-osvoboditelnoe dvizhenie v tropicheskoi i iuzhnoi Afrike", <u>Sovetskaia etnografiia</u>, Moscow, no. 1, 1950, p.24.

[38] Ivan Potekhin, "Etnicheskii i klassovoi sostav naseleniia zolotogo berega", <u>Sovetskaia etnografiia</u>, Moscow, no.3, 1953, p.113.

scholarly analysis imposed on the Soviet Union by Stalinism. For a major Africanist and Soviet pioneering researcher of Ghana's history and politics to view Nkrumah and the CPP in that light was both unfortunate and distortive. How would he have evaluated the United Gold Coast Convention (UGCC), a party from which Nkrumah and his "veranda boys" broke away to found the CPP in 1949? Did he deliberately ignore Nkrumah's political activities, in Britain, particularly during the 5th Pan-African Congress at Manchester in 1945? Did he also disregard the philosophical content of Nkrumah's policies between 1947 and 1951?

Leading Soviet ideologists in the first decade following the war of 1939-1945 maintained that only a socialist revolution could redeem Africa and Africans from the yoke of colonialism. However, after Stalin's death in March 1953 the CPSU began to realize the impotence of its foreign policy. It became obvious to the CPSU that a negation of the "two camps" doctrine was imperative. For example, in July 1952, when the Egyptian army toppled the government in Cairo and seized power, the Soviet Government condemned the military takeover as western inspired: "In the night of July 22, 1952, power was seized in Cairo by a reactionary group of officers connected with the United States."[39] However, in 1954 when Moscow was convinced that the "reactionary officers" were

---

[39]   Bolshaia sovetskaia entsiklopediia, vol XV, Moscow, 1952, p.460. It is interesting to note that Anwar el-Sadat, a participant in the military takeover and later president of Egypt (1970-1981), revealed in his autobiography that he and his colleagues who effected the July 23, 1952 revolution decided to get "in touch with the Americans (even at dawn on July 23) to give them an idea of the objectives and nature of our revolution." Jefferson Caffery, "the U.S. ambassador invited us to have dinner with him at his place and we all accepted." Anwar el-Sadat, In Search of Identity. An Autobiography, London, 1978, p.108. The Soviets did not know about this in 1952 when they condemned the military coup as western inspired. Soviet criticism in 1952 was conditioned by Stalinism.

not receiving U.S. support, the Soviet Government proceeded to recognize the military officers and signed a series of trade agreements with Egypt.

Policy Rehabilitation: Khrushchev

Stalin's death on March 5, 1953 caused a serious problem for the Soviet Union as the CPSU had no established guidelines on leadership succession. However, Nikita S. Khrushchev emerged as the head of the CPSU with the title of First Secretary, and not General Secretary as Stalin was, while G. M. Malenkov became the Chairman of the Council of Ministers (Prime Minister). Stalin had occupied both positions. This arrangement represented a compromise between the contending forces that had crystallized following Stalin's death: the pro-Stalinists and the anti-Stalinists. Even though all the leaders including Khrushchev and Malenkov were "true Stalinists" prior to March 5, 1953, the death of "the Leader" necessitated an intra-party power struggle among his disciples as to which faction was best suited to either advance Stalinism or expose its ills. The compromise was only a temporary measure as each faction of the troubled alliance sought ways to outsmart its "ally."

The first noticeable break with Stalinism occurred in July 1953. At a Plenum of the Central Committee of the CPSU (CC CPSU), Malenkov delivered a major political speech condemning the "anti-party services" of certain party members which were said to be "in the interest of foreign capital." Lavrenty Pavlovich Beria, who was Stalin's hatchet man as head of the secret police and first deputy prime minister under Malenkov, was ousted from the CC, expelled from the CPSU and relived of his offices on July 10, 1953 "as an enemy of the Communist Party and the Soviet people."[40] Beria's case was referred to the USSR Supreme Court which ordered his

---

[40]   Kommunisticheskaia partiia sovetskogo soiuza v resoliutsiiakh i resheniiakh sezdov, konferentsii i plenumov Tsk. Vol. 6 (1941-1954, Moscow, 1971, p.384.

execution by firing squad on December 23, 1953. With his execution the anti-Stalin faction started to gain momentum within the party. Some contradictions over national policies, East-West relations, the question of rapprochement with Yugoslavia and foreign policy in general, led to the resignation of Malenkov in 1955 and the rise of the short-lived Khrushchev-Bulganin alliance. [41] Malenkov refused to accept de-Stalinization in exchange for Yugoslavia's friendship which Moscow lost in 1948 over the Stalin-Tito discord. His resignation in February 1955 therefore paved the way for Bulganin, as Premier, to accompany Khrushchev to Belgrade in May 1955. The Belgrade Declaration signed by Tito and Bulganin on June 2, 1955, had far-reaching implications in the process of de-Stalinization which was already gaining grounds in Moscow. The most significant section of the declaration was the recognition of different paths to socialism adhered to by both Soviet and Yugoslav governments. [42] Moscow had hitherto maintained that the "only" path to scientific socialism was the rigid application of the Soviet model.

Two other events of international importance also took place in 1955. These had greater impact on shaping Soviet policies toward bourgeois nationalism and neutralism. These were the Bandung Conference in April 1955 and the East-West Summit at Geneva in July 1955.

The Bandung Conference (April 18-24, 1955) of African and Asian countries and national liberation movements significantly influenced Soviet behaviour at Geneva. The Conference, which was initiated by Burma, India, Indonesia, Pakistan and Ceylon, was attended by 29 African and Asian countries including leaders of some national liberation movements and the People's Republic of China. This was the first gathering of Afro-Asian countries in which the participants attempted to construct a common strategy to

---

[41] For a detailed analysis of the power struggle in the Kremlin and its impact on immediate post-1953 Soviet policy, see W. Leonhard, The Kremlin since Stalin, New York, 1962.

[42] See Pravda, June 3, 1955.

combat colonialism and military blocs. The participants expressed their support for the Magrib anti-French independence movement. Moscow was impressed with the Bandung Declaration which was basically anti-western in tone. The Soviet Government quickly proceeded to ally itself with Bandung and to exploit its Declaration to enhance Soviet position in Africa and Asia. Writing in May 1955, Zhukov, the author of the pro-Stalinist address of June 8, 1949, to the USSR Academy of Sciences, began a process of self-criticism geared toward the rehabilitation of Leninist principles that Stalin had discarded and which the Khrushchev leadership was rehabilitating. Zhukov sought to establish a correlation between the 1917 October socialist revolution and the Bandung Declaration of the "bourgeois nationalists" of Africa and Asia.[43]

As a result of the impact which the Bandung Declaration had on the alliance structure of global politics, the Soviet Government began to initiate contacts with the key participants of the conference. Pandit Nehru was invited to Moscow in June 1955, while Khrushchev and Bulganin paid official visits to India and Burma in November 1955. It was at Bandung that President Abdel Nasser first requested for arms from a communist state—China. He discussed his request with the Chinese Premier Chou en-Lai who transmitted it to Moscow. Two months later, June 1955, Nasser formally asked the Soviet Union for military aid.

Besides Bandung, the year 1955 also witnessed a movement toward the normalization of East-West relations. Molotov was still Soviet Foreign Minister (1939-1949; 1953-1956). However, he had begun to lose credibility in the Kremlin where his policies were considered to be detrimental to Soviet declared policy of lessening international tensions. According to Soviet sources, he was against the signing of the State Treaty with Austria in 1955 and was accused of playing "into the hands of reactionary imperialist circles that

---

[43]   See E. Zhukov, "The Bandung Conference of African and Asian Countries and its historical significance", <u>International Affairs</u>, No.5, Moscow, May 1955, pp.18-22.

were determined to intensify international tensions . . ."[44] In 1955 the Soviet Government felt that it had taken sufficient measures to discard the negative traits of Stalinism, and was therefore prepared to press for the reduction of international tensions by promoting peaceful coexistence and detente. The Soviets could now state:

> After discarding the personality cult of Stalin which had negative consequences in foreign policy, the Communist Party of the Soviet Union and the Soviet Government, with enormous clearness of purpose and energy, engineered the struggle for peace for the prevention of world wars and for the settlement of disputed international questions through honest negotiations taking into consideration the interests of both sides.[45]

It was in pursuance of "honest negotiations" as a means of resolving international conflict that the Soviet Government decided to attend the Four Power Summit of 1955—The Geneva Conference—which grappled with pressing international issues. Before going to Geneva, the Soviet Government signed the State Treaty with Austria on May 15, 1955, that re-established an independent and democratic Austria. The Geneva Conference of July 18-23, 1955, was the first major East-West meeting since Potsdam. One of the products of the "spirit of Geneva" was Soviet diplomatic recognition of West Germany on September 13, 1955, even though the western powers did not reciprocate by recognizing East Germany.

Between 1953 and 1955 we have witnessed a systematic shift in Soviet foreign policy from that of promoting a violent two camps thesis to peaceful coexistence as a responsible or tactical response to the realities of contemporary international politics. It should be stressed, however, that this was not a new policy, but rather a return

---

[44]   Mezhdunarodnye otnosheniia posle vtoroi mirovoi voiny, vol.2, Moscow, 1963, p.637.

[45]   Ibid., p.264.

to the Leninist principles of international politics. According to the dialectics of societal change, the symptoms of a new society begin to crystallize at the decaying stage of the old society. This is also true between two opposing regimes of the same polity. A perceptive analyst of Soviet politics observed this phenomenon as early as 1953 when a reappraisal of Soviet immediate post 1945 policies was necessitated by Moscow's failure to blockade Berlin in 1948.[46] The setback of Soviet policy during the Korean War, and the ultimate prestige of the Asian neutral states during this conflict compelled the Soviet Union to readjust its policies toward neutrality. As assessed by Ginsburg, Soviet policy toward neutrality changed "from initial distrust to reluctant tolerance to whole-hearted approval."[47] It was in this atmosphere of positive reappraisal that the Soviet Government endorsed neutrality at the 1955 Geneva Conference, gearing itself to woo the emerging nations of Africa and Asia. Bulganin declared at the Conference:

> It is a fact that for some time a movement in favour
> of a policy of neutrality, a policy of non-participation
> in military blocs and coalitions, had been gaining
> ground in some countries. Experience shows that some
> states which pursued a neutral policy in time of war
> were able to ensure security for their peoples and play
> a positive role. This was confirmed, in particular, by
> the experience of the Second World War, although the
> neutrality of some countries was not beyond reproach.
> The Soviet Government is also of the opinion that any
> nation desiring to pursue a policy of neutrality and

---

[46] See George Ginsburg, "Neutrality and Neutralism and the tactics of Soviet Diplomacy", The American Slavic and East European Review, XIX, 4, 1960, pp.537-540.

[47] Ibid., p.542. See also E.I. Selezneva, Politika neprisoedineniia molodykh suverennykh gosudarstv Azii i Afriki, Moscow, 1966, pp.51-92.

non-participation in military groupings, while these groupings exist, raises the question of having their security and territorial integrity guaranteed, the Great Powers should accede to these wishes.[48]

To underscore the basic tenets of Moscow's endorsement of neutrality, Foreign Minister Molotov, in his speech at the Geneva Conference, emphasized the reason for Soviet recognition by stressing the "peaceful" aspect of neutrality which began to dominate Soviet policy. He opined:

> In many countries the desire to preserve a neutral policy is mounting, and this is one of the forms of a negative attitude to the policy of forming military blocs. As the Soviet Government has said, this tendency deserves every support, for it works in the interest of slacking international tensions and strengthening peace.[49]

A Soviet scholar, B. V. Ganiushkin underlined this position when he asserted that: "In contemporary situations after world war ll, the main criterion of evaluating neutrality is the relationship of the neutral countries to the maintenance of peace and the prevention of wars—this is the main objective of sincere peace-loving states in their foreign policies."

Soviet abandonment of its anti-neutralist policy at the Geneva Conference was endorsed by the CPSU at its 20th Congress in February 1956. Armed struggle was low-keyed as a viable option for the colonies, instead the "parliamentary path" to socialism was considered more practicable. In his address to the Congress, Khrushchev described the parliamentary path to socialism in "many

---

[48]   Izvestia, July 19, 1955. See also Ginsburg, loc.cit., pp.544-545.

[49]   Ginsburg, p.545N. See also B.V. Ganiushkin, Neitralitet i neprisoedinenie, Moscow, 1965, p. 8.

capitalist and former colonial countries" as a progressive step.[50] According to Richard Lowenthal, the upgrading of a parliamentary path to socialism was "a decisive step to free communism from a doctrinaire prejudice"[51] which had hitherto inhibited the development of Soviet Marxism as a universal model.

Khrushchev's "secret" speech at the 20th CPSU Congress, in which he strongly condemned Stalin's policies, climaxed the process of de-Stalinization in the Soviet Union. The political and ideological condemnation of Stalin and the Stalinist "cult of personality" led to the rehabilitation of ideas, concepts and personalities destroyed by Stalinism in the period between 1924 and 1953. Histories and textbooks were re-written with the "heroic" role of Stalin in previous editions subjected to complete ridicule. The "secret" speech caused grave political and ideological disarray in East European communist states. Viewed as a signal for ideological liberalism, political leaders in these countries became publicly critical of the continued Stalinist policies of their respective leaders. The Hungarian revolt of 1956 was a product of Moscow's de-Stalinization policy. Even though the Soviet Government intervened and crushed the revolt, the process of de-Stalinization which it initiated in 1956 contributed significantly to polycentrism in the international communist movement which nourished independent Marxist analysis in different countries vis-à-vis Soviet Marxism.

The Congress also regarded "bourgeois" national liberation movement in the colonies as an integral part of its anti-imperialist struggle. It further endorsed "peaceful coexistence" as Moscow's approach to international politics. With the CPSU Congress providing the ideological legitimization, Soviet scholars now shifted grounds to claim that:

> the national bourgeoisie is not always ready to betray the
> cause of national independence; indeed on the contrary

---

50   *Pravda*, February 15, 1956.
51   Richard Lowenthal, _, New York, 1964, p.25.

it is the natural and practically irreconcilable enemy of imperialism.[52]

Potekhin now had the opportunity to engage in self-criticism. He argued that:

> The gaining of political independence is only the first step on the road to attaining real independence, but it is a very important step. A sovereign state is the most powerful means of developing the national economy and of attaining economic independence by such a path. Already the very fact of the formation of a sovereign state limits the power of the imperialist powers and ties their hands.[53]

Thus began the process of rehabilitating Lenin's policy toward national liberation movements in Africa (and Asia) in post-Stalinist Soviet politics. Communism was to unite with bourgeois nationalism in an unholy alliance against western imperialism. In 1957, E. Zhukov, who was a staunch apologist of the Stalinist school of thought, was now compelled to regard an alliance between the national bourgeoisie and the communist working class as a progressive historical necessity which could hasten the collapse of capitalism in Africa and Asia.[54] This alliance, quite to Moscow's

---

[52]   See Helene Carrere d'Encasusse, "Soviet Foreign Policy in the Moslem East", in Oliver J. Frederiksen, ed., <u>Problems of Soviet Foreign Policy</u>, p.120

[53]   Ivan Potekhin, "Politicheskoe polozhenie v strannakh Afriki", <u>Sovetskoe vostokovedenie</u>, Moscow, no.1, 1956, p.32.

[54]   See E. Zhukov, "The October Revolution and the rise of the National Liberation Movement", <u>International Affairs</u>, Moscow, no.9, September 1957, pp.39-44; V. Cheprakov, "Nekotorye voprosy sovremennogo kapitalisma", <u>Kommunist</u>, no.1, January 1956, pp.93-108.

displeasure, constituted a dilemma to the Soviet Government as the bourgeois nationalists in power in most African countries continued to persecute local communists as agents of Soviet Marxism. This dilemma posed a series of fundamental ideological questions for Soviet policy makers. First, should the Kremlin cease to cooperate with African bourgeois nationalists? Second, would a Soviet refusal to cooperate tantamount to a tactical withdrawal from a potentially fertile ideological ground? Third, what would be the utility of a tactical withdrawal in the absence of viable re-entry points into the respective African countries? Fourth, how could the CPSU continue to assist local Marxist-Leninist organizations without Moscow's official diplomatic presence in these bourgeois African countries? If we view these questions in terms of policy options available to the Soviet Union in the wake of de-Stalinization and beyond, option four would seem undoubtedly the most viable one to pursue. Moscow's official diplomatic presence afforded the CPSU a channel to communicate with the local communists. Table 2 demonstrates a risk-incentive analysis of Soviet Marxist ideological interest as per the four options:

Options 1 and 3 were high risks for communist organizational work and ideological agitation as the given bourgeois nationalist African government could easily shift to a position of extreme reactions detrimental to Soviet Marxism. This is based on the assumption that contiguous countries to the given African regimes were particularly hostile to Marxism or any progressive thinking. Besides, the adoption of either option 1 or 3 created a conducive atmosphere for the U.S. and its allies to have a field day in the given country. While option 2 tended to represent a balanced position reflective of the correlation of forces in the given African country, it also was subject to a periodic swing from left to right of the political spectrum depending on the alignment of endogenous and exogenous class forces. Thus, option 4 presented itself as the most viable one for the Kremlin to pursue. It was on the basis of this that the Soviet Government proceeded to negotiate a series of economic, cultural and technical agreements with these countries, thus facilitating the influx of Soviet apparatchiki into the respective

African countries. The risk here was controllably low because of the opportunity to quickly adjust.

It should be stressed, however, that the computation of these options was strongly influenced by the basis and superstructure of the given African polity.

TABLE 2. RISK-INCENTIVE INTEREST MATRIX

Options at Stake	Intensity of Risk-Incentive:		
	High	**Moderate**	**Low**
Non-cooperation with bourgeois African governments	Risk		Incentive
Tactical withdrawal		Risk/Incentive	
Absence of re-entry points	Risk		Incentive
"Friendly" relations with bourgeois African governments	Incentive		

For example, option 1 would be the most appropriate course to pursue with regard to the then apartheid regime of the Republic of South Africa (RSA). As has been argued elsewhere,[55] non Marxist recognition of apartheid RSA coupled with a highly intensified urban guerrilla warfare targeted at the military-industrial installations would have a higher probability of compelling the apartheid regime and its western allies to seek a face saving device to dismantle

---

[55] See O. Igho Natufe, "Africa and South Africa: Policy Options", <u>Departmental Seminar Papers</u>, Department of Political Science, University of Benin, Benin City, Nigeria, February 5, 1981.

apartheid. Ian Smith's racist regime collapsed mainly as a result of such a policy. A sustained urban guerrilla warfare with highly destructive capabilities will force the apartheid regime to negotiate, hoping to retain a foothold, and institute a liberal multi-racial regime in Pretoria thus setting the stage for the second phase of the national liberation process.

In view of the above dilemma, and the need for strategic planning on the basis of the decisions of the 20th CPSU Congress, in 1960 the Kremlin policy makers formulated an ideological position, the doctrine of a "state of national democracy", which was conceptualized as a "united front" of national liberation in non-communist countries. Writing in 1960, perhaps to coincide with the formulation of this concept, Potekhin opined: "The gaining of political independence is the most important precondition for resolving all other tasks of the national revolution."[56] Except for a greater portion of the Stalinist era, Soviet analysts had always dichotomized (African) national bourgeoisie into competing groups. Such dichotomization became a matter of policy in post 1956 as a faction of the bourgeoisie allied itself with western imperialism while the other faction, though temporarily remaining bourgeois in form and content, opposed western imperial interests. It was this latter group that Moscow sought to cooperate with.[57]

The struggle for power in the immediate post-Stalinist era, i.e., 1953-1958, was not merely a question of who to replace Stalin but,

---

[56] Ivan Potekhin, "1960 reshaiushchii god natsionalnoi revoliutsii v Afrike", Sovremenny vostok, no.12, December 1960, p.5.

[57] See N. Savalev, "O roli burzhuazii v natsionalno-osvoboditelnom dvizhenii", Mirovaia ekonomika i mezhdunarodnye otnsheniia, (hereinafter referred to as Meimo), no.5, May 1962, pp.97-102; Ivan Potekhin, "On African Socialism: A Soviet View", in Friedland and Rosberg, Jr., eds., African Socialism, p.105; N. Postukhov, "Volia narodov Azii i Afriki k miru i edinstvu", Kommunist, no.5, May 1956, pp.88-95; I. Potekhin, "Vozrastaiushchee znachenie Afriki v mirovoi ekonomike i politike", Kommunist, no.6, June 1957, pp.100-113.

more importantly, who can either consolidate Stalinist policies or de-Stalinize and prove to be a more authentic Leninist. As the first socialist country and the leader of the international communist movement the victory of either faction was bound to have a corresponding risk\incentive correlate in Soviet global politics. For the leaders of the pro-Stalinist faction, Molotov and Malenkov, the socio-political consequences of de-Stalinization vis-à-vis their future role in Soviet politics was a nightmare which they dreaded. The thought of committing them to trial for crimes against the Soviet state, as per the Stalinist purge and show trials of the 1930s, was a constant reminder about the consequences of Stalinism. In the external arena this group also felt that de-Stalinization would cause the Soviet Union to lose its leadership role in the international communist movement. On the other hand, the anti-Stalinist group, led by Khrushchev and Anastas Mikoyan, was not only convinced that de-Stalinization would re-establish Soviet credibility as a global (communist) power, but, more significantly, it would endear the Soviet Union to the hearts of both the international communist movement and the leaders of the various bourgeois nationalist anti-colonial liberation movements. The incentive of de-Stalinization that was driven by the Leninist policies formulated at the 2nd Comintern Congress significantly out weighted any risk.

Between the 20th and 21st CPSU Congresses of 1956 and 1959 respectively, the pro-Stalinists made desperate efforts to seize political power. Referred to as the "anti-Party group" in subsequent Soviet writings, these leaders, including Premier Bulganin, Malenkov, Molotov and L. M. Kaganovich failed in their attempt to overthrow Khrushchev in 1957. Khrushchev, in surviving the first organized attempt to oust him, removed Bulganin and his allies from their respective positions and gradually began to consolidate his grip on power. He took over the premiership and, like Stalin before him, became both the Premier and leader of the CPSU. With his position seemingly enhanced, Khrushchev proceeded to formulate the policies of the 21st CPSU Congress, the Statement of the 81 Communist and Workers' Parties (1960), and the 22nd CPSU

Congress (1961) which ensured, in his own thinking, the complete process of de-Stalinization.

The concept of a "state of national democracy" was formulated by the Soviets and endorsed by the representatives of 81 Communist and Workers' Parties at their Moscow conference in November-December, 1960.[58] It was conceived as a Marxist stratagem for the seizure of political power in the less developed countries. To achieve an "independent state of national democracy", Marxists in Africa, Asia and Latin America were required to organize a broad national front in alliance with the national bourgeoisie. As defined in the 1960 Statement, a "state of national democracy" is:

> A state that consistently defends its political and economic independence, that struggles against imperialism and its military blocs, against military blocs on its territory; a state that struggles against the new forms of colonialism and the penetration of imperialist capital; a state that rejects dictatorial and despotic methods of administration; a state in which the people enjoy the broadest democratic rights and liberties (freedom of speech, of the press, of assembly, of demonstration, of forming political parties and social organizations), in which they have the possibility to strive for land reforms and for the implementation of other demands for democratic and social transformations and for participation in shaping public policy. The rise and consolidation of national democratic states gives them a chance to advance quickly on the road of social progress and to play active role in the struggle of the peoples for peace, against the aggressive policy of the capitalist camp, and for the complete liquidation of the colonial yoke.[59]

---

[58] See "Statement of the Conference of 81 Communist and Workers' Parties", Pravda, Moscow, December 6, 1960.

[59] Ibid. See also Richard Lowenthal, "On National Democracy: Its function in Communist Policy", Survey, London, no.47, April 1963,

With the exception of the last sentence, the above definition is both superfluous and ideologically contradictory. For example, the struggles "against imperialism and its military blocs" <u>and</u> "against military blocs on its territory" referred to two different phenomena. While the first is specific, the second is general. Thus, the former excluded the WTO, while the latter did not. The policies of France within NATO and that of Rumania in the WTO clearly illustrated the above contradiction. Furthermore, the reference to "a state that rejects dictatorial and despotic methods of administration" did not include identical regimes under socialism.

In the Statement it was underscored that, to achieve a complete "state of national democracy", the country in question must institute a total "extirpation of the economic roots of imperialist rule", pursue a "peace-loving foreign policy" and establish a permanent "economic and cultural cooperation with the socialist countries." As a Marxist stratagem the Statement envisaged to accomplish the following:

1. Local Communists and progressive forces in non-communist states must unite to liquidate the presence of "imperialist capital" in their countries.

2. The accomplishment of (1) and the abolishment of "imperialist military blocs" in non-communist countries would not only mean a pro-Soviet neutralist stance in international politics, but would easily facilitate the influx of <u>communist capital</u> into these countries, and thus create a fertile ground for the propagation and growth of communism.

3. Since the concept of a "state of national democracy" formed an integral part of Moscow's definition of a "non-capitalist path of development" which, according to Khrushchev, "will ultimately lead to socialism", local communists, in order to achieve (1) and (2), are to work with the national bourgeoisie and the peasantry in a united front during which

---

p.119.

period the Communists must consolidate their power-base
and be prepared to seize political leadership of the front.

This strategy was the first attempt by a Soviet leadership since 1924
to base its ideological thinking on the theses enunciated by Lenin
at the 2nd Comintern Congress of 1920. It also related favourably
to Lenin's proposal in his letter of September 1917 to the Central
Committees of the Bolshevik party in Petrograd and Moscow:

> The Bolsheviks, having obtained a majority in the Soviets
> of Workers' and Soldiers' Deputies of both capitals,
> can and <u>must</u> take state power into their own hands.
> They can, because the active majority of revolutionary
> elements in the two chief cities is enough to carry the
> people with it, to overcome the opponent's resistance, to
> smash him, and to gain and retain power.[60]

The abandonment of Stalinist ideological stance was influenced
by the fortunes of local communists in Africa and Asia. The strategy
proposed in 1960 was an ideological extension of the policies of the
20th CPSU Congress. However, it must be stressed that in 1960 the
revolutionary regimes in Africa—Egypt, Ghana, Guinea, Mali, and
Algeria—either did not have or had disbanded their communist
parties. In his address at the 22nd CPSU Congress in October 1961,
Khrushchev offered a solution to this problem:

> In the present era, practically every country, irrespective
> of the level of its development, can take the path leading
> to socialism . . . Marxist theoretical thought, profoundly
> studying the objective course of development, has
> discovered the form in which the unification of all the

---

[60]   Lenin, <u>Selected Works</u>, 2, p.362. Italics in the original.

healthy forces of a nation can be most successfully achieved. This form consists in the national democratic state.[61]

It was at the 22nd Congress that the CPSU took the final step of de-Stalinization. The Congress resolved to remove Stalin's body from the Mausoleum in Moscow's Red Square where it had been lying next to Lenin's since 1953. According to the resolutions of the Congress, the "serious violation of Leninist advises" by Stalin, his "abuse of power, the massive repression against honest Soviet citizens and other actions in the period of the personality cult made it impossible to allow" Stalin to continue lying next to Lenin in the Mausoleum.[62]

A linkage with Leninism was re-established. In his speech, Khrushchev echoed Lenin to provide an ideological credence for the thesis of a non-capitalist path of development. Lenin had declared in 1920:

> Not only should we create independent contingents of fighters and party organizations in the colonies and the backward countries, . . . but the Communist International should advance the proposition, with the appropriate theoretical grounding, that with the aid of the proletariat of the advanced countries, backward countries can go over to the Soviet system and, through certain stages of development, to communism, without having to pass through the capitalist stage.[63]

It was vital for Khrushchev to demonstrate his legitimacy as the authentic continuator of Leninism, and also to bolster his position

61 *Pravda*, October 19, 1961.
62 *Kommunisticheskaia partiia sovetskogo soiuza v rezoliusiiakh i resheniiakh sezdov, konferentsii i plenumov Tsk.* vol. 8 (1959-1965), Moscow, 1972, p.325.
63 Lenin, *Selected Works*, 3, 459.

globally as the leader of the world communist and working class movement. It was particularly important for him to project this image in the emergent countries of Africa, Asia and Latin America where the concept of the **non-capitalist path of development** was considered most relevant.

Notwithstanding the propagation of a non-capitalist path of development, Aleksandr Sobolev argued in 1963 that all African countries were basically capitalist oriented. He postulated that the quest for progressive development compelled some African political leaders to profess "socialism", but their "understanding of socialism is still very far from scientific" socialism. Nasser's Arab socialism and the African socialism of other African leaders constituted an attempt to escape from the agonies of capitalism, because, opined Sobolev:

> . . . a majority of these concepts were formulated in the process of desperate struggle with imperialism as a reflection of their poignant search for effective methods to quickly solve the urgent problems[64]

of building a democratic society. Sobolev contended that these African leaders should be encouraged since the content of their struggle was "anti-imperialistic", and there were the prospects that the future generation could lead Africa toward scientific socialism. He further argued that the state of national democracy is the most appropriate form of social organization that countries pursuing the non-capitalist path of development could establish because it

> is the real reflection of the victory of patriotic democratic forces over reaction, i.e., over imperialism, compradors,

---

[64] A. Sobolev, "Natsionalnaia demokratiia - put k sotsialnomu progressu", <u>Problemy mira i sotsializma</u>, Moscow, no.2, February 1963, p.41.

feudals, which is the first stage of genuine people's sovereignty.[65]

The Soviet Union viewed such a state as a union of all democratic forces made up of different classes and parties that are united in a popular front for the struggle against colonialism and imperialism. It is envisaged that the Marxist party would play the leading role in the united front. The concept of unity and struggle of opposites applies to the united front, and the local Marxists could reckon on the support of the Soviet Union and the international communist movement for the gradual but systematic elimination of non-Marxists from the united front.[66] This strategy is based on Lenin's slogan of an "alliance between the working class and the peasantry in the hegemony of the proletariat." In the Soviet view "the movement for the non-capitalist path would begin under the leadership of any democratic class", but the

> completion of the process, and the transition to socialism,
> is possible only under the leadership of the working
> class, on the basis of its union with the proletariat, at the
> head of which is the Marxist-Leninist vanguard.[67]

Thus, it is the core group of "professional revolutionaries", to use Lenin's phrase, that <u>determines</u> the timing of a socialist revolution and not the masses who, in all probability, do not understand class consciousness. Mongolia was frequently cited by Soviet scholars to illustrate the point that a successful socialist revolution could be engineered independent of the existence of a Marxist proletarian

---

[65]   <u>Ibid</u>., p.43.
[66]   <u>Ibid</u>., pp.44-45.
[67]   <u>Ibid</u>., p.46. See also <u>Afrika v mirovoi ekonomike i politike</u>, Moscow, 1965, p.85. For a Marxist critique of this Soviet position, see Mahmoud Hussein, <u>Class Conflict in Egypt, 1945-1970</u>, New York, 1973.

working class. It was argued that since the "historical mission of a working class and, in some aspects, of the socialist state for the Mongolian People's Republic was fulfilled by the brotherly Soviet Union",[68] less developed countries could also rely on the Soviet Union to play the same role. Marx never envisaged that a socialist revolution would take place in a less developed country; neither did he foresee that agrarian and backward Russia was to become the world's first socialist state. However, as Lenin repeatedly pointed out, Marxism is a theoretical and not a dogmatic guide which each country could interpret to suit its own domestic conditions. Writing in 1899 he declared:

> We do not regard Marx's theory as something completed and inviolable; on the contrary, we are convinced that it has only laid the foundation stone of the science which socialists must develop in all directions if they wish to keep pace with life. We think that an <u>independent</u> elaboration of Marx's theory is especially essential for Russian socialists; for this theory provides only general <u>guiding</u> principles, which, in particular, are applied in England differently than in France, in France differently than in Germany, and in Germany differently than in Russia.[69]

Lenin's analysis of Marxist theory applies to any other theory of social development. But the value of his analysis was ignored by a group of Sovietologists in their critique of Soviet politics.

---

[68]   Sobolev, "Nekotorye problemy sotsialnogo progressa", <u>Problemy mira i sotsializma</u>, no.1, January 1967, p.22. See also Y. Tsedenbal, "From Feudalism to Socialism: What we can learn from the Non-Capitalist Development of Mongolia", <u>World Marxist Review</u>, 4, 3, March 1961, pp.11-18.

[69]   Lenin, <u>Collected Works</u>, Moscow, 1960, vol.IV, pp. 211-212. Italics in the original.

The seeming decline of Marxian revolutionary ideology in the industrially advanced capitalist countries, vis-à-vis the growth or popularity of Marxism in the less developed countries, had compelled some western Marxologists to conclude that Leninism, and not Marxism, applies to the conditions of the latter group of countries. In their view Leninist "voluntarism" was an ideological departure from Marxist "economic determinism." Thus, the 1917 Russian socialist revolution is constantly referred to as a "proof" of this thesis, coupled with the non-existence of a working class in many less developed countries.[70] These scholars further argue that Marxism "is not" relevant to "traditional" African society, and that African leaders should be contented with the "democratic" process and the establishment of a welfare state following the pattern of some western capitalist countries.[71] It is not surprising that the concept of <u>class</u> is understood differently by opposing ideological scholars: Marxists and non-Marxists. For example, those in the advanced capitalist countries whom the Marxists refer to as <u>working class</u> resent this appellation. They do not deny they are <u>workers</u>, but would deny they are <u>working class</u>. Marxists do not appreciate this position because they conceptualize <u>class</u> as the determinant rather than the aspiration. In the Marxist view, most elements of the working class in advanced capitalist countries have constituted themselves into the mainstay of the bourgeois status quo and monopoly capitalism. This has become the case, essentially because the economic system of contemporary capitalism offers shares to the workers in companies and corporations, a phenomenon which has built in the workers a state of false consciousness vis-à-vis the general economic system of capitalism. They therefore seem to live a

---

[70] See R. N. C. Hunt, <u>A Guide to Communist Jargon</u>, New York, 1957, p.164; G. Sabine, <u>A History of Political Theory</u>, London, 1963, p.806.

[71] See David E. Apter, ed., <u>Ideology and Discontent</u>, London, 1964; A. M. Kamarck, <u>The Economics of African Development</u>, New York, 1967.

more "comfortable life" than the bourgeois class of the less developed countries. This phenomenon has led anti-Marxist social theorists to advance the concepts of "controlled exploitation", "limited exploitation", and "regulated capitalism"[72] in their justification of the benefits of capitalism. The class struggle concept is the most significant element in Marxian revolutionary ideology. This is captured in the <u>Communist Manifesto</u> which refers to the history of society as the history of class struggle. While Marxists conceptualize a society in class terms, non-Marxists do not but maintain that Marxism encourages social conflict instead of "class harmony." It is therefore logical as it is inevitable for Marxism to oppose other variants of socialism.

Some African leaders and non-Marxist Africanists are struggling to deny socialism of its Marxian ideology by propagating the concept of "African socialism." Julius Nyerere, the former President of Tanzania and a leading exponent of this school of thought, insists that the Marxian concept of class struggle does not apply to Africa because, in his view, Africa has "no classes" and that Marxism generates "class antagonism" and not class harmony. "Ujamaa", according to Nyerere, "is opposed to doctrinaire socialism which seeks to build its happy society on a philosophy of inevitable conflict between man and man."[73] Contradicting himself, Nyerere argues that "it is essential that the ruling Party should be a Party of peasants and workers." Therefore, concludes Nyerere, "for a country to be socialist, it is essential that its government is chosen and led by the peasants and workers themselves."[74] It is interesting that Nyerere does not see classes in contemporary Africa, but yet argues for a government of "peasants and workers." Nyerere's position is reflective of the trend in Africa to combat Marxism. As Kenneth

---

[72] For a critique of the Western anti-Marxist position, see <u>Theories of "Regulated Capitalism"</u>, Moscow, ND.

[73] Julius Nyerere, <u>Ujamaa - Essays on Socialism</u>, Dar-es-Salaam, 1968, p.12.

[74] <u>Ibid</u>., pp.16-17.

W. Grundy has argued: "In short, the denial of the presence of antagonistic social classes", by exponents of African socialism, "is a device utilized by ruling elites to bolster their regimes."[75] This device is being advanced as a substitute for reasoned ideological thinking. However, the conclusion drawn from such ideological non-clarity usually exposes the illogical premise upon which the argumentation is based.

This position is reflective in the rationalization provided by Bede Onuoha, a Nigerian Priest. He argued that ". . . African socialism is but an attempt to recapture and modernize the communitary way of life practised by the Negro races before the coming of the Europeans."[76] In order to "recapture and modernize" Africa's past Onuoha proposed the following developmental strategy for African countries:

> Private enterprise, yes; Communism, no. Public control
> of the economy, yes; Communism, no.[77]

It is significant to note that Onuoha negates both capitalism and communism but endorses "private enterprise" (a vital aspect of capitalism) and "public control of the economy" (a key determinant of communism). Onuoha's postulate gained currency in Africa as a "mixed economy" with disconnected ideological prism. How can the public exercise control over an economy that is based on private enterprise? An Egyptian Marxist, Mahmoud Hussein, has produced

---

[75]   Kenneth W. Grundy, "The 'Class Struggle' in Africa: An Examination of Conflicting Theories", Journal of Modern African Studies, 2, 3, 1964, p.392. See also Idris Cox, Socialist Ideas in Africa, London, 1966, p.71; Thierno Amath, "Class Structure in Tropical Africa", World Marxist Review, 9, 2, 1966, pp.25-29.

[76]   Bede Onuoha, The Elements of African Socialism, London, 1965, p.30.

[77]   Ibid., p.135.

a brilliant analytical indictment of the "mixed economy" bogey[78], while, in pursuance of an anti-Marxian thesis Charles F. Andrain advanced the widely known bourgeois position that Marx's theory applied only to "mid-nineteenth century capitalism":

> In particular, the theory of the class struggle is not relevant to Africa. Although there may exist castes or stratification based on religion, traditional Negro African society has no classes founded on wealth. Whereas European workers experienced class subjugation, the masses of African peoples came under racial domination[79]

The thesis advanced by Andrain, Onuoha and Nyerere is primarily designed to isolate Africa from the universal historical process by a falsification of Africa's social and political history. If Africa had "no classes founded on wealth" before European colonization of the continent, and if the main contradiction in Africa was (or is) "racial domination", one then wonders what were the basis and superstructure of slavery and feudalism as these socio-economic systems existed in Africa long before the European colonial era of African history.[80] One of the key ideological weapons employed by Andrain et.al to distort the class base of African society is to explain Africa's social strife solely within the context of "racial domination", "ethnic" or "religious domination" as if these phenomena were indigenous to Africa and alien to Europe.

While we concede that class consciousness is low in Africa, it is analytically fraudulent to raise "ethnic domination" to the level

---

[78] See Mahmoud Hussein, Class Conflict in Egypt, 1945-1970. Note pp.184-241 where Hussein seriously questioned Moscow's policies in Egypt on this subject.

[79] Charles F. Andrain, "Democracy and Socialism", in David E. Apter, ed., Ideology and Discontent, p.178.

[80] See I. I. Potekhin, "On African Socialism: A Soviet View", p.109; and I. I. Potekhin, African Problems, Moscow, 1968, pp.94-121.

of an explanatory variable of Africa's socio-economic and political problems. Those who conceptualize African polity mainly in terms of "ethnic domination" are deliberately ignoring the sharp class confrontation within respective African ethnic groups. It is interesting to note that this technique is a strategic device employed by the bourgeois elites to continue the class domination of their respective ethnic folks, by constantly reminding them that their main enemy is not the particular ethnic capitalist but rather members of the opposing ethnic group. Thus, ethnicity is used as a shield to conceal class domination. Let us illustrate.

The Urhobo and Itsekiri ethnic groups in the Delta State of Nigeria are neighbours. They have inter-married so much over the centuries that it is commonly said that every Itsekiri has an Urhobo blood. The territorial dispute between them has not prevented this inter-marriage. Most of those who are vocal in propagating either an anti-Itsekiri or an anti-Urhobo policy are, ironically, off-springs of this inter-marriage and also have their spouses from the "opposing" ethnic group, including the chief spokesmen of the revolving Itsekiri-Urhobo territorial dispute—Daniel Okumagba (Urhobo) and O. N. Rewane (Itsekiri). While they have succeeded in keeping aflame the Itsekiri-Urhobo ethnic conflict, in order to maintain a semblance of their respective ethnic cohesion, they are, on the other hand, staunch allies in the arena of class politics. The financial rewards accruing from the Urhobo-Itsekiri territorial dispute do not go to the oppressed workers of either ethnic group, but to the pockets of individual Itsekiri and Urhobo capitalists whose interest it is to keep the conflict alive.

Let us return to the thesis of Nyerere and Onuoha. Their argument that African society prior to European colonization was "communalistic" indicates that "communalism" was a social system peculiar only to Africa, whereas it is a universal phenomenon that every nation experienced at a particular stage of its socio-economic development. Marx and Engels addressed this issue in The German Ideology:

> The first form of ownership is tribal ownership . . .
> The social structure is therefore limited to an extension

of the family; patriarchal family and chieftains; below
them the members of the family. The second form is
the ancient communal and state ownership which
proceeds especially from the union of several tribes into
a city . . .[81]

The thesis of Nyerere and Onuoha is nothing but an unscrupulous
stratagem of Africa's elites to protect their privileges vis-à-vis the
working class. L. S. Senghor, the former president of Senegal
(1960-1980), attempted to "prove" the non-existence of classes in
Africa. He argued that ideology is a reflection of a people's culture
expressed in philosophical terms. In his view, there is no ruling
class ideology as opposed to the working class in Africa.[82] Speaking
in Sofia, Bulgaria, in May 1962, Khrushchev responded to the
apologists of African socialism:

Many of the leaders of the countries that have their
national independence are trying to pursue a kind of
fence-sitting policy, which they call non-class, are trying
to ignore the class structure of society and the class
struggle, which are matters of fact in their countries.[83]

Unlike Senghor, Kwame Nkrumah (Ghana's premier 1957-1960,
and president 1960-1966) made an ideological distinction between
philosophy and culture. He perceived philosophy as an ideological
manifestation of a particular class expressed as an ideological
class struggle. Thus, Nkrumah was arguing for the application
of Marxism in contemporary Africa.[84] Nkrumah had previously
defined the ideology of the CPP along the general framework

---

[81] Marx and Engels, The German Ideology, p.9.
[82] See L. S. Senghor, On African Socialism, New York, 1964.
[83] N. S. Khrushchev, "Speech in Sofia", Pravda, May 20, 1962.
[84] See Kwame Nkrumah, Consciencism, New York, 1965. Note chapter
3, "Society and Ideology."

of African socialism; in its 1962 programme the CPP endorsed "scientific socialism"—Marxism—as the party's ideology.[85]

Marxists have always maintained that "scientific socialism" was the only acceptable brand of socialism. However, as we have observed since the Yugoslav-Soviet rapprochement of 1955, the Soviet Union conceded that each country could map its own path to socialism based on the country's peculiar conditions. This decision was merely a re-statement or rehabilitation of Lenin's position of 1899 referred to above in this chapter. Based on this, Potekhin thus rationalized:

> There are no grounds therefore to oppose "African Socialism" to scientific socialism if all that is meant by "African Socialism" is the specific paths and means of proceeding to socialism that correspond to African reality.[86]

There is no general theory of African socialism. Proponents of African socialism have consistently opposed Marxism on the grounds that the latter breeds class confrontation. Arthur Jay Klinghoffer's analysis of the relationship between Marxism and African socialism conflicts with the position of the latter. He argued:

> In fact, African socialists do not deny the applicability of Marxism to Africa. They often claim that Marxism is definitely relevant to their continent but that Marxism is not a dogma and its lessons must be put into practice in accordance with different national conditions.[87]

---

85   See <u>Work and Happiness. Programme of the Convention People's Party</u>, Accra, 1962, p.7; The Spark, Accra, November 13, 1964.

86   Potekhin, <u>African Problems</u>, p.42. Note pp.35-44.

87   Arthur Jay Klinghoffer, <u>Soviet Perspectives on African Socialism</u>, Madison, Ill., 1969, p.70.

Klinghoffer would seem to be advancing a position that contradicts the main tenets of African socialism as enunciated by Nyerere, Onuoha and Senghor whose works define the ideological world outlook of African socialism. Since African socialists reject the Marxist concept of class struggle, the cornerstone of Marxism, it is ideologically incongruous to conclude that they "do not deny the applicability of Marxism to Africa", as claimed by Klinghoffer. Furthermore, Klinghoffer argued that there is no difference between the state of national democracy and the non-capitalist path of development, but failed to indicate the difference. In fact, these concepts represent the two sides of a coin. The non-capitalist path of development is the socio-economic formation which determines the character of the political superstructure—the state of national democracy.

Though Marx and Engels did not provide any theory on the non-capitalist path of development, we can extrapolate from the general outlines of Marxist revolutionary strategy some elements of tactical significance which link Marxism to this concept. Marcuse opined that "two main factors" influenced "the emergence of Leninism as a new form of Marxism", which gave birth to non-capitalist development. These factors, according to Marcuse, are:

> the attempt to draw the peasantry into the orbit of Marxian theory and strategy, and (2) the attempt to redefine the prospects of capitalist and revolutionary development in the imperialist era. The two main current of Leninist thought are closely interrelated; the viability of advanced capitalism (unexpected from the traditional Marxist point of view) and, consequently, the continued strength of reformism among the proletariat in the advanced capitalist countries called almost inevitably for s shift in Marxist emphasis to the backward countries, which were predominantly agricultural and <u>where the</u>

weakness of the capitalist sector seemed to offer better chances for a revolution.[88]

Potekhin's analysis of this "shift in Marxist emphasis" substantiates Marcuse's conclusion. His central theme, and indeed Moscow's argument for advocating that African and other less developed countries should proceed to socialism by-passing capitalism is based on the following premise: 1) it would take these countries centuries to attain advanced capitalism and catch up with the more advanced capitalist countries; and 2) they would be subjugated to centuries of continued exploitation by the West. The Soviets had projected socialism as the short-cut to solving Africa's socio-economic and political problems. They argued that "the world socialist system" had created conducive objective conditions for this process.[89]

In the preceding analyses Potekhin, as the founding Director of the Institute of Africa of the USSR Academy of Sciences (1959-1964), emerged as the main academic articulator of Soviet policies toward Africa. In fact, the establishment of the Institute of Africa in 1959 was through the personal efforts of Potekhin who succeeded in convincing the Kremlin about the desirability of such an Institute. Prior to 1959 Soviet researchers on African affairs had operated from both the Institute of Oriental Studies and the Institute of Ethnography. Potekhin was the Deputy Director of the Institute of Ethnography from 1949 to 1959. With regards to Soviet African policy of the Khrushchevian period, Potekhin, without a doubt, provided the intellectual materials Khrushchev needed for an effective policy formulation and articulation. It was rather ironic that this intellectual-politician collaboration came to an abrupt end in 1964. Potekhin died on September 17, 1964, while Khrushchev was overthrown from power by a Kremlin palace coup on October 14, 1964. On October 14 the Plenum of the CC CPSU

---

88   Marcuse, op. cit., p. 29. Italics mine.
89   I. Potekhin, "On African Socialism", International Affairs, Moscow, no.1, 1963, p.73.

ousted Khrushchev from his offices of First Secretary of the CC CPSU <u>and</u> Premier (Chairman, Council of Ministers) of the Soviet Union, including his membership of the Presidium on the grounds of "advancing age and deteriorating health."[90] The fact that this decision taken on October 14 did not appear in <u>Pravda</u> on October 15, but on October 16, testified to the power tussle in the Kremlin. It could also suggest that the Plenum took the decision in the early hours of October 15. In 1964 Khrushchev was 70 years old, and was in a better physical condition than Leonid Brezhnev was at 68 years old in 1974, or at any time from 1974 to 1982 when he, Brezhnev, died in office of "advancing age and deteriorating health."

Policy Consolidation: Brezhnev

The ouster of Khrushchev from power, and the role Brezhnev played in the process was perceived by Soviet analysts as a move to stir the Soviet Union along the path of qualitative advancement in domestic and international affairs. Though Khrushchev significantly contributed toward the enhancement of Soviet credibility in international politics, particularly in Africa, his reign also registered some abysmal setbacks in domestic and external policies.[91] For example, the decisions of the 20th CPSU Congress courted the friendship of the national bourgeoisie in Africa and Asia and, at the same time, produced a bitter split in the international communist movement: the Sino-Soviet schism. The problems caused by Soviet handling of both the Berlin and Cuban crises overshadowed the political points scored in the 1963 Moscow Test Ban Treaty.

But why did I decide to refer to the Brezhnev leadership as a period of policy consolidation? While Khrushchev's de-Stalinization policy rehabilitated Leninism and facilitated the publications of

---

90 <u>Pravda</u>, October 16, 1964.
91 See, for example, the analysis of Roy A. Medvedev and Zhores A. Medvedev, <u>Khrushchev: The Years in Power</u>, London, 1977, pp.94-128.

such literary works as A. Solzhenitsyn's <u>One Day in the Life of Ivan Denisovich</u>, for example, Khrushchev and his policy makers failed to provide effective ideological guidance to control the euphoria created by de-Stalinization. The key question that arose was: How do you promote de-Stalinization and at the same time formulate and implement policies that would reflect, ideologically, a firm grip of the socialist polity? For the regime regulators, it became vitally important for them to <u>consolidate</u> the gains of the socialist polity, by instituting an effective monitoring mechanism to checkmate any possible excess of "dangerous liberal" tendencies emanating from uncontrolled de-Stalinization.

Following the example of the power structure in the immediate post Stalin years (1953-1958), the post Khrushchev CPSU in October 1964 established a collective leadership system. Brezhnev and Alexie N. Kosygin took over Khrushchev's offices of First Secretary of the CC CPSU and the Premier of the USSR, respectively, while Mikoyan replaced Brezhnev as the titular Head of State—Chairman of the Presidium of the USSR Supreme Soviet in 1964-65, only to be replaced by N. V. Podgornyi in 1965. The Brezhnev-Kosygin—Podgornyi triumvirate initially worked well as a collective with each performing specific functions. Thus, while Brezhnev was in-charge of party domestic and external affairs, Kosygin took care of government-to-government relations, and Podgornyi functioned as the ceremonial Head of State receiving the credentials of foreign ambassadors and, above all, the traditional 21-gun salute as Soviet Head of State when on official visits abroad. At the 23rd CPSU Congress (March 29-April 8, 1966) Brezhnev's title of First Secretary was changed to General Secretary—a return to the title under Stalin. As head of the party which defined policies for the government (Kosygin) to implement, it was clear to all observers that Brezhnev was the *primus inter pares* of the collective leadership. The 1968 Czechoslovakian crisis and its resolution, coupled with the subsequent Brezhnev Doctrine, significantly enhanced Brezhnev's power and authority within the party.

Though the pre-eminence of the General Secretary did not immediately disband the collective leadership, Brezhnev gradually and systematically began to usurp the functions of the state (Podgornyi) and the Government (Kosygin). The three of them, for example, undertook diplomatic assignments abroad in 1971: Brezhnev visited East European socialist states, Podgornyi visited North Africa, and Kosygin visited Ottawa, Canada, while Podgornyi visited Somalia in 1974. This was an excellent display of the collectivist spirit of Soviet leadership. However, in very crucial and more substantial issues it was Brezhnev who dealt directly with western heads of states/governments. This process began with the visit of the U.S. President, Richard M. Nixon, to Moscow in May 1972. It was Brezhnev who negotiated, and also signed the bilateral agreement with Nixon. His return visit to the U.S. in 1973 placed him in the role of Soviet's Head of state and government, at least *de facto*.

This role was formalized in October 1977 when a new, revised Soviet Constitution was adopted. Brezhnev "ousted" Podgornyi from the presidency and combined the office with his. Though this act could be viewed as a "coup" against Podgorny, it was, in fact, the establishment and recognition of the real function of the General Secretary of a communist party. Lenin underestimated the office of party secretary; Stalin did not. Khrushchev, like Stalin, recognized the enormous powers of the party secretary but lacked the clout to manifest this. The general (or first) secretary of a Communist party is, for all practical purposes, the chairman of the party, and as such, for the avoidance of role conflicts, it is imperative that he combines the office of the head of state to his. It is essential that all students of communism, irrespective of their ideological orientation, understand and recognize this fact.

Brezhnev presided over four Congresses of the CPSU—the 23rd (1966), the 24th (1971), 25th (1976) and the 26th (1981)—before his death on November 10, 1982. He also presided over the International Meeting of Communist and Workers' Parties, in Moscow, 1969, and the Conference of European Communist Parties, in Berlin, 1976.

During the Brezhnev era, Soviet analysis of African politics gradually began to be more systemic oriented. A higher level of scholarly debate became noticeable among Soviet scholars. G. B.

Starushenko, the Deputy Director of the Institute of Africa, emerged as the undisputed chief Africanist in the Brezhnev era. It was interesting to note that two prominent Soviet analysts specializing on African (and Asian) affairs, R. A. Ulianovskii and K. N. Brutents had direct access to Brezhnev. Under Brezhnev, they were both secretaries of the CC CPSU and also senior party officials in the International Department of the CC CPSU. Though, as usual, the decisions of the CPSU Congresses will form the basis of our analysis, we shall also rely on the analyses of Moscow's experts in discussing the issues in Soviet African policy during the Brezhnev era.

A party congress serves dual functions in Soviet politics, both as an occasion of stock-taking and for articulating future policy options. The party secretary utilizes the occasion to inform the international community of the successes/problems of Soviet foreign policy since the preceding congress, and also to formulate new strategies for the succeeding years. It was also, more importantly, an occasion for the Soviet Union to re-emphasize its class position on the vital question of the eradication of colonialism and imperialism. Soviet official pronouncements and scholarly analyses emanate from the resolutions of the CPSU congress. These resolutions are indispensable source materials for every Sovietologist.

From October 15, 1964, when Khrushchev was dropped from office, to March 29, 1966, when the 23rd CPSU Congress was opened, Brezhnev and his colleagues struggled to reassure the socialist Commonwealth of Nations, and the international communist and working class movement, including the independent countries of Africa, of continued Soviet support. At the Congress, Brezhnev underlined the need for closer relations between the Soviet Union and these countries as vital to the success of the Soviet led anti-colonial struggle.[92] In his report Brezhnev stressed the growing "international authority" of the world socialist system and

---

[92] See L. I. Brezhnev, "Otchetnyi doklad tsentralnogo komiteta KPSS XXIII sezdu kommunisticheskoi partii sovetskogo soiuza", in <u>Materialy XXIII sezda KPSS</u>, Moscow, 1966.

its "influence on the faith of mankind." While recognizing the unity of the socialist camp, he also regretted the "unsatisfactory" nature of Soviet relations with the socialist states of China and Albania.[93]

He acknowledged the task confronting the communist movements in African, Asian and Latin American countries and reiterated Moscow's aid to ensure the defeat of imperialism. With regard to Africa, he condemned the "disgraceful colonial orders" in Angola, Mozambique, and the so-called "Portuguese" Guinea, including the racist regimes of South Africa and Southern Rhodesia. Promising Soviet assistance to the anti-colonial forces in Africa, Brezhnev declared:

> Our Party, the Soviet people actively support this struggle, and are rendering, and shall continue to render, the peoples struggling against the foreign land grabbers for their freedom and independence, a real all-round assistance. We firmly know that the day is not far off when the remnants of colonialism shall be destroyed and on the liberated territories the people will hoist the banner of national freedom. This is the verdict of history, and it is irreversible.[94]

He praised the "progressive social development" of the countries that have opted for the non-capitalist path of development. Among these he mentioned Egypt, Algeria, Congo (Brazzaville), Mali, Guinea, and Burma (now Myarmar) as countries that have "implemented serious social transformations."[95] The anti-socialist coup engineered by the U.S. that toppled Kwame Nkrumah on February 24, 1966, led to the exclusion of Ghana from this group of countries. He further stated that the Soviet Union will continue to maintain "close and friendly relations" with the countries that have

---

[93] Ibid., pp. 5 and 9.
[94] Ibid., p.19.
[95] Ibid., p.22.

"chosen the course of socialism" while the CPSU shall increase its ties "with the revolutionary democratic parties of these countries."[96] In condemning the global conspiracy of imperialism "especially on the African continent", and underlining the role of the Soviet Union in the anti-imperialist struggle, Brezhnev confirmed that:

> Our Party and the Soviet state shall henceforth: continue to render all conceivable assistance to the peoples struggling for their freedom, and to secure the urgent granting of independence to all colonial countries and peoples; develop an all-round co-operation with countries that have achieved national independence, and assist them in the development of their economy, in the training of national cadres, in their struggle against neo-colonialism; strengthen the fraternal ties of the CPSU with the communist parties and the revolutionary democratic organizations of the countries of Asia, Africa and Latin America.[97]

In conclusion he opined:

> The successes of the national liberation movements are inextricably linked with the successes of world socialism and the international working class. The lasting and inviolable union of these great revolutionary forces guarantee the definitive triumph of the national and social liberation of the peoples.[98]

Brezhnev's speech at the 23rd CPSU Congress was an assurance of continued Soviet assistance to the anti-colonial revolutionary movement. As a process of strategic consideration, the Soviet Union

---

[96]   Ibid.

[97]   Ibid., p.23.

[98]   Ibid.

undertook to also assist African and other less developed countries in the training of their human resources. The in-built calculation here was that some of the "class conscious" Soviet-trained cadres will embrace Marxism-Leninism and constitute the core of the "revolutionary democratic" organizations of these countries. These "revolutionary democrats", in the Soviet stratagem, will be the centrifugal force in the broad-based national democratic front. In dialectical terms, this force will simultaneously transform itself into a centripetal force in the development of a Marxist-Leninist party as soon as the objective and subjective conditions for a socialist revolution attain maturity in the broad-based national democratic bloc.

It is significant to note that Brezhnev used the concept "*revolutionary democratic*" instead of "*national democratic*" as was the case in the Khrushchevian era. This shift from national democracy to revolutionary democracy is of vital importance in our understanding of the tactics and strategies of a socialist revolution. As a concept, national democracy includes both revolutionary socialist forces and the forces of bourgeois nationalism. The extirpation of revolutionary democracy from the broad-based concept of national democracy was considered by the Soviets, under Brezhnev, as a qualitative process in contemporary Marxist-Leninist political analysis. While socialists are revolutionary democrats, not all democrats are socialists since, according to the Soviets, the majority of those espousing national democracy are in fact bourgeois nationalists. An understanding of this dichotomy is essential in our analysis of contemporary African revolutionary process. Since the 23ʳᵈ Congress, the definition of the role and function of revolutionary democracy dominated Soviet analysis of African, Asian and Latin American politics in the Brezhnev era.[99] Though, for tactical reasons, Moscow still maintained an

---

[99] See, for example, the following works by Soviet scholars. Akademiia nauk SSSR. Institut gosudarstva i pravo, <u>Nekapitalisticheskii put razvitiia stran Afriki</u>, Moscow, 1967; R.A. Ulianovskii, <u>Ocherki natsionalno-osvoboditelnoi borby. Voprosy teorii i praktiki</u>, Moscow, 1976; K.N. Brutents, <u>National Liberation Revolutions Today</u>, 2 vols.,

alliance with national democracy (i.e. bourgeois nationalists), it was obvious that its main class allies were the revolutionary democrats. We shall present a detailed analysis of revolutionary democracy later in the succeeding pages.

The Soviets increasingly viewed the less developed countries as an area for a *quick* socialist revolution. With considerable caution in their analyses, Soviet scholars did raise contradictory arguments on this question.[100] A text by the Soviet Institute of State and Law argued that: "As a rule, a revolution cannot succeed in a country in the absence of subjective prerequisites" since this "creates a historical problem for the formation of transitional forms of political organizations of society leading to socialism through an intermediary stage of general democratic transformation."[101] In conclusion, the authors of the text rationalized that since, "At the same time the people cannot remain inactive, can no longer endure the poverty, a doom to which colonialism has condemned them"[102] a socialist revolution remains the only viable option. V. Solodovnikov, who succeeded Potekhin as the Director of Moscow's Institute of Africa (1964-1974), and later Soviet ambassador in Lusaka, Zambia, advanced a reason why the Soviet Union considered the less developed countries ripe for socialist revolution:

> Non capitalist path toward socialism is possible in countries where there are no conditions for a quick

---

Moscow, 1977; G.B. Starushenko, <u>Mirovoi revoliutsionnyi progress i sovremennoe mezhdunarodnoe pravo</u>, Moscow, 1978; <u>XXV sezd KPSS i problemy ideologicheskoi borby v strannakh Azii i Afriki</u>, Moscow, 1979; and N.B. Bikkenin, <u>Socialist Ideology</u>, Moscow, 1980.

[100] See, for example, V. Solodovnikov, "Leninizm i osvobodaiushchiasia Afriki", <u>Meimo</u>, Moscow, no. 4, 1970, pp.67-78; and N.B. Bikkenin, <u>Socialist Ideology</u>, p.73.

[101] <u>Nekapitalisticheskii put razvitiia stran Afriki</u>, p.21.

[102] <u>Ibid</u>.

victory of socialist revolution, but where revolutionary forces are striving for a socialist orientation.[103]

Furthermore, basing his analysis on Leninist postulates, he argued that the prospects for a socialist revolution are greater in these countries than in the more advanced capitalist states:

> This is explained by the fact that in the underdeveloped countries the basis of the socio-economic formation, which determines the character of the political superstructure, is still in its embryonic stage.[104]

Solodovnikov based his analysis on an objective articulation of contemporary international politics. Soviet scholars were understandably critical of bourgeois political theorists who suddenly became "Marxists" by arguing that Leninism had "distorted" Marxism. According to N.B. Bikkenin, the arguments of bourgeois political theorists "also reflect the overall strategic thrust of imperialist policy aimed at the de-Leninization of the world communist movement by playing Lenin off against Marx."[105]

In <u>Principles of Communism</u>, written in 1847, Engels stated that a "communist revolution" will occur simultaneously in the "civilized" countries—England, France, America, and Germany. This conclusion was based on an analysis of the prevailing conditions in mid-19th century. However, on the global effect of this "communist revolution" Engels opined:

---

[103] Solodovnikov, <u>loc.cit.</u>, p.74.

[104] <u>Ibid</u>.

[105] Bikkenin, <u>op.cit.</u>, p.67. See also M.A. Suslov, "Leninism and the Revolutionary Remaking of the World", <u>Leninism and the World Revolutionary Working Class Movement</u>, Moscow, 1971, p.37.

It will also have an important effect upon the other
countries of the world, and will completely change and
greatly accelerate their previous manner of development.
It is a world-wide revolution and will therefore be
world-wide in scope.[106]

The relationship of Marxism to Leninism shall remain a topical issue
in contemporary political theory. We encountered a non-Soviet
analysis of this phenomenon in the preceding pages. However,
what Lenin did, especially in the 1899-1917 period, was to apply
Marxian theory to the realities of 20th century social and political
development. Elaborating on this, M. A. Suslov, the ideologist of
the CPSU, wrote:

> "Having emerged as a continuation of Marxism at a
> time when capitalism had entered its last, imperialist
> state, Leninism expressed the objective requirements of
> world social development."[107]

Lenin held a contrary view from Marx and Engels, who argued
that a socialist revolution will occur "simultaneously" in a number
of advanced capitalist countries. He maintained that a successful
socialist revolution can occur in a single country and spill over
to other countries. Marxists view international capitalism as an
organic whole. For example, both the USA and Zaire belong to
the same capitalist organism, each fulfilling different functions
with the latter as the periphery. It is, therefore, not crucial for a
socialist revolution to occur in the centre before occurring in the
periphery. The counter argument is even more valid. A socialist
revolution can take place in any of the peripheries of the capitalist
organic whole. The world capitalist system is like a village, and any

---

[106] K. Marx and F. Engels, The Socialist Revolution, Moscow, 1978,
p.52.
[107] Suslov, loc.cit., pp.37-38.

section of the capitalist village can opt out and proceed to socialism, irrespective of its particular level of social development. Capitalist exploitation is more brutal in the periphery than it is in the centre. The question, according to Marxists, is neither to make capitalism "less" brutal in the periphery nor to "reform" it in the centre, but rather to dismantle it as a socio-economic system. The inhabitants of both the periphery and the centre jointly experience exploitation under the conditions of advanced capitalism. To ignore this fact is to engage in intellectual subjectivism. Even within the confines of a single advanced capitalist country, like Canada, it is obvious to all observers that the province of Ontario, for example, constitutes the centre of Canadian capitalism while the impoverished provinces of Newfoundland and Prince Edward Island are in the periphery, not to mention the appalling sub-third world social conditions of Canada's Inuit and Indians. Would it be anti-Marxist for any of Canada's provinces to opt out from Canadian capitalism and proceed to socialism? Would it be anti-Marxist for an economically less-developed African country to quit the global capitalist village and proceed to socialism? In fact, the inevitability of some countries attaining socialism, by-passing the capitalist stage of development did not escape Marx and Engels.[108]

One of the problems that an analyst has to grapple with as he strives to untangle the web of Soviet politics is the value of Soviet post-mortem analysis of Moscow's ally. While the cases of Ghana, Egypt, and Somalia shall be examined in chapters 6 and 7, a brief comment on the Malian case is considered appropriate here. In the 1960s, Ghana, Guinea, Mali, Algeria, Tanzania, Congo (B), and Somalia were categorized as "socialist oriented" states. In the 1970s, the Republic of Benin (formerly Dahomey) was included in this group, Egypt was dropped, Ethiopia replaced Somalia, and new members included Libya, Angola, Mozambique, and Guinea Bissau.

---

[108] See R.A. Ulianovskii, <u>Ocherki natsionalno-osvoboditelnoi borby. Voprosy teorii i praktiki</u>, p.121; and also Ulianovskii, <u>Sotsializm i osvobodivshiesie strany</u>, Moscow, 1972, <u>passim</u>.

In assessing the demise of the Malian experiment, Solodovnikov and Gavrilov claimed that the extreme "leftist" policies of the regime led to the collapse of Mali's "socialist orientation" in 1968,

> . . . when Modibo Keita's ruling group tried to launch a "vigorous revolution, using voluntaristic methods" in tackling the country's tangled economic, political and social problems.[109]

Solodovnikov and Gavrilov are prominent Africanists whose analyses were bound to influence Soviet policy-makers. By accusing the late Modibo Keita of launching a "vigorous revolution using voluntaristic methods", without citing examples of Keita's alleged "voluntarism", is a disservice to scholarship and Marxist analysis. It should be noted that, in January 1966 Boris Paveltsev, another prominent Soviet Africanist, had strongly argued that the army "cannot revolt against the regimes of Ghana, Guinea and Mali" because in those countries "the army is regarded as an inalienable part of the national political forces." He was more emphatic regarding Guinea and Mali where, according to him, "the ruling parties are in full control of the army and are responsible for its political training."[110] But when the army struck and toppled Modibo Keita in November 1968, V. Kudryavtsev, Izvestia's chief Africanist, challenged Paveltsev's claim when he, Kudryavtsev, declared: "The Military Liberation Committee consists of 14 men, mostly army captains and lieutenants whose political views are practically unknown."[111] From the above, it would appear that Paveltsev did not know the Malian

[109] V. Solodovnikov and N. Gavrilov, "Africa: Tendencies of Non-Capitalist Development", International Affairs, Moscow, no.3, 1976, p.32.

[110] Boris Paveltsev, "The Military Coups in Africa", as cited in O. Igho Natufe, "Nigeria and Soviet Attitudes to African Military Regimes, 1965-70", Survey, vol. 22, no. 1(98), Winter 1976, p.98.

[111] V. Kudryavtsev, "After the Coup in Mali", as cited in Natufe, loc.cit., p.101.

army and thus based his analysis on mere ideological enthusiasm, as demonstrated in Kudryavtsev's bewilderment; and that the conclusion of Solodovnikov and Gavrilov is an example of reckless ideological conjecture.

The question of non-capitalist path of development <u>and</u> the socialist orientation of political systems significantly transformed the neutralist postures of many African countries. This phenomenon was observed by Y. Etinger when he wrote in 1973 that:

> . . . some African countries, which have embarked on non-capitalist development, are beginning to come to the conclusion that today there is hardly any good reason to regard their neutralist course in the traditional sense of the word based on the concepts of late 1950s and early 1960s. It is believed that for some of these states, neutralism in their foreign policy has become, to a certain extent, a thing of the past, and that the present foreign policies of the countries of socialist orientation can hardly be fitted into the traditional framework of the policy of neutralism.[112]

Neutralism as a foreign policy orientation of member-states of the non-aligned movement has undergone tremendous transformation since its inception in 1961 at the Belgrade Conference. If in the immediate post 1945 era it served its early exponents as a useful instrument of internal soul searching, and in the first decade following the Year of Africa (1960) it also afforded the emerging African countries an opportunity to locate their footsteps in the mines of international politics and diplomacy, it has, however, since the early 1970s become a worthless analytical tool of foreign policy. This is not to suggest that the non-alignment of either Kenya or Guinea in the early 1960s was not pro-West or pro-East respectively,

---

[112] Y. Etinger, "African Countries: Anti-Imperialist Foreign Policies", <u>International Affairs</u>, Moscow, no.8, 1973, p.76.

but the growing rate of bilateral military pacts between individual African non-aligned countries and the USA and USSR, respectively, made a mockery of the non-aligned movement. The dynamics of class politics dictates the pattern of foreign, non-African troops' involvement in African domestic conflicts, especially since 1975. We witnessed this phenomenon in Angola, Chad, Egypt, Ethiopia, Morocco, Somalia, and Zaire, for example. Contending parties in those conflicts assumed opposing ideological positions even at the expense of non-alignment which supposedly united them. It was on the basis of this that R. A. Tuzmukhamedov rationalized the "supremacy" of the socialist principle of proletarian internationalism in a conflict situation with non-alignment, notwithstanding the fact that, in principle, non-alignment "reflects the general democratic position of the anti-imperialist forces."[113] African member-states of the non-aligned movement have, accordingly, assumed their respective ideological stance in intra African conflicts. Witness the opposing role of, for example, both Libya and Zaire in Chad (1980-1982), and the questionable role of the Nigerian-led OAU "peacekeeping force" which facilitated the ouster of President Goukouni Weddeye and installed Hissene Habre as president in June 1972. The above cases demonstrated the importance of ideological orientation, and not the nebulous and moribund concept of non-alignment, in determining the foreign policies of African states. The super powers recognized this fact hence they spent billions of dollars in supplying African countries with military aid to pursue the ideological warfare between capitalism and socialism. The Soviet Union propagated the concept of "socialist orientation" to define its African allies.

According to Solodovnikov and Gavrilov, socialist orientation is not a special social formation, but a "stage of transition from pre-capitalist or early capitalist phases to socialism" via several intermediate stages; "it is the highest stage of the national-democratic revolution." They concluded:

---

[113] Tuzmukhamedov, Neprisoedinenie i razriadka mezhdunarodnoi napriazhennosti, p.79.

119

> The movement along that way is headed by the
> revolutionary democrats, who rely on the awakening
> sections of the peasantry, the working class, the petty
> bourgeoisie, and the patriotically-minded national
> bourgeoisie, including the military.[114]

Based on the elevation of "revolutionary democracy" and the relegation of "national democracy" under Brezhnev, Solodovnikov and Gavrilov accorded revolutionary democracy a higher ideological consideration. But the concept of revolutionary democracy raises two main problems. It suggests that only "pre-capitalist or early capitalist" states that have opted to pursue the non-capitalist path of development can be considered to be socialist oriented. Conceptually it excludes the situation whereby, for example, a progressive regime emerges in an advanced capitalist country and elects to pursue a Marxist socialist oriented policy. This definitional limitation ruptures the ideological import of the concept. Secondly, the inclusion of the military underscored Moscow's recognition of the progressive role a section of the military can play in the development of Africa.

A perennial problem in African countries that pursued the non-capitalist path of development was that these countries had banned communist parties, while the working class was yet to attain any appreciable level of mass organization required for serious ideological agitation and propaganda. While there was a consensus among Soviet scholars on how the Soviet Union would assist those countries, it is significant to note that there also existed a discordant voice in Soviet assessment of the non-capitalist path of development. N. B. Bikkenin rejects the skipping of a stage or stages in the social development scale. Writing in 1980, he averred:

> An ideal in socialist practice thus has a two-fold (dual)
> significance: on the one hand it shows that pragmatism

---

[114] Solodovnikov and Gavrilov, loc. cit., p.33. Italics mine

is wrong as it fails to open up future prospects, and on the other, it demonstrates that voluntarism is also wrong since it implies the artificial introduction of new social forms disregarding the degree of maturity of material conditions and social consciousness at the given point in time, and means an attempt to by-pass, "skip" objectively necessary stages and phases of historical development.[115]

The above analysis is a profound one, particularly coming from a leading Soviet theorist. It is logical in classical Marxist terms, but potentially dangerous if applied as a framework of analysis in projecting the strategies of contemporary Marxist-Leninist revolutionary theory. Bikkenin's reference to "an ideal in socialist practice" articulates the prerequisites of a socialist revolution as espoused by Marx and Engels which, of course, Lenin had revised to fit into the realities of contemporary international political economy. For Marxist-Leninists, Bikkenin's analysis would seem to lend credence to the well-known bourgeois thesis on the vital question of the relevance of Marxism in contemporary political analysis. Bikkenin's book, Socialist Ideology, is a well written synthesis of Leninism even though he did not succeed in making himself explicit in the key issues at stake. Soviet Marxists, as a whole, argued for the defeat of capitalism at its embryonic, intermediate or advanced stages. Ulianovskii underlined this position in one of his publications in 1978—Sovremennye problemy Azii i Afriki. For social process to be meaningful and constructive it must be linked with anti-imperialism, he opined. It must, above all, possess a fundamentally structured ideological construct as a socio-economic and political system. These cannot be achieved by either idealistic argumentation or by "reforming" capitalism.[116]

---

[115] Bikkenin, op.cit., p.73.
[116] See Ulianovskii, Sovremennye problemy Azii i Afriki, Moscow, 1978, pp.71-73.

Soviet social theorists in the Brezhnev era generally became extremely concerned with the formulation of concrete strategies for the enhancement of Marxist-Leninist revolutionary doctrine. This was very evident in their analyses of the social processes and development of the "third world." The blending of revolutionary democracy and the non-capitalist path of development was a crucial element in this process. The concept of non-capitalist path of development posed a problem of strategic alliance building among the various forces involved in the process. The shift from *national democracy* to *revolutionary democracy* was made by Brezhnev. Ulianovskii and Brutents, two prominent Soviet social theorists with direct access to Brezhnev, helped to elucidate these key issues of non-capitalist path of development and revolutionary democracy, respectively. All other Soviet scholars that wrote on these themes revolved their analyses around Ulianovskii and Brutents. Though Ulianovskii did not shift from the definition of non-capitalist path of development of the Khrushchev era, he however proceeded to identify "*tri glavnye opasnosti*" ("three main dangers") which must be tackled in evaluating and analysing the applicability of the concept in African and Asian countries. The tri glavnye opasnosti are:

1. ". . . an underestimation of the reactionary role of the feudal-landlord system, the patriarchal-feudal and clannish relations, which restrain the revolutionary spontaneous activity of the peasantry and the country's advancement, especially its agrarian peasant structure, toward social progress, which leads to the alienation of the revolutionary leadership from the peasantry, that is, from the main mass of the population."
2. ". . . an underestimation of the multiplicity and diversity of the elements of capitalism dissipated in different stages and forms in the country's economy . . ."
3. ". . . the ignoring of the ethnic, national and cultural, historical peculiarities, the psychological mentality of a people gradually retreating from the capitalist path of development and striving toward a progressive society of socialist orientation. The importance of this danger is great. First of all, it is evident in

the mechanical imitation of the experiences of the transition to socialism of developed and medium-range developed capitalist countries, and, consequently, in oblivion of the fact that the general natural development of every transitional period is manifested and realized in time (phase and speed of transition) and in space (local and regional peculiarities)"[117]

Two years before Ulianovskii enunciated his *tri glavnye opasnosti*, Leonid Brezhnev, in his address at the 25th CPSU Congress on February 24, 1976, acknowledged:

> A complicated process of class differentiation is under way in many liberated countries, with the class struggle gaining in intensity. It is taking different forms. New progressive changes have occurred in the economy and the political life of the socialist-oriented Arab, African and Asian countries. But there are also countries where development follows the capitalist way.[118]

Brezhnev's speech and Ulianovskii's *tri glavnye opasnosti* were evidently influenced by the following social and political developments that occurred in Africa, the Middle East, and Asia between the 24th and 25th congresses of the CPSU:

- Nigeria had just emerged from a bloody civil war (1967-1970) and was grappling with the social consequences of reconstruction, rehabilitation and reconciliation. Soviet military assistance to the Nigerian federal government was crucial in the victory of the federalist forces.

---

[117] Ibid., pp.88-89.

[118] Leonid Brezhnev, "Report of the CPSU Central Committee and the Immediate Tasks of the Party in Home and Foreign Policy", Documents and Resolutions: XXVth Congress of the CPSU, Moscow, 1976, p.15

■ The Pakistani civil war (1971-1972) gave birth to a pro-Soviet state of Bangladesh, formerly East Pakistan.

■ The expulsion of Soviet military advisers from Egypt in 1972 by President Anwar Sadat was a huge setback for Soviet policy in Africa and the Middle East.

■ The 1973 Middle East war and the gradual retreat of Egypt from its pro-Soviet position to rapprochement with Israel.

■ The Ethiopian creeping revolution of 1974 that toppled Emperor Haile Selassie, and led to the emergence of a socialist oriented military regime in Addis-Ababa.

■ The antagonism between two socialist oriented states—Ethiopia and Somalia—compromised Soviet strategic position in the Horn of Africa.

■ The "revolutionary" posture of Nigeria's head of state, General Murtala Mohammed, in the OAU in favour of the MPLA in Angola.

■ The sharpening of class contradiction in Africa as a result of the US-South African-Chinese collusion against the MPLA in 1975-1976.

■ The withdrawal of the US from Vietnam following its defeat in 1975.

The above cases caused various types of class alliances in Africa that led to the shifting of Soviet power and influence in the international community. On the basis of these, there arose the need to organize the disorganized and the imperative to reorganize the organized in terms of revolutionary theory and practice. The attendant problems of this process were what Ulianovskii identified as the *tri glavnye opasnosti*. A central fundamental problem of the *tri glavnye opasnosti* in contemporary African "revolutionary spontaneous activity" is the inability of the socialists to have a sustained movement. This vital deficiency can be viewed from two perspectives. First, the continued fragmentation of the rank and file of an African socialist movement into various splinter groups linked to external control centres reduces them to a status of permanent rebuilding. Second, and as a product of the first, the US-led imperialist forces have easy access to intensify their destabilisation policies within a given African socialist movement.

The Nigerian socialist movement of the 1960s compounded its domestic problems of internal squabbles by fragmenting into pro-Soviet and pro-Chinese groups which hindered its ability to make a dent in the political landscape of Nigeria's first republic (October 01, 1963-January 15, 1966). During the second republic (October 01, 1979-December 31, 1983) Nigerian socialists constantly grappled with the need to organize the disorganized. There existed an appalling tendency among Nigerian socialists to apply Marxism dogmatically, while the "I must lead" mentality of most of the academic Marxists frustrated relations with non-academic members of the socialist movement, a phenomenon which reduced the effectiveness of the socialist movement to sustain and advance its agitation in the electoral process.

One of the issues we encountered in the analysis and function of revolutionary democracy was the role of opposing classes in a united front. As a concept, revolutionary democracy superseded national democracy of the 1960s. In the Soviet view, it represented a higher level of ideological articulation. Revolutionary democrats may not have completely assimilated Marxism to constitute a class and be able to successfully oppose bourgeois national democrats, hence its tactical alliance with the latter in the united front. In this scenario, Marxist-Leninists recognize the historically defined progressive role played by bourgeois nationalism, while only a segment of the bourgeoisie is identified as an "ally" in the strategic struggle. The regimes in Algeria, Congo, Ethiopia (post 1974), Somalia (1969-1977), Angola, Mozambique, and Libya, for example, were considered revolutionary democratic regimes because of their declared maladaptive ideological positions vis-à-vis colonialist status quo in Africa. Brutents succinctly captured the essence of these regimes when he observed that ". . . the parties and political organizations that revolutionary democrats have created are largely national anti-imperialist coalitions (fronts) that are inter-class

conglomerations, aggregates of the most diverse social forces."[119]
Ethiopia under the military administration of Haile Mengistu
exemplified this type of regime. To clarify the class position of
revolutionary democracy and its expected role in the front, Brutents
declared:

> Whatever the case, one thing is already clear: the
> revolutionary democrats' doctrines can be neither an
> alternative nor an antipode to scientific socialism, but
> a stage in the passage to the latter—if, of course, these
> doctrines are free or are freed of anti-communism.[120]

The location of revolutionary democrats in the class struggle is very
crucial, and the tilt depends on the correlation of the "diverse social
forces" in the polity. According to the Soviets, this would require
an uncompromising support for communism. A key component
of this imperative is the *national* and *international* alliance between
revolutionary democrats and foreign communists in order to enhance
and advance the political and ideological strength of the former. At
the national level, with the guidance of foreign communists, the
alliance between revolutionary democrats and local communists
serves two functions of vital significance. First, it facilitates the
emergence of an ideological unity, and thus a propensity of a move
toward the left. Second, it helps to build a politically conscious and
an ideologically disciplined party organization of Marxist-Leninist
professional revolutionaries. On the other hand, fraternal
cooperation between revolutionary democracy and international
communism is designed to enhance the prestige of revolutionary
democrats as important participants in the global anti-imperialist
movement. (See diagram 2 below).

---

[119] Brutents, vol.2, p.140.
[120] Ibid., p.92.

Diagram 2: Revolutionary Democracy and International
Communism

International Communist Movement

Communist of   Revolutionary Democrats of
African State "A"   African State "A"

The Soviet conception of nationalism vis-à-vis revolutionary
democracy in the post 1966 period was a bit perplexing. Zhukov's
definition of nationalism in the Stalinist era was altered in 1956.
Brutents admits that prior to Stalin's death, and particularly since the
20th CPSU Congress, "the view was fairly widespread in literature
that nationalism was a reactionary ideology and a policy of fanning
mistrust and hostility among nations, and no more. This view was
one-sided and imprecise in theoretical and epistemological terms,
and politically considered virtually only reactionary nationalism,
to which it reduced nationalism in general."[121] Brutents'
dichotomization of nationalism into reactionary and progressive
categories informed Soviet strategic class collaboration policy, a
dichotomy which N. D. Kosukhin did not seem to recognize as he
wrote in 1979:

> In contemporary Africa the main ideological trend
> is nationalism which, although still maintains its
> anti-imperialist trend, has become the weapon of the
> narrow class interests of the national bourgeoisie.[122]

---

[121] Ibid., vol.1, p.94. Italics in the original.
[122] N. D. Kosukhin, "K voprosu o stanovlennii revoliutsionno-
demokraticheskikh vzgliadov v stranakh sotsialisticheskoi orientatsii
tropicheskoi Afriki", in XXV sezd KPSS i problemy ideologicheskoi
borby v stranakh Azii i Afriki, Moscow, 1979, p.113.

Kosukhin was a political aide in Brezhnev's office, from where he was transferred to the Institute of Africa in Moscow for his first encounter with African studies. Like Zhukov's in 1949, it is obvious that Kosukhin's analysis is, in the words of Brutents, "one-sided and imprecise in theoretical and epistemological terms." While Brutents identified the use of <u>nationalism</u> in national integration, and classified and located its respective exponents in the overall strategy of the class struggle, Kosukhin disregarded this important task and allied his thought with that of pre 1953 Zhukov.

In the preceding pages, we had examined and analyzed the key issues in Soviet African policy. Soviet disposition towards these issues evolved significantly since the days of Stalin. As was demonstrated above, this evolution was ideologically legitimized by each Soviet leadership while, at the same time, negating the previously legitimized policy of its predecessor. This posed enormous problems for the Soviet Union in its dealings with African countries. The various policy changes initiated were calculated to enhance Moscow's position vis-à-vis the Western powers in the "new scramble for Africa." We shall examine the content of this scramble as it unfolded in the first decade following the war of 1939-1945: a decade of the decolonization process and the cold war.

CHAPTER FOUR

AFRICA IN SUPER POWER RIVALRY, 1945-1955

One word which has featured prominently in post 1945 international politics is DECOLONIZATION. Simply defined, decolonization means the disbandment of colonial bondage and the restoration of the independence of a colonized people. In principle, all colonial powers *endorse* decolonization, but disagree on the *politics* of the process which determines the result of decolonization. Without any sustained pressure on the colonial powers, decolonization would be difficult to attain as the colonial powers would not, on their own, want to quit the colonies. For this pressure to be meaningful, the anti-colonial movement has to utilize an external support system as a leverage to compel the imperial powers to decolonize. Naturally, such an external support system has to emanate from an influential international organization, and a non-colonial international actor that is powerful enough to vigorously pursue a consistent anti-colonial policy which constitutes a threat to the imperial powers. In post 1945, decolonization found such a support in both the United Nations Organization (UNO) and the Soviet Union, respectively. Soviet power and influence substantially increased after 1945 following the emergence of socialist states in Europe and Asia. As the Western powers strove to contain the spread of communism and limit Soviet power in international politics, a fierce ideological battle between

the forces of capitalism and socialism dominated the course of post 1945 political intercourse, thus intensifying the cold war.

Cold war as a concept of contemporary international politics describes the unfriendly relationship between conflicting global ideological centres represented by socialism and capitalism, led by the USSR and US, respectively. Thus, as a concept it denotes a state of permanent hostility reflected in the foreign policy actions of the ideological protagonists for hegemony and influence in the international system. Viewed from this perspective, therefore, cold war describes a strained relationship between international political actors as a result of their irreconcilable class, ideological orientations. The main protagonists of the cold war, Moscow and Washington, engaged in ideological warfare to undercut or obliterate the power and/or influence of their class enemy in global politics.

Though the term *cold war* is frequently used to describe Soviet-US relations in the post 1945 period, it is conceptually wrong to do so. The cold war phenomenon defines the relationship between the Soviet Union and the capitalist world *after* the October 1917 Russian socialist revolution, especially following the abortive US-led intervention to crush the emergent Soviet socialist state. As a concept in international politics, therefore, the end of the civil war in Soviet Russia and the failure of the West's military intervention to subvert the Soviet state should be regarded as the origin of the cold war. While the guns were silenced following this episode, both the Soviet Union and the Western powers engaged in ideological warfare by supporting the centrifugal forces in the opposing camp. This state of mutual hostility acquired a new dimension in post 1945 with the emergence of socialist states in Europe and Asia.

Ideologically speaking, the balance sheet of the war of 1939-1945 favoured communism. With the collapse of Nazism and fascism, and the division of Germany, the prestige of the Soviet Union in world politics was significantly enhanced. The Soviet Union emerged as the most powerful state in Europe, a situation which caused grave panic in Western Europe and North America. If prior to the outbreak of the war in 1939 Soviet leaders feared a *capitalist encirclement* that was constantly posited as a threat to Soviet survival, the reverse was the case after 1945. At Rapallo the Soviet Union succeeded in breaking the chains of isolationism but did not constitute a serious military threat to the West. However, the spread of communism beyond Soviet frontiers in post 1945 posed a challenge to Western imperial interests. Winston Churchill, (then) British Prime Minister, in a speech at Fulton, Missouri, USA, on March 5, 1946, attacked what he perceived as "Eastern imperialism" and coined the "iron curtain" as a term describing the establishment of socialist states in Eastern Europe and the Soviet Union. He called on the West to halt the spread of communism.[1] The policy of "containment" which was later adopted by the US government was an expression of the strategic measures proposed in Churchill's speech as the West sought ways "to hold the USSR and its Communists satellites within their existing boundaries, . . ."[2] Confident that it had dismantled the *capitalist encirclement* psychology, the Soviet Union could now talk of a real socialist camp opposed to a capitalist camp within the confines of the "two camps" doctrine. As a follow up to the policy of containment, the West established NATO in 1949 as a politico-military alliance system to halt the spread of Communism, and to abort the anti-colonial liberation movements in the colonies. NATO's military bases were dotted all over West European member states at strategic striking distance from key Soviet cities. Greece, Turkey, and Berlin became the initial testing grounds of cold war muscle flexing.

To curb the Soviet "threat" and to combat Marxism in the international system, the U.S. Secretary of State, Dean Acheson, postulated the concept of force[3] by proposing "total diplomacy" as

---

[1]   W. S. Churchill, <u>The Sinews of Peace. Post-war Speeches</u>, edited by Randolph S. Churchill, London, 1948, p.100.

[2]   Julius W. Pratt, <u>A History of United States Foreign Policy</u>, Englewood Cliffs, New Jersey, 1955, p.719.

[3]   See D. Acheson, "'Total Diplomacy' to Strengthen U.S. Leadership for Human Freedom", <u>Department of State Bulletin</u>, March 20, 1950, pp.427-430.

Washington's foreign policy which he defined as a "defence against Communism."[4] In pursuance of this objective Acheson argued that the United States must achieve world "peace through strength"[5] by weakening the Communist bloc and the anti-colonial movements in Africa, Asia, Latin America and the Caribbean. Furthermore, the U.S. "liberation" concept based on anti-communism was even regarded as a progression of the Monroe Doctrine[6], while J. Burnham, in his <u>Containment or Liberation?</u>, advanced the idea of "liberating" the citizens of socialist countries from Marxism, by encouraging internal strife within the Communist states, and also to curb the spread of Marxism by outlawing "Communist activities" in non-Communist states[7], particularly in the colonies.

From the Soviet perspective, the victory of the anti-Hitler alliance created greater opportunities for Marxism. While the West was formulating its strategy of containment, the Soviet Union was negotiating a series of bilateral economic and military agreements with its East European communist allies in order to consolidate the emergent socialist Commonwealth of Nations. With the containment of the *capitalist encirclement*, Soviet *pactomania* of the 1930s was again evident in the 1940s. These agreements differed substantially from those of the 1930s.[8] In response to NATO, the socialist states established a counter politico-military alliance in

---

[4]   D. Acheson, "Tensions between the United States and the Soviet Union", <u>Department of State Bulletin</u>, March 27, 1950, pp.473-478.

[5]   D. Acheson, "Peace Through Strength. A Foreign Policy Objective", <u>Department of State Bulletin</u>, June 26, 1950, pp.1037-1041.

[6]   See T. K. Finletter, <u>Power and Policy. U.S. Foreign and Military Power in the Hydrogen Age</u>, New York, 1954, p.124.

[7]   J. Burnham, <u>Containment or Liberation? An Inquiry into the Aims of United States Foreign Policy</u>, New York, 1963, pp.31-34; 130-140.

[8]   For a detailed discussion on the formation of the socialist commonwealth and the initial treaties between the Soviet Union and East European Communist states, see Kazimierz Grzybowski, <u>The</u>

1955—the WTO. As both opposing alliances began the process of arming themselves with destructive weapons systems, the main ideological battle grounds shifted from Europe to Africa, Asia, Latin America and the Caribbean.

During the debates on decolonization at the UNO, the Soviet Government made a bid to obtain Libya, a former Italian colony, under a UNO trusteeship. Libya's strategic importance appealed to both the Soviet Union and the West. In presenting its claim, the Soviet Union argued that as an important factor in the anti-Hitler alliance it was entitled to trusteeship rights over a colony of a defeated enemy. The Soviet Government referred to Togoland, Cameroon, Tanganyika, and South West Africa, which were placed under the trusteeship of France, Britain, and South Africa following the defeat of Germany in the war of 1914-1918. Though the Soviet Government had historical precedence to support its claim, it was obvious that its ideological orientation was more of a concern to the West than any argument based on precedence. To grant Soviet trusteeship request over Libya would have been tantamount to deliberately establishing a Soviet communist regime right under the belly of NATO. However, when Soviet bid for trusteeship collapsed, the Soviet Government then proceeded to pursue a policy of preventive imperialism by championing the cause for immediate independence for Libya.

The *loss* of India, Burma and Indonesia weakened the colonial empires of Britain and the Netherlands, while the defeat of France in Vietnam further discredited imperialism in the universal anti-colonial movements which gained momentum after 1945. The immediate post 1945 East-West ideological conflict and the independence of these countries significantly influenced the tempo of the anti-colonial movements in Asia and Africa. As the myth of European invincibility was destroyed in Vietnam and Indonesia, colonial Africa began to acquire a new dimension in

---

Socialist Commonwealth of Nations: Organizations and Institutions, New Haven, Conn., 1964.

the West's strategic thinking. With respect to Africa, North Africa fell within the immediate strategic concern of NATO. Because of their close proximity to NATO member-states, Italy, Greece and Turkey, North African countries were considered vital elements in NATO's anti-Soviet strategic planning. This explains why the West vehemently rejected Soviet trusteeship request over Libya. A new strategic alliance system began to crystallize in international politics as the question of independence for the colonies was championed by the Soviet Union, while the U.S. and its West European allies thought of how to either delay the process of decolonization and/or involve the newly independent countries in the West's global anti-Communist crusade. Thus, Africa was viewed by both competing ideological alliance systems as an important object in the cold war. In the opinion of S. Possony, a leading U.S. Sovietologist, the "correct course for the West is neither to retreat nor to withdraw, but the formulation of an acceptable decision to remain . . ."[9] in the colonies. Thus, the imperial powers began to propagate the thesis that the colonized peoples were *not yet ready for self-government.* Imperial powers with colonies in Africa further tightened their grip in the exploitation of Africa's resources in their attempt to lessen the burden of U.S. economic domination in Western Europe in the immediate post 1945 period. While the West was battling to retain a moribund colonial system that was fast disintegrating, the Soviet Union was marshalling its ideological offensive which allied it to the interests of the colonized peoples and territories.

Egypt and North Africa

Egypt occupies a strategic position as the Northern Gate of Africa, a fact which seems to have plagued its history as it gradually became a bone of contention among external powers in global politics. Since its completion in 1869, the Suez Canal has increased

---

9   S. Possony as cited in E. D. Modrzhinskaia, Ideologiia sovremennogo kolonializma, Moscow, 1961, p.90.

Egypt's strategic importance as it provided the shortest naval and commercial routes between Europe and Asia. Following the war of 1939-1945, both the Soviet Union and the United States replaced two former imperial powers—Great Britain and France—as the dominant powers in North Africa and the Middle East, with Egypt and Israel as the main targets. The Israeli victory against the Arabs in 1948-1949 and the West's support for Israel ultimately made the Soviet Union an external source of support for the Arabs. This did not begin to crystallize until 1954. However, Michael Brecher states that:

> It was Soviet bloc weapons that enabled Israel to withstand the initial Arab assault in 1948; and it was Soviet bloc weapons to Egypt and Syria (since 1945) that catalyzed an inflationary spiral in the arms race within that subordinate system.[10]

Brecher's analysis seems to ignore the role played by Western weapons and policy in the militarization of Israel between 1948 and 1955.

Western policy in the Middle East and Africa in the decade following the end of the war dictated the tune of Soviet diplomacy in these regions. For example, Britain could not rationally define the policy of the Arab League which was formed under strong British pressure in late 1944 vis-à-vis the Palestine Arab and the Jewish question. Rather, the British Government was compelled

> to call on the United States for help in dealing with the civil war in Greece, and in backing Turkey and Persia against post-war Russia pressure. This help and the economic aid she needed herself also meant that Britain must pay greater attention to American views

---

10   Michael Brecher, <u>The Foreign Policy System of Israel</u>, New Haven, Conn., 1972, p.26.

on Palestine and face the fact of American public and
political support for Zionism.[11]

Zionism began to determine the West's policy toward the Middle
East. The Western powers' Tripartite Declaration of 1950, which was
intended to minimize armed conflict in the region by maintaining
a military balance between Israel and the Arab nations, found itself
concerned by a rising Soviet influence in the region. The decision of
the West to establish a defence system hostile to Soviet interest

> marked the beginning of the dilemma or confusion in
> the Middle East for the next decade and to accelerate its
> decline and the rise of Russian influence in the area.[12]

Beginning from 1944 the Western powers started to discuss a series
of drafts for the formation of a Middle East Defence Pact involving
all countries in the region. In 1946-1947 the British Government
succeeded in creating a quadripartite alliance system, the so-called
London-Ankara-Baghdad-Amman axis.[13]

In response to the Israeli victory in the 1948-1949 war, the
Muslim Brotherhood instigated a series of anti-British riots in Cairo.
When Premier Nekrashy ordered the dissolution of the Brotherhood,
he was assassinated on December 28, 1948. Anti-Communist and
anti-Zionist hunts were propelled while attempts were made by
Premier Hadi to establish a correlation between the Brotherhood
and the anti-government faction in the Egyptian army.[14] Gamal

---

[11] Robert Stephens, <u>Nasser. A Political Biography</u>, London, 1971, p.70.
See also V. B. Lutskii, <u>Anglo-amerikanskii imperializm na blizhnem
vostoke</u>, Moscow, 1968.

[12] Robert Stephens, p.93.

[13] 13The Anglo-Jordan treaty of 1946; Iraqi-Turkish treaty of 1946;
Jordan-Turkish treaty of 1947; and the Iraqi-Jordan treaty of 1947.
See <u>Diplomaticheskii slovar</u>, Moscow, vol.1, 1960, pp. 84; 562; 564.

[14] Stephens, pp.88-89.

Abdel Nasser, in his <u>The Philosophy of the Revolution</u>, stressed the primacy of Egyptian security and the concept of Arab brotherhood when his faction in the Egyptian army decided to aid the Palestine Arabs in 1948-1949. He stated that his group was motivated by

> neither sympathy with our Arab Brethren nor love for adventure—it was solely the clear consciousness of our confirmed conviction that . . . our security made it necessary for us to defend the frontiers of our Arab Brethren with whom we were destined to live in one and the same region.[15]

A revolt by a group of young officers of the Egyptian army overthrew the government and exiled King Farouk from Egypt in July 1952. Nasser emerged as the leader of the military coup that was anti-British in orientation, and abrogated the notorious Anglo-Egyptian Treaty of 1936.[16] If the first two years portrayed Nasser as an "anti-Arab" nationalist in the British orbit of influence (witness the Anglo-Egyptian Agreement of 1954 and the Sudan), subsequent years proved the contrary. He emerged as the undisputed leader of the Arab world and also established himself as one of the pioneering leaders of contemporary Africa. However, it is interesting to note that the July 23, 1952 Egyptian coup that ousted King Farouk and Britain from Egypt was condemned by the Soviet Government:

---

[15] Nasser, as cited in Stephens, pp.85-86.

[16] The Anglo-Egyptian Treaty of 1936 legalized the stationing of British troops in Alexandria, Cairo, and in the Suez Canada region. Both contracting parties agreed to aid the other if attacked by a third power. However, as far as Egypt was concerned, the treaty symbolized a "colonial regime" in the country. See <u>Diplomaticheskii slovar</u>, vol. 1, 81-82.

> In the night of July 22, 1952, power was seized in Cairo
> by a reactionary group of officers connected with the
> United States.[17]

Mohamed H. Heikal, writing in 1973, revealed that the leaders of the July 23 coup forewarned the Americans of the impending coup and assured them that it was an internal affair.[18] Heikal, a prominent Egyptian journalist, was considered a confidant of President Nasser. In his autobiography, Anwar el-Sadat, Nasser's successor as President, corroborated Heikal's account. Sadat confirmed that he and his colleagues who effected the 1952 revolution decided to get "in touch with the Americans (even at dawn on July 23) to give them an idea of the objectives and nature of our revolution." Jefferson Caffery, "the U.S. ambassador invited us to have dinner with him at his place and we all accepted."[19] It is highly improbable that the Soviet Government knew this detail in 1952. Thus, Soviet condemnation of the coup was entirely in line with then Soviet policy of dissociating itself from the bourgeois nationalists. In keeping with its "two camps" doctrine, Moscow viewed all bourgeois nationalists as "lackeys" of western imperialism. As was demonstrated in the preceding chapter, this policy was reversed in 1956 hence, for example, G. Mirsky, a Soviet expert in African and Asian studies, could write in 1962 that:

---

[17]   Bolshaia sovetskaia entsiklopediia, 2nd. edition, vol. XV, Moscow, 1952, p.460.

[18]   Mohamed H. Heikal, The Cairo Documents. The Inside Story of Nasser and his Relationship with World Leaders, Rebels, and Statesmen, New York, 1973, pp.33-34.

[19]   Anwar el-Sadat, In Search of Identity. An Autobiography, London, 1978, p.108.

The military coup organized in 1952 by a group of army officers led by 34-year-old Lieutenant-Colonel Nasser put an end to the pro-imperialist clique of Farouk.[20]

Why did the coup plotters reveal their plan to the U.S. government? It was obvious that the "young officers" had serious misgivings about the British just as much as they despised Soviet communism. They had to assure the U.S. of the safety of the latter's interests, especially as the U.S. had emerged in post 1945 as a major global power with geostrategic interests in the region, but without the imperial guilt of Britain and France.

After Egypt abrogated the Anglo-Egyptian Treaty of 1936, the Western powers failed to persuade it to endorse and join the projected Middle East Defence Organization (MEDO). MEDO was perceived as an anti-Soviet military alliance with strong linkage to NATO. In pursuing anti-Soviet policies in the region, Western powers "failed to understand that Arab nationalist sentiment regarded both Israel and Western military bases as greater threats than Russia or Communism."[21] Britain limited the technical advancement of the Egyptian army within the minimum range of enforcing law and order in a British dependency, taking measures to curb its development as a force inimical to British imperial interests. For economic and geostrategic reasons, Nasser began to develop closer relations with the Soviet Union and other Communist states, but did not hesitate to condemn the Soviet Government when he felt the need to do so. The expansionism and ultra-security consciousness of Israel between 1953 and September 1955, manifested in the Bat Galim incident, the Lavon affair, and a series of sporadic armed conflicts in the Gaza strip, coupled with Western powers' indecision (Britain) and unwillingness (USA) to arm Egypt at a time when

[20]   G. Mirsky, "The U.A.R. Reforms", <u>New Times</u>, no.4, Moscow, 1962, p.12.
[21]   Stephens, 143.

Israel was receiving substantial arms from the West, compelled Nasser, rather reluctantly, to seek Soviet aid.

In quest of Soviet aid an Egyptian delegation was despatched to Moscow in January 1954. The delegation, led by the Deputy War Minister, Brigadier Hassan Ragab, had previously visited other communist states: Poland, Czechoslovakia, East Germany, and Hungary. Simultaneously with the Moscow mission, Egypt sent a similar mission to the West. The trade agreements reached with the Soviet Union and Rumania were ratified in Cairo in March 1954. They provided for a barter of Egyptian cotton for petroleum from Moscow and Bucharest. A Soviet-Egyptian trade pact was signed in Cairo, March 27, 1954, which provided for Soviet export to Egypt of industrial, agricultural equipment, and also motor cars, iron and steel products including timbers and petroleum products for an exchange of Egyptian rice, cotton and leather.[22] This agreement established the basis for Soviet-Egyptian cooperation and led to Soviet recognition of the "reactionary group of officers connected with the United States" in Cairo. Both Egypt and the Soviet Union recognized the need for closer, mutual cooperation. While the Soviet Union was seeking for an ally to counter Western influence in Africa and the Middle East, Egypt's primary concern, on the other hand, was the question of acquiring aid for its development and security.

At a meeting of the UN Security Council on March 29, 1954, the Soviet Union vetoed a Western sponsored resolution which demanded the lifting of Egyptian restrictions on Israeli bound ships in the Suez Canal. This event was hailed in Cairo as a sign of Soviet goodwill toward Egypt, and viewed as an indication of future Soviet action against Israel. The Soviet veto came two days after the signing of the Soviet-Egyptian trade agreement, and twelve days after Egypt had agreed to elevate the diplomatic representation between both countries to the rank of embassy. D. S. Solod, who had hitherto been Soviet Minister in Cairo, thus became the first Soviet Ambassador

---

22 See The Times, London, January 18, 1954; Soviet News, Embassy of the USSR, London, April 2, 1954.

to Egypt, while A. el-Massri was appointed Egyptian Ambassador to the Soviet Union. This diplomatic elevation was regarded in the Kremlin as a move aimed at "strengthening and developing relations between the two countries."[23]

Meanwhile in Egypt an organization calling itself the Democratic Movement for National Liberation (DMNL) was challenging the government of Nasser. In its manifesto the DMNL called for the abolishment of capitalism, the overthrow of Nasser, and the institution of a "Soviet state in Egypt." The drive to smash the DMNL led to the discovery of a communist cell in Alexandria which was alleged to have been financed by the Cominform.[24] The Alexandria cell was the first DMNL underground to be discovered outside Cairo and its effectiveness caused grave concern for Nasser's nationalist government. Between January and May 1954, 252 Communists were prosecuted in Egypt. The anti-communist hunt became a national movement as an editorial in the semi-official Cairo newspaper, Al Ahram stated:

> It is not enough for the state security agents to contain Communist activity and drag Communists to court. It is the duty of all of us to answer each rumour they spread, or each appeal they make. The anti-Communist struggle should become our unfailing duty if we do not want new victims to fall prey to lies and threats.[25]

At one of the trials in a Cairo court where 36 members of the DMNL were sentenced to various terms of imprisonment, the condemned Egyptian communists shouted: "We will fight for freedom with the

---

23 Pravda, Marc 21, 1954
24 The Times, London, February 1, 1954; March 18, 1954.
25 See O. M. Marashian, "Egypt Unwraps Drive on Reds", Christian Science Monitor, June 9, 1954.

Soviet Union against Western imperialism."[26] It is interesting to note that President Nasser adopted this slogan in the 1960s

The persecution and execution of Communists in Egypt did not jeopardize Soviet-Egyptian economic cooperation. The CPSU had abandoned its "two camps" doctrine and recognized the nationalist leaders as the most important factors in the national liberation movements in Africa and Asia. This posed a serious threat to Marxism and compelled Communists to go underground, thus creating a situation similar to the effect of the Nazi-Soviet Pact on German Communists. Nasser's political status and CPSU's anti-Stalinism compelled the Soviet Government to strengthen its ties with Egypt despite the latter's strong anti-communism. In the Soviet view, cooperation with these bourgeois nationalists would enhance Moscow's international image and lead to the isolation of the Western powers from these regions. An ideological justification for this policy was provided at the 20th Congress of the CPSU in February 1956.

The colonial powers had banned communist activities in their respective African colonies which were choreographed to play a predetermined role in the cold war in favour of colonialism. The anti-colonial struggle for independence in the colonies was construed by the West as a communist inspired movement, thus implicitly suggesting that the colonized peoples "preferred" to remain under colonial yoke. It was from this perspective that, for example, France viewed the national liberation movements in Algeria, Morocco, and Tunisia. France therefore granted the U.S. the right to build four military bases in Morocco in 1950. As the national liberation movement gained momentum in North Africa, France protested that "the Soviet Union and its agents are seeking to intensify disorder and revolt in an area that is strategically important to the West." Furthermore, in November 1954, in an attempt to involve NATO, France argued that their interest in North Africa "is consonant with the interests of the Atlantic Alliance since it includes military

---

[26]   The Daily Worker, London, December 31, 1954.

control of part of the strategically important Mediterranean areas."[27]
To emphasize the significance of North Africa to NATO's global
strategy in the cold war, French officials in the region posited:

> The four big American bases in Morocco, capable of
> bombing any spot in the globe including all of the Soviet
> Union, are of topmost value to the free world because
> they are farther away from Russian counter-attack than
> any spot in Europe or North Africa. Loss of them would
> be a grave blow.[28]

It is obvious from the above that the decolonization process had
to be aborted by the West in order to utilize African colonies as
buffer zones in its anti-communist crusade. Besides geostrategic
consideration, this policy was also influenced by economic factors.
In 1954, U.S. Vice President, Richard Nixon expressed concern
for the fate of imperialism when he claimed that the Communists
"have begun to concentrate their forces" in Africa, and predicted
that "as the world's resources move toward depletion, Africa will
become decisive."[29]

It was evidently clear that the policy of the West was based on
mere conjecture and political speculation in an attempt to "justify"
the continued presence of imperial powers in Africa. For example, it
was alleged that a meeting between North African "Communists and
intermediaries for the Soviet Union" took place in December 1954
in Amsterdam, Holland, where the "Chinese volunteer" technique
was approved as a means of combating French imperialism in
Africa. According to Arnold Beichman, a Western anti-communist
journalist, after the 1954 Indo-Chinese armistice, north Africans
who had served in the French Foreign Legion and the French Army,

---

[27] The New York Times, November 12, 1954.
[28] See Barrett McGurn, "Reds Aiding Arab Revolt in North Africa",
New York Herald Tribune, December 6, 1954.
[29] Sunday Mail, Salisbury, Rhodesia, January 3, 1954.

but subsequently deserted to join the Ho Chi Minh forces, were "sent into the Soviet Union where they were lodged in Soviet army barracks and given extensive military training" before they were despatched as "peoples volunteers" to north Africa."[30]

This rather baseless assertion was made at the time when Moscow was still actively pursuing a pro-French policy in Africa as the Soviet Union needed French support in Europe to undercut NATO. Besides, the Soviet Government failed to exploit North African conditions to expel the French. Though Moscow had demanded the independence of Libya and other colonies when Soviet bid for trusteeship over Libya was rejected, the Soviet Government did not seize the opportunity to ally with Libya when the latter attained independence in 1952. On two occasions, September 16, 1952, and December 13, 1955, the Soviet Government vetoed Libya's application for UN membership.[31] Diplomatic relations were not established between the Soviet Union and Libya until September 4, 1954. It is logical to argue that had Moscow voted for Libya's seating in the UNO, Soviet officials would have been in a better position to aid the nationalists in Tunisia, Algeria, and Morocco. However, the Soviet Government was not prepared for this in 1954-1955. For example, in an interview published in Pravda, Nikita Khrushchev called for a "correct decision" of the north African question which he said could be solved by taking into consideration the "*legitimate rights and national interests*" of the people concerned in the conflict.[32] He refrained from any criticism of France. His mild remarks toward France and his preference for the colonialist term "French Union" rather than "French colonial empire" was indicative of Soviet harmonious relations with France. Khrushchev preferred to

[30] Arnold Beichman, "Reds Plan for African Told", Christian Science Monitor, January 31, 1955.

[31] Institute for the Study of the USSR, Soviet Diplomatic Corps, 1917-1967, Metuchen, New Jersey, 1970, pp.215-216.

[32] Pravda, October 3, 1955. Italics mine.

mollify the French in light of French Foreign Minister Pinay's assertion that Soviet Foreign Minister Viacheslav M. Molotov had promised to abstain on the Algerian vote in the United Nations in October 1955.[33]

While European colonial powers banned communist activities and arrested suspected communists in their African colonies, as the anti-colonial movements intensified the struggle for independence, the Soviet Union failed to exploit these opportunities in the immediate post 1945 period. The Stalinist "two camps" doctrine was still dominant in Soviet strategic thinking. Moscow perceived the world in an either-or (socialist or capitalist) situation, and considered the nationalist leaders in the anti-colonial movements as "lackeys of imperialism." The Bandung Conference of 1955 and its Declaration impressed the Soviet Union thus compelling a policy reversal in the Kremlin.[34] However, prior to the policy reversal in 1956 the Soviet Union had benefited from the anti-colonial movements in the colonies irrespective of Moscow's non-recognition of those movements. Writing in 1977, K. N. Brutents, Kremlin's expert on national liberation theory, admitted:

> In the post-war period, especially in the early years, the tide of national liberation revolutions dealt heavy blows at the imperialist policy of aggression, helped substantially to thin out the forces of imperialism and to create more favourable international conditions for the

---

[33] Wellas Hangen, "Moscow's Policy on Algeria Given", The New York Times, October 4, 1955; Marguerite Higgins, "Russians Give View on Algeria: Respect Interests of French Union", New York Herald Tribune (European Edition), October 4, 1955; The Times, London, October 5, 1955.

[34] See E. Zhukov, "The Bandung Conference of African and Asian Countries and its Historical Significance", International Affairs, no. 5, Moscow, 1955, pp.18-32.

effort to rehabilitate the USSR's economy and build up
the emerging socialist community.[35]

Thus, while the imperialist powers were diverted by the anti-colonial
movements, Africa's independence struggle functioned as a tactical
ally of the Soviet Union throughout the cold war period.

It was only in July 1956 that the Soviet Union began to support
the Algerian National Liberation Front (FLN). At a Kremlin
reception held in honour of Prince Norodim Sihanouk of Cambodia,
which was attended by the French ambassador, Maurice Dejean,
Soviet leaders publicly declared Moscow's support for the FLN.
Pravda recalled the fruitless trip to Moscow, May 1956, of French
Premier, Guy Mollet, when he sought Moscow's continued support
for Paris' North African policy. The Soviets declared: "The Arabs,
who comprise the indigenous population of Algeria and are the
lawful masters of their land, no longer wish to tolerate their unequal
position"[36] with French imperialism. It must be stressed that while
the above declaration signalled a departure from Moscow's previous
policy, it did not indicate a total commitment vis-à-vis the FLN. As
we shall see in the next chapter Moscow was still cautious in dealing
with both France and the FLN.

West Africa[37]

The anti-communist witch hunt witnessed in North Africa was
also executed by British colonial administrations in both Ghana

---

[35] K. N. Brutents, National Liberation Revolutions Today, vol. 1,
Moscow, 1977, pp.65-66.

[36] Pravda, July 7, 1956.

[37] Only Nigeria and the Gold Coast (now Ghana) are discussed in this
section. For factual coverage of French-speaking west African countries,
see Ruth S. Morgenthau, Political Parties in French-Speaking West
Africa, London, 1964; Legvold, Soviet Policy in West Africa.

(then the Gold Coast) and Nigeria. Though the CPSU had no direct contact with the socialist and communists of these countries, the British Government believed the contrary. Political leaders in both countries carried out the colonial diktat of Britain vis-à-vis communism.

When Kwame Nkrumah won a decisive election in 1951 and became leader of Government Business in Parliament, he immediately launched a campaign against suspected communists and banned Ghanaians from attending communist sponsored seminars abroad. It was in criticism of this policy that Ivan Potekhin wrote in 1953 accusing Nkrumah and his CPP of collaborating "with English imperialism."[38] In 1954 Nkrumah banned the employment of anyone "with Communist leaning" in most vulnerable ministries and positions in Ghana. He denounced the actions of "certain persons" whom he claimed were in communist pay and repudiated the award of "scholarship . . . to Gold Coast citizens to attend conferences and seminars organized by Communists" abroad.[39] The Ashanti Pioneer, a conservative newspaper published in Kumasi, Ghana, which had traditionally attacked Nkrumah, strongly criticized Nkrumah's communist witch hunt. According to the Ashanti Pioneer, Nkrumah's anti-communist policy was hypocritical since "his National Propaganda Secretary, Mr. N. A. Welbeck, attended a similar conference in Vienna in 1952 . . ." while at home Nkrumah was employing "Communist tactics" as an indication of his belief "in one party government."[40]

Meanwhile in Nigeria, in July 1954, the British Colonial Office instituted a ban on "Communist activity"; ordered the seizure of passports of Nigerians suspected of "Communist connection", and banned the importation of Communist literature into the country.

---

[38] Ivan Potekhin, "Etnicheskii i klassovoi sostav naseleniia zolotogo berega", Sovetskaia etnografiia, no. 3, Moscow, 1953, pp. 112-133. Note p.113.

[39] The Times, London, February 26, 1954.

[40] Ashanti Pioneer, February 27, 1954. See also ibid., July 12, 1954.

H. P. Adebola, a member of the Western Nigerian House of Assembly, and Secretary of the Station Staff Union of the Nigerian Railways, tabled a motion in the House stating that "the All-Nigerian Trade Union Federation is opposed to Communism . . ." and that the Federation should declare "its determination to exterminate this ideology in the Nigerian Trade Union Movement."[41] In September two prominent leaders of the United Working People's Party (UWPP), Meke Anabogu and S. G. Ikoku were detained by the Nigerian colonial government as the UWPP was accused of "communist connection."

When the African Newsletter, an organ of the British Communist Party, was banned by the British colonial regime in Nigeria, the British Communists promptly protested against the ban. In its letter to J. S. MacPherson, the British colonial Governor in Nigeria, the British Communist Party argued:

> As there is no legal discrimination in Britain against the Communist Party, this prohibition has no basis in British law and it is a flagrant violation of the United Nations Charter of Human Rights to which the British Government has given its signature . . . and we call for the immediate withdrawal of the order in question.[42]

The colonial office did not lift the ban. While the British Communist Party functions uninhibited in Britain, the logic of imperialism dictated the prohibition of communist activities in the colonies. The colonial government headed by Abubakar Tafawa Balewa readily executed British imperial policies in Nigeria. In a policy statement issued in October 1954 Balewa declared:

> After careful examination of the situation in Nigeria and in other countries, particularly those

---

41 The Times, London, July 16, 1954.
42 The Daily Worker, London, August 13, 1954.

in the British Commonwealth which are on the
threshold of self-government or have recently become
self-government territories, the Council of Ministers
has reached the conclusion that steps are necessary to
prevent the infiltration of active Communists into post
in the service of the country in which divided loyalty
might be dangerous to the interests of Nigeria.[43]

According to the Nigerian government,

the first loyalty of a Communist lies not to Nigeria, but
to a foreign Communist organization, the objective of
which is the political, economic and social subjugation
of Nigeria.[44]

Every dissent was perceived as communist-inspired, and
anti-communism was elevated to the level of statesmanship. In such
a situation logic and reason gave way to illegal and irrational policies.
It became a mark of statecraft to uncover a communist. Writing in
October 1954 Colin Legum, a respected British journalist, alleged
that a Nigerian "shadow cabinet" was set up in London with the
purpose of seizing power in Nigeria. This "cabinet", according to
Legum, was headed by a "Moscow trained Secretary General, a
young Nigeria student" then resident in London.[45] It is interesting
to note that Legum did not provide any evidence to substantiate this
allegation; neither did he give the name of the Nigerian student. This
was probably a calculated misinformation to direct and intensify the
anti-communist British policy in Nigeria.

Unlike French African colonies where the French Communist
Party (PCF) penetrated, the British communists had no contact with

---

[43] The Times, London, October 14, 1954.
[44] Ibid.
[45] Colin Legum, "Anti-Communist Moves in West Africa", Scotsman,
October 19, 1954.

communists in British African colonies. The absence of Africans at the London conference of the Communist Parties of the British Empire in 1947 indicated the nonexistence of contacts between the British Communist Party and communists in British African colonies.[46] Neither was there any evidence linking the CPSU with most communists on the African continent.

It was significant to most Western political analysts that the measures to proscribe communist activities in Accra and Lagos were taken by African leaders themselves. The fact that these countries were then British colonies was completely ignored. However, it should be stressed that while Balèwa's anti-communism was expected due to the feudal-conservative basis of his political party, the Northern People's Congress (NPC), Nkrumah's anti-communism was revealing given his background in Pan African and radical political movements. Balewa remained consistent throughout his political career, while Nkrumah later had a "comradely" relationship with the Soviet Union and the international communist movement. It was clear that the pressure of cold war politics dictated the pattern of political behaviour in the emergent African states. Africa was becoming a fertile ground for East-West ideological warfare as the two main superpowers, the Soviet Union and the U.S., prepared for a "new scramble" for Africa.

---

[46]   See William H. Lewis, "Sub-Saharan Africa", in Cyril E. Black and Thomas P. Thornton, eds., Communism and Revolution. The Strategic Use of Political Violence, Princeton, New Jersey, 1974, p.372; Walter Kolarz, "The West African Scene", Problems of Communism, X, 6, Washington, DC, 1961, p.17

CHAPTER FIVE

AFRICA IN SINO-SOVIET CONFLICT

The People's Republic of China and the Soviet Union became engaged in ideological conflict after the 20th CPSU Congress of 1956. At the Congress, the Soviet Union denounced Stalin and Stalinism, and endorsed the so-called *three peacefuls*: *peaceful competition, peaceful coexistence*, and the *peaceful transition* from bourgeois parliamentary democracy to socialism. China condemned these policies as an attempt by the Soviet Union to "revise" Marxism-Leninism and a conspiracy against the international Communist movement.[1] The conflict, which began as an ideological confrontation between the CPSU and the Communist Party of China (CPC) took a political twist that endangered Sino-Soviet inter-state relations. This was evident in the armed border clash in early 1969. Essentially, the conflict was over *tactical*, not *strategic*, implementation of Communist ideology. It was centred on the issues of *war, peace,* and *revolution.* It was within this framework that Beijing criticised Moscow's concept of "parliamentary path" to socialism which the latter argued was now possible in the colonies. In the Chinese view, this was a negation of the armed struggle movement of the oppressed peoples and colonies as it constituted a victory for bourgeois, parliamentary democracy.

---

[1]   See Donald S. Zagoria, *The Sino-Soviet Conflict, 1956-1961*, Princeton, New Jersey, 1962, pp.225-235.

The CPC considered the resolutions of the 20th CPSU Congress a deviation from Marxism-Leninism. While the Soviets had argued that "revolution is impossible without a nationwide crisis"[2] it was still the view in the Kremlin that: "Although world wars are unthinkable without revolutions, revolutions are fully possible without wars."[3] After the 20th Congress, the Central Committee of the CPSU established commissions to re-write texts in conformity with the resolutions adopted at the Congress. One of such texts was *The Fundamentals of Marxism-Leninism,* a Communist handbook of tactics and strategy which the Kremlin insisted should be used by all Marxists-Leninists. The Soviets propagated peaceful coexistence and the peaceful transition from capitalism to socialism as objective policies that defined the foreign policy of Communist states as well as all peace-loving forces in the international community. In 1956 the concept of peaceful coexistence was rehabilitated. It was first employed by G.V. Chicherin (Soviet Foreign Minister, February 1918-July 1930), but was more amplified by Lenin in all his writings on Soviet foreign policy. It thus became the cornerstone of Soviet foreign policy before the outbreak of the war of 1939-1945. The doctrine of peaceful coexistence implies the lessening of international tensions and the peaceful coexistence of states irrespective of their social, economic and political systems. However, after 1945 the Stalinist **two camps** concept downgraded peaceful coexistence as Moscow propagated the armed struggle concept. Thus, by returning to Lenin's concept of peaceful coexistence in 1956, the CPSU was rejecting Stalin's *two camps* theory. The concept of peaceful transition to socialism was endorsed by the CPSU as a stratagem to mollify the anti-colonial bourgeois nationalists in Africa and Asia. This political compromise was sought in order to improve the ideological stance of local Communists. Even though in the short run it meant the decline of the role of local Communists, its long term objective was

---

2   The Fundamentals of Marxism-Leninism, Moscow, 1960, p.607.

3   *Ibid.,* p.606.

recognized in the Kremlin. Beijing challenged this policy and argued that it was an obliteration of revolutionary Marxism, citing Lenin:

> Not a single great revolution in history has been carried out without a civil war, and no serious Marxist will believe it possible to make the transition from capitalism to socialism without a civil war.[4]

The controversy over Communist global strategy became pronounced in 1957. Soviet achievements in space and weaponry in 1957 convinced China that, militarily, Communism was superior to capitalism, and wanted the Soviet Union to distribute its arms among Communists for a final bloodbath with the West.[5]

The systematic deterioration of relations between the CPC and the CPSU led to a split within the rank and file of the international Communist movement. As a result of this split the pro-Beijing faction within a national Communist movement identified itself as a "Communist Party (Marxist-Leninist)." In an article written by the Editorial Departments of *Renmin Ribao* and *Honggi*, organs of the CPC, the CPSU was accused of gradually systematizing its "revisionist" policy adopted in 1956 and insisting that fraternal parties follow the Soviet line.[6] The Chinese protested:

> Without any prior consultation with the fraternal Parties, the leadership of the CPSU drew arbitrary conclusions; it forced the fraternal Parties to accept a fait accompli and, on the pretext of "combating the personality cult", crudely interfered in the internal

---

[4]   Long Live Leninism, Peking, 1960, p. 36.

[5]   See Zagoria, pp.152-171.

[6]   See "The Origins and Development of the Differences Between the Leadership of the CPSU and Ourselves", Peking Review, VI, 37, September 13, 1963, pp.6-20.

affairs of fraternal Parties and countries and subverted
their leadership, . . .[7]

It was alleged by the CPC that the CPSU's original draft of the
1957 Declaration was based on the resolutions of the 20th CPSU
Congress on the "peaceful, parliamentary" transition to socialism.
According to the Chinese, the inclusion of the phrase "non-peaceful
transition" was at the insistence of the CPC. They argued:

> While indicating the possibility of peaceful transition,
> the Declaration also points to the road of non-peaceful
> transition and stresses that 'Leninism teaches, and
> experience confirms, that the ruling classes never
> relinquish power voluntarily.' Secondly, while speaking of
> securing a 'firm majority in parliament', the Declaration
> emphasizes the need to 'launch an extra-parliamentary
> mass struggle, smash the resistance of the reactionary
> forces . . .[8]

The CPC was not satisfied with these changes in the Declaration
regarding the transition from capitalism to socialism, but only
conceded after the "repeatedly expressed wish of the leaders of the
CPSU that the formulation should show some connection with that
of the 20th Congress of the CPSU."[9] Besides the desire to maintain
the *unity* of the international Communist movement, the leadership
of the CPC did not elaborate on the ideological justification for the
political concession made to the CPSU since, one may postulate,
it implied a tactical victory for peaceful revolution vis-a-vis the
Chinese concept of armed struggle.

From 1956 to 1959 Sino-Soviet disputes grew systematically
to a freezing point and became noticeable in Sino-Soviet state

---

[7]   *Ibid.*, p.8.
[8]   *Ibid.*, p.11.
[9]   *Ibid.*

relations. In October 1957 China and the Soviet Union contracted an agreement that would have developed and modernized Chinese weaponry and provided China the atomic bomb, but on June 20, 1959, the Soviet Government unilaterally abrogated the agreement. Soviet decision to discontinue its nuclear development project in China had grave impact on Chinese economic and military development as the Soviets attempted to force China into submission. China had only two alternatives: either to pursue an independent policy and refer to the Soviet Union as a "social imperialist" or agree to play second fiddle to the Kremlin. The latter option was rejected. It was not surprising, therefore, when in early September 1959 the Soviet Union declared its support for India during the Sino-Indian border crisis, and condemned China of "wanton aggression" against India whose policy of neutralism seemed to be aiding the forces of peaceful coexistence.

The unilateral abrogation of the Sino-Soviet agreement in June 1959, and the pro-Indian position of Moscow in September 1959 indicated the primacy of Soviet national interest over proletarian internationalism. Since both actions were taken on the eve of Nikita Khrushchev's celebrated visit to Washington (September 1959) where he discussed arms control and world peace with U.S. President Dwight Eisenhower, it was obvious that Moscow's policy toward Beijing between June-September 1959 was calculated to assure Washington of Soviet preparedness to achieve peace and to use its atomic weapons for only peaceful purposes. It thus appeared the Soviet Union was using China as a bargaining instrument in its foreign policy machinations.[10] The Chinese did not conceal their disappointment when

Khrushchev lauded Eisenhower to the skies, hailing him as a man who "enjoys the absolute confidence of

---

[10] See Donald S. Carlise, "The Sino-Soviet Schism", <u>Orbis</u>, VIII, 4, Winter, 1965, pp. 790-815.

his people" and who "also worries about ensuring peace just as we do."[11]

It is interesting to note that Khrushchev flew directly to Beijing from Washington after his Camp David meeting with Eisenhower, to brief Mao and Chou en-Lai on the outcome of his discussions with Eisenhower. However, the absence of a joint communiqué following his Beijing visit indicated the complete failure of both parties to reach a compromise. This was reflected in Khrushchev's farewell speech in Beijing:

> We Communists of the Soviet Union consider it our sacred duty, our primary task . . . to utilize all possibilities in order to liquidate the cold war.[12]

Khrushchev did not elaborate on what he meant by "all possibilities." From the Chinese perspective, Soviet desire "to utilize all possibilities in order to liquidate the cold war" meant sacrificing Chinese interest on the altar of Soviet-U.S. relations.

Both China and the Soviet Union recognized the impact of their disputes on the international Communist movement as well as on international relations. At different stages of the conflict they took some measures to resolve their differences through a series of bilateral talks.[13] But as Tenh Hsiao-ping arrived in Moscow leading a Chinese

---

[11] "The Origins and Development of . . .", Peking Review, p.12.

[12] Pravda, October 5, 1959.

[13] See "The Letter of the Central Committee of the CPSU to the Central Committee of the CPC" February 21, 1963, Peking Review, VI, 2, March 22, 1963, pp.8-10, and the reply of the CPC to the CPSU, ibid., 6-8. See also The Open Letter of the Central Committee of the Communist Party of the Soviet Union, July 14, 1963, Moscow, 1963. "The Letter of the CC of the CPC in Reply to the Letter of the CC of the CPSU of March 30, 1963", Peking Review, VI, 25, June 21, 1963, pp.6-22.

delegation to one of the bilateral meetings, renewed polemics arose over some fundamental issues[14] thus completely overshadowing the Sino-Soviet meeting of July 5-20, 1963. Soviet leaders refused to publish the Chinese letter of June 14, 1963 in the Soviet press even though Soviet anti-Chinese letters, accompanied by Chinese replies, were routinely published in Chinese newspapers. When five Chinese nationals, including three diplomats, decided to print and circulate the Chinese letter of June 14, among Soviet citizens, they were arrested and declared *persona non grata* and returned to Beijing in July 1963. China protested against the "unreasonable Soviet" expulsion of its diplomats, and accused the CPSU leadership of disservice to Soviet citizens by refusing to publish Chinese letters in the Soviet press.

The Anglo-US-Soviet nuclear test ban treaty signed in Moscow on July 25, 1963, came under severe condemnation in China. Moscow had hailed the signing of the treaty as a victory for peace and its policy of peaceful coexistence. For the Chinese, the test ban treaty was "a big fraud to fool the people of the world", and an Anglo-US-Soviet "attempt to consolidate their nuclear monopoly and bind the hands of all peace-loving countries subjugated to the nuclear threat." According to China, the treaty was "by no means a victory for the policy of peaceful coexistence" but a "capitulation to US imperialism."[15] China continued to view the test ban treaty as a plot by Western "imperialists" and Soviet "modern revisionists" to dominate the world. This viewpoint was extensively propagated in Africa as China sought to ally with Africa against Soviet overtures in the continent.

---

[14] See "Statement of the Central Committee of the CPSU" of July 9, 1963, and "Statement of the Central Committee of the Communist Party of China" of July 10, 1963, Peking Review, VI, 28, July 12, 1963, pp.7-8.

[15] For the full text of China's reaction, see "Statement of the Chinese Government" of July 31, 1963, Peking Review, VI, 31, August 2, 1963, pp.7-8; and VI, 32, August 9, 1963, pp.10-11.

In studying the place of Africa in Sino-Soviet schism it is imperative that attention be directed at, primarily, Africa's national liberation movements and, secondly, Chinese and Soviet attempt to woo independent African states. Both China and the Soviet Union sought to win the support of existing African Communist parties. Of the five African Communist and Workers' Parties that were present at the International Communist Meeting in Moscow in June 1969, three were considered pro-Soviet (Algeria, Tunisia, and Sudan) while one (Morocco) maintained an independent stance in the Sino-Soviet conflict. The schism caused a split in the Nigerian Socialist Workers' and Farmers' Party (SWAFP) though its general secretary, Tunji Otegbeye, representing the pro-Moscow faction, attended the Meeting.

China, like the Soviet Union, entered Africa through the Northern Gate—Egypt. The Nasser-Chou en-Lai conversation during the 1955 Bandung Conference led to the establishment of diplomatic relations between Egypt and China in May 1956.

Sino-Soviet divergence in Africa surfaced for the first time in 1958 in their contending approaches toward the Algerian war of independence. The armed struggle in Africa was identical to China's armed struggle concept of national liberation and ran counter to Soviet cautious policy during the Algerian war. Soviet policy toward Algeria was determined by current Franco-Soviet relations. The Soviet Union was aware that a belligerent policy toward France in Algeria would reduce the prospects of Franco-Soviet cooperation in European politics. The Kremlin leadership was also exploiting De Gaulle's anti-Americanism in its strategy to weaken NATO in Europe. Nevertheless, Moscow did manage, under the auspices of the International Red Cross, to ship food and medication to Algerian refugees in Morocco and Tunisia. The fact that Franco-Soviet courtship compelled Moscow to slow-pedal in Algeria caused Beijing to condemn Soviet policy of peaceful coexistence as a betrayal of the national liberation movements. China was quick to endorse the political line of the Algerian FLN and the anti-imperialist struggle in Africa and Asia. It should be stressed that, long before there was a People's Republic of China and the emergence of a Sino-Soviet dispute in Africa, the Chinese had, since the late 1930s, argued that their approach to revolution "stands as a paradigm for all anti-imperialist liberation movements."[16]

De Gaulle's proposal of self-determination for Algeria was denounced by China as "nothing but a sugar-coated poison"[17]; while the Soviet Union endorsed the proposal saying that it "could play an important part in the settlement of the Algerian question."[18] In refuting the Chinese statement that the Soviet Government and the CPSU were abandoning the national liberation movement to promote peaceful coexistence, M.A. Suslov, CPSU's chief ideologist, stated before a Central Committee meeting:

> The warriors of the heroic national liberation army
> of Algeria, the armed forces of Indonesia, Yemen and
> other countries, well know whose weapons have helped
> in the struggle against the colonisers for freedom and
> independence.[19]

Suslov's statement, when viewed against the background of the Algerian war of independence, obviously posed a dilemma in any critical analysis of Soviet behaviour vis-a-vis major national liberation movements. Unlike China, the Soviet Union hesitated to state publicly its policy and the arms support it was rendering to Algeria. The main issue was not Soviet *secret* arms deal with Algeria but rather the centrist or pro-French policy which Moscow consistently pressed the Algerians to adopt. By doing so the Soviet Union was

---

16   "The Chinese Revolution and the Communist Party", in Mao Tse-tung, <u>Selected Works</u>, London, 1954, vol. III, p.97, cited by Richard Lowenthal, "China" in Zbigniew Brzezinski, ed., <u>Africa and the Communist World</u>, pp. 142-143.

17   New China News Agency, October 17, 1959.

18   N. S. Khrushchev, Address to the Supreme Soviet, Moscow Radio, October 31, 1959, cited by Lowenthal, "China", p.172.

19   Pravda, April 3, 1964.

calculating to win on both fronts by appeasing Algeria (the arms deal) to accept De Gaulle's moderate proposal (thus appearing non-committal before the French) which had been rejected by the leadership of the FLN. Under this scenario, Moscow was compelled to walk on both sides of the street at the same time, thereby exposing itself to charges of pro-imperialist manipulations. Marx and Engels stated that Communists and workers engaged in armed struggle have nothing to lose but their chains. Since the Sino-Soviet dispute surfaced in the public, China had identified itself with this Marxian dictum while the Soviet Union seemed concerned with maintaining its status as a super-power and unwilling to lose its *chains* through violent, armed revolution.

Moscow's peaceful and gradual process could not match Beijing's armed struggle concept. The Kremlin leadership was worried that its reformist philosophy would collapse before China's revolutionary policy. This led Moscow to accuse Beijing of "discrediting the USSR" in Africa.[20] According to S. G. Yurkov, a Soviet expert on Chinese politics, it was wrong of China to propagate the Algerian armed struggle as an example to be emulated by African countries in their struggle against Western imperialism. To do so, he argued, would be to the detriment of the international Communist movement.[21]

The two Communist giants were prepared to *unite* by supporting the only political movement in a given African country. The table on page 156 illustrates Sino-Soviet divergence in African national liberation movements. The respective counter alliance systems which these organizations contracted with both the Soviet Union and China gravely limited their effectiveness in the anti-colonial

---

[20] S.G. Yurkov, Pekin: Novaia politika?, Moscow, 1972, p.111. See also B. Zanegi, A. Mironov, Y.Mikhailov, Developments in China, Moscow, 1968; Maoizm glazami kommunistov, Moscow, 1969; Y. Bogush, Maoism and its Policy of Splitting the National Liberation Movement, Moscow, 1970; Opasnyi kurs: O politike pekinskikh rukovoditelei, Moscow, 1971.

[21] See Yurkov, p.70.

struggle. Some of their attempts to *unify* the divergent groups did not yield tangible results. In Angola, for example, both the MPLA and UNITA failed in their efforts to resolve their differences. In 1973-74 their attempt to create a *common front* against Portugal collapsed. When Angola attained independence in November 1975 with the MPLA as the governing party, UNITA intensified its war against MPLA with the tripartite assistance of the U.S., South Africa, and China. This formidable sources of support hardened UNITA's resolve to continue its war against the MPLA government. Especially during the presidency of Ronald Reagan, the U.S. treated Jonas Savimbe, UNITA's leader, with the honours of a head of state. Soviet military, economic, and political assistance, coupled with Cuban armed intervention sustained the MPLA government of Augustino Neto in power. This support continued after the death of Neto in September 1979 in Moscow.

In Zimbabwe, ZAPU and ZANU leaders established a *common front* that fought the war against the white minority racist regime in what was southern Rhodesia. Irrespective of this, however, they maintained their respective alliances with Moscow and Beijing as exemplified by their separate training camps in Tanzania in the anti-colonial/racist regime. It is interesting to note that the ZAPU camp at Morogoro was staffed with Soviet instructors, while the ZANU camp at Intumbi Reefs, near Mbeya, was staffed with Chinese instructors.[22] The ZANU-ZAPU coalition government that emerged following the Lancaster House agreement and the elections of early 1980 saw the gradual demise of ZAPU (Soviet influence) in the post independent era.

---

[22] See <u>Strategic Survey</u> 1970, London, 1971, p.57.

AFRICAN NATIONAL LIBERATION MOVEMENTS SUPPORTED BY THE USSR AND CHINA

COUNTRY/ ORGANIZATION	SOURCES OF SUPPORT			
	USSR	CHINA	SINO-SOVIET	INDEPENDENT
ANGOLA:				
MPLA	*			
UNITA		*		
GRAE				*
ETHIOPIA:				
MEISON	*			
EPRP		*		
GUINEA BISSAU:				
PAIGC			*	
MOZAMBIQUE:				
FRELIMO	*			
COREMO		*		
NAMIBIA:				
SWAPU	*			
SWANU		*		
SOUTH AFRICA:				
ANC	*			
PAC		*		
ZIMBABWE:				
ZAPU	*			
ZANU		*		

Following the overthrow of Emperor Haile Sellasie and the abolishment of the monarchy in Ethiopia, the contending forces for power sought and obtained the support of Moscow and Beijing respectively. While the All-Ethiopian Socialist Movement (MEISON) was aligned with the Soviet Union, the Ethiopian People's Revolutionary Party (EPRP) relied on China. MEISON had proposed a programme for a *National Democratic Revolution* (NDR) which appealed to Mengistu Haile Mariam and the *Dergue*. Though EPRP supported the NDR concept, it however predicated its participation on "the elimination of the Dergue from the political scene"[23] and demanded the proclamation of a democratic provisional people's government with Marxist ideological trappings. The EPRP was a threat to the pre-eminence of the Dergue in Ethiopia in the late 1970s. The *Dergue*, which had secured Soviet support during this period, immediately allied itself with MEISON "and urged it to liquidate EPRP."[24] This gave rise to the notorious Ethiopian *Red Terror* of 1976-1978. While the Sino-Soviet conflict vividly reflected itself in the rank and file of the above nationalist movements, the consensus of the rest of Africa was to remain neutral.

We should, at this juncture, discuss the impact of the Sino-Soviet schism on the Afro-Asian People's Solidarity Organization (AAPSO) since it was the *vehicle* that brought China to Africa. It was at Bandung in 1955 that Chou en-Lai first met with President Nasser of Egypt and other African leaders attending the Bandung Conference. Moses Kotane represented South Africa's African National Congress (ANC) at Bandung. From the Chinese perspective, constant meetings between Africans and Asians were considered advantageous. Apart from the relationships which might ultimately develop, a forum of African and Asian leaders also afforded China an opportunity to propagate its ideology, especially in Africa where it was, in the words of Chou en-Lai, a "late comer."

Egyptian writers attending the Asian Writers' Conference in New Delhi in December 1956 had persuaded the participants, including the Soviet Union and China, to change the name of the existing organization, Asian Solidarity Committee, to the Afro-Asian Solidarity Committee which later became AAPSO. The organization was a forum for both Soviet and Chinese delegates to lay counter accusations with the ultimate aim of winning Afro-Asian nations to support their respective policies. Since the Sino-Soviet conflict was more ideological than political, any support for either side was

---

[23] Bereket Habte Selassie, "The Dergue's Dilemma: The Legacies of a Feudal Empire", <u>Monthly Review</u>, 32, 3, July-August, 1980, p.15.

[24] *Ibid.*

capable of jeopardizing the proclaimed neutrality of most African (and Asian) nations.

The first conference of AAPSO was held in Cairo from December 1957 to January 1958. Kuo mo-jo of China, in his maiden speech clearly negated Soviet peaceful coexistence policy and argued that in

> the Afro-Asian countries the struggle for national independence and against imperialism and colonialism forms an integral part of our movement for safe-guarding peace. We must first obtain independence and equality, and then we can live in peace.[25]

At AAPSO's executive meeting in December 1961 China began to challenge Soviet participation in the organization, arguing that the Soviet Union was not an Asian country. Even though Soviet territory included a substantial part of Asia, the Chinese argued that Soviet Asian republics were integral parts of a "European" political entity. The Soviet Union was a "white" man's country, argued Beijing, while the Chinese belong to the "coloured" oppressed race of the world. This racial solidarity theme was reinforced by the "similarities" in Chinese and African societies and the colonialization of both societies by the Europeans. The Soviets immediately labelled the Chinese "racists" for exploiting racism in AAPSO.

During the executive meeting of AAPSO's Solidarity Council held in Nicosia in September 1963, Soviet delegates laboured very hard to discredit the "racial" policy of China. China's policy was propagating "war" not "peace", and it encouraged Western imperialists to intensify their aggression in countries struggling for independence, maintained the Soviets. In the Soviet view, China was a "war monger." The Soviets called upon all peace-loving peoples to fight the "yellow peril." China, on the other hand, reiterated its

---

[25]   *Conference de Peoples Afro-Asiatiques, 26 decembre 1957 - Janvier 1958, Principaux Rapports*, Cairo, 1958, cited in Lowenthal, "China", p.170.

attack on the nuclear test ban treaty and accused the Soviet Union of collaborating with the West to undermine the significance of the national liberation movements in Africa and Asia:

> World peace can be won only through struggle by the people of all countries and not by begging the imperialists for it. Peace can be effectively safeguarded only by relying on the masses of the people and waging a tit-for-tat struggle against the imperialist policies of aggression and war.[26]

However, the Nicosia Declaration was considered a victory for Soviet policy. AAPSO expressed its

> loyalty to the principle of peaceful coexistence between independent states with different social and political systems . . . in the struggle for peace, complete and universal disarmament and the banning of nuclear tests and the liquidation of military bases.[27]

Soviet victory in Nicosia did not deter China from further attacking the Soviet Union. Six months after the Nicosia meeting, the Solidarity Council convened in Algiers in March 1964. Kuo Chien of China challenged the pro-Soviet Declaration adopted at Nicosia. She declared:

> A certain outside force . . . has been trying to impose on us an erroneous line which leaves out anti-imperialism and revolution. It spreads the nonsense that Afro-Asian peoples' task of opposing imperialism and old and new colonialism has been completed . . . It propagates the

---

[26] "Two Different Lines on the Question of War and Peace", <u>Peking Review</u>, VI, 47, November 22, 1963, p.13.

[27] <u>Pravda</u>, September 14, 1963. See also Yurkov, p.131.

> view that the main task now confronting the Afro-Asian
> peoples in their struggle is "peaceful coexistence" with
> imperialism and old and new colonialism, and general
> and complete disarmament. This erroneous line in fact
> meant that the oppressed nations must for ever suffer
> imperialist plundering and enslavement.[28]

In the Chinese view, imperialist unjust wars must be halted in order
to ensure freedom and independence in former colonies *before* peace
could be attained. Secondly, "complete and universal disarmament"
could only be attained *after* the possession of nuclear weapons by
all countries. It is interesting to recall that Syria had made a similar
proposal at the UN in 1955. During the 10th session of the UN
General Assembly, Ahmed el-Shukairy of Syria demanded that the UN
establish an "international pool of arms and military equipment" to
be distributed "equitably" among the "haves" and the "have-nots."[29]

China's plan was to oust the Soviet Union from AAPSO. The
proposed "Second Bandung" scheduled for June 29, 1965 in Algiers
was postponed and permanently abandoned primarily because of the
issue of Soviet participation. Though the military coup that ousted
Ben Bella on June 19, 1965, dictated the original postponement
till November 1965, it did not, however, determine the complete
abandonment of the "Second Bandung."

For both the Soviet Union and China the period between
1957 and 1961 was filled with optimism. They overestimated
the revolutionary movement in Africa. It was during this period
that Moscow and Beijing began to clash in Africa. In Moscow, the
Department of African Countries was established in the Soviet
Foreign Ministry in 1958, while the Institute of Africa was founded

---

[28] *Hsinhua*, March 26, 1964, cited in George A von Stackelberg,
"Afro-Asian Solidarity and the Sino-Soviet Dispute", <u>Bulletin</u>,
Institute for the Study of the USSR, Munich, XI, 8, August 26, 1964,
p.22.

[29] <u>Christian Science Monitor</u>, October 4, 1955.

in 1959 with Professor Ivan Potekhin as the first Director. Potekhin and China's Yang Shou attended the Accra Conference of 1958 where contacts were established with revolutionary Africa. China accorded diplomatic recognition to Guinea on October 4, 1959, on the first anniversary of Soviet recognition of Guinea. Twelve months later Sekou Toure was in Beijing to receive a $25 million credit over a 10 year period.

The Congo crisis of 1960 was the second open confrontation in Sino-Soviet African policies. Both Communist states had recognized the government of Patrice Lumumba and were both expelled from the Congo in September 1960 by Joseph Mobutu's military junta. The Communist states and a few African states, Ghana, Guinea, Mali, and Egypt, recognized the pro-Lumumba regime in Kisangani which was headed by Antoine Gizenga, Lumumba's former deputy. However, this Lumumbist regime was defeated when Gizenga joined Cyril Adoula to form a coalition government in August 1961. While the Soviet Union and other East European communist states *moved* their embassies to Kinshasa, China denounced the newly formed coalition government and criticized the Soviet Union for maintaining an embassy in Kinshasa. The Chinese argued that the Lumumbist regime in Kisangani had ceased to exist with the formation of a coalition government, and that recognition of Adoula's coalition government was a legitimization of the anti-Lumumba regime in Kinshasa.

In 1963-1964 China moved for increased bilateral contacts with African countries. Chou en-Lai led a Chinese government delegation that visited ten African countries between December 14, 1963 and February 4, 1964. Vice Premier and Foreign Minister Chen Yi represented China at Kenya's independence celebrations in December 1963, before joining Chou en-Lai in Cairo on December 14, 1963. Chou visited the Soviet-built Aswan High Dam in Egypt. At Aswan he recalled past trade relations between Egypt and China as far back as the second century. He deliberately low-keyed his visit especially in countries where the Soviet Union seemed well established. His main theme throughout his African tour was the identification of similarities between China and African countries. Speaking in Cairo on his arrival on December 14 he declared:

> The new emerging independent Asian and African
> countries share the common experience of suffering
> from imperialist aggression and oppression and face the
> common task of continuing the fight against old and
> new colonialism.[30]

The identification of Afro-Asian *similarities* with the constant reference to "old and new colonialism" was used by China as a pointer against Soviet participation in AAPSO. Soviet leaders were aware of the intent of Chou en-Lai's speech; and while he was still in Egypt Nikita Khrushchev announced his decision to visit Egypt in the spring of 1964. Khrushchev's visit to Egypt in May 1964, planned to coincide with the blocking off of the Nile River at the site of the Aswan Dam, was meant to neutralize any impact of Chou en-Lai's speech.

Addressing the Press in Cairo on December 20, 1963, Chou en-Lai explained that his visit was motivated by the desire to seek "friendship and cooperation" with African countries in order to facilitate Sino-African understanding and joint actions in international politics. He repeatedly stated, as he did throughout his tour of Africa, that Sino-African relations were based on the Chinese five principles of peaceful coexistence. He reiterated the Chinese position on the Anglo-US-Soviet 1963 "nuclear blackmail." However, while answering a question on Sino-Soviet disputes he responded in a cautious tone that indicated the ideological commitment of both China and the Soviet Union:

> We do have serious differences with the leaders of the
> Communist Party of the Soviet Union on questions
> of principles of Marxism-Leninism. It is our belief,
> however, that these disputes will be resolved in the
> end on the basis of Marxism-Leninism and on the

---

[30] Peking Review, VI, 52, December 27, 1963, p/ 8. For the full text of the China-UAR Joint Communiqué, see *ibid.*, pp.9-11.

revolutionary principles of the 1957 Declaration and
the 1960 Statement. Some countries want to profit by
these differences; they are doomed to failure. China
and the Soviet Union, the two big powers, are both in
the socialist camp. They have between them a Treaty of
Friendship, alliance and Mutual Assistance. In the event
of emergency, the Chinese and Soviet peoples will stand
by each other, shoulder-to-shoulder, hand-in-hand.[31]

If such optimism existed in the early 1960s, it evaporated following
the Sino-Soviet border armed conflict of early 1969. It is significant
to note that Chou referred to both China and the Soviet Union
as "the two big powers"; however, China resented the "big power"
appellation since the late 1960s in its attempt to detach itself from
Soviet-U.S. "big power" politics.

Nasser and Chou reached agreements on a series of issues
without impact on the Sino-Soviet dispute. It was in Algiers that
Chou got a public rebuff of Chinese policy. Welcoming Chou in
Algiers on December 21, 1963, Ben Bella informed his guest that
"Algeria supports the policy of peaceful coexistence pursued by
the socialist camp under Moscow's leadership."[32] In his address to
Algerian FLN cadres four days later, Chou completely disregarded
Ben Bella's policy statement of December 21. Instead, he stressed
the similarities between the Chinese and Algerian armed struggle
concepts and argued that this was a tacit negation of Soviet "peaceful"
coexistence policy. He hailed the Algerian revolution as an example
for all oppressed countries:

> The independence of Algeria in our era is a great event in
> the African national liberation movement. For the other

---

[31]   *Ibid.*, p.14.

[32]   *Le Monde*, Paris, December 24, 1963, cited by Mian-Dhin'am, "The
       Results of Chou en-Lai's Visit to Africa", <u>Bulletin</u>, Institute for the
       Study of the USSR, Munich, XI, 7, July, 1964, p.43.

African peoples, it has set a brilliant example of daring
to wage an armed struggle and daring to seize victory,
and indicates to the oppressed nations throughout
the world the correct road to win independence and
freedom. The great victory of the revolutionary struggle
of the Algerian people shows that the new-born
revolutionary forces, though seemingly weak at first,
can ultimately defeat the outwardly strong but decadent
counter-revolutionary forces . . . and that confronted
with imperialist armed suppression, the oppressed
nations can win independence and liberation only by
fighting the counter-revolutionary armed forces with
revolutionary armed forces. The Algerian revolutionaries
have defeated colonialism precisely because they firmly
relied on the peasants and all revolutionary people,
launched and persisted in armed struggle with the
countryside as their base, and combined the other forms
of struggle with armed struggle.[33]

In the above speech Chou negated the Soviet position which,
according to Ben Bella, was endorsed by Algeria. Addressing himself
to the Kremlin leaders and other proponents of *peaceful coexistence*
Chou underlined that armed struggle was the only "correct road
to win independence and freedom." The ideological confrontation
between Chou and Ben Bella compelled the Chinese Premier to
define China's concept of *peaceful coexistence* in Rabat, Morocco, on
December 27, 1963:

We believe that it is possible for countries with different social
systems to coexist peacefully. The Chinese Government
has persistently pursued a policy of peace aimed at

---

[33] Chou en-Lai, "African Peoples' Example of Daring to Wage Armed
Struggle and Seize Victory", <u>Peking Review</u>, VII, 1, January 3, 1964,
p.34.

bringing about peaceful coexistence with all countries on earth, including the Western countries, on the basis of the following five principles: mutual respect for sovereignty and territorial integrity, non-aggression, non-interference in internal affairs, equality and mutual benefits, and peaceful coexistence. On the basis of these principles, China has already brought about peaceful coexistence with certain Asian, African and European countries whose social systems are different from our own.[34]

In the Chinese argument *peaceful coexistence* is one of the five principles that regulate *peaceful relations* between states. It is the last to be achieved, as the other four principles function as prerequisites of *peaceful coexistence*. This was the fundament difference between the Soviet and the Chinese concepts of *peaceful coexistence*.

Leaving Morocco on December 30, 1963, Chou visited Albania (December 30, 1963-January 9, 1964); Tunisia (January 9-10, 1964); Ghana (January 11-16, 1964); Mali (January 16-21, 1964); Guinea (January 21-26, 1964); Sudan (January 27-30, 1964); Ethiopia (January 30-February 1, 1964); and Somalia (February 1-4, 1964). It was the most extensive visit to Africa to be ever undertaken by any world leader. It underscored the Chinese determination to establish its presence in Africa.

Speaking before a large crowd in Mogadishu, Somalia, on February 3, 1964, Chou declared Africa was ripe for revolution.[35] This remark caused grave political concern in East Africa where, on January 22, a People's Democracy was proclaimed on the Island of Zanzibar, and the armies had mutinied against the governments in Tanganyika, Kenya, and Uganda. The Soviets quickly condemned Chou's statement as political adventurism amidst speculations

---

[34]   Le Monde, Paris, January 1, 1964, cited by Mian-Dhin'am, "The Results of Chou en-Lai's Visit to Africa", p.42.

[35]   Chou en-Lai, "Revolutionary Prospects in Africa Excellent", Peking Review, VII, 7, February 14, 1964, pp.5-8.

of Chinese "involvement" in East African politics. According to Mian-Dhin'am, Julius Nyerere of Tanganyika and Jomo Kenyatta of Kenya accused China of involvement in the "mutinies of their respective armies" hence Chou's proposed visits to Tanganyika and Kenya were cancelled.[36] Mian-Dhin'am's conclusion was based on mere conjecture that was completely devoid of any evidence. There existed a high probability that the erroneous assumption of Chinese "involvement" and, perhaps more important, the presence of British *imperialist* troops in Tanganyika and Kenya, which Beijing condemned may have compelled China to cancel the planned visits of Chou. In fact, it was the Chinese Government that actually cancelled the visits:

> The postponement of the visits of Mr. Chou en-Lai, the Chinese Prime Minister, to Tanganyika and Kenya, which were planned for February 2 and February 7 respectively, was decided by the Chinese Government and not at the request of Tanganyika and Kenya.[37]

There was a handicap in Chinese competition with the Soviets in Africa. China lacked the economic and technological power to offer grandiose aid and construct huge projects like the Soviet Union. This limitation was recognized in Beijing. This may have informed the Chinese constant insistence on *self-reliance* and the reference to China as a paradigm for emerging African countries. The Soviets, however, systematically exploited this limitation in order to enhance their position in Africa. The Soviets realized that African countries needed economic and technical aid which China was not able to afford. S. G. Yurkov argued that:

> Besides "leftist" phrases on armed struggle, Chinese leaders have nothing to tell the peoples of emerging countries

---

[36]   Mian-Dhin'am, p.42.
[37]   The Times, London, January 30, 1964.

about the paths of better future development. They have no positive ideas which could help the progressive forces in former colonies to strive for socialism.[38]

Soviet leaders were very prompt in their attempt to obliterate Chou's inroads in Africa. In January 1964, a month after the Ben Bella-Chou confrontation in Algiers, the Soviet Government presented the Algerian President with an Ilyushin 18 plane and invited him to Moscow in late April 1964. During the traditional May Day Parade in Moscow, President Leonid Brezhnev read a decree of the Supreme Soviet awarding President Ben Bella the title of *Hero of the Soviet Union* in appreciation of his "outstanding services in the struggle for freedom and in strengthening and developing Algerian-Soviet friendship."[39]

Both China and the Soviet Union constantly opposed each other in Africa by taking different positions on major issues. For instance, in Somali the Soviet Union failed to support the *Greater Somali* concept **openly** so as not to antagonize Ethiopia and Kenya, while leaders of the Somali Youth League (SYL) were given sanctuary in Moscow. China, on the other hand, declared its support for the SYL whose philosophy is to unite all Somalis in East Africa, including those presently in Kenya and Ethiopia, in a Somali state.[40] Sino-Soviet dispute was also evident during the Nigerian-Biafran civil war. While Nigeria fought the war primarily with Soviet weapons, China supported secessionist Biafra in its "struggle against imperialism and revisionism" and was convinced that the civil war was engineered by the "coalition of the imperialism of the USA, Britain, and Soviet revisionists for the division of spheres of influence in Africa."[41]

---

[38] Yurkov, p.124.

[39] Soviet News, Embassy of the USSR, London, May 4, 1964.

[40] See Mahdi Ismail, "My Communist Schooldays", Observer, February 18, 1962.

[41] As cited in Africa Report, Washington, DC, 13, 8, November 1968, p.36. For a detailed analysis of Soviet policy toward the Nigerian civil

CHAPTER SIX

THE KHRUSHCHEV YEARS

The analysis of Soviet African policy in this chapter covers the period from 1955 to 1964, when Nikita S. Khrushchev was CPSU First Secretary and Prime Minister of the Soviet Union. This was the period when Africa was appropriately referred to as The Lion Awakes.[1] In implementing Soviet African policy during this period Khrushchev was guided by the following:

- The decisions of the 20th CPSU Congress of 1956;
- The 1957 Declaration of the International Communist Movement; and
- The 1960 Statement of the 81 Communist and Workers' Parties Meeting in Moscow.[2]

Armed with these guidelines Khrushchev sought to implement Soviet Policy in Africa in order to:

---

war, see O. Igho Natufe, "Nigeria and Soviet Attitudes to African Military Regimes, 1965-70", Survey, 22, 1(98), London, 1976, pp.93-111.

[1] Jack Woddis, Africa. The Lion Awakes, London, 1961.

[2] See "Policy Rehabilitation: Khrushchev" in chapter three.

1. neutralize and/or obliterate Western capitalist power and influence;
2. institute Soviet power and influence; and
3. collaborate with progressive African governments to achieve 1 or 2 above.

To realize the above, the Kremlin's game plan was the persistent pursuance of the following policy options:

Option A:
Close collaboration and fraternization with a pro-Moscow neutral and anti-Western regime headed by the national bourgeoisie.

Option B:
In the absence of Option A, maintain close fraternal relationship with pro-Moscow socialist/workers'/communist parties.

Option C:
Reliance on the armed forces of the country concerned to cause a socialist revolution irrespective of the socio-economic level of development.

The period was very volatile for both Africa and the Soviet Union, as the former was struggling to find its feet in the mines of international politics while the latter was equally struggling to keep the Western imperialist powers out of Africa. Both parties agreed, *in principle*, to keep out the imperialist powers from Africa, but disagreed on the modalities to achieve this objective. According to a U.S. expert on Soviet African policy,[3] this was the era of Soviet policy experimentation as it grapples to comprehend Africa's reality. However, this does not suggest that *policy* experimentation is a conclusive process since, in dialectical terms, the process of theory ➤ practice ➤ theory ➤ practice is a continuous phenomenon in

---

[3] See Robert Legvold, <u>Soviet Policy in West Africa</u>.

social and political development. In as much as any given period in foreign policy study can rightly be tagged a period of policy experimentation in relation to the preceding period, the current policy experimentation period becomes a policy formulation period for the succeeding period. Thus, it is imperative that foreign policy be understood in dialectical terms if we seek to deduce meaning from the behaviour of states in the international political system. It is on the basis of this that Soviet African policy is discussed and analyzed in the present study.

As we indicated in the preceding pages, Soviet-Egyptian relations were normalized as Western support for Israel compelled Nasser to seek closer co-operation with the Soviet Union. Nasser was an anti-communist; he was also a nationalist opposed to Western imperialism. Notwithstanding his anti-communist policies, the Soviet Government sought to cooperate with him on the basis of his anti-Western imperialist policies. However, when Nasser began to criticize Soviet policies, frictions developed in Soviet-Egyptian relations as Egypt's neutralism posed a problem for the Soviet Government.

The Soviet Government formally abandoned its hostile policy toward neutralism and the national bourgeoisie in 1954-1955 and allied with African neutralism and nationalism in order to combat Western imperialism. As we demonstrated in chapter three, this change was necessitated by the impact of the Bandung Conference, the Geneva Conference of 1955, and the growing importance of the neutrals in international politics. Moscow had to repudiate its Stalin's "two caps" concept and ally with neutralism. At the 20th CPSU Congress in 1956, the Soviet Government formally endorsed neutralism and proposed to cooperate with African and Asian bourgeois nationalists leaders.

Moscow's contact with Africa south of the Sahara had an ironic twist to it: Liberia, a country which the Soviet Union had long considered the "main stay" of U.S. imperialism in Africa, was the first Soviet contact in Africa south of the Sahara. Members of the Soviet delegation to Monrovia, for the third inauguration of William Tubman as President of Liberia, utilized their presence in Liberia to promote Soviet-Liberian bilateral relations. It is interesting to note that the Soviet Government had declined a previous invitation, in 1952, to attend the second inauguration of Tubman. This was not surprising, as Stalin and Stalinism were still in power in the Kremlin. But in the immediate post Stalinist era, Moscow was now prepared to pursue a policy of peaceful coexistence with the "main stay" of U.S. imperialism, as the Soviet leaders decided to offer "disinterested" aid to Liberia in 1956 and proposed the establishment of diplomatic relations at ambassadorial level.

Alexander Volkov, the leader of the Soviet delegation to Monrovia, extended Soviet Government's invitation for President Tubman to send a good-will mission to Moscow for both countries to "develop friendly relations." This was followed by an economic agreement with Liberia that would have led to a small, but significant Soviet presence in West Africa. This package was rejected by Liberia; although the commercial setback was mitigated somewhat when both Liberia and the Soviet Union agreed to establish diplomatic relations in January 1956—the first Soviet embassy at ambassadorial level in Africa south of the Sahara.[4] While the Soviets were cautious in their appraisal of the establishment of diplomatic relations with Liberia, the Chinese hailed the event as a communist "success" in the campaign to oust the West:

> Liberia is setting an example for other countries in Africa. This will have a far reaching effect on the whole continent. Africa has long been in the grip of Western imperialism.[5]

However, Volkov who negotiated the Soviet-Liberian accord displayed concealed optimism when questioned on the significance

---

4   For the exchange of Notes between Liberia and the USSR, see <u>Soviet News</u>, Embassy of the USSR, London, January 26, 1956.

5   <u>New China News Agency</u>, January 25, 1956.

of diplomatic relations between Liberia and the Soviet Union. He stated at a Kremlin interview:

> But we believe that establishment of normal diplomatic relations will provide the opportunity to reach agreement on other forms of contact, not only trade and other forms of technical cooperation, but also cultural contacts could be of interest.[6]

Volkov underlined the importance of "cultural contacts" in Soviet policy. Through cultural cooperation the Soviet Union sought to ally with Africa in the latter's struggle to regain and restore its cultural heritage which was plundered by West European imperial powers who destroyed Africa's culture and undermined its traditional value systems. This was a central theme in Soviet policy in Africa as Moscow argued that it could assist African countries to regain their culture. The Soviets always pointed to the central Asian Soviet republics as indicative of Soviet, Communist policy in promoting the cultural development of a hitherto oppressed people.

Though Moscow's attempt to establish close relations with Monrovia did not yield the expected results, it however portrayed the Kremlin's growing desire to establish friendly relations with African states irrespective of the ideological differences. Soviet leaders were aware of strong U.S. influence in Liberia, but seemed willing to cooperate with the bourgeois ruling class of Liberia.

Meanwhile in North Africa the Soviet Government was making its presence felt, outside Egypt and Algeria. Moscow offered to build two hospitals in Libya and to admit Libyan students to study in Soviet higher institutions. This offer cost the Soviet Union over $2.8 million. The hospitals, built in Tripoli and Bardia (Cyrenaica) were equipped and staffed by the Soviets, while Libyan medical students were being trained in the Soviet Union. This aid to Libya was prompted by an appeal by the UN for the industrially advanced

---

[6] The Times, London, February 2, 1956.

countries to assist the emerging nations of Africa and Asia.[7] It is significant to note that, on two occasions, September 16, 1952 and December 13, 1955, the Soviet Government had vetoed Libya's seating at the UN.[8] However, on this time around, Moscow seized the opportunity to assist Libya in the hope that such assistance will create an inroad for Soviet presence in Libya. In September 1958, the Soviet Union offered Libya financial and technical assistance for the latter's economic development, and proposed that both countries "should strengthen economic relations through a commercial agreement."[9]

The year 1960 has often been referred to as the YEAR OF AFRICA, primarily because seventeen nations on the continent regained their independence and became members of the UN. It also manifested in itself the crisis of independence as African states, in search of internal stability and political unity, became engulfed in East-West cold war intrigue. African states were divided over the Franco-Algerian war; the Congo Crisis; and the Morocco-Mauritanian conflict. The polarization of conflicting ideologies in Africa between 1960 and 1963 led to the emergence of rival blocs that were partially resolved in May 1963 with the formation of the Organization of African Unity (OAU). In September 1999, the OAU was renamed the African Union (AU) by a declaration of African heads of state and government meeting in Sirte, Libya.

The October 1960 meeting of French-speaking African states (excluding Guinea and Togoland; Mali sent an observer) in Abidjan urged moderation in the Franco-Algerian war but sided with France; and came out supporting Mauritania vis-à-vis Morocco; and Joseph Kasavubu against Patrice Lumumba in the Congo. French atomic tests in the Sahara were endorsed. The Abidjan group reconvened in Brazzaville in December 1960 without Mali. Morocco was

---

7   Egyptian Mail, March 29, 1958.
8   See, Institute for the Study of the USSR, The Soviet Diplomatic Corps, 1917-1967, pp. 215-216.
9   The Times, London, September 5, 1958.

compelled to host a counter summit in Casablanca in January 1961 with Ghana, Guinea, Mali, Egypt and Algeria in attendance. Thus emerged the Casablanca and Brazzaville (later Monrovia) blocs that dominated African politics in the early 1960s.[10] In demonstration of its support for the emerging Casablanca bloc, and against the pro-Western Brazzaville bloc, the Soviet Government vetoed Mauritania's seating at the UN on December 4, 1960.[11]

The emergence of new states in Africa saw the increase of Soviet diplomatic activities on the continent, as the Soviet Government offered diplomatic recognition to these states and pushed for the conclusion of economic and technical agreements. At the same time, several Soviet leaders were attending celebrations in African capitals: N. P. Firiubin, Soviet deputy Foreign Minister (former Soviet Ambassador to Yugoslavia), led a Soviet delegation to Cameroon's independence celebrations; N. A. Mukhitdinov headed a top level Soviet delegation to Liberia for the fourth term inauguration of President Tubman in January 1960. While in Monrovia Mukhitdinov was able to establish personal contacts with some African leaders attending the inauguration. For example, Slyvanus Olympio of Togoland invited the Soviet Government, through Mukhitdinov, to attend Togoland's independence celebrations in mid-1960.

In early 1960 it was announced that Khrushchev would visit Africa toward the end of the year. His planned visit to Guinea was not a surprise, neither was his proposed visit to Ethiopia as Emperor Haile Selassie was Khrushchev's guest in Moscow in 1959. In order to include Liberia in the visit, the Soviet Government invited Tubman to visit Moscow; Tubman accepted and in return invited Khrushchev to visit Liberia during his projected African tour. While in the Soviet Union, the Ghanaian parliamentary delegation

[10]   See I. William Zartman, <u>International Relations in the New Africa</u>, Englewood Cliffs, New Jersey, 1966; G. V. Fokeev, <u>Vneshniaia politika stran Afriki</u>, Moscow, 1968; Igho Natufe, "Diplomatiia i vneshniaia politika Afrikanskikh gosudarstv, 1963-1968 gg".

[11]   <u>See The Soviet Diplomatic Corps</u>, p.217.

extended Nkrumah's invitation to Khrushchev to visit Accra. The long list also included Egypt. Khrushchev cabled Africa's Heads of States attending the Second Conference of Independent African States in Addis Ababa:

> We look forward with confidence to the time now approaching when the whole great continent of Africa will be free . . . The peoples of African continent can be sure they have in the USSR the most loyal and most disinterested friend and ally in their righteous struggle for the freedom of the African continent from the blight of imperialism.[12]

However, Khrushchev's proposed African trip was never realized.

Soviet diplomatic activities in 1960 indicated both anxiety and optimism on the part of the Soviet Government to establish friendly relations with African states. The legacy of colonialism and the relative economic under-development of African countries led the Soviets to conclude that a majority of these emerging states would prefer Soviet economic and technical assistance. Since West European colonial powers had underdeveloped Africa, the Soviets reasoned, the new states would reject Western aid in favour of Soviet aid. Furthermore, the Soviet model of development, especially in the Soviet central Asian republics, was viewed relevant to the African situation. However, the year 1960 also marked the beginning of growing setbacks for Moscow in Africa. In Egypt, President Nasser was doing battle with Soviet Marxism; in the Congo, the Soviet alliance with Lumumba met with disastrous failure, while the expulsion of ambassador Solod from Guinea did not help to substantiate Soviet claim of friendship and cooperation.

The proclamation of Nigerian independence on October 1, 1960 was considered a milestone in Africa's political history.

---

12   See Richard C. Wald, "Khrushchev Plans Tour of Africa", <u>New York Herald Tribune</u> (European Edition), June 18, 1960.

However, the fanfare was not as grand as Ghana's independence in 1957. Most Nigerians, as well as foreign observers had envisaged that Nigeria would assume leadership of the African anti-colonial movement given its population and rich human and natural resources. Nigeria's trade unions were considered the most organized and articulated in Africa south of the Sahara (except South Africa), but their ideological platforms were to inhibit the realization of any hope of leadership in the emerging African radical trade union movement. For example, Ghana with a lesser population was able to assume leadership of Africa's radical trade unionism because of its anti-colonial ideological basis. John K. Tettegah was the Secretary General of the All-African Trade Union Federation (AATUF) and also Secretary of the Ghanaian Trade Union Congress (GTUC). On the other hand, Nigeria's major political parties—the Northern Peoples' Congress (NPC), National Council of Nigerian Citizens (NCNC), and the Action Group (AG)—were all suspicious of Soviet policy in Africa. Britain had projected Nigeria as the showcase of African democracy, and viewed Nigeria as a defender of Western liberal capitalist ideology in Africa. Nigeria's neutralism meant closer cooperation with Western powers and the rejection of Soviet invitation for establishing friendly relations. It was not accidental that the first countries to host Nigerian embassies were Britain, the U.S., and Saudi Arabia.

However, the Soviet Government sent a high profile delegation to Nigeria's independence celebrations. The delegation included Soviet Vice President, S. M. Arushanian, and Deputy Foreign Minister Yakov Malik. It was revealed that Khrushchev was to head the Soviet delegation to Lagos, but his pre-arranged visit to North Korea in early October made this impossible. It is interesting to note that the Soviet Union was represented at Ghana's independence celebrations in 1957 by a junior minister, Benediktov, while a vice president was despatched to Nigeria in 1960. This was indicative of the role the Soviets envisaged Nigeria would play in global politics. Soviet policy analysts had observed the nucleus of a class struggle in Nigerian politics prior to October 1960, and, with the aid of the Trade Unions, it was anticipated that the philosophical concept of the struggle could be brought to the surface. Even though northern Nigeria was feudal, the economic indicators pointed to a gradual growth of an industrial working class in the south where a mixture of patriarchal, feudal and capitalist tendencies was noticed by Kremlin advisers.[13] It was expected that a carefully planned propagation of Marxist ideology would unite the emerging southern intelligentsia and the progressive elements of the Trade Unions in the fight against both the southern and northern "compradors".

Speaking in the House of Representatives on Foreign Policy debate, the Prime Minister, Abubakar Tafawa Balewa, revealed that Yakov Malik had presented him a letter from Khrushchev requesting that the Soviet Union be permitted to open an embassy "forthwith" in Nigeria. He rejected Khrushchev's request and retorted that Nigeria "will not be bullied" by any foreign power. According to Balewa, the Nigerian Government would consider a more formal diplomatic approach on the question of establishing diplomatic relations. He later reported that Nigeria had received such a "formal request" from the Soviet ambassador to Ghana, S. D. Sytenko, which the Nigerian Government was to consider in line with Nigeria's interest.[14] Nigeria's rejection of Soviet initial request was not reported in the Soviet press. Mention was only made of Foreign Minister Andrei A. Gromyko's letter to Balewa in which the Soviet Government "officially proposed" the establishment of diplomatic relations between both countries. According to Gromyko, the Soviet Government was prepared to "accept an Embassy of the Federation of Nigeria in the Soviet capital," and negotiations toward this could be held "either in Accra or London, or any mutually agreed place."[15]

The line of communication between Lagos and Moscow on the question of establishing diplomatic relations was not as smooth

---

[13] Noveishaia istoriia Afriki, Moscow, 1968, pp.353-361.

[14] See The Times, London, November 3, 1960; and The New York Times, November 3, 1960.

[15] Soviet News, Embassy of the USSR, London, November 15, 1960.

as Moscow had wanted. For example, Somalia agreed to establish diplomatic relations with the Soviet Union in October 1960—three months after it attained independence and the first Soviet ambassador, G. I. Fomin, arrived in the Somalian capital on November 24, 1960. It was obvious that the political situation in east Africa influenced Somalia to quickly establish diplomatic relations with the Soviet Union. The concept of a Greater Somalia—the unification of all Somalis in east Africa under a single Somali state—has been the main political platform of Somalia's leaders. This meant the *re-acquisition* of Kenyan and Ethiopian territories inhabited by ethnic Somalis. Somalia had hoped that closer ties with the Soviet Union would counter balance the strong influence of Britain and the U.S. in the region, particularly since these western powers were supporting Kenya and Ethiopia. In West Africa, Nigeria had no such factors pressing it to establish closer ties with the Soviet Union. However, in view of Nigeria's proclaimed neutrality in global politics there was a strong domestic movement demanding that Nigeria establish diplomatic relations with the communist states. The Anglo-Nigerian Defence Pact signed in 1960 put Nigeria in the NATO orbit inimical to both Soviet interests and neutralism. This was a challenge to Balewa's neutrality, but the Nigerian Prime Minister was not prepared to play ball. Moscow accused Britain and "reactionaries" in Nigeria for the delay in establishing diplomatic relations between Nigeria and the Soviet Union.

The Anglo-Nigerian Defence Pact was condemned by the AG and the newly formed Nigerian Youth Congress (NYC) led by Tunji Otegbeye, a Lagos-based medical practitioner with Marxist-Leninist pretensions. Public protests and demonstrations organized by the NYC and the National Union of Nigerian Students (NUNS) compelled Balewa to abrogate the Pact in 1961. When the Nigerian Government finally agreed to exchange representatives at the ambassadorial level "at a time convenient to both", Balewa stipulated that Soviet embassy staff in Lagos was not to exceed ten officials.[16] Nigeria agreed to establish diplomatic relations with the Soviet Union on April 3, 1961, and the first Soviet ambassador to Nigeria, F. P. Dolya, a seasoned diplomat with the rank of ambassador extraordinary and plenipotentiary, who had been in the Soviet diplomatic service since 1938 and had served in Afghanistan, Thailand, and India, arrived in Lagos on October 20, 1961.[17] Prior to his arrival, leaders of the Opposition and the NYC attending the All-Nigerian Peoples Conference (ANPC) in Lagos, in August 1961, demanded that the numerical strength of the Soviet embassy be raised to equal that of Britain and the U.S.[18] This, they argued, would give credibility to Nigeria's neutralism. Despite the public pressure on his government, Balewa was not prepared to accord the Soviet embassy similar status enjoyed by both Britain and the U.S.

Between 1958 and early 1962 the Kremlin leadership encountered serious setbacks in Soviet-African relations. The conflict with Egypt in 1958-1961, which grew from the Khrushchev-Nasser counter recriminations, led to a gross deterioration of Egypt-Soviet relations and affected Soviet prestige in North Africa. The expulsion of Soviet diplomatic representatives from the Congo in September 1960, and ambassador Solod from Guinea in December 1961 were disappointments Moscow did not expect to receive from emerging African states in the 1959-1961 period. The Soviet Government had assumed that the growth of anti-western sentiments in Africa, particularly in Egypt, Guinea, and the Congo, would automatically lead to conformity in African-Soviet relations. The withering away of the Kisangani regime in the Congo, and the diplomatic defeat manifested in Mikoyan's trip to Guinea in January 1962 ruined Soviet early expectations in Africa. Presidents Nasser's and Sekou Toure's policies between 1959-1961 and 1961-1962, respectively, pointedly reflected the miscalculations of western powers in writing

---

16   Pravda, March 3, 1961; The Daily Worker, March 4, 1961.
17   The Soviet Diplomatic Corps, pp. 49 and 89.
18   See Claude S. Phillips, Jr., The Development of Nigerian Foreign Policy, Evanston, Ill., 1964, pp.57-58.

off Nasser and Toure as pro-Communists. What became evident was these leaders' determination to pursue a policy of positive neutrality. Expressing Soviet disappointment over Africa's stance in international politics, D. D. Degtia, who replaced Solod as Soviet ambassador to Guinea (January 9, 1962-November 25, 1964), declared: "Anyone can understand neutralism. But what on earth do these people mean by positive neutrality?"[19]

The setbacks suffered in this period compelled Soviet foreign policy strategists to shift gradually their areas of priorities in Africa: Ben Bella, and not Sekou Toure, became Moscow's favourite. During the last two years of Khrushchev's leadership, Soviet analysts and Soviet leaders began to deal rather cautiously with Africa. In the middle of the Congo crisis the Soviet Government tried to persuade "moderate" African leaders to accept Soviet proposals. Sudan, primarily because of its proximity to the Congo, especially to the Kisangani regime of Antoine Gizenga, was courted by the Soviet Government to open up a Sudanese corridor leading to Kisangani. President Ibrahim Aboud of Sudan was invited to Moscow on July 17, 1961 to discuss, among other things, the Congo crisis. At a Kremlin reception he hailed the "peaceful" policy of the Soviet Union and the Soviet position during the historic 25th session of the UN. Sudan's neutralism and anti-military bloc policy were praised by President Leonid I. Brezhnev since they "meet with the Soviet Government's understanding and support." On the basis of this, the Soviet Government offered to assist Sudan "to eliminate the political and economic consequences of colonialism."[20] In anticipation of Soviet aid which Brezhnev had promised, Aboud declared:

---

[19]   19As cited by Aidan Crawley, "The Russian Gamble for Africa", Sunday Times, London, April 15, 1962.

[20]   Soviet News, Embassy of the USSR, London, July 20, 1961.

We know that the Soviet Union is not a state which
exploits other peoples . . . we believe in its friendship
and cooperation with it.[21]

The promptness of Brezhnev's return visit to Khartoum
indicated the high strategic premium the Soviet Union placed
on the Sudan vis-à-vis the corridor project. Brezhnev arrived in
Khartoum on November 15, 1961, on a 7-day state visit. Though
Gizenga had dissolved his Kisangani regime to become a deputy
premier in Cyril Adoula's central government in the Congo since
August 1961, the Soviet Government was still pressing Aboud
to open a Sudanese corridor leading to Kisangani. This was to
facilitate the movement and transportation of personnel and goods
to Gizenga who was to continue a pro-Lumumba struggle. While
both presidents were discussing Soviet-Sudanese and Afro-Asian
politics, members of Brezhnev's entourage were engaged in
ideological work by distributing specially designed badges to the
Sudanese. The badges displayed pictures of a Soviet sputnik and
a mosque, a red star and hammer and sickle. While the sputnik
represented Soviet technological achievement, the red star, hammer
and sickle emphasized the supremacy of communism over other
social systems. The insertion of a mosque on the badge was the
most significant aspect of the ideological propaganda. It was meant
to appease the Sudan, a predominantly Muslim country, and to
underline the existence of religious freedom in the Soviet Union
which also has a substantial Muslim population. Brezhnev ended
his visit on November 20 after signing an agreement that fetched
the Sudan a $20 million Soviet credit. Under the agreement the
Soviet Government undertook to build three grain elevators, three
canning factories, a cement factory, a cotton factory, and a veterinary
research centre. However, Brezhnev failed to get Aboud's agreement
on the corridor project.

---

[21] Ibid.

In the period under review African states considered to be in the forefront of radical political thought were Ghana, Guinea, Mali, Egypt, Algeria, Congo (Brazzaville), and Tanzania. Soviet relations were not however confined to the states in this avant-garde group. There was also the quest to establish friendly relations with other African states:

- Mamadou Dia, Senegalese Premier, was in Moscow on June 5, 1962, for a 10-day visit. His visit and the talks that followed culminated in the decision of both parties to establish diplomatic relations at the ambassadorial level.
- The Republic of Benin's (formerly Dahomey) decision to accommodate a Soviet embassy in Porto Novo, six months after the Solod affair, was welcomed in Moscow.
- A team of ten Kenyan politicians was invited to Moscow in April 1962. The delegation, which included five members of the Kenyan African National Union (KANU) and a representative of the Kenyan African Democratic Union (KADU), also visited Poland and East Germany. The delegation was impressed by Soviet economic development.
- Oginga Odinga, Kenya's leader of the opposition attended the conference of the World Peace Council in Moscow, July 6-9, 1962. Odinga, whose passport was seized in 1960 by British colonial officials because of his previous visits to East European communist states, was compelled to travel to Moscow on Ghanaian documents.

The preceding pages provide a broad overview of Soviet African policy in the 1955-1964 period. With this background knowledge we shall now proceed to analyse Soviet policy towards selected African states.

Egypt: A Troubled Partnership

In 1954 Egypt and the Soviet Union signed a trade agreement that set the basis for Egypt-Soviet cooperation. At the UN Security Council the Soviet Government defended the rights of Egypt as opposed to western support for Israel. This became the cornerstone of Egypt-Soviet relations. The partnership, which was essentially an alliance against the West, should also be viewed as a tactical move by Moscow to have an ally in the strategic north-eastern portion of Africa. The Suez Canal is a vital waterway, and control of it in times of international crisis would be of tremendous value to the controlling power. For the Soviet Union, it would be an important spot from where it could counter western policies in both Africa and the Middle East. Though it could be regarded as a move that "halted" the advancement of Egyptian communists' struggle for power, from the Soviet perspective the partnership had a long term objective which was intended to strengthen the cause of its ideology in Egypt.

After the Bandung Conference of 1955, Nasser contacted the Soviet Government for military aid. Nasser's request for military aid was made through China at the Bandung Conference. It has been clear to Nasser, since the Arab-Israeli war of 1948-1949, that reliance on the West for military aid to check Israeli expansionism was a futile idea. It was Nasser's belief that the basis for cordial Israeli-Egyptian relations did not exist without Israeli withdrawal to its boundaries as at the pre 1948 war. Thus, the question of a homeland for the Palestinians inside Palestine was inextricably linked to Egypt's policy under Nasser. Nasser strove to remain equidistance between Moscow and Washington. Irrespective of his reliance on Soviet military aid, Nasser did not curtail Egypt's anti-communist campaign.

In an interview with a foreign correspondent Nasser confirmed that Egyptian Police had arrested communist leaders and that there were "15,000 Communists" in Egypt who "could have dominated the masses" had his government been liberal toward communism. When asked why he refused to ally with the West in an anti-Communist crusade, Nasser declared: "We have been dominated and occupied for too long. Now we are suspicious—Egypt needs a breathing space."[22]

On July 21, 1955, D. T. Shepilov, then the Editor-in-Chief of *Pravda*, arrived in Cairo for talks with President Nasser. He brought with him an invitation from the Kremlin for Nasser to visit Moscow. Considering Nasser's political stand, his Moscow visit could only mean a manifestation of Egypt's policy of neutralism, a neutralism hitherto condemned but now embraced by the Kremlin as an ally in the global anti-colonial movement. For the Soviets, however, it was considered a justification of their policy to attain rapprochement with all anti-colonial and peace-loving states and peoples. Nasser's acceptance of Moscow's invitation, according to K. Petrov, pleased the "Soviet Government and people" who began to wish that the visit would result in the "further strengthening of friendly relations between the two countries and serve the cause of world peace."[23] While presenting his credentials to M. P. Tarasov, Soviet Vice President, Muhamed A. el-Kouny stated that the "great sympathy and good-will of the government and peoples of the Soviet Union towards" Egypt "is unquestionably highly gratifying . . ." and agreed with Petrov that the spring 1956 visit of Nasser to Moscow "will strengthen friendly relations between our two countries and will serve the cause of peace."[24] In a gesture indicative of Soviet willingness to cooperate with Egypt, a team of Soviet Muslim pilgrims visited Cairo in August 1955, and invited Sheik Ahmed Hassan el-Bakouri to visit Moscow.[25] Just like every marriage is a marriage of convenience, the Soviet-Egyptian marriage was necessitated by the imperatives of geostrategic considerations thrust upon both parties by the external environment. Each had

---

[22] News Chronicle, August 10, 1955.

[23] K. Petrov, "In the interest of promoting friendly relations between the USSR and Egypt", Izvestia, August 21, 1955

[24] Soviet News, Embassy of the USSR, London, August 29, 1955.

[25] The New York Times, August 20, 1955.

its own specific and conflicting agenda to survive, but agreed to contract a wedlock that unites them against a common foe.

A perennial problem with colonial powers in formulating a strategic agreement with their former dependencies is their total refusal or reluctance to recognize the capability of the former dependencies to make their own policy choices. Imperialism would lose part of its being it if fails to impose its will on the peripheral states. Egypt, and indeed the Palestinian question, exemplifies the debility of British and U.S. policies in their attempt to rope Egypt into their anti-Soviet campaign, but failed to grapple with the Palestinian question. If, in the 1949-1955 period, the West had taken meaningful steps to restore a Palestinian homeland in Palestine and respect Egypt's sovereign right as a state, Nasser would have been hard pressed to justify his rapprochement with the Soviet Union. Witness the British Government attitude toward Premier Mustapha Nahas' proposal for a revision of the Anglo-Egyptian Treaty of 1936 which led to a *cul de sac* in the negotiations, and Nahas had to take decisions befitting a sovereign state: Egypt abrogated the treaty in October 1951. The policy objective of both Britain and the U.S. was specially tailored to tie Cairo to a western defence alliance system in the Middle East, a condition which they placed on the flow of western economic aid to Egypt.[26] In 1953, two years before the arms deal with the Soviet Union, Nasser reacted bluntly to the basic premise of Anglo-U.S. policy:

> The so-called "free world", particularly the United States, proclaim they are helping to attain self-determination and are helping underdeveloped countries to advance. We consider such talk as opium administered by the "free world" to enslave peoples so that they remain under its domination and not seek liberation.[27]

---

[26] See Keith Wheeleck, Nasser's Egypt: A Critical Analysis, New York, 1960, pp.208-214; 228-230.

[27] As cited in ibid., p.215.

The U.S. Secretary of State, John Foster Dulles, arrived in Cairo in May 1953 to discuss the Arab-Israeli conflict with Nasser. However, the top priority of Dulles was not to seek any solution to resolve the conflict, but rather to enlist Egypt in an encirclement of "the Soviet Union with military and political alliances."[28] According to Mohamed H. Heikal, a close confidant of Nasser, the leaders of the July 23, 1952 coup briefed the Americans about the impeding coup[29], which obviously suggested the willingness of Nasser and his colleagues to cooperate with the U.S., but the latter failed to formulate policies to retain a willing ally without subjugating him to a colonial status. As far as Nasser and his colleagues were concerned, the Israeli raid of February 1955 of an "Egyptian army camp at Gaza" killing "37 Egyptian soldiers"[30], coupled with Washington's refusal to grant Egypt economic aid, <u>and</u> the formation of the Baghdad Pact clearly demonstrated American anti-Egyptian policy.

Nasser's policy was to establish a solid economic and political base in Egypt, and also a national defence force to counter Israel. He perceived the western sponsored military pact as basically a pro-Israeli military pact. It was on the basis of this that a Soviet-Egyptian alliance began to crystallize in 1955. The Soviets were well aware of Nasser's anti-communist policy. But they considered him an independent nationalist leader hostile to western imperial machinations in Africa and the Middle East, a factor which suited Soviet policy in both regions. When Nasser and Soviet ambassador D. S. Solod discussed the question of Soviet arms sale to Egypt on May 21, 1955, neither of them was under the illusion that their countries were *ideological allies*. However, the motif of the arms deal was to check the aggressive policies of a third force hostile to both Cairo and Moscow. On Soviet advice the arms negotiations shifted to Prague, with Czechoslovakia

---

[28]   Mohamed H. Heikal, <u>The Cairo Documents. The Inside Story of Nasser and his Relationship with World Leaders, Rebels, and Statesmen</u>, p.31.

[29]   <u>Ibid</u>., pp. 33-34.

[30]   <u>Ibid</u>., p.46.

representing the Soviet Union to negotiate with Egypt in order not to jeopardize the Four Power Geneva Summit of July 18-23, 1955. This consideration led Karen Dawisha to conclude that the shift to Prague was a "Soviet decision to dissociate itself from the deal . . ."[31] There is no evidence to corroborate Dawisha's conjecture. However, it was obvious that the Soviet Government preferred secret arms negotiations, as it did not want the Western powers to use the negotiations as an excuse to derail the Geneva summit.

In the Soviet view, partnership with Egypt was to include all aspects of bilateral relations. The Soviet Union was very adept at using cultural propaganda to advance foreign policy objectives. The unearthing of the fact that Fouad El-Awal University (now Cairo University) "was the brainchild of a Russian, the Count Prozor" had a huge psychological effect favouring the Soviets in Egypt. Count Prozor, with the assistance of Kasim Amin, spearheaded the founding of the university.[32] In a move geared towards friendship consolidation with Egypt, members of the Soviet Ballet Company, during their performances at Cairo's Opera House in October 1955, ended their programme with a series of songs sung in Arabic, songs which reflected Egyptian patriotism. This elevated the Egyptians who pointedly remarked that western powers had failed to appreciate the culture of less developed countries.[33] Soon after this event the Soviet Union was permitted to open a consulate-general in Port Siad.

Following the Egyptian revolution of 1952 the western powers gradually became suspicious of Nasser, especially after March 1954 when the Soviet-Egyptian trade agreement was signed in Cairo. Basing its policy on mere conjecture Britain, for example, castigated Egypt in March 1956 for an "offence" it did not commit. When King Hussein of Jordan, in response to popular public demand, dismissed General Glubb Pasha, commander of the Arab Legion, on

---

[31]   Karen Dawisha, <u>Soviet Foreign Policy Towards Egypt</u>, London, 1979, p.11.

[32]   <u>Dawn</u>, Karachi, December 18, 1955.

[33]   <u>The Times</u>, London, October 11, 1955.

March 1, 1956, British Prime Minister Anthony Eden "declared a personal war on President Abdel Nasser" accusing him of instigating the General's dismissal[34], whereas Nasser had no knowledge of the dismissal.[35] Even a conservative British analyst, Wilfrid Knapp, lamented that, on Glubb's dismissal, the British Government placed "too much" emphasis on Nasser's policies "and too little on the spontaneous nationalism which had spread through the Arab world, and to the concentrated bitterness of the Palestinian Arabs in Jordan."[36]

Britain, France and the U.S. had agreed to aid Egypt to finance the construction of the Aswan High Dam, but with political strings attached which Egypt rejected. The political preconditions included: 1) Egypt to abrogate its arms deal with the Soviet Union; and 2) Cairo to conclude peace with Tel Aviv. The western powers had warned Nasser not to accept Soviet arms. The gulf between Egypt and the Anglo-Franco-U.S. alliance over the above issues led the latter to turn down Egypt's request for economic aid on July 19, 1956. In response, Egypt nationalized the Suez Canal. Nasser's nationalization speech of July 26, 1956 was a rejection of western imperial machinations. Moscow's first comment on the Suez Canal crisis was on July 28 when the Soviet Government declared its recognition of "the sovereign rights of Egypt."[37] Assuring Britain and France of U.S. support against Egypt, Dulles stated that the

---

[34] The Times, London, April 29, 1967. See also A. S. Protopopov, Sovetskii Soiuz i suetskii krizis 1956 goda, Moscow, 1969, p.83.

[35] Heikal, op.cit., p.81.

[36] Wilfrid Knapp, A History of War and Peace, 1939-1965, London, 1967, p.401.

[37] SSSR i Arabskie strany, 1917-1960gg. Dokumenty i materialy, Moscow, 1961, pp. 190; 142-144. See also Tareq Y. Ismail, The U.A.R. in Africa. Egypt's Policy Under Nasser, Evanston, Ill., 1971; Uri Ra'anan, The USSR Arms the World. Case Studies in Soviet Foreign Policy, Cambridge, Mass., 1969.

western powers must decide "to make Nasser disgorge what he was attempting to swallow"[38], referring to the Suez Canal.

Opened in 1869, the Suez Canal was initially operated by Ferdinand de Lesseps before it was acquired by the Suez Canal Company. It was to become Egyptian property after 99 years, i.e.in 1968. Thus, Egypt had only 12 more years to wait before claiming complete ownership over the Suez Canal. Did the nationalization of the Canal precipitate the crisis? Was the deterioration of relations between Egypt and the West the origin of the crisis? The Suez crisis was part of a larger Middle East political conflict that emerged after 1945. The creation of Israel in 1948, and Washington's determination to support Israel vis-à-vis the Arab states increased the polarization of the Middle East conflict. No attempt was made by the West to assuage Arab nationalism, even though the results of the 1948-1949 war dictated such a policy. It was clear that Western political failures in this conflict were positively utilized by Nasser in his drive to consolidate his power.

Britain and France resorted to dual diplomacy; while publicly "exploring" means to resolve the Suez Canal crisis, both were interested in ousting Nasser from power. The London conferences summoned to discuss the Suez Canal question failed to reach a compromise favourable to Egypt and the West. Egypt did not attend the conferences. Prior to the opening of the first London Conference of August 16-23, 1956, British and French military leaders met in London on August 7-9 to discuss their coordinated policy toward Egypt, while at the same time Britain referred the Suez Canal question to the United Nations. After encouraging Israel to attack Egypt on October 29, 1956, Britain and France issued a joint ultimatum on October 30 requesting both Israel and Egypt to withdraw their forces ten miles from the Canal region for the "temporary" occupation of Port Said, Suez, and Ismailia by Anglo-French troops. The strategy of the Anglo-Franco-Israeli forces was obvious: Israel was employed to invade Egypt so that British

---

[38]   Dulles, as cited in Knapp, op.cit., p.409.

and French troops would occupy the Suez Canal region. British and French forces were ordered to bomb Egypt on October 31 following Egypt's rejection of the ultimatum. On November 5 British and French forces joined the war against Egypt. However, under strong international reaction, both in and out of the U.N., Britain, France and Israel were compelled to halt their aggression against Egypt.

The British Government's primary intention was to *dispose* of President Nasser in order to entrench British rule in the region. According to Peter Wright, a former Assistant Director of British MI5, Prime Minister Anthony Eden "gave his approval" to MI6's plan "to assassinate Nasser using nerve gas" at the beginning of the Suez Canal crisis. He however annulled this plot "when he got agreement from the French and Israelis to engage in joint military action" against Egypt. Wright continued:

> When this course failed, and he was forced to withdraw, Eden reactivated the assassination option a second time. By this time virtually all MI6 assets in Egypt had been rounded up by Nasser, and a new operation, using renegade Egyptian officers, was drawn up, but it failed lamentably, principally because the cache of weapons which had been hidden on the outskirts of Cairo was found to be defective.[39]

It is difficult to imagine if Eden had thought he could have resolved the Suez Crisis by assassinating Nasser. The mere articulation of an assassination option revealed the poverty of thought which permeated the consciousness of British foreign policy making.

In its several declaratory statements throughout the crisis, the Soviet Government expressed its support for Egypt's position as exemplified in its notes to Britain and France. From the Soviet perspective, the capitulation of the West (Britain and France)

---

[39] Peter Wright, <u>Spy Catcher. The Candid Autobiography of a Senior Intelligence Officer</u>, Toronto, Canada, 1987, p.160.

"demonstrated the debility of imperialist powers' policy of crushing" the forces of nationalism and the national liberation movement.[40] However, in a critical review of Soviet attitude toward the crisis Anwar el-Sadat revealed that the Soviet Union refused "to extend a helping hand to Egypt" during the critical days of the Suez Canal crisis, a revelation which contradicted Egypt's statement in the immediate post crisis era. He declared:

> This made me believe, from that moment on, that it was always futile to depend on the Soviet Union. On November 5 Eisenhower intervened and asked Britain and France to withdraw at once. When the Soviet Union learned that Britain and France had responded to the U.S. President's request, it addressed a warning—known as the Khrushchev-Bulganin Ultimatum—to both countries. It was nothing in effect but an exercise in muscle-flexing and an attempt to appear as though the Soviet Union had saved the situation. This was not, of course, the case. It was Eisenhower who did so.[41]

Peter Wright offered a different angle to this issue. He revealed that the British MI5 had installed a listening device inside the Egyptian Embassy in London in order to have first-hand information about the intents of Egypt and its allies during the Suez Canal Crisis. The information gathered by MI5 through this process "detailed a meeting between the Soviet Foreign Minister and the Egyptian Ambassador in which the Russians outlined their intentions to mobilize aircraft in preparation for a confrontation with Britain." He continued:

---

[40]   Mezhdunarodnye otnosheniia posle vtoroi mirovoi voiny, vol. 3, Moscow, 1965, p.46.

[41]   Anwar el-Sadat, op.cit., p.146.

The panic provoked by this cable, which was handed
straight to the JIC, did as much as anything to prompt
Eden into withdrawal. Similarly, since all GCHQ
product was shared with its American counterpart, the
National Security Agency (NSA), the intelligence, I am
sure, did play an important part in shaping American
pressure on Britain to end the crisis.[42]

The timing of the crisis seemed to constrain Moscow's ability
to act more forcefully as the Soviet Union was busy fighting a
counter-revolutionary uprising that threatens to overthrow the
socialist regime in Hungary. This fact lends credence to Sadat's
analysis of Soviet position as Moscow would not have got itself
involved on two fronts at the same time. The retention of Hungary
within the Soviet orbit was more vital to Soviet security interests
than Egypt and the Suez Canal. Thus, it was highly probable that
the Soviet Government was deliberately engaged in *disinformation*
knowing that its discussions with the Egyptian Ambassador in
Moscow were being monitored by the British through its device
in the Egyptian Embassy in London. Wright alluded to this
in his book.[43] It is unlikely, therefore, that the information on
Soviet-Egyptian discussions provided by the British intelligence to
the U.S. NSA "did play an important part in shaping American
pressure on Britain to end the crisis" as Wright alleged. In my view,
intra imperialist contradiction was evident in U.S. attitude towards
Britain and France in the Suez Canal crisis. While in principle
the U.S. supported Britain and France as exemplified in Dulles'
statement cited above, Washington was reluctant to demonstrate
its support beyond that, and in fact asked its allies to halt their
aggression. The White House's reluctance to endorse the military
action of its allies did not in any way imply U.S. endorsement of
Nasser's policy, rather it was influenced by Washington's stratagem

---

[42]   Wright, p.85.
[43]   *Ibid.*, 85-86.

to dislodge its allies as the dominant Western powers in the Middle East. The realities of post 1945 global politics compelled London and Paris to scramble for a back seat behind the new imperial power—Washington. Thus, the U.S. desertion of its allies during the Suez Canal crisis was designed to:—

■ limit Anglo-French prestige in the Middle East; and
■ ally with the anti-colonial forces in the U.N.[44]

In Cairo, government leaders began denouncing the so-called "communist menace" which had hitherto been endorsed. However, government policy remained hostile toward communism as many Egyptian communists who took advantage of Nasser's mass mobilization of Egyptians to combat the aggressors of 1956 were arrested when they attempted to usurp the initiative in Egypt's domestic affairs. Nevertheless, in answering a question posed by an American correspondent, an Egyptian government spokesman stated:

> All we know is that we have been attacked by your allies,
> Britain and France, and Israel still occupies our territory.
> This is the aggression we fear. We are aware of Soviet
> ambition in our area but the Russians are not threatening
> us. We will not allow them to spread Communism in
> Egypt but they have offered to help without political
> strings.[45]

This statement made in early 1957 remained the basis of Cairo's policy: Soviet aid was welcomed and appreciated while efforts were exerted to prevent the spread of Marxist ideas in Egypt. However, the pro-Soviet content of Egypt's policy was considered a good

---

44 See A. P. Baryshev, <u>Strategiia belogo doma i OON</u>, Moscow, 1972, p.99.
45 <u>New York Times</u>, February 17, 1957.

omen in the Kremlin. On his return from Moscow on September 4, 1957 Ambassador E. D. Kiselev underlined Soviet position on anti-western international cooperation in an interview in Cairo:

> It is in the interest of Russia and all the peoples to eradicate international imperialism and unify the efforts of the Asian, African and Arab peoples against this beast.[46]

Kiselev had returned to Moscow on June 4 amidst speculations of a rupture in Soviet-Egyptian relations which was thought to be linked to Egypt's desire to increase its trade with the West. The fact that Kiselev stayed in Moscow for three months, and not for his "annual month-long holiday" as stated by the Soviet embassy in its bulletin, gave credence to the speculations. Interestingly, a month after Kiselev's statement, Egypt and the Soviet Union signed a cultural agreement in Cairo on October 19, 1957. Egypt also signed similar agreements with Bulgaria and Czechoslovakia in Cairo on the same day.

In July 1957 Soviet Minister of Defence, Marshal Zhukov, invited Egypt's Major-General Abdel Hakim Amer to Moscow for the celebrations of the 40th anniversary of the October Revolution. However, when Amer arrived in Moscow with his 30-man delegation on November 1, Marshal Zhukov was no longer in the Defence Ministry: Amer was welcomed by Marshal R. Y. Malinovskii, Zhukov's successor. It is interesting to note that; while it was Marshal Zhukov who had invited General Amer to Moscow, TASS, the Soviet News Agency reported that Amer was invited by Marshal Malinovskii, Zhukov's successor.[47]

---

[46] Ambassador E. D. Kiselev's interview, Egyptian Mail, September 7, 1957

[47] See The Times, London, July 29, 1957; and The New York Times, November 2, 1957.

General Amer did not conceal Egypt's desire to employ Soviet weaponry for its ant-imperialist struggle in North Africa.[48] At a meeting in the Soviet Defence Ministry he discussed with Soviet military chiefs the issue of training Egyptian army officers in the Soviet Union, while at a reception in the Egyptian Embassy to thank the Soviet Government for its policy; he pointedly underscored the significance of Soviet military aid in Egypt's policy. Addressing an audience that included CPSU First Secretary Khrushchev, Premier Bulganin, Defence Minister Malinovskii, and Foreign Minister Gromyko, Amer declared:

> Your army is struggling for the sake of universal peace. But our army in the Middle East is trying to defend the Arab people looking forward to freedom and to save them from the forces of imperialism and Israel, the tool of imperialism. These are the reasons uniting us. We are now two friendly states, two friendly peoples and two friendly armies.[49]

Amer's statement suggested the emergence of a Soviet-Egyptian holy alliance geared towards the capitulation of the West and Israel in Middle Eastern politics. Prior to his departure for Cairo, the Soviet Government granted Egypt a $2 million loan to assist Egypt in its five-year industrialization programme. Payment on the loan was to commence five years after the conclusion of the agreement, with instalments extending over a 12-year period. Reflecting on the loan and the prospects of enhancing Soviet-Egyptian relations, Izvestia, the Soviet Government newspaper, editorialized:

> The favourable perspective of Soviet-Egyptian economic cooperation testifies that in the struggle for economic

---

[48] Egyptian Gazette, November 6, 1957.

[49] Ibid., November 17, 1957.

> independence the Arab countries will always find in the
> Soviet Union a loyal friend and disinterested help mate.[50]

While the development of cordial Soviet-Egyptian relations was raising Soviet optimism in Egypt, the Egyptians were concerned in the gradual recession of trade with the West. Soviet aid policy was considered more favourable than western aid policy as the former involved the construction of factories and the manufacture of mining equipment while the former strove to limit, or restrict Egypt's independence. However, Egyptian leaders expressed the view that "if the West had been a bit more sensible" Egypt would not have fallen into the Soviet economic orbit.[51] This position reflected a strong desire by a group of Egyptian leaders to re-think Egypt's policy towards the two conflicting ideological power blocs. It was increasingly felt in Egypt that Moscow's continued reference to its "disinterested help" was a misnomer since *aid*, particularly foreign aid in general, has an objective and more so since the Soviet Union was very much interested to see Egypt remain a strong Soviet ally both in Africa and the Middle East in order to counter Western imperialist incursions.

President Nasser had an open invitation since 1955 to visit the Soviet Union, which had been postponed twice because of the deterioration of the Middle East crisis. The success of General Amer's trip and the relative relaxation of tensions in the Middle East dictated the timing of Nasser's long-awaited trip to Moscow. Nasser left Cairo for Moscow on April 29, 1958, on an 18-day visit. Prior to his departure he instituted some policy measures to underline Egypt's neutrality. The anti-Western propaganda in the Egyptian press was gradually ceased. Nasser's last minute cancellation of his plans to attend the Accra Conference of Independent African States, where he would have had to champion, along with Nkrumah,

---

50 Izvestia, November 21, 1957.
51 The Times, London, November 22, 1957.

Africa's anti-imperialist movement, was no doubt a policy meant to mollify the West.

President Nasser had a triumphant entry into Moscow on April 29. A squadron of Soviet jet fighters escorted his TU-104 as the "Hero of the Arab world." Apart from the British, French, and Israeli ambassadors in Moscow, "partners in the 1956 aggression against Egypt", all heads of diplomatic missions accredited to the Soviet Union were officially informed of the date and time of Nasser's arrival in Moscow.[52] Nasser was housed in the Kremlin, an honour never before accorded any visiting head of state.

While Nasser's anti-colonial posture favoured the Soviet Union, he nevertheless articulated a neutralist foreign policy. He did not want the rapprochement with the Soviet Union to become a catalyst for communist penetration in Egypt; neither did he want communist influence to spread in North Africa and the Middle East. It was clear that his position on this fundamental question did not receive Soviet endorsement. Thus, this policy disagreement led to frictions in Soviet-Egyptian relations in mid-1958. Two developments that occurred in 1958 in the Middle East engineered these frictions: the formation of the United Arab Republic (UAR), and the Iraqi revolt.

In early 1958, Nasser succeeded in manoeuvring Syria into forming a union, the short-lived UAR, a move motivated by the desire to crush the powerful Syrian Communist Party which Nasser regarded as a Soviet front organization in the region. According to Heikal, it was a group of Syrian nationalists that approached Nasser in Cairo, in January 1958, with the idea of a union between Syria and Egypt in an attempt to halt the growth of Syrian Communists. But Heikal did not identify these "Syrian nationalists" and their relationship to state power in Syria, but merely stated that Nasser endorsed the plan on the proviso that: 1) Syria abolishes all political parties, and 2)

---

[52]   Egyptian Gazette, April 29, 1958.

de-politicize its army.[53] Thus, the UAR, with Nasser's support, was formed in 1958 primarily as an anti-communist union.

Nasser was visiting Marshal Broz Tito in Brioni, Yugoslavia, when news of a revolt in Iraq reached him on July 14, 1958. General Abdel Karim Kassim emerged as the leader of a military coup that toppled Iraqi pro-western monarchy. With this development, and the U.S. Six Fleet sailing toward Lebanon, Nasser decided to cut short his stay in Yugoslavia and returned to Cairo on board his yacht, Al Hourya (Freedom). Tito cabled him while at sea.

> Please do not proceed any further at sea. I think it is very dangerous to go on. I suggest you turn back to the nearest Yugoslav port and maybe we can arrange for a very powerful plane to take you to Cairo.[54]

Nasser agreed and returned to Pola, Yugoslavia. On Tito's suggestion the Soviet Government despatched a TU-104 jet fighter to Yugoslavia to take Nasser to Egypt; but he decided instead to fly to Moscow to brief the Soviets on the situation. Nasser and his entourage arrived in Moscow on July 17, 1958 and held discussions with Deputy Premier Mikoyan and General I. A. Sedov. Since Nasser's visit was considered "secret" the Egyptian ambassador, el-Kouny, was "smuggled" to the talks. Khrushchev was convinced that Nasser engineered the Iraqi coup. He told Nasser: "They are your men in Iraq."[55] Nasser denied any knowledge of, or involvement in the coup. However, he pleaded with Soviet leaders to issue an ultimatum to the West vis-à-vis its reactions over the coup. The Soviet Government refused, but agreed to stage a military manoeuvre along the Bulgarian-Turkish border. At the airport to see Nasser off in the early hours of July 18 Khrushchev reminded Nasser:

---

[53] Heikal, 123-124.

[54] Ibid., 129.

[55] Khrushchev as cited in ibid., 133.

It is only a manoeuvre. Please, Mr. President, keep it in
your mind that it is nothing more than manoeuvres.[56]

Twenty Soviet army divisions participated in the manoeuvres
which were designed to demonstrate Soviet readiness to intervene
in support of Egypt, should the West mount a military operation
against Egypt as a result of the Iraqi coup.

Meanwhile, a power tussle had emerged in Iraq between General
Abdel Salam Arif and General Kassim who were regarded as the
Nasser and the Naguib of Iraq, respectively. Baghdad withdrew
from the Baghdad Pact. Kassim legalized the Iraqi Communist
Party (ICP) as Iraqi communists began to gravitate toward him,
while Arif was portrayed as a Nasserite nationalist and anti-Kassim.
Though Nasser welcomed the anti-West coup in Iraq, he did not
appreciate Kassim's legalization of the ICP.

In view of the above developments, Nasser began to attack
communism publicly. In Port Said, on December 23, 1958, he
delivered a speech in which he attacked "international communism"
and its agents in the Middle East. Following this speech over 200
communists in the UAR—Egypt and Syria—were arrested. Nasser's
renewed anti-communism caused concern in the Kremlin, just as
his neutralism was suspected in both Moscow and Washington.
The Soviet Government, which had endorsed neutralism as the
foreign policy of African and Asian states, was now faced with the
realities of Egypt's positive neutralism. According to the Soviet
perspective on neutralism, the policies of a neutral state and the
Soviet Union were considered compatible since both were allies
in the global anti-imperialist struggle. However, it was clear that
Egypt's neutralism was challenging Soviet policy in the Middle East
as Nasser did not want to become a victim of Soviet Marxism. In
his Note to Khrushchev, sent through ambassador Kiselev who was
returning to Moscow to attend the 21st Congress of the CPSU,
Nasser declared:

---

[56]   Khrushchev in ibid. See also el-Sadat, op.cit., p.153.

> We consider that the fate of Iraq affects us and we are
> not going to leave it under the Communists at any price.
> But we do not want this to be the cause of a quarrel
> with the Soviet Union. You must decide whether you
> want to deal with the Arab people or only a few isolated
> communist parties.[57]

It should be emphasized that Nasser's strong anti-communist position occurred at a time when the Soviet Union (in December 1958) had just signed an agreement with Egypt to build the Aswan High Dam, a project upon which Egypt's future economic and technological development very much depended, and which the West had bluntly refused to finance. Nasser's Port Said speech and his Note to Khrushchev dominated part of the proceedings of the 21st Congress of the CPSU in January 1959. In his address to the Congress, Nikita Khrushchev opined:

> We can only express our concern that in several countries
> a campaign is being carried on against progressive forces
> under the false banner of anti-Communism. In as much
> as attacks been recently made on Communism in the
> United Arab Republic, . . . I as a Communist consider it
> necessary to point out that . . . no one is more steadfast
> and devoted to the cause of the struggle against the
> colonialists than the Communists.[58]

Khrushchev's speech bolstered the morale of Egyptian and Syrian communists whose network Nasser had committed himself to destroy. Syrian Communist leader, Khalid Baldash, also used the platform of the CPSU Congress to attack Nasser.

In March 1959 General Abdel Wahab Shawaf engineered an anti-Kassim revolt in Mosul, northern Iraq. In the wake of the

---

[57] Nasser as cited in Heikal, 140.
[58] Materialy vneocherednogo XXI sezda KPSS, Moscow, 1959, p.69.

Mosul revolt Nasser got increasingly involved in a battle against Khrushchev. The tactical alliance between Egypt's Arab nationalism and Soviet Marxism which Moscow had sought began to show signs of disintegration. The suppression of the "pro-Nasser" Mosul revolt of March 8 sparked violent anti-communist demonstrations in Libya and other North African states. The Egyptian government perceived the conflict as a "struggle between communists supported by Moscow and Arab nationalists" while Arab communists were accused as "agents of the Communist Party in Moscow."

Meanwhile in Moscow, at a Kremlin press conference on March 19, Khrushchev predicted that Nasser's anti-Soviet policy was "doomed to failure." Answering a question posed by Mr. Shapiro of the United Press International (UPI) as to whether good relations with the UAR (Egypt) could be maintained in view of Nasser's anti-Sovietism, Khrushchev stated:

> We are not interfering; we are only defending our ideas—the teachings of Communism . . . As a Communist, I have the right to defend our Communist teaching . . . If the President of the UAR could exercise patience, and not allow the UAR to interfere in the internal affairs of Iraq and other Arab states, they would arise greater possibilities for the Arab states to unite in their struggle to maintain their independence . . . We have always been, and shall continue to be on the side of those fighting for independence[59]

Khrushchev's attack on Nasser was the fiercest the Soviet Government had ever addressed to its ally in Africa, or indeed to any of its allies in the "Third World", besides China. "President Nasser is young and rather hot-headed", continued Khrushchev, "and this is harmful. He takes upon himself even more than his stature allows him. He might strain himself." In the Soviet view, as articulated

---

[59]   Pravda, March 20, 1959.

by Khrushchev, Kassim was "manifestly leading his country along the path of progress" while Nasser was suppressing "freedom-loving aspirations not only in the UAR but also in other countries."[60]

As a result of Khrushchev's anti-Egyptian statement, Egypt recalled its ambassador, el-Kouny, from Moscow. It is interesting to note that, notwithstanding the serious deterioration of relations between both countries, Soviet aid to Egypt was not discontinued, neither was there any threat to the Aswan High Dam which the Soviets had undertaken to construct. Though Khrushchev frequently stated that Soviet aid to Egypt was meant to promote the cause of communism and not for Nasser, it must, however, be emphasized that Moscow's decision to continue its aid to Egypt favourably contrasted with Western aid policy of economic strangulation usually pursued under similar circumstances.

Soviet attack on Nasser was on ideological grounds. On the basis of this, Soviet writers reminded Egypt of Soviet support during the 1956 Suez Canal crisis. For example, this line of attack featured in a Pravda article signed by "Observer" in March 1959. According to "Observer", in 1956, "the USSR and the People's Republic of China not only aided the Egyptian people economically and politically but also declared their readiness to despatch volunteers to assist Egypt" during the Suez Canal crisis[61] The author of the Pravda article argued that Nasser and other Egyptian leaders had repeatedly applauded Soviet "disinterested aid". Pointing out that Nasser had denounced the West and hailed Moscow as the real friend of Egypt, the author cited Nasser's speech at Damascus on March 21, 1959 in which the Egyptian President maintained that no foreign state "including the USSR" had helped Egypt during

---

[60] Ibid. See also Henry B. Ellis, "Nasser caught in Red Vise", Christian Science Monitor, March 20, 1959; The New York Times, March 20, 1959.

[61] "Observer", "The Unity of Arab Peoples in their struggle for independence is a pledge of victory", Pravda, March 30, 1959. "Observer" is the appellation given to official view of Soviet policy.

the 1956 crisis, and that the Egyptians had only "relied on Allah."
Nasser's apparent self-contradiction was confusing to the Soviets.
The Soviet Government argued that it was impossible "to partition
the Arabs from other people" since their struggle was allied to the
universal anti-imperialist struggle. In a bid to undermine Nasser's
anti-Sovietism, the author concluded: "The USSR will continue
to pursue its policy of sincere friendship toward Egypt, other Arab
states and the peoples of Asia and Africa . . ."[62]

The circulation of "Observer's" article in Moscow prompted a
counter attack from Nasser. While addressing an Officers' Meeting
in the Cairo suburb of Heliopolis on March 30, 1959, Nasser
reminded the Soviets:

> Those who talk about democracy today must remember
> what happened in their country in 1917 when Parliament
> was dismissed by force of arms. Now they forget their
> history and their Chief stands up and attempts to stir up
> feelings against us . . .[63]

Nasser disclosed that during his 1958 visit to Moscow, he had rejected
Khrushchev's appeal to legalize communist activity in Egypt. "As we
crushed the imperialist agents we will also crush the Communist
agents", declared Nasser at Heliopolis. Referring to the 1956 Suez
Canal crisis, Nasser stated that the Soviet Union only rendered Egypt
"moral assistance", and argued that communism posed "a greater
menace because it seeks to impose foreign domination on us from
within, whereas the Anglo-Franco-Israeli attack was over aggression
from without." The Egyptian press began a systematic attack on the
Soviet Union. For the first time in Egypt, Khrushchev's anti-Stalin
"secret" speech at the 20th Congress of the CPSU was published
accusing Khrushchev of liquidating "his fellow leaders" as Stalin
did. It was revealed that the Soviet Government had attempted to

---

[62] Ibid.
[63] The Times, London, and The New York Times, March 31, 1959.

establish military bases in the Middle East on the pattern of Western military bases.[64]

President Nasser revealed that his security forces had uncovered a "Communist master plot" supported and financed by the Soviet Government to overthrow his regime and establish a Communist Federation of Iraq, Syria, Jordan, Kuwait and Lebanon. He also condemned the British Government of "being anti-Communist and at the same time pro-Kassim." He underlined the foreign policy objective of Egypt:

> Our minimum demand of Moscow, as indeed of Washington and London, is that they understand Arab nationalism, appreciate its dignity and independence, and support rather than subvert our stand on positive neutrality.[65]

Commenting further on Soviet global strategy, Nasser alleged that there was a Soviet plot to infiltrate Africa and South America through Egypt, and set up a Communist state in Israel. According to Nasser, the U.S. Government was "playing straight into the hands of the Soviet Union" by financing Jewish emigration from east Europe.[66]

The disarray in Soviet-Egyptian alliance illustrated the type of fundamental contradictions that could arise from an ill-conceived alliance devoid of serious ideological commitment. Even where a Marxist progressive bourgeois nationalist alliance is desirable, it is imperative that the parameters are clearly understood by members of the alliance. Nasser's anti-Marxism was clear to Moscow, but it was anticipated that he would not articulate this publicly to embarrass the Soviet Government. Nasser, on his part, had hoped that Khrushchev would not *push* him to defend Egypt's positive

---

[64] Observer, London, April 5, 1959; The Hindu, April 67, 1959.

[65] Daily Telegraph, London, and The Daily Worker, London, April 17, 1959.

[66] See The Times, London, April 18, 1959.

neutrality. What emerged from the conflict was the obvious dislike of positive neutrality in the Kremlin, as the Soviet Government did not appreciate Egypt's positive neutralist international politics.

However, in mid April 1959, Moscow and Cairo began to explore moves to lessen the tensions. Kiselev, Soviet Ambassador to Cairo who was recalled during the conflict, returned to his posting in April conveying a personal message from Nikita Khrushchev. Ambassador Muhamed el-Kouny returned to Moscow on May 14, 1959, with a Note from President Nasser. The return of the envoys to their respective stations, and the messages they carried along, indicated a joint desire to find an acceptable *modus operandi*. Khrushchev sent a warm message to Nasser on the occasion of the Muslim New Year:

> I sincerely hope to see the good relations existing between our two countries as the extensive economic cooperation successfully develop in the best interest of the peoples of our two countries and world peace.[67]

On August 3, 1959, less than a month after Khrushchev sent the above message, Vladimir Yerofeiev, a seasoned diplomat and member of the Soviet diplomatic corps since 1939, replaced Kiselev as Soviet Ambassador in Cairo. Prior to his Cairo posting, he was the head of the Department of Middle East Countries in the Soviet Ministry of Foreign Affairs.[68] It was expected that Yerofeiev would be able to manage Soviet crisis relationship with Nasser. While the Soviet Government perceived its investment in Egypt as a nucleus for the realization of Communism's long term objectives, the continued aid and support of the Egyptian cause in international relations considerably affected Soviet stance in the international communist movement. Leaders of the Arab Socialist Union (ASU)—Egypt's only political party—invited to CPSU Congresses

---

67   New York Herald Tribune (European Edition), July 10, 1959.
68   The Soviet Diplomatic Corps, 165.

were ceremoniously received in the Kremlin, while leaders of the proscribed Communist Party of Egypt were denied similar treatment in Moscow. This was considered a *de facto* recognition of the status of the Egyptian communists. However, following the 1960 Statement, the Soviets began to reconsider their policy toward this vital issue as the Egyptian Government continued to persecute and imprison Egyptian Communists. In 1961 friction again developed in Soviet-Egyptian relations over Nasser's persecution of Egyptian communists.

The 1961 spring issue of the World Marxist Review, and the Russian edition of Problems of Peace and Socialism, (Problemy mira i sotsializma), began a systematic attack on Nasser and described Egypt as a "dictatorship." These criticisms of Egypt, in Soviet-sponsored international theoretical Marxist journals, were designed to remove the Soviet-Egyptian schism from a bilateral level of analysis and placed it squarely within the universal framework of ideological struggle. As a follow-up to these orchestrated condemnations, Mr. "Observer" wrote on May 31, 1961 that Nasser's anti-communist movement would not eradicate the "great mission which the Soviet Union is fulfilling in African countries." Using the Aswan Dam to substantiate his argument, "Observer" pointedly reminded Egyptian leaders that the "age-long dream of the Arabs was being fulfilled with Soviet aid by the means of Soviet loans and credits . . ." and therefore warned the Egyptians "not to cut down the tree that provides the shade."[69] The Soviet All-Union Central Council of Trade Unions denounced "the arbitrary actions" of the Egyptian government "against imprisoned patriots, democrats and militants of the labour movement."[70] The Egyptian response was plain and

---

[69] Observer, "Vylaska klevetnikov", Pravda, May 31, 1961.

[70] Soviet News, Embassy of the USSR, London, June 7, 1961. See also The Daily Worker, April 5 and June 8, 1961; Daily Telegraph, May 12 and May 24, 1961; The Guardian, May 5 and June 8, 1961.

blunt: "We treat Russia as a bank. The bank which grants me a loan has no right to interfere in my own affairs."[71]

In late April 1961 Anwar el Sadat, then Speaker of Egypt's National Assembly, led a Parliamentary Delegation to Moscow at a time when schism started to develop in Soviet-Egyptian relations. Egypt was consistently attacked in the Soviet press for alleged inhuman treatment of communists in Egyptian prisons. It is significant to note that Soviet attack was intensified following the December 1960 Statement of 81 Communist and Workers' Parties Conference in Moscow in which the Soviet-proposed concepts of "national democracy" and "national front" were adopted by leading Communist parties as a Marxist strategy in non-Communist states. This decision envisaged the participation of Communists in a national democratic front as a prelude to their seizure of political power in the given anti-colonial struggle. Thus, the persecution and exclusion of Communists from the Egyptian political process was gravely resented in Moscow, as Soviet criticism of Egypt's political system became more systemic after December 1960. The Soviet Government and the CPSU therefore sought to put pressure on Nasser to accept Egyptian Communists as allies in Egypt's "national front."

According to the Egyptians, the Moscow-Cairo polemics was initiated by Khrushchev during Sadat's visit to Moscow in April 1961. Sadat was reported to have angrily left a dinner party in his honour and flew from Moscow "without any official goodbye" after Khrushchev had ridiculed Arab nationalism and stated that he (Khrushchev) "can hardly have confidence in your Nasser when he is losing his grip on the country and not solving his country's problems."[72] The text of Khrushchev's statement to the Egyptian delegation on May 3, 1961 was published in the semi-official

---

71   As cited in David Morison, The USSR and Africa, London, 1964, p.19.

72   The New York Times, June 8, 1961.

Cairo newspaper, <u>Al Ahram</u>. In an attempt to justify the benefits of Communism before his Egyptian guests, Khrushchev declared:

> You probably believe I want to turn you from Arab nationalism to the Communists. Of course I do not want to do this now. But I feel that some of you present here will turn Communists in the future . . . If our people are living a better life than yours under the banner of Communism, how can you declare you are against Communism?[73]

When Sadat cited the low standard of living in the Soviet Union as compared to leading capitalist countries, Khrushchev ignored the comparison and insisted that his guests must understand the implication of his ideological attack as he predicted the triumph of Communism in Egypt:

> History will be the arbiter between us. We are Communists. You do not belong to this creed . . . Your people will ask you to step aside and demand they handle their own affairs. I am warning you. I am saying this because Communism is sacred.[74]

The above represented the deep ideological cleavage between Soviet and Egyptian leaders which had become public since December 1960. The CPSU newspaper, <u>Pravda</u>, did not repudiate "the Khrushchev remarks" revealed by <u>Al Ahram</u>, but merely accused the Egyptian newspaper of attempting to drift toward the U.S. <u>Pravda</u> warned that any attempt to make Egypt pro-U.S., thus anti-Soviet, was

---

[73] <u>Al Ahram</u>, as cited in <u>The Guardian</u>, and <u>New York Herald Tribune</u> (European Edition), June 10, 1961; <u>The New York Times</u>, June 10 and June 11, 1961.

[74] <u>Ibid</u>.

a slippery road which has nothing in common with the national interests of the peoples of the United Arab Republic, who understand how important it is to maintain good relations with the USSR in order to strengthen their independence.[75]

Since the 1917 revolution the Soviets had always underlined the "progressiveness" of the citizens of a foreign capitalist state vis-à-vis their respective governments. Thus, the "national interests of the peoples of the United Arab Republic", in *alliance* with the USSR, were considered inimical to the interest of President Nasser's government in Cairo. This ideological position had its origin in Lenin's Peace Decree of 1917. In effect, Pravda was challenging the ideological basis of the Egyptian government.

However, Moscow had still to be cautious after such a strong statement in Pravda. The Soviets were of the opinion that continued economic aid to Egypt and support for the anti-Marxist government would strengthen the position of Egypt in international politics, preserve the state of Egypt and, hopefully, create favourable internal conditions for the local "Communists and democrats" to eventually seize political power and "handle their own affairs." The validity of this interpretation was buttressed by Khrushchev's message to Nasser on the 9th anniversary of July 23, as the Soviet leader mollified Nasser and his colleagues. Khrushchev remarked that it gave him

special satisfaction to note that the friendly relations between our countries, which have stood the test of time, continue developing successfully, providing a graphic example of mutually advantageous cooperation of states with different social and political systems—cooperation based on . . . non-interference in internal affairs.[76]

Khrushchev's message was an indication of Soviet desire to maintain good relations with Egypt at all cost. The language of

---

75 Pravda, June 17, 1961.
76 Soviet News, Embassy of the USSR, London, June 24, 1961.

the message was diplomatic and business-like, and demonstrated Moscow's difficulty in shifting from a *comradely* style to a *friendly* tune. It was the first time that the Soviet Government used the phrase, "states with different social and political systems", in a congratulatory message to Egypt which clearly defined the current level of relations between Moscow and Cairo.

The events of the 1958-1961 period of Soviet involvement in Egypt showed the inherent problematics encountered by Soviet foreign policy strategists as they embraced Africa's bourgeois nationalist leaders, who continuously insisted on implementing anti-Marxist policies. In the midst of Africa's anti-colonial movements, and in an attempt to implement the three peacefuls of the 20th Congress of the CPSU, the 1957 Declaration and the 1960 Statement, Soviet ideological posture towards Africa wavered. Moscow's invitation of the ASU to CPSU's congresses gave the ASU a false status, and this falsity made it to assume a *comradely* and *fraternal* relationship with other Marxist-Leninist parties at the expense of the proscribed Egyptian Communist Party which was excluded from CPSU congresses. The ideological contradiction is obvious. It was on the basis of such contradictions that Mahmoud Hussein, an Egyptian Marxist, criticized Soviet policies and referred to Soviet advisers in Egypt as a "bureaucratic bourgeois class." While Hussein's criticism of some aspects of Soviet policies cannot be faulted, his categorization of Soviet advisers as a "bureaucratic bourgeois class" in alliance with Egyptian bourgeoisie raises a fundamental problem in contemporary Marxist scholarship.[77]

The 1958-1961 period was crucial for U.S. and Soviet African policies. Even though Nasser's anti-communism posed a problem for Soviet leaders, his staunch anti-imperialist position was considered a valuable asset to Soviet policies in Africa during this period. For example, the Cairo-Moscow alliance during the Congo crisis of 1960-1962 was a vital element in maintaining a strong

---

[77] For an incisive analysis of this problem, see Mahmoud Hussein, <u>Class Struggle in Egypt, 1945-1970</u>.

anti-imperialist front. Secondly, the volatile nature of international politics was such that Nasser could have turned to other donors had Moscow elected to ditch him. The Soviet decision to sign the final agreement to construct the Aswan Dam in 1960 was not unconnected with the agreement Egypt had just got from the Federal Republic of Germany on this project. Though Soviet involvement in the Aswan Dam was highly valued in Egypt, especially in the early stages when the West failed Nasser, it is however significant to note that the entire Soviet contribution toward the Dam was $325 million, or 27.8% of the total cost.[78]

Almost a year before his visit to Egypt in May 1964, Khrushchev was able to convince Nasser to relax his anti-communist policies and to release imprisoned political prisoners, particularly communists. In August 1963 Nasser released these prisoners and allowed them to join ASU, Egypt's only legal political party. This decision was well received in the Kremlin where it was considered a tactical victory of communist participation in Egypt's united front.[79] Khrushchev's state visit was timed to coincide with the completion of the first phase of the Aswan Dam. However, when he was told that he would be met on arrival at Cairo airport by Marshal Amer, he felt dejected and wondered: "They are applying protocol to me. Nasser is in Cairo and only Marshal Amer will meet me because I am not a head of state."[80] It is significant to note that irrespective of this feeling of dejection, Khrushchev awarded Nasser the *Order of Lenin* and declared him a *Hero of the Soviet Union*, a move which generated mixed reactions in the Kremlin given that the latter award was the Soviet Union's most prestigious honour. He also awarded Marshal Amer *the Order of Lenin*. According to the Soviet Constitution, only the Presidium of the Supreme Soviet was empowered to confer such awards. Khrushchev's personal diplomacy had run into a *cul de sac*,

---

[78] See Marshall L. Goldman, Soviet Foreign Aid, New York, 1962, p.67.

[79] See Pravda, August 16, 1963.

[80] As cited in Heikal, 154.

and when he was relieved of his offices in October 1964 his posturing in Egypt topped the list of illegal actions levelled against him.

Notwithstanding the cracks in Soviet-Egyptian relations both countries remained firm allies, especially under Nasser's regime in Egypt. The correlation of forces in the international political scene in the 1960s, including the deterioration of the Palestine issue helped to explain the continued alliance Nasser was able to maintain with the Soviet Union.

Algeria: Alliance Building

On November 1, 1954 the Algerian Front de Liberation Nationale (FLN) launched the Algerian war of independence against French colonial rule. By this act the FLN positioned itself as the champion of Algerian nationalism under whose platform other nationalist parties must function.[81] In 1958, as the war entered its fourth year, the Soviet Government expressed its "grave concern" but was restrained to act. While China had publicly and ferociously condemned French colonial war in Algeria, the Soviet Union maintained a cautious policy for fear of jeopardizing Franco-Soviet alliance in European politics. The Soviet Union needed French support in order to undermine NATO's (USA's) aggressiveness and to curb the growing influence of West Germany in European politics. It was obvious that the European theatre had more serious consequences for Marxism, and thus was considered by Moscow to be of vital ideological primacy than Algeria's anti-colonial war of independence. However, a closer examination of the question reveals that the Soviet Union was searching for a political compromise in the interest of Marxism.

---

[81] For a discussion of the rivalry between contending Algerian nationalist parties, see Marnia Lazreg, The <u>Emergence of Classes in Algeria. A Study of Colonialism and Socio-Political Change</u>, Boulder, Colorado, 1976, pp. 61-68.

The establishment of NATO in 1949 was primarily designed to curtail Soviet and communist influence in Europe. This made the Soviet State vulnerable as the erosion of the state would mean the withering away of communism in Europe. Therefore, it was considered politically expedient for the Soviet Union, a communist state, to ally with France, a capitalist colonial power, against a greater threat to international communism. This was a tactical ideological move by Moscow, which Beijing viewed as a manifestation of Soviet "revisionism" and "opportunism." It was clear that China still possessed the revolutionary zeal that was characteristic of Soviet policy immediately after the October 1917 revolution.

Moscow confined itself to acting within the framework of the International Red Cross Organization as the Soviet Union utilized its membership in the Red Cross to foster its policy interest in Algeria. In February 1958 the Soviet Red Cross and Red Crescent Societies donated food and clothing valued at about $250, 000 to help Algerian refugees in Morocco and Tunisia. The executive committees of both Soviet humanitarian organizations

> expressed on behalf of the Soviet public the hope that
> this gift will alleviate the lot of the victims of the war in
> Algeria and strengthen the ties of friendship between the
> peoples of the USSR and Algeria.[82]

Ten days after the Soviet Red Cross offer, French pilots bombed the Tunisian border village of Sakiet Sidi Youssef where Algerian refugees were housed. Soviet press quickly condemned this action as "brutal and barbarous."[83] Since Moscow's consideration was to prevent France's "dirty war" in Algeria from spreading to other areas thereby "endangering world peace", the Soviet Government

---

[82] New York Herald Tribune (European Edition), February 5, 1958.

[83] Pravda, Izvestia, Red Star, February 11, 1958.

requested a UN Security Council debate on the Franco-Algerian war to ensure a "peaceful settlement" in north Africa.[84]

The Soviet Red Cross gift of food, clothing and medical supplies were unloaded in Tunis on February 17, 1958 for distribution among Algerian refugees in Tunisia and Morocco. The frequency of these donations and the condemnation of France in the Soviet press reflected Moscow's growing political interest in the Algerian crisis. It was difficult for France to accuse the Soviet Union of intervention in Algeria since every country sends its humanitarian gifts to war victims through the Red Cross, even though it was obvious that Soviet intention was to undermine French rule in Algeria. The development in Algeria favoured Soviet policy in Africa; a continent which the Soviets argued "has being encouraged in its struggle with the modern slavers by the mighty socialist camp headed by the Soviet Union and by its peaceful policy."[85] While the Soviet Red Cross donated $3,000 to the Tunisian Red Cross "to be spent on assistance to the air raid victims", Baimuhamet Tugusbayev, a prominent Soviet Muslim, expressed "profound sympathy for the Tunisian people on behalf of Soviet Muslims" during his sermon at a Mosque in Ufa, USSR.[86] This was meant to assuage Arab Muslim nationalism in North Africa and the Middle East, especially at a time when Nasser's Arab nationalism was challenging Soviet Marxism in the region. It was one of the many occasions when the Soviet Government employed religious sentiments in aid of its foreign policy objectives in Africa and the Middle East. Even though the Soviet State was atheistic, the Kremlin found it politically expedient to unite religion and Marxism in its foreign policy. In the Soviet Marxist world outlook, this was viewed as a manifestation of the philosophical concept of the "unity and struggle of opposites."

Moscow's action in Algeria was still limited, and did not pose any serious threat to French policy in the colony. When the FLN

---

[84]   Pravda, February 15, 1958.

[85]   Ibid., February 17, 1958.

[86]   Soviet News, Embassy of the USSR, London, February 18, 1958.

proclaimed the Provisional Government of the Algerian Republic (GPRA) in September 1958, the Soviet Government slow pedalled while China promptly recognized *de jure* the independence of Algeria. In an interview with the Washington correspondent of Sabah, a Tunisian newspaper, Soviet Foreign Minister Andrei Gromyko promised that the

> Soviet Union will soon recognize the Provisional Government of the Algerian Republic which represents the unanimous desire of the Algerian people.[87]

At a Moscow rally on September 24, 1958, Soviet Trade Unionists voted in support of the resolution passed at the Cairo Conference of the International Trade Union Committee for solidarity with the workers and people of Algeria. The Soviet trade unions underscored the ambiguity of Soviet policy in Algeria by declaring that "the proclamation of the Algerian Republic and the establishment of a Provisional Government mark an important stage in the Algerian people's just struggle . . ." and stressed that France's colonial war in Algeria must come to an end through "talks between the governments of France and the Algerian Republic in a spirit of understanding and respect for each other's interests."[88] While, officially, the Soviet Government was still oscillating between Paris and Algiers, its agents, Soviet trade unions, were unequivocal in their support for the GPRA. This seemingly contradictory policy was based on Soviet's dual approach in the conduct of Moscow's foreign policy which Lenin had formulated in 1918. The essence of this approach allowed the Soviet Government to concentrate on **government-to-government** relations, while the so-called non-governmental organizations of the Soviet Union concentrated

---

[87] Egyptian Gazette, September 22, 1958. For an analysis of the Algerian revolution, see David and Marina Ottaway, Algeria. The Politics of a Socialist Revolution, Berkeley, California, 1970.

[88] Soviet News, Embassy of the USSR, London, September 26, 1958.

on **people-to-people** relations. This was meant to create the impression that the latter's views did not represent those of the Soviet Government.

Trade unions and religion were important instruments of Soviet foreign policy. The Soviet Government had its first high-level contact with the GPRA in Cairo in late September 1958. Muritdin A. Mukhitdinov, a Soviet Muslim and member of the Presidium of the Supreme Soviet, was visiting Cairo as President Nasser's guest when he conferred twice with the Algerian Minister of the Interior, Abdalla Ben Tobal, and the Minister for North African Affairs, Amid Mehkri.[89] Mukhitdinov's discussions with the Algerian leaders were timed to coincide with another proclamation of support by Soviet Muslims as they wished "the best success to the people of Algeria and to our Muslim brothers" and "hope that the day is not far off when Algeria will become free and independent."[90] Notwithstanding the promise of Andrei Gromyko and the series of support from the USSR, the Soviet Government was inhibited by the complex nature of European politics which dictated its cordial relations with France, and was therefore compelled to delay recognition of the GPRA. The anti-French crusade in Soviet newspapers was relaxed in early 1960, well in advance of Khrushchev's visit to Paris in the spring of 1960 to attend the Four Power Summit. When the Soviet Government elected to recognize Algeria in 1960, it was merely a *de facto* recognition.

Premier Ferhat Abbas of Algeria was disturbed by Soviet shifts of priority as exemplified in the Kremlin's indecision to give total commitment to the GPRA. Soviet shifting attitude also significantly influenced the French Communist Party (PCF) in its relations toward France and Algeria. For example, in 1956 the PCF, on Soviet advice, supported Premier Guy Mollet's policy toward Algeria, while in 1959, in conformity with Moscow's belligerent policy toward France, the PCF publicly demanded self-determination for Algeria.

---

[89] Pravda, September 27, 1958.

[90] Egyptian Gazette, September 28, 1958.

This was shortly after Maurice Thorez, the French Communist leader, had returned from Moscow. Soviet dilemma in Algeria had several dimensions. The Kremlin could not locate a prototype of the PCF in Algeria; neither could Algerian Communists shift grounds like their French comrades, a policy which would have resulted in a major setback for them in view of the mass popularity of the FLN. The Algerian propaganda centre, and the **Voice of the Algerian Republic** based in Cairo, frequently publicized Soviet support for Algeria as a tactical move to put the Soviet Government in a discomforting situation before France. The GPRA was aware that the Soviet Government was handicapped to justify French colonial policy in Algeria as this would have negated Soviet endorsement of the Bandung Declaration and constituted a possible loss of face in African and Asian countries. Besides, a certain degree of hesitancy was also apparent in Soviet policy. Moscow's confrontation with Arab nationalism which led to the open Khrushchev-Nasser counter recriminations in 1959 informed the contents of Soviet strategy. Moscow therefore opted for a cautious approach in dealing with Algeria.[91]

On his way to Beijing to attend the Chinese 11th National Day Celebrations, Premier Abbas stopped in Moscow on September 28, 1960 for talks with Soviet deputy Premier Alexei Kosygin. He returned to Moscow on October 6 after the Chinese celebrations. At a reception in his honour hosted by Admed Meshiri, the Tunisian Ambassador in Moscow, which was attended by Kosygin and D. S. Polianski, Abbas reminded the Soviets that it was "not by chance that representatives of the Provisional Government of Algeria find themselves in Moscow." He opined:

> We are here because we consider that at the moment
> the world is divided into two camps—the camp of the

---

91   See Robert Stephens, "World crisis fear over Algeria." <u>Observer</u>, April
      24, 1960.

imperialists and the camp of peace—and the Algerians
believe that Moscow is the camp of peace.[92]

It should be noted that while Abbas sought to link the USSR with
the destiny of Algeria's anti-colonial war, and to obtain Moscow's
de jure recognition of the GPRA, Kosygin merely reaffirmed Soviet
support for the struggle of oppressed peoples and wished the
Algerians success in their anti-colonial war. The Soviet Government
rejected Abbas' plea to open an Algerian Permanent Mission in
Moscow probably in recognition of President de Gaulle's threat to
severe diplomatic relations with the Soviet Union should such a
mission be opened. However, both Kosygin and Abbas appeared
satisfied with the Soviet Government's *de facto* recognition of the
GPRA.[93] Soviet aid to Algerian refugees in Tunisia and Morocco
was continued.

Soviet *de facto* recognition of the GPRA generated deterioration
in Franco-Soviet relations. Paris was disappointed by the
Abbas-Kosygin talks, and de Gaulle expressed French indignation
when he remarked in Nice that "another empire was interfering"
in the Algerian question,—a statement which Moscow promptly
deplored. In a Pravda article published on November 3, 1960, and
signed by **observer**, the Soviet Government accused de Gaulle
of discarding "the idea of initiating negotiations on a peaceful
settlement of the Algerian question . . ." It was further stated that
President de Gaulle, "on whom so many Frenchmen pinned their
hopes of peace in Algeria" was bringing "the Algerian question to
an impasse . . ." A TASS statement, which carried the weight of

---

[92] Osgood Caruthers, "Algerian Rebel Leader Hailed on surprise arrival
in Soviet Union," The New York Times, October 7, 1960. See also
Soviet News, Embassy of the USSR, London, October 11, 1960.

[93] Soviet News, Embassy of the USSR, London, October 13, 1960.

Soviet Government policy, denounced France for its "criminal acts in Algeria."[94]

What motivated such a drastic shift in Soviet policy toward Algeria? It was not a coincidence that the USSR pursued a strong anti-French policy in October 1960 over Algeria. The Kremlin was cultivating a fertile ground to exploit the political situation in Africa at this time. Seventeen African countries had just joined the UN in 1960; the political crisis in the Congo was considered a threat to world peace and a battle ground for East-West ideological rivalry. Nikita Khrushchev had just returned from the UN 15th Session in New York City where he bitterly condemned Western colonial rule in Africa, Asia, and Latin America. Algeria and the Congo dominated his speech at the UN. It is significant to note that his personal diplomacy ensured that prominent political leaders of Africa, Asia, and Latin America—Modibo Keita, Sekou Toure, Nkrumah, Nasser, Sukarno, Nehru, and Fidel Castro—were present at the UN 15th Session.

The 15th Session of the UN General Assembly was a great historic event for both the UN and the global decolonization process. The Soviet Government scored a major diplomatic victory before the "Third World" as Khrushchev did not only condemn the West but proposed the "immediate" liquidation of colonialism and the granting of independence to the colonies. He challenged member-states of the UN that really "stand for peace and progress" to support the Soviet initiated Declaration on the Granting of Independence to Colonial Peoples and Countries. "Either the demands are recognized by all States, or the oppressed peoples, with the support of their many friends in the world, will achieve freedom and independence."[95] This was the strongest indication of support

---

[94] Soviet News, Embassy of the USSR, London, December 16, 1960. See also ibid., December 20, 1960, for Khrushchev's message to Ferhal Abbas.

[95] SSSR i strany Afriki, 1946-1962gg., vol. 2, p.744. Note pp.737-747. See also David W. Wainhouse, Remnants of Empire. The United

from the Soviet Government for the GPRA. Its value laid in the positive impression it was designed to create in the anti-colonial movement, as was dictated by the imperatives of the cold war, even though it was obvious that the Soviet Government would not intervene to force the course of events in Algeria. We witnessed a similar sentiment during the Congo crisis, as Moscow was not in a position to alter the trends in the Congo beyond issuing mere declaratory statements of support and misguided intents.

When Franco-Algerian talks resulted in French withdrawal and the "granting" of independence to Algeria, the Soviet Government congratulated the GPRA and declared that the USSR now "recognizes the GPRA *de jure* and expresses its preparedness to establish diplomatic relations with the GPRA."[96] Both countries agreed to establish diplomatic relations at an ambassadorial level, and the first Soviet ambassador, A.N. Abramov, arrived in Algiers on October 30, 1962. Thus, the ambiguity which had clouded Soviet policy in Algeria since 1954 was resolved as the Kremlin formally recognized the GPRA. It was obvious in Moscow that cordial relations with France were crucial for harmonizing anti-U.S. and anti-NATO policies in Europe. However, Soviet reluctance to recognize the GPRA *de jure* between September 1958 and March 1962 was still questionable, especially since the GPRA was a prominent member of the radical "pro Soviet" Casablanca bloc of African states that was opposed to the West and Kasavubu in the Congo. Soviet cautious approach could be explained as a tactical move geared towards the maximum exploitation of available opportunities without jeopardizing Franco-Soviet relations, irrespective of the strong condemnation it drew from Beijing.

Nations and the End of Colonialism, New York, 1964, pp.148-149. When India invoked the Declaration to justify its seizure of Goa in December 1961, the Soviet Union was the only world power to endorse the Indian move: Wainhouse, pp.17-19.

[96]   Izvestia, March 19, 1962.

Khrushchev's quarrels with Sekou Toure and Nasser influenced Soviet posture in Africa in the early 1960s. It was therefore expedient for the USSR to embrace Algeria given that the Algerian war of independence was universally acclaimed as a heroic anti-colonial war. The CPSU gradually began to develop "comradely" relations with the FLN. A policy of consolidating the gains of the war and to direct Algeria towards socialist construction became dominant in Soviet calculations. The anti-colonialism of the FLN was therefore linked with the ideological prism of the CPSU world outlook.

Houari Boumedienne, (then) first deputy chairman of Algeria's Council of Ministers and Minister of Defence, led a government delegation to Moscow on September 30, 1963. The Soviet-Algerian joint communiqué of October 6, 1963 reported the "frank" talks between Boumedienne and Soviet leaders—L. I. Brezhnev, A. N. Kosygin, and Defence Minister Marshal R. Ia. Malinovski—and emphasized the friendship between the USSR and Algeria and their commitment in the global anti-colonial struggle. The characterization of the talks as "frank" was an indication of the absence of agreement on key political issues. We could only conjecture that Boumedienne may have raised the issue of Soviet delayed recognition of the GPRA, and that he may also have indicated Algeria's brand of socialism. However, the USSR and Algeria signed an Economic and Technical Cooperation Agreement which fetched Algeria a long term credit, and guaranteed Soviet assistance in the construction of Algeria's industrial enterprises and the development of its agricultural and transport systems.[97]

Prior to Boumedienne's trip to Moscow, the Algerian Government had clarified its position on the issue of East-West ideological struggle. In April 1963 President Ben Bella declared:

> We are not Communist and do not belong to the Communist camp, but neither are we hostile to Communist ideology. On the contrary, we take a

---

[97]   Pravda, October 6, 1963.

229

friendly attitude towards the Communist camp and cooperate with it on the basis of the principles of peaceful coexistence and positive neutralism.[98]

Khrushchev was aware of Algeria's policy as articulated by Ben Bella. In his address to Boumedienne's delegation in Moscow he praised the "courage and heroism of the Algerian patriots who stopped at no sacrifices to national freedom and the independence of their country."[99] In an obvious reference to Moscow's ideological quarrel with Cairo, the Soviets hoped that Ben Bella would be a strong supporter of socialism who will not allow "anti-Communism" in Algeria.[100]

The joint communiqué of October 6, 1963 had set the basis for the development of friendly relations between Algeria and the USSR. On the invitation of the CC CPSU and the Soviet Government an Algerian party-government delegation led by Ben Alla, FLN Politburo member and Chairman of Algeria's National Assembly visited Moscow on December 18-28, 1963. The delegation was received by Khrushchev, and met with Kosygin, N.V. Podgorny and B.N. Ponomarev. The talks were held in an atmosphere of "friendship" unlike the "frank" talks of October 1963 between Boumedienne and Brezhnev. The Ben Alla-led delegation was able to secure another agreement on Economic and Technical Cooperation, according to which the Soviet Union agreed to aid in building Algeria's national cadres. In the joint communiqué the Soviet Union stated that it "highly values Algeria's progressive and revolutionary role in Africa."[101]

[98] Ben Bella as cited in D. Petrov and L. Yakovlev, "The Algerian Republic Gains in Strength," International Affairs, Moscow, no. 8, 1963, pp.73-74.
[99] Khrushchev as cited in N. Chibisov, "The Impact of the Algerian Revolution," New Times, Moscow, no.44, 1963, p.5.
[100] Ibid., p.6.
[101] Pravda, December 30, 1963.

The two agreements signed in 1963 laid the basis for Soviet-Algerian cooperation in most fields. On the ideological plane, the FLN was now recognized as an ally of the CPSU even though the Algerian Communist Party (ACP) was banned by the FLN government. The Soviets were guided by the resolutions of the 20th Congress of the CPSU which had rationalized the dialectics of such an alliance in the struggle for socialism. Since the movement towards socialism had to be nurtured, it was imperative for the CPSU to portray the FLN as a national democratic front.

A month before Ben Bella's state visit to Moscow in April 1964 Soviet ideologues intensified their analyses of FLN's *progressive* policies. It was the view in the Kremlin that the progressive elements of Algerian society, including the workers, peasants and small merchants, were "united . . . within the ranks of the National Liberation Front, the political organization expressing Algeria's popular aspirations."[102] The ideological implication of Soviet endorsement of the FLN was that the ACP had to concede the role of leading Algeria towards socialism to the FLN. But such a concession also implied that Algerian Communists had to work within the framework of the FLN and aspire to attain the objectives of Marxism utilizing the existing instrumentalities of power.

The in-fighting within the ruling FLN on the path of Algerian development accentuated the class struggle in Algeria. According to N. Kuznetsov, a leading Soviet Africanist, the "petty-bourgeois elements vacillated in choosing ways for the country's development." In his view:

> Most (National) Council Members; *especially the military* reflecting the sentiments of the poor peasants, the agricultural labourers and urban workers, demanded a deep-going land reform and expropriation of the big bourgeoisie. The fact that 80 per cent of the National

---

[102] N. Kuznetsov, "Algeria Chooses her way ahead," <u>International Affairs</u>, Moscow, no. 3, 1964, p.47.

Liberation Army consisted of fellahs was decisive in the adoption of the Council's programme which called for a non-capitalist path of development.[103]

The Soviets were pleased that the Algerian Constitution of September 1963 had endorsed socialism. Ben Bella took measures to deprive the big landlords and bourgeoisie of their means to exploit the masses by nationalizing most of their properties. Landless peasants now owned lands. The ACP had no grounds to oppose the FLN government. The fact that the ACP was banned did not seem to concern the Soviets. They still manage to craft a role for the ACP in Algeria. Kuznetsov argued:

> Together with all honest revolutionary patriots, this position of the FLN leadership in the present situation is shared and approved by Algerian Communists. Guided by the supreme interests of the nation, the Communists are doing everything to bolster the forces which advocate a non-capitalist road of development, uniting them in a progressive party capable of solving the intricate problems of the transitional period.[104]

It was apparent that the CPSU had faith in the FLN as a progressive party "capable of solving the intricate problems of the transitional period" leading to socialism. Thus, the CPSU had forgotten that, fundamentally, the FLN was a *nationalist* party ideologically opposed to communism and as such could not be expected to lead Algeria to socialism. The Soviet Government was prepared to disregard this ideological imperative perhaps as a strategic move in its desire to transform Algeria into a client state. The war of independence had done serious damages to Algeria's economy; the task of reconstruction was expensive and Algeria's decision to

---

[103] Ibid. Italics mine.
[104] Ibid., p.50.

pursue a *non-capitalist* path of development effectively ostracized it from Western investment and aid. However, the Soviets were optimistic that a "Soviet loan on easy terms will help consolidate the republic's economic independence",[105] since "the progressive core of the National Liberation Front led by Ben Bella" had opted for a socialist-oriented economy.[106] The Soviets were convinced that the Algerian public management committees set up in March 1963 to take over the abandoned French enterprises had put Algeria "on the road of socialist revolution."[107]

From the above it was apparent that the Soviet Government had placed the FLN in the forefront of the African revolution. It was against this background that Ben Bella visited the Soviet Union in April-May 1964. By early 1964 Ben Bella had emerged as one of the closest Soviet allies in Africa. When Chou en-Lai, the Chinese Premier sought to enlist Algeria's support in China's anti-Soviet crusade in December 1963, Ben Bella informed Chou that Algeria supported Soviet "peaceful coexistence policy." While in Moscow he also announced to his Soviet hosts that Algeria had "entered the path of socialism." This undoubtedly must have flattered Khrushchev as he became to address Ben Bella as "comrade President" even though Ben Bella addressed him as "Dear Friend."

At a Kremlin reception Khrushchev condemned the "machinations of external enemies" in Algeria, and promised that the "difficulties caused by an acute shortage of funds and of trained staff and a lack of experience in economic construction" would be supplemented by "the experience of the Soviet Union" in

---

[105] Ibid., p.51.
[106] V. Kuznetsov, "Algeria Today," International Affairs, Moscow, no. 6, 1964, p.106.
[107] Alger Republicain as cited in G. Mirsky, "Algeria: Yesterday, Today, Tomorrow," New Times, Moscow, no. 17, 1964, p.9. See also V. Kudryavtsev, "Algeria's Revolutionary Path," New Times, Moscow, no. 44, 1964, pp.8-10.

terms of assistance and aid.[108] Khrushchev and Ben Bella continued their talks in Yalta. In the Yalta agreement the Soviet Government undertook to provide Algeria with military aid. Ben Bella was convinced that the agreement would make "it possible to protect Algeria from the forces which are trying to throw it off its chosen path of socialist construction," while Khrushchev perceived the agreement as a blow to the "imperialists and internal reaction" that were plotting to subjugate Algeria to the "yoke of oppression."[109] Ben Bella's trip fetched Algeria a Soviet long term loan of $13.8 million. The agreement caused concern in Rabat given that Morocco and Algeria had not settled their territorial disputes. The armed conflict between them in 1963 demonstrated the weakness of Algeria. Thus, the Soviet-Algerian arms deal of 1964 was viewed in Rabat as an anti-Moroccan policy.

For the Soviets, the Ben Bella trip came at an opportune time as it coincided with Soviet Government's policy readjustment in Africa. Since 1962 Soviet leaders began to assume a more realistic stance in their African policy.[110] The problems encountered in Egypt, Guinea and in the Congo necessitated a shift of emphasis in policy formulation. The decision to cooperate with Algeria was perhaps compelled by the desire to influence other African states. Towards the end of 1962 Ben Bella had emerged as Africa's most charismatic leader whose actions were influencing the course of Africa's political development. Moscow grasped the implication of Ben Bella's leadership in Africa as most young African political activists regarded the Algerian President as the living symbol of Africa's anti-colonial struggle. The number of African students that lined the streets of Moscow to welcome Ben Bella surpassed those that welcomed other

---

[108] Soviet News, Embassy of the USSR, London, April 29, 1964.

[109] Izvestia, May 5, 1964. For the complete English text of the Soviet-Algerian Yalta Agreement, see Soviet News, Embassy of the USSR, London, May 14, 1964, pp.99-102.

[110] See Helen Desfosses Cohn, Soviet Policy Toward Black Africa. The Focus on National Integration, New York, 1972.

African heads of states. Furthermore, the frustrating experience of the Soviet Union in Africa south of the Sahara must have persuaded Soviet leaders to concentrate on Algeria. For example, in March 1964 the Government of Guinea ordered the Soviet Press Agency, Novosti, to refrain from distributing its bulletin to Guinean citizens maintaining that the Bulletin contained items detrimental to Guinea's relations with other African states.[111]

The Congo Crisis

The Congo, a former Belgian colony, gained its independence on June 30, 1960. However, the constitutional arrangements reached as of that date seemed to have planted the seeds of conflict for the ensuring disarray that transformed the emergent state into an ideological battle ground of the cold war. These arrangements or compromises which provided that Patrice Lumumba be the Prime Minister, Joseph Kasavubu to be the President, and Moise Tshombe to be the President of the province of Katanga were based on the Belgian perceptions of the Congo as a neo-colonial entity, and on the overall West European strategic calculation in Africa. Belgian perceptions informed the choices of leaders (Kasavubu and Tshombe) and other key government officials that Belgium imposed on Prime Minister Lumumba. The main expectation of Belgium was the retainment of Congo as a neo-colonial country whose natural resources would be exploited for the development of Belgium and other West European economies, and the perpetual underdevelopment of the Congo. The sandwiching of Lumumba between Kasavubu and Tshombe was designed to create a hotbed of instability favourable to Belgian and West European colonial interests. Thomas Kanza, who served as Congo's Ambassador to the UNO under Lumumba's government, summed up the compromise as follows:

---

[111]   See The New York Times, March 26, 1964.

Lumumba's submission to the will of Belgium and equally
Belgium's acceptance of him as Prime Minister, were
both purely tactical steps. The atmosphere was one of
mutual mistrust, misunderstanding, and denigration.[112]

With Africa's *head*, Egypt, already an ally of the Soviet Union,
and Africa's *feet*, the Republic of South Africa, entrenched in the
international capitalist design, the Congo, situated in the *heart*
of Africa, had natural appeal to the competing global ideological
blocs for the following reasons. First, the province of Katanga has
valuable mineral resources essential for the West's economic and
military development with strong Belgian, French and British
interests. Second, Congo shares its southern borders with Angola
and northern Rhodesia then Portuguese and British colonies,
respectively. Third, the Benguela railway system links the mine
fields of Katanga with the Angolan port of Benguela. And finally,
Lumumba's presence as the leader of a 3-man delegation of the
Movement Nationale Congolais (MNC) at the first All African
Peoples Conference (AAPC) in Accra in November 1958, caused
grave concern to Western interests in the Congo, the central and
southern African colonies as well as in the apartheid regime of
South Africa. Delegates from these countries were also at the Accra
conference whose main objective was the decolonization of Africa.
It is interesting to note that in February 1959, two months after
the Accra conference, the Nyasa African Congress (NAC) organized
a demonstration demanding the independence of Nyasaland (now
Malawi Republic) and the disintegration of the colonial Federation
of Rhodesia and Nyasaland. Many demonstrators were killed in
a combat with the police. For the apologists of colonialism the
Accra conference must have instigated this demonstration! Roy
Welensky, the Prime Minister of the Federation, blamed the Accra
conference:

---

[112] Thomas Kanza, The Rise and Fall of Patrice Lumumba. Conflict in
the Congo, London, 1978, p.98.

> I want to go on record as saying that the Accra Conference
> was attended by a number of African leaders from
> Rhodesias and Nyasaland. The public ought to know
> that at the Accra Conference the Russians had a strong
> team . . . We have it from factual evidence that direct
> contact was made between Russian representatives and
> certain of the African leaders from the Federation.[113]

Thus, it was the view of the colonial powers that Lumumba's *contact*
with Kwame Nkrumah and "Russian representatives" at the AAPC
must have influenced his independent posture vis-a-vis Belgian
design in the Congo. This qualified him to be regarded by the West
as an ally of the East, even before June 30, 1960.

Prior to independence it could be said that political discourse
by Congolese nationalists was almost non-existent. In 1950, a
cultural organization, the Association pours la Sauvegarde de la
Culture et des Interests des Bakongo (ABAKO) was founded with
Kasavubu as its leader. In 1956 ABAKO was transformed into a
political movement agitating for the unification of the Bakongo
ethic group in the two Congos (Belgian and French) and Angola
for the creation of a Kongo state, a reincarnation of the ancient
Kongo Kingdom. The main national independence movement,
the MNC, was founded in Leopoldville (now Kinshasa) in 1958
with Lumumba as its president. Also in 1958 Tshombe established
his Confederation of Tribal Association of Katanga (CONAKAT)
with Belgian support. Of the above political groups the MNC was
considered a threat to Belgian interests.

In July 1959 Albert Kalonji, with Belgian support, engineered a
split in the MNC and began to promote Baluba ethnicism as opposed
to MNC's nationalist policies, and conspired to oust Lumumba from
the presidency. This led to the emergence of two MNCs: MNC(L)
and MNC(K), with L and K representing Lumumba and Kalonji,
respectively. The anti-Lumumbist elements from the above political
organizations decided to establish another movement known as the

---

[113] The Guardian, March 11, 1959.

O. Igho Natufe

Parti solidaire africain (PSA) which was a "federation ... of political groups whose bases were tribalist but whose declared sympathies were for Christianity, federalism, and anti-communism."[114] Antoine Gizenga, who in 1960 became Lumumba's deputy prime minister, was elected president of PSA with Pierre Mulele as the secretary general.

Any analysis of the Congo crisis must understand the dialectics of political relations, internal and external, that were represented in the above alliance construct prior to June 30, 1960. Lumumba was aware of the membership and strategy of each competing alliance system. He accepted Kasavubu, a Belgian protégé as president perhaps hoping that after independence, with himself entrenched as head of government, he would be in a better position to ostracize Kasavubu. As events were to prove, he grossly underestimated his enemies as the Belgian-Kasavubu-Tshombe forces began the process of humiliating Lumumba on independence day. For example, the head of government, Lumumba, was ignored by Belgium in matters of protocol relating to the independence celebrations. As the prime minister, Lumumba should have had a prior knowledge of the contents of Kasavubu's speech. This was not the case, and the showdown took place at the independence celebrations.

After the Belgian King and Kasavubu had read their respective speeches, which were paternalistic in tune, Lumumba, in his speech, attacked Belgian colonialism which he described as a catalogue of "deprivation, suffering ..." He declared that Congolese "independence has only been won by struggle . . ." and that the battle for independence "was a noble and just struggle, which was needed to bring to an end the humiliating slavery imposed on us by force. Such was our lot for eighty years under the colonialist regime."[115] While it is conceded that Lumumba was not diplomatic,

<hr/>

[114] See Kanza, *op.cit.*, p.35.
[115] *Ibid.*, p.37. For the texts of the speeches of King Baudouin of Belgium and President Kasavubu, see *ibid.*, pp.155-157 and 157-160 respectively.

it should be recognized, however, that his speech reflected the aspirations of millions of Congolese and Africans who had endured the suffering and pillage of colonialism. Did his speech provoke the crisis? It is essential to understand that the Congo crisis would still have occurred in 1960 had Lumumba been diplomatic, and the fact that it did occur unquestionably confirmed the fears and aspirations contained in Lumumba's anti-colonialist pronouncements.

The continued exploitation of the Congo was considered vital for the economic well-being of Belgium and, to a certain extent, to both France and Britain. It should be noted that, prior to the proclamation of independence, U.S. government officials met with Kasavubu, Tshombe, Kalonji and other leading anti Lumumbists emphasizing the need to protect "American capitalist interests" in the Congo after June 30, 1960.[116] On the other hand, the Communist bloc used the Belgian Communist Party as a link between itself and Congolese nationalists considered hostile to capitalist interests. However, as argued by Kanza, the use of the Belgian Communist Party in this operation was "a grave mistake . . . for the Belgian Communist Party was larded with double agents . . . Some of its leaders differed from the leaders of other Belgian parties only in the rhetoric with which they denounced Belgian colonialism."[117] Thus, in terms of class solidarity, the forces of anti-imperialism in the Congo were at a serious disadvantage given that their "comrades", Belgian Communists, had allied themselves with Belgian interests. The Belgian government knew this, while the Lumumbists knew it after the betrayal. Such was the correlation of forces in the Congo at independence.

The events scholars refer to as the Congo crisis or, in the words of Colin Legum, Congo Disaster (London, 1960), occurred between July 5 and September 4, 1960:—

---

[116]   *Ibid.*, p.161.

[117]   *Ibid.*, 139-140.

1. On July 5 Congolese nationals in the Armee Nationale Congolaise (ANC) mutinied against Belgian "colonial masters."
2. On July 10, at the invitation of Tshombe, Belgian troops landed in Katanga and systematically began to disarm Congolese troops.
3. On July 11, Tshombe declared the "independence" of Katanga, thus seceding from the Republic of Congo.
4. On September 4, Kasavubu dismissed Lumumba as prime minister.

What was Lumumba's government response to these developments? What was the nature of the competing domestic power blocs vis-a-vis these developments? How did the opposing ideological power centres—Moscow and Washington—react to the crisis? Because of their strong linkages, an answer to one of these questions invariably has to deal with the others.

Robert Murphy led the U.S. delegation to the independence celebrations on June 30. One of those in the delegation was Clark Timberlake, U.S. ambassador-designate to the Congo. A 12-man Soviet delegation to the independence celebrations was led by Mirzo Rakhmatov, a vice president of the USSR Supreme Soviet. The inclusion of an ambassador-designate (USA) and a vice president (USSR) in the respective delegations of the two major powers indicated the significance of the Congo in the strategic planning of Washington and Moscow. It would be recalled that the U.S. had established contacts with prominent anti Lumumbists with the view of constructing an alliance hostile to communist interest in the Congo. It is interesting to note that, forty-eight hours before the proclamation of independence it was reported that the Soviet Union had made an offer of economic and technical aid to the Congo amidst speculations that Lumumba was contemplating establishing diplomatic relations with Moscow, Beijing, and other socialist states in order "not to be a stooge of the Western powers."[118] The subsequent Rakhmatov-Lumumba discussions resulted in the establishment of diplomatic relations between the Soviet Union and the Congo on July 8, and the Soviet delegation returned to Moscow on July 9, 1960.

However, prior to the departure of the Soviet delegation the Congo was thrown into political disarray as the ANC mutinied on July 5 against its Belgian officials, demanding the indigenization of the ANC. The mutiny was part of the *expectations* of independence as the mutineers perceived independence to mean an end of Belgian involvement in all aspects of governance, including the armed forces. Belgium immediately exploited the mutiny and alleged that Lumumba had brought in Soviet soldiers. Soviet delegates to the independence celebrations were humiliated and searched at the airport as their aircraft was suspected of carrying arms and soldiers to aid Lumumba and the ANC mutineers. The Council of Ministers, with Kasavubu in the chair, met on July 8 to discuss the mutiny. The decision to indigenize the ANC was unanimous and Joseph Mobutu, Lumumba's private secretary, was appointed Chief of Staff of the Army and immediately catapulted to the rank of colonel. According to the communiqué of the Council of Ministers:

> After soon discussion, the Head of State and members of the government have decided to give positions of command to Congolese soldiers, so as to create a national army directed and commanded by its own people . . . The Council of Ministers wants to make it clear that these reforms do not involve the dismissal of any Belgian commanders and officers prepared to serve the Congo loyally. The government guarantees them their income and security, and the safety of their families and goods. All that is asked of them is to work with the new regime

---

[118] See <u>Daily Telegraph</u>, June 28, 1960.

which is part of the natural working-out of Congolese independence.[119]

Though the communiqué was both moderate and conciliatory, yet it did not seem to satisfy the Belgian government which had decided to exploit the ANC mutiny in order to undermine the independence of the Congo. Belgium began to consolidate its stronghold in the province of Katanga. Declining to withdraw its troops from the Congo after June 30, the Belgian government systematically started to position its troops in the country. On Tshombe's invitation Belgium troops landed in Katanga on July 10 and began to disarm Congolese troops loyal to the central government of Lumumba. As a result of this development the central government sent a request for aid to the UNO on July 10, while Tshombe declared the "independence" of Katanga on July 11. Belgian and Western support for Tshombe, who had refused to place Katanga under the central government of Lumumba, encouraged him to disregard Lumumba, as the country gradually slipped into a series of riots and disorders. Belgian and Congolese troops were engaged in a military showdown. In a move to assess the crisis and assure Congolese of the central government's determination to restore law and order, as well as safeguard the territorial integrity of the Congo, Lumumba and Kasavubu toured the country and met with both political and military leaders. It is interesting to note that Belgian Ministers and U.S. ambassador Timberlake attended the Council of Ministers' meetings of July 11 and 12 which were chaired by Gizenga.[120] The participation of Belgian ministers and the U.S. ambassador in these deliberations was suspect as it demonstrated the extent to which the West had succeeded in penetrating into, and manipulating the government of the Congo.

Kasavubu and Lumumba dispatched a second telegramme to the UN requesting its intervention to oust Belgium from the Congo.

---

[119] Kanza, 141.
[120] *Ibid.*, 194 and 201.

They also sought military aid from Ghana on July 13, and appealed to both Moscow and Washington for assistance in persuading Belgium to withdraw from the Congo. Ghana accepted, but informed Belgium, and outlined its desire to work within the framework of an international body. The refusal of Belgium to withdraw, with the apparent endorsement of the West, provided an opportunity for the Soviet Government to condemn Western powers in the crisis as Moscow took measures to display its support for Lumumba. The Soviet Foreign Ministry summoned the Belgian ambassador to Moscow, J. Cools, and the U.S. *charge d'affaires*, E. L. Freers. The Soviets accused Belgium of "committing a flagrant violation both of the territorial integrity and of the political independence" of the Congo, while the U.S., through its NATO connection, was accused of supporting Belgium in the latter's design in the Congo. The Soviets alleged that Belgian troops under NATO command in the Federal Republic of Germany were deployed in the Congo as the Soviet Government appealed to the UN to halt western aggression in the "interest of peace" and to "restore the sovereign rights of the independent republic" of the Congo.[121] The Belgian Government argued it was intervening to fulfil "its sacred duties, imposed by law and morals, to protect its compatriots in extreme danger" since, in its opinion, Lumumba's government was unable "to stop or control" the disorders; while Bonn refuted Soviet allegation and accused Moscow of waging "ideological aggression" with the explicit purpose of making the Congo "one of its colonial satellites."[122] The arguments advanced by Belgium in justification of its aggression in the Congo indicated its disinclination to forfeit its imperial grip in the country. If its *reason* to intervene was purely to "protect its compatriots" it is instructive that the Belgian Government did not make any move to evacuate "its compatriots" from the Congo. This

---

[121] Soviet News, Embassy of the USSR, London, July 14, 1960. See also The New York Times, July 14, 1960.

[122] The New York Times, July 16, 1960.

tactic is normally employed by colonial powers to justify an inept policy.

The Katanga-Belgian alliance which was supported by the West paralyzed the efforts of Lumumba to govern the country. This seemed to compel the Congolese government to seek the assistance of non-western forces. Kasavubu's and Lumumba's joint appeal to the Soviet Government for aid to stop the aggression was accepted by Moscow, on the proviso that the aggressors "continue their criminal actions" in the Congo.[123] This was *after* Lumumba was "rebuffed by the Eisenhower administration" of the U.S.[124]

The UN Security Council resolution of July 14, 1960, requested Belgium to withdraw its forces from the Congo. It also authorized the Secretary-General, Dag Hammarskjoeld, "*in consultation* with the government of the Republic of the Congo to provide that government with such military assistance as may be necessary, with the technical assistance of the United Nations until the national security forces are able, in the *opinion of the government*, to meet fully their tasks."[125] The Security Council resolution made it explicitly clear that the intensity or level of UN involvement in the Congo was to be determined by the legitimate government of Lumumba that sought for UN military intervention. As part of the UN contingents General H. T. Alexander, a Briton and head of Ghana's armed forces, arrived in the Congo on July 14. It is ironical that Kwame Nkrumah, the leading African anti-colonial crusader should in 1960; three years after Ghana's independence, still have a Briton as head of his armed forces, a Briton who did not conceal his hostility toward African independence and the anti-colonial movement. While in the service of Ghana, General Alexander

---

[123] See Soviet News, Embassy of the USSR, London, July 18, 1960.
[124] See D. N. Chatterjee, Storm over the Congo, New Delhi, 1980, p.13.
[125] As cited in Kanza, 208. Italics mine.

contributed to the overthrow and the eventual assassination of Lumumba, Nkrumah's ally![126]

Kasavubu and Lumumba returned to Léopoldville from their cross country tour on July 15. Meanwhile, Ghana's General Alexander, who was the *de facto commander* of the UN contingent, had ordered the disarming of the mutinous ANC soldiers. The Congolese parliament was divided on its support for Lumumba. The Chamber of Representatives under Joseph Ileo was against Lumumba as the internal forces began to position themselves in the ensuing alliance formation.

On July 20 Lumumba flew to New York to personally appeal before the UN Security Council for Belgian troops to be withdrawn from his troubled country. He seemed to have had some faith in the UN peace keeping effort, but stipulated that the Secretary-General must evacuate the UN troops once his government was convinced that the situation was under its control in accordance to the Security Council resolution of July 14. The withdrawal of Belgian troops still remained the top priority of Lumumba's government. But the UN could not compel Belgium to adhere to the Security Council resolution, and neither was the West interested in Belgian withdrawal from the Congo.

Lumumba's appeal to the U.S. Government was also a failure, as Washington argued that its peace efforts were channelled through the UN. However, the U.S. did promise to render economic aid; but adopted a wait-and-see attitude and refused to condemn Tshombe's secession or Belgian policy. While the Soviet Government opposed the presence of U.S. troops in the UN operation, Lumumba remained pragmatic and hoped for the restoration of peace to the Congo. In a Washington Press Conference he reiterated his government's decision

---

[126] See Lumumba's letter to Nkrumah on this subject, in Kwame Nkrumah, <u>Challenge of the Congo</u>, London, 1967, p.39. See also W. Scott Thompson, <u>Ghana's Foreign Policy, 1957-1966. Diplomacy, Ideology, and the New State</u>, Princeton, New Jersey, 1969, pp.125-128, & 139.

to welcome "American troops" whose task, he had hoped, would be to compel Belgium to withdraw immediately from the Congo.

By the end of July 1960, it became evident that the UN forces were determined to defy Lumumba's government. While still in Washington, Lumumba received a cable from his deputy, Gizenga, informing him that the "United Nations troops were disarming Congolese and leaving the Belgians their arms",[127] and that the UN command's action was aiding Tshombe's rebellion. Hammarskjoeld and the West were criticized by Moscow and Africa's radical states—Ghana, Guinea, Mali, and Egypt. The crisis had polarized the international community along the East-West ideological divide. In August 1960, the Soviet Government despatched a plane to airlift Ghanaian troops to the Congo. This operation almost coincided with the arrival of Soviet Ambassador M. D. Yakovlev in Leopoldville.

Lumumba's discussion with Hammarskjoeld in New York was acrimonious. On his way from New York in August 1960, he visited Tunisia, Morocco, Liberia, Guinea, Ghana, and Togoland to drum up diplomatic support for his government. Sekou Toure promised that Guinean UN troops would be placed under the complete jurisdiction of his (Lumumba's) government. Though this was the type of encouragement the Congolese government had expected from other African states, it was clear that these states lacked the power to compel the withdrawal of Belgian troops from the Congo. The Lumumba-Nkrumah meeting of August 8 seemed to confirm Lumumba's political aspirations to defeat the Hammarskjoeld-Belgian-Tshombe triple alliance. Nkrumah called for the formation of an African High Command outside the UN to assist Lumumba. This was followed on August 10 by a Declaration of the Ghanaian Government to withdraw its troops from the UN command and place them in readiness to assist Lumumba. The gesture of Toure and Nkrumah appeared progressive but it lacked the power of implementation, while the pro-Western African states viewed it as a

---

[127] See <u>The Times</u>, London, and <u>The New York Times</u>, July 29, 1960.

hypocritical act by Guinea and Ghana to publicize their ideological stance in African politics. The conference of Independent African States which convened in Leopoldville to discuss the crisis had failed to reach unanimity as most African states, for obvious ideological reasons, reaffirmed their confidence in the UN command.

Towards the end of July 1960 it was clear to most perceptive analysts that the UN Secretary-General, Dag Hammarskjoeld, was piloting the UN Operation in the Congo to favour U.S. and Western interests. It was however odd that Thomas Kanza, Lumumba's Ambassador to the UN, failed to observe this, even though he had had several discussions on the Congo with Hammarskjoeld. He seemed to believe in Hammarskjoeld's *goodwill* in resolving the crisis. He accompanied Hammarskjoeld from New York to the Congo in late July. According to him, Hammarskjoeld stated that:

> I don't know what you think about the United States,
> but it seems to me right now that America is the only
> ally the central Congolese government can count on, the
> only one that sincerely supports what the UN is doing
> in the Congo.[128]

Why did Hammarskjoeld make the above statement? Why did Ambassador Kanza trust Hammarskjoeld, especially as there was no evidence to sustain Hammarskjoeld's allegation that the U.S. was "the only ally the central Congolese government can count on." What about France and Britain in the Security Council? What about the USSR? Why did the Soviet Government refuse to contribute its financial quota to maintain the UN Operation in the Congo? Was there an intra-capitalist rivalry that compelled both Paris and London to suspect Washington's calculations in the Congo? It should be recalled that Lumumba had failed to secure the support of the U.S. Government during his visit to New York and Washington, and that his discussion with Hammarskjoeld in New

---

[128] As cited in Kanza, 244.

York was acrimonious. That the Secretary-General of the UN would make such a statement was suggestive of an ulterior motive. These were vital questions which Kanza failed to answer, but to which the Indian Ambassador in Washington (and later in Leopoldville in 1962), D. N. Chatterjee addressed in his study.[129]

Frustrated by the U.S., and Hammarskjoeld's UN command, Lumumba became increasingly dependent on Soviet support. The failure or reluctance of the West to support the legitimate government of the Congo drove Lumumba into Moscow's embrace, just as a similar blunder by the West had driven Sekou Toure to Moscow. On August 15, 1960 the Soviet Government sent Lumumba an IL-4 plane, and on August 16 he declared he was assuming complete power to resolve the conflict without the UN troops. On August 18 the UN command reacted by putting under its control all radio stations and deprived Lumumba the use of these facilities. The conflict was no longer a conflict between Lumumba and Tshombe, but a conflict which Lumumba must grapple with on two fronts: against the UN command <u>and</u> against the Tshombe-Belgian alliance. Hammarskjoeld's interpretation of UN's role would seem to confirm his complicity in a design to undermine the government of Lumumba. For example, when P. D. Morozov, the Soviet deputy permanent representative in the UN confronted Hammarskjoeld on the presence of Belgian troops in the Congo, Hammarskjoeld responded that the UN had taken over the Belgian bases in Kamina and Kitona, but had asked the Belgians, who were occupying the bases, "to remain as part of the UN organization."[130] This act of Hammarskjoeld was a violation of the Security Council Resolution of July 14 that demanded the withdrawal of Belgian troops from the Congo. Hammarskjoeld's assimilation of Belgium into the UN military command was also an unfriendly act against the central government of the Congo as it gave credence to the allegation of a UN-Belgian conspiracy to overthrow Lumumba.

---

[129] See Chatterjee, *op.cit.*, pp.20-21, and 26.

[130] <u>New York Herald Tribune</u> (European Edition), September 2, 1960.

Meanwhile, Kasavubu and Lumumba were involved in a constitutional tussle that further aggravated the conflict. On September 3 Kasavubu announced he had dismissed Lumumba, even though he only had the required constitutional two signatories to do so on September 6. In a speech before parliament on September 7 Lumumba accused both Kasavubu and Hammarskjoeld of conspiracy to undermine Congo's legitimate government. It is interesting to note that the "Western pressure groups" condemned the parliamentary initiative to reconcile Kasavubu and Lumumba, while U.S. President Eisenhower accused "the Soviet Union rather than Belgium of causing anarchy in the Congo."[131] As a prelude to the overthrow of Lumumba, Kanza reported that Andrew Cordier, a U.S. citizen and Hammarskjoeld's assistant in the Congo, took effective control of the Congolese government.[132]

Hammarskjoeld's decision to place Belgium in command of the Kamina and Kitona bases in the secessionist province of Katanga raised the morale of Tshombe, and encouraged him to further defy the authority of the central government of Lumumba. It was no longer in doubt that the UN was in support of Tshombe. Barely a week after this decision the Soviet Government sent 15 IL-14 planes to Lumumba. The arrival of these planes, with the inscriptions **"Republique du Congo"**, underlined Lumumba's determination to extirpate Tshombe's secessionist regime in Katanga. To foil Lumumba's plans, Hammarskjoeld banned all non-UN planes, including those belonging to the Congolese government, from UN controlled airports and bases, not excluding the important Kamina base in Katanga. This decision strongly restricted the movement and actions of the legitimate government, and constituted a *de facto* recognition of the Tshombe regime in Katanga. Kasavubu appointed Joseph Ileo to replace Lumumba as premier on September 10.

Hammarskjoeld's decision to ban Lumumba's government from all radio stations and airports had two fundamentally pathetic

---

[131] Kanza, 301.

[132] *Ibid.*

consequences. First, it permitted Belgium to operate in the Congo, especially in the province of Katanga. Second, it was implemented by Ghana's UN troops! In his letter of September 11 to Nkrumah, Lumumba complained bitterly about the hostility of the Ghanaian troops headed by General Alexander that prevented him and his loyal soldiers from taking control of the radio stations. Lumumba lamented:

> In the circumstances, I feel obliged to renounce the help of your troops in view of the fact that they are in a state of war against our Republic. Instead of helping us in our difficulties, your soldiers are openly siding with the enemy to fight us.[133]

In his reply, Nkrumah regretted the use of Ghana's troops by the UN to "tie" down Lumumba. He made the following proposal to Lumumba:

> If Ghana's troops are to be placed completely at your disposal, then you and your government must find some way to declare that in this struggle Ghana and the Congo are one.[134]

This proposal by Nkrumah conflicted with the August 10 Declaration of the Ghanaian Government in which Ghana committed its troops to assist Lumumba. In another note to Lumumba on September 12, Nkrumah advised him to be tactful and less harsh in dealing with his opponents. He advised Lumumba to be "as cool as a cucumber" and adopt "tactical action" in his struggle to consolidate his forces to a position of strength before pushing out the enemies.[135] Nkrumah's advice to Lumumba in the

---

[133] Nkrumah, *op.cit.*, 39.

[134] *Ibid.*, 42.

[135] *Ibid.*, 43.

critical days of August and September was perhaps misguided, given the fact that the framework for implementing an anti-colonial stratagem he had in mind could not be sketched out at this time. In all likelihood, the "tactical action" Nkrumah was advocating in September could have yielded tangible results in early July, but not in September when Lumumba found himself completely trapped in a hostile encirclement. On September 13 the Congolese parliament passed a vote of confidence in Lumumba. Unfortunately, this act lacked the military might it required to keep Lumumba in power. The UN military command in the Congo was implicated in corrupt practices as it financed the Mobutu-led military coup that toppled Lumumba's government on September 14. Ambassador Chatterjee had this to say about money and politics: "In international affairs, it is no secret, money is a useful lubricant and widely employed by the cynic and the virtuous." Depending on the stakes and the quality of services rendered, a leader is either "bought" or "rented."[136] On September 14, 1960, Mobutu was *rented* by the West to perform its dirty work in the Congo.

The Soviet Government was in a predicament as it could not formulate any sustained policy to deal with the creeping Congo crisis. It is interesting to note that Moscow condemned Kasavubu for dismissing Lumumba, but when Mobutu ordered the Soviet Union and Czechoslovakia to close their embassies within 48 hours, the Soviet Government reversed its position arguing that its ambassador was accredited to Kasavubu and not to Mobutu! On September 16 Kasavubu formally signed a statement dismissing all Communist ambassadors and journalists from the Congo, and also authorized the closure of their missions. Soviet response was an attempt to undermine the significance of Kasavubu's statement. From its perspective, the expulsion of Soviet diplomats and the closure of its mission did not signify a severance of diplomatic relations between the Soviet Union and the Congo. In an official statement designed for domestic consumption, the Soviet Government maintained that

---

[136] Chatterjee, 9.

it had "decided to recall temporarily the staff of the Soviet Embassy" as a result of the political unrest and the "imperialist manoeuvre" which had made it "impossible for the Embassy of the USSR . . . to function normally." and that the decision to "withdraw temporarily" did not affect Soviet-Congolese relations as "the Soviet Union's attitude to the young African Republic . . . remains one of invariable friendship."[137]

The Soviet Government began to exercise extreme caution in its appraisal of the crisis. While it continued to blame the West for the closure of its embassy, and for the increasing anarchy in the Congo, it exhibited a firm determination to remain loyal to Lumumba in the hope that Congo's anti-western sentiments would eventually enhance Moscow's prestige in the country. It is difficult to establish whether the Soviet Government was convinced of Lumumba's success at this stage of the crisis. However, what seemed vital to Moscow was to align its actions with those of Ghana, Guinea, Mali, and Egypt, and the general wave of African anti-imperialism that was sweeping through the continent. Thus, the Soviet Government hoped that the Congo crisis would set the basis for its future ideological alliance with Africa's anti-colonial movement.

Viewed from the context of the East-West ideological struggle, the anti-Lumumba military coup *and* the expulsion of Soviet (and Communist states')diplomats signified a victory for the West in the Congo. Clarke Timberlake, the U.S. Ambassador, was alleged to have urged Mobutu to expel the Soviet diplomats and those of other Communist countries, and had insisted that a complete U.S. "victory" over the Soviet Union would be meaningful only when "the Lumumba question is settled once and for all". Was this a rationalization of U.S. involvement in the conspiracy to assassinate Patrice Lumumba? Timberlake's "victory" was regarded as U.S. "amends for the American fiasco of the U-2 flight" and a "breathing

---

[137] <u>Soviet News</u>, Embassy of the USSR, London, September 20, 1960.

space" for the West in the Congo.[138] The arrest of Lumumba and his colleagues, Okoto and M'polo, their torture and subsequent air-lifting as "three packages" to Tshombe's Katanga, where they were finally murdered and their bodies quickly disposed of, portrayed the complicity of the UN "peace-keeping" force as a tool of western imperial design. The West and Hammarskjoeld could not exonerate themselves from blame as the architects of the assassination of Lumumba. This prompted the Soviet Government to demand the replacement of Hammarskjoeld as UN secretary general. In his place Moscow proposed a *troika* system of a secretary-generalship: one each from the East, West, and the non-aligned bloc. This, and Moscow's other proposal that an African military command be commissioned to replace the UN in the Congo[139] failed to generate any sustained interest and support in the international community.

Meanwhile, political development in the Congo was gravitating towards a balkanization of the country: Lumumba's deputy, Gizenga had established a Lumumbist government in Stanleyville; Tshombe was still in control in Katanga; Cyrille Adoula had replaced Ileo in Leopoldville, while Kalonji had established a power base in Kasai province. The Soviet Union, China, Poland, Czechoslovakia, Yugoslavia, Ghana, and Guinea were represented by their respective charge d'affaires in Stanleyville, while Mali and Egypt had ambassadors also in Stanleyville. Belgium was firmly in control of Katanga with strong Anglo-French capital investment in the mines. Kalonji's regime was a mere protest symbol without super power encouragement or support, while Adoula was having difficulty managing Leopoldville. This was the relative strength of the respective alliance formation in the Congolese political chessboard following the assassination of Lumumba.

---

[138] See Donald Seaman, "This was the invisible victory," <u>Daily Express</u>, September 21, 1960.

[139] See <u>Soviet News</u>, Embassy of the USSR, London, January 21, 1961, and February 16, 1961.

Through a Sudanese corridor the Soviet Union and its allies began the shipment of security support systems to Gizenga's regime in Stanleyville. However, this was not enough to confront the combined forces of the West and Hammarskjoeld's UN command that were aiding Mobutu and Tshombe. For the West, especially for the U.S., its strategic concern was the obliteration of communist influence in the Congo as a prelude to a war against communism in Africa. This became a vital policy objective for Washington. It was obvious that an *overt* U.S. support for Tshombe would strengthen the pro Lumumbist forces in Stanleyville, neither was it considered viable to control Katanga and Kasai without Leopoldville. While U.S. policy was opposed to Tshombe in Katanga, it did not exclude Tshombe in a *united* Congo with zero communist influence and a *controlled* leverage of Belgian, French, and British capitalists dependent on Washington. Thus, in Washington's calculation, Lumumbists had to go, so also was secession; a stratagem which implied U.S. continued support for Mobutu and Kasavubu. Washington did not want a Congo without Katanga. Ambassador Chatterjee pointedly stated:

> America wanted a strong, not necessarily a democratic, government in Léopoldville. America did not want fabulously rich Katanga secede under Tshombe who was being financed, guided, and encouraged in his treasonable enterprise not merely by necessary adventurers but by respectable "western" allies of America.[140]

Meanwhile, Congolese political leaders were busy crafting a coalition government that they hoped would restore peace and stability to their country. In August 1961 such a government was formed with Adoula as premier, and Gizenga as deputy premier. This was hailed by Moscow as a progressive development and the Soviet Government took immediate measures to respond to it. In

---

[140]   Chatterjee, 20-21.

its statement of August 31 the Soviet Government argued that since Adoula was the successor of the "great patriot Lumumba", Moscow was prepared to maintain cordial relations with the new coalition government. In Moscow's view, the normalization of relations between Adoula and Gizenga meant the restoration of political stability in the Congo. As a result of this development all the pro Lumumba countries, excluding China, decided to "move" their embassies from Stanleyville to Leopoldville. The Chinese maintained that the murder of Lumumba and the collapse of Gizenga's regime had negated the concept of Beijing's diplomatic representation in the country, accusing the Soviet Union of betraying the cause of national liberation. The Soviets dismissed the Chinese position as a gross oversimplification and a failure to take proper cognisance of the necessity to exploit even the minutest opportunities available in the Congo. The Congolese crisis further intensified the Sino-Soviet schism as both communist states found themselves engaged in bitter rivalry to support in Africa.

The traumatic experience of September 1960 did not seem to deter Moscow from Congolese politics. The slain Patrice Lumumba became an international hero in the anti-colonial movement. Following Lumumba's assassination, African students at the Friendship University in Moscow persuaded Soviet authorities to ascribe the name of Lumumba to the institution in early 1961. To immortalize the name of Lumumba, the Soviet Government named the People's Friendship University, established on February 5, 1960 in Moscow, after Patrice Lumumba. It had been erroneously stated by Alexander Dallin that the university was established in 1960 *primarily* to train African students.[141] This was part of the general western misinformation strategy to denigrate the institution as a worthwhile centre of learning. It should be noted that the following number of students graduated from the University between June 1965 and June 1969:

[141] See Alexander Dallin, "The Soviet Union: Political Activity," in Brzezinski, ed., <u>Africa in the Communist World</u>, 22.

593 from Latin America including the Caribbean;
517 from Asia;
450 from Africa;
422 from the USSR; and
317 from Arab countries.[142]

Following the re-establishment of diplomatic relations in December 1961, the Soviet Government began to seek for a way to strengthen the pro-Lumumbist forces in the Adoula-Gizenga coalition government. In Moscow the coalition was regarded as a sort of "national front" that could be utilized to advance the anti-imperialist struggle. The concept of a *national front*, which was formulated in Moscow at the December 1960 meeting of 81 Communist and Workers Parties, envisaged the coming together of all anti-imperialist forces in the national liberation movement. It was calculated that the pro-Marxist elements in the *national front* would be able to use it as a stepping stone to acquiring political power through the systematic elimination of the anti-Marxist forces. However, the political alliance system in the Congo did not offer the Soviet Government any prospect of exploiting the *national front*. The U.S. and its allies still remained in full control of the Congo, as a result of which some Lumumbists were either compelled to escape to neighbouring countries or were politically interned in the country.

It was difficult for Moscow to operate successfully in the Congo, even under the Adoula-Gizenga coalition government. Toward the end of 1963 an alleged Soviet inspired "plot" to topple Adoula's regime was uncovered. Two Soviet diplomats, Boris Voronin and Yu. Miakotuykh were arrested and detained on their return from Brazzaville. They were accused of smuggling anti-government documents into the country, while Miakotuykh was alleged to have had discussions with Christopher Gbenge, a Lumumbist who fled

---

[142] See The Patrice Lumumba People's Friendship University for 10 Years, Moscow, 1970, pp.18-19.

to Brazzaville in September 1963. According to Premier Adoula, the documents revealed plans of the Lumumbists to overthrow his coalition government.[143] Both diplomats were expelled from the Congo, and Voronin was forced to board a Brussels bound plane without proper clothing and shoes. Adoula demanded the replacement of Soviet Ambassador S. S. Neimchina. The Kremlin's response to Adoula's action was symptomatic of Soviet disappointments in Africa in the early 1960s. While Soviet authorities mobilized foreign students in Moscow to protest against the pro-Western policies of Adoula, the official Soviet Government Note on the situation was rather mild and did not reflect the public mood in Moscow. In the Note, the Soviet Government condemned Adoula's action as "illegal and unfounded" but, because of the "deep sympathy and friendly disposition" of the Soviet Union toward the Congo, the Kremlin agreed to replace the expelled diplomats and promised that no retaliatory action would be taken against Congolese diplomats in Moscow.[144]

What was the political significance of the Soviet Note? It seemed to demonstrate the maturity of Soviet diplomacy borne out of historical experiences. The Soviet Government was aware that a retaliatory action could precipitate a rupture of diplomatic relations with the Congo. Moscow was determined to maintain its mission in the Congo, irrespective of the anti-Soviet policies of Adoula's government. This determination was based on the assumption that the Congolese people would grow to understand and appreciate Soviet Union's friendly policy toward *them*. A similar policy was pursued toward Egypt in the 1958-1961 period. Another factor that influenced the Soviet Union to remain in the Congo was China. The Soviets were aware that a severance of diplomatic relations with the

---

[143] For different versions of the incident, see Izvestia, November 20, 1963; The Times, London, November 21, and November 22, 1963; The New York Times, November 21, 1963.

[144] Soviet News, Embassy of the USSR, London, November 25, and November 29, 1963.

Congo would have confirmed the "correct political line" of Chinese non-recognition of the Adoula-Gizenga coalition government. Therefore, the motif of the Note was primarily an attempt to justify Soviet decision to stay in the Congo, at least temporarily until favourable objective conditions necessitated a contrary move.

The Congo crisis was still a major issue in international politics in 1964. The Soviet Union continued to condemn Belgian and U.S. policies in the Congo. Even U. Thant, who had replaced the deceased Hammarskjoeld as UN Secretary-General in 1961, was also accused of complicity in aiding Western powers in the Congo.[145] The OAU Resolution of September 1964 to explore peaceful means of solving the crisis was given wide publicity in the Soviet press, and the decision to bar Moise Tshombe from attending the OAU Conference of Heads of States and Governments in Cairo, in November 1964, was hailed as a victory of Africa's anti-imperialist struggle. In November 1964 the western powers launched a military intervention in support of their puppet regime and to safeguard their economic interests in the Congo. In a strange twist of irony, the Soviet Government demanded the closure of the Congolese embassy in Moscow on the basis of the Western military intervention, while the powers invo[146]lved—U.S., Britain, and Belgium—only had their embassies defaced by Soviet inspired demonstrators. African students in Moscow had demanded the closure of these embassies as a protest against the military intervention, an action which the Soviet Government was not prepared to undertake. G. Nyambani, the Congolese charge d'affaires, left Moscow on December 22, 1964. It is significant to note that only a handful of African diplomats visited him before his departure, but none was at the airport when he finally left the Soviet Union. The fact that British, U.S., and Belgian diplomats were at the airport increased Soviet *verbal* criticism of the West.

---

145   Pravda, September 4, 1964.
146   See The Times, London, December 23, 1964.

In analysing the Congo crisis, there is the temptation to blame Lumumba for lack of tact in dealing with Belgium and its allies. It should be made clear, however, that he displayed tact and willingness to cooperate hence his acceptance of the Belgian candidate, Kasavubu, as president of the Congo. As it turned out, this proved to be his waterloo. His belief in the UN was genuine; but the UN demonstrated itself as a tool of western imperialism by its subsequent actions in the Congo. The UN Operation in the Congo completely discredited the concept of a *peace-keeping force* as a mechanism for the peaceful resolution of conflicts. The UN *peace keeping force* in the Congo turned out to be a cover for western intervention and the elimination of Lumumba. Ambassador Chatterjee opined:

> As everyone knows, or should know, the great powers never "interfere"; they are however, frequently obliged to "intervene" for global good.[147]

The obligation to *intervene* in political conflicts is dictated by the dynamics of competing *class* interests. Thus, ideology as a principle of thought and action must be seen as the justifier of policies.

From Guinea to Ghana

In the 1960s Guinea and Ghana were the main Soviet allies in West Africa, and the governments of these countries seriously pursued anti-imperialist policies geared toward the realization of socialist objectives in Africa. Though the leaders, Admed Sekou Toure (Guinea) and Kwame Nkrumah (Ghana), did not permit the formation of communist parties in their respective countries, their political parties, the PDG (Guinea) and the CPP (Ghana) enjoyed close comradely relations with the CPSU. They considered themselves (African) Marxists.

---

[147] Chatterjee, 103.

The contrasting Anglo-French colonial policies made themselves clear in West Africa in the 1950s. While nationalist leaders in former British colonies were demanding independence, their counterparts in French colonies were negotiating with France on *fruitful* ways of cooperation between Paris and the colonies. It was obvious that the paternalistic policy of France manifested itself in the perception of most Africa nationalists in former French colonies. However, a dramatic development occurred in 1958 in West Africa as the French Government put forward its constitutional proposal on which the immediate political future of the colonies depended. France offered its colonies an "opportunity" to decide their future by either voting "yes" or "no" on the proposal which envisaged continued "partnership" between France and the colonies. Only Guinea voted "no", and was instantly declared independent on September 28, 1958. Sekou Toure, besides campaigning against President De Gaulle's constitution, gave Guineans the freedom they had long expected, and made Guinea a proud nation among other former colonies in West Africa. The independence vote signalled a *complete* break with France.

The Soviet Union was the first world power to establish diplomatic relations with Guinea on October 4, 1958. Moscow's first ambassador, P. I. Geresimov, arrived in Conakry on March 7, 1959, but was replaced by the Soviet Middle East expert, Ambassador D. O. Solod, on December 30, 1959. In Khrushchev's telegramme to Sekou Toure on October 5, 1958, the Soviet Government "gladly" recognized the Republic of Guinea and offered to give Guinea immediate economic and technical assistance. France's hostile attitude toward Guinea as a result of the independence vote was readily exploited by the Soviet Union which was in search of an ally in Africa, especially at a time when Moscow's political alliance with Iraq's Abdel Karim Kassim was causing serious frictions in Soviet-Egyptian relations.

It is significant to note that Sekou Toure did not display any noticeable enthusiasm over Kremlin's recognition. He delayed the publication of the Soviet Note, and was awaiting French recognition as he "did not want to appear to be playing a game of international blackmail."[148] De Gaulle considered Guinean independence a personal defeat; and France was not prepared to recognize Toure's government, instead France engineered an anti-Guinean campaign in Western Europe as well as in its African colonies. Felix Houphouet-Boigny of Ivory Coast was very instrumental in the French campaign against Guinea and he obstructed any sign of a rapprochement between Paris and Conakry. Irrespective of this development, Guinea was willing to maintain an *association* with France and also to remain in the Franc zone. Faraban Camara, Toure's aide and Secretary for France, pointedly underscored the consequences of French and Western powers' anti-Guinean policies: "If Guinea becomes the door to Africa for the Soviets, it will be the fault of Europe."[149] This was a strong indication of Sekou Toure's desire to cooperate with France and the West, as it equally demonstrated his dilemma in deciding what to do with the Soviet Union. This dilemma was a reflection of Toure's ideological bewilderment. He was a strong anti-colonialist who seemed to prefer working within the framework of western democratic institutions irrespective of his socialist tendencies. He was not a *socialist* in the Soviet sense, but a *democratic socialist* in the tradition of West European political philosophy. Thus, when he eventually walked into Khrushchev's embrace it was not because of any initial ideological commitment, but rather because of his rejection by the West. Naturally, this was a welcome development in the Kremlin as the Soviet Union was compelled to accelerate its activities in emerging African states following the Sino-Soviet schism in Algeria in 1958. In March 1960 Guinea decided to quit the Franc zone.

France succeeded in isolating Guinea from other French-speaking West African states. In late 1958 Toure visited Accra and Monrovia

---

148 Thomas F. Brady, "Guinea awaiting move by France," The New York Times, October 7, 1958. For a detailed analysis, see Ruth S. Morgenthau, Political Parties in French-Speaking West Africa, London, 1964.

149 Brady, loc.cit.

in search of allies and aid. He tried, but failed, to obtain U.S. aid by using President William Tubman of Liberia as a go-between. De Gaulle had pressurized Washington and other western nations to reject Guinea's plea for economic assistance. However, Toure's trips to Accra proved to be a success. Both he and Nkrumah needed allies. Nkrumah was setting the stage for his maladaptive anti-colonial policies in Africa as was reflected by the tone of the two conferences he had hosted in 1958. It was therefore expedient for him to appreciate Toure's independence vote against France. He regarded the Guinean leader as a potential ally in his anti-colonial stratagem. During Toure's visit to Accra in November 1958, he and Nkrumah agreed to establish a Ghana-Guinea Union; and Guinea got a Ghanaian loan in the tune of $28 million. A political union of West African states had long been the aspiration of Nkrumah dating back to his activities at the 5th Pan-African Congress in Manchester, England. Toure, on the other hand, was not known to have expressed such a desire prior to his Accra visit. Given that his trips to Monrovia and Accra were undertaken purely to secure economic assistance, and not to enter into a political union, it would be safe to postulate that his acceptance of Nkrumah's Ghana-Guinea Union proposal was a *quid pro quo* for obtaining the Ghanaian loan. When the Mali Federation was dissolved in 1960, the Republic of Mali joined Ghana and Guinea to form the Union of African States (Ghana-Guinea-Mali) in Accra in April 1961.[150]

Following the independence vote of 1958 Guinea gradually began to occupy a prominent position in Soviet African policy. The Soviet Government seized the opportunity created by the West's ostracization of Guinea. The Soviet-Guinean economic and technical agreements signed in 1959 provided for the construction of roads, rails, mining and the building of a technical college. A huge stadium, like the Soviet-built stadium in Djakarta, Indonesia, was also a part of Soviet aid to Guinea. The Soviets spent over

---

[150] The last meeting of the Union took place in June 1961 in Bamako, Mali.

$100 million in the process. The huge Soviet aid accorded Guinea between 1959 and 1961 demonstrated the significance of Guinea in Soviet African policy. Though Guineans questioned the quality of Soviet goods, the vacuum they filled was of considerable economic benefit for Guinea, especially after the West had abandoned Guinea. Soviet-Guinean cooperation reached its peak in 1960 as both countries exhibited a high degree of policy congruity on major issues of international politics, especially on the Congo crisis, notwithstanding the fact that Sekou Toure consistently maintained that Guinea was non-committal in the East-West ideological conflict. He defined Guinea's policy as *positive neutralism* which was conceptualized as the freedom to condemn the aggressive policy of *any nation.*

The initial conformity of ideas and policies between Conakry and Moscow caused grave concern in the West. It was feared in the West that the Soviets would use Guinea as a springboard to spread Marxist ideology across West Africa. The close cooperation between both parties during the Congo crisis in 1960-1961 underlined their growing ideological alliance. Sekou Toure's state visit to Moscow, September 6, 1960, coincided with the deterioration of the Congo crisis. He arrived in Moscow barely twenty-four hours after Kasavubu had dismissed Lumumba as premier in the Congo. The subsequent Soviet-Guinean communiqué of September 10, 1960, underlined the commitments of both parties in their support for Lumumba. Both countries joined in the condemnation of Western "imperialist aggression" in Africa at the UN General Assembly. During his Moscow visit, the Soviet Government awarded Sekou Toure the *Order of Lenin*, Soviet Union's highest award, in recognition of his role in the international struggle for peace. This gesture did not only portray Toure as a "champion of the African revolution", but was also intended to remind President Nasser that there was *a* reliable Soviet ally in Africa other than Egypt. Soviet-Egyptian relations were in limbo in between 1958 and 1961, and Moscow needed to strengthen its ties with a promising radical leader like Sekou Toure in order to compensate for the setbacks it was experiencing in both Egypt and the Congo. Soviet alliance with Lumumba was in jeopardy as the dismissal, arrest and the subsequent assassination of Lumumba seriously fractured Soviet policy in the Congo.

Before his departure from Moscow, Sekou Toure invited the President of the Supreme Soviet of the USSR, Leonid Brezhnev, to visit Guinea in early February 1961. Brezhnev would be visiting Guinea two months after the UN Declaration of December 14, 1960, which had posited the Soviet Union as *the* champion of the anti-colonial struggle. The invitation was regarded as a political gain for the Soviet Union. It was the first visit by a Soviet Head of State to Africa. The choice of Guinea symbolized its significance in Soviet African policy, given the increasing political affinity between Conakry and Moscow. The wide publicity accorded the visit in the Soviet press, and the booklet (Sovetskii Soiuz—iskrennii drug narodov Afriki) later published about it, clearly demonstrated Soviet optimism during this period.

Brezhnev's first stop in Africa was at Rabat where he had talks with King Muhammed V of Morocco on February 9-10, 1961. En route to Rabat, France inadvertently *drew* the Soviet Union into its conflict with Algeria as French military planes attacked Brezhnev's official plane as he was flying over northern Algeria. This incidence was very well utilized by the Soviet Union to further discredit French war against Algeria. The Soviet Government condemned the attack as an "act of international banditry" and demanded that the "criminals" be punished.[151] France expressed its "regrets", but maintained that the Soviet plane had flown off the designated course previously agreed upon by Moscow and Paris. The Soviets dismissed the French argument as "malicious lies devoid of any foundation."[152] We have no way of ascertaining whether Brezhnev's plane actually flew off the designated course. But if the French position is correct, it would suggest that the Soviet Union *deliberately* lured the French military planes in order to provoke a crisis that would enhance Moscow's prestige in Africa's anti-colonial movement. However, it

---

[151] Izvestia, February 10, 1961; Pravda, February 11, 1961.
[152] Izvestia, February 11, 1961.

was clear that France had unwittingly played into Soviet anti-western policy. This undoubtedly lent credence to Moscow's accusation of western "aggression", given that it occurred nine months after the U.S. spy plane piloted by Gary Powers was shot down in Soviet territory on May 1, 1960. Thus, France's "banditry" action helped to enhance the ideological linkage between Moscow's *peace policy* and Africa's anti colonialism, as well as popularized Brezhnev's name in Africa. Leonid Brezhnev, who was relatively unknown in Africa, received a hero's welcome in Rabat, Conakry, and Accra, where he was warmly received as a *victim* of French "aggression."

President Sekou Toure underlined this point when he welcomed Brezhnev to Guinea on February 11, 1961:

> Your presence in Guinea is the realization of your government's principles in foreign policy which have made the USSR a constant and persistent defender of our human rights and a natural ally of all oppressed peoples.[153]

In his response Brezhnev assured Toure that the Soviet Government would continue its economic and political cooperation with Guinea, and declared that the "Soviet-Guinean friendship is based on the identity of views on questions concerning the struggle against colonialism" and other related problems in international politics.[154] In their joint communiqué both parties condemned Dag Hammarskjoeld, the UN Secretary-General, the NATO powers, and expressed their support for the regime of Antoine Gizenga in the Congo.[155] Brezhnev was awarded the Guinean *Order of the*

---

[153] Sovetskii Soiuz - iskrennii drug narodov Afriki, Moscow, 1961, p.49.
[154] Ibid., 57-67.
[155] For the full text of the Soviet-Guinea Joint Communiqué, see Soviet News, Embassy of the USSR, London, February 18, 1961.

Fighter for Independence in recognition of Soviet support for Africa's anti-colonial struggle.

However, Soviet expectation of ideological inroads began to wither away gradually as the Kremlin encountered some fundamental problems in its African policy. The Soviet Government had embraced and supported Africa's anti-colonialism as a strategic manoeuvre for the advancement of Marxism in Africa, but the Soviet concept of *political cooperation* was not appreciated by many African nationalist leaders. Egypt was challenging the Soviet Union over this issue, just as the Congo had proved elusive. If Moscow had failed to comprehend Arab nationalism, as manifested in the Soviet-Egyptian conflict, it had also underestimated the political problematique of African states south of the Sahara as was exemplified in both the Congo and Guinea.

Soviet-Guinean *friendship* which was the theme of Brezhnev's speech in Conakry began to dwindle in late 1961 in the wake of political unrest in Guinea. Sekou Toure's positive neutralism came under increasing attack by the left wing of Guinean politics. The Guinean National Union of Teachers had staged a demonstration against this policy arguing that it was impossible for a country to be neutral in East-West conflict. The union demanded a swing to the left that would put Guinea squarely within the Soviet orbit. At a conference of the Guinean Trade Union Federation (CNGT) on November 16, 1961, a pro-Marxist memorandum was distributed challenging Toure's policies. The ensuing demonstration caused the government of Sekou Toure grave political concern. The report of a Government Commission of Inquiry blamed "an embassy of Eastern Europe" for instigating and financing the anti-Toure demonstration. Following Toure's meeting with the heads of East European diplomatic missions on December 16, 1961, Soviet Ambassador D.S. Solod was declared *persona non grata* and expelled from Guinea. The expulsion of Ambassador Solod, one of Moscow's most experienced diplomats, was an embarrassment to the Soviet Union, particularly as the expulsion was ordered by the government of a friendly country. It occurred exactly one year after the Moscow meeting of Communist and Workers' parties which had advanced the concept of a *state of national democracy*. Since December 1960 the Soviet Union had been referring to Guinea as a *state of national democracy* pursuing the *non-capitalist path of development*. When Guinean students in Moscow demonstrated against the expulsion of Ambassador Solod, President Toure threatened to withdraw them and stop the influx of Guinean students to the Soviet Union.

While *Radio Conakry* claimed that Ambassador Solod was expelled in connection with the left-wing demonstrations in Guinea, the Guinean ambassador in Paris denied the linkage and stated that Solod's exit was for "personal reasons."[156] It was difficult to ascertain the reasons for these contradictory statements. It reflected some conflict over the issue within the Guinean cabinet indicating, perhaps, that a section was still interested in maintaining friendly relations with the Soviet Union. However, while Guinean leaders appeared reluctant to link the expulsion with the pro-Marxist demonstrations, it was rather odd that *Radio Conakry* maintained its position that the Soviet Union was the outside "organizer" of the demonstrations. Nevertheless, the "expulsion" or "exit" of Solod was a serious setback for Soviet policy in Africa. It caused the Soviet Government more embarrassment than Moscow's experience in the Congo in September 1960.

The oddity of the Solod affair is not that it took place, but rather that it was generally assumed that it was organized by the Soviet Union. This assumption raises a number of fundamental questions to which we may not necessarily have the answers. Did the Soviet Union really organize the demonstrations? Is it possible that the demonstrations were organized by a western power as a means to implicate the Soviet Union in order to discredit its relations with Guinea? We live in a complicated world of political intrigue and deliberate misinformation. The *cold war* was a *hot war* in the 1960s

---

[156] Daily Telegraph, December 20, 1961; The Times, London, December 21, 1961. See also Colin Legum, "Soviet Setback in Africa," O.F.N.S, no. 17635, December 22, 1961. (O.F.N.S. stands for Observer Foreign News Service).

and the main protagonists, Moscow and Washington, did not exclude the use of all *means necessary* to tarnish the reputation of the other camp. The financing of demonstrations was one way of doing so. But if our speculation is off target; and the Soviet Union actually masterminded the demonstrations, we can only conclude that it was an inept policy initiative at a critical time when the Soviet Union was just recovering from its setbacks in both Egypt and the Congo. The experiences of the Egyptian and the Congo crises should have dictated the pursuance of a cautious policy, and not a policy of self-inflicted wounds which the Solod affair surely represented. The Soviet Union was now in hunt for another African ally. It began to shift its preference from Guinea to Ghana.

The independence of Ghana (the former Gold Coast) on March 6, 1957, was the most significant event of the year in Africa. Ghana was the first African state south of the Sahara to attain political independence in the 20th century. The event did not receive much attention in Moscow as the Soviet Government delegation to the independence celebrations was led by I. A. Benediktov, a junior official in the Ministry of Agriculture, while the U.S. delegation was led by vice president Richard Nixon. Nkrumah and Benediktov "unofficially" agreed to the establishment of diplomatic relations between Ghana and the Soviet Union, but the implementation of this intent was delayed by the Ghanaian Government. It appeared that Ghana was not in a hurry to establish diplomatic relations with the Soviet Union, given the cool reception that was accorded Dmitri F. Safonov, the first secretary at the Soviet Embassy in London, who arrived in Accra in November 1957 to discuss the issue with the Ghanaian government.

Both Moscow and Accra seemed to have reasons to be cautious in the early days of Ghana's independence. While Nkrumah's declaration on March 6 that Ghana's independence was meaningless without the complete liberation of Africa was considered a *threat* to western imperial holdings in Africa, it is significant to note that the Soviet Union did not seem to display any enthusiasm. Soviet nonchalant attitude could be explained by the presence of George Padmore and British expatriates in Nkrumah's government, especially in the foreign ministry.[157] The Soviets were particularly uneasy in dealing with Nkrumah, given the prominent role which Padmore occupied in the formative stage of Ghana's political development. They recalled his break with Soviet Marxism and harsh condemnation of the Nazi-Soviet Pact of 1939, which Padmore categorized as an *imperialist* pact. Since then Padmore had devoted his time to developing a *Pan-Africanist socialism*. Besides the presence of Padmore, it was obvious that the Soviet Government was still having some ideological problems in dealing with Nkrumah, an African *bourgeois nationalist,* twelve months after the 20th CPSU Congress when the Soviet Union had supposedly made peace with bourgeois nationalism. The Soviets perhaps could not reconcile Nkrumah's anti-colonialism with his expressed faith in Britain and the British Commonwealth, an institution which the Soviet Union regarded as a vehicle of British imperialism. Soviet scholars, especially Potekhin, the doyen of Soviet Africanists and the leading expert on Ghana, were yet to articulate a conceptual base for dealing with Ghana. Potekhin's earlier evaluation of the CPP as an "agent" of British imperialism was still prevalent in the Kremlin.

Throughout 1957 Ghana remained politically isolated in West Africa. Nkrumah's crusade for African independence was to wait another year before securing an ally in the sub-region—Guinea. On independence day Nkrumah had declared his intention to host Africa's first conference of independent states as a vehicle to push for the total decolonization of the continent. Padmore's organizational skills acquired during his activities with the Comintern and the Pan-African Movement were valuable assets to Nkrumah in this enterprise.

The first Afro-Asian Conference in Cairo (1957) and the first Conference of Independent African States (CIAS) in Accra (1958) were events of major concern to the West and the white racist regimes

---

[157] See Robert Legvold, pp.40-45. For further analysis, see Dennis Austin, Politics in Ghana, 1949-1960, London, 1964; David E. Apter, Ghana in Transition, Princeton, New Jersey, 1972.

of southern Africa. Unlike the Bandung Conference of 1955, the Soviet Union was represented at both conferences in Africa. The Western powers, particularly Britain, felt threaten by the seemingly penetration of Africa by Moscow. In London, Nkrumah's loyalty to the British crown was considered hypocritical. The racist regimes and West European colonial powers were searching for strategies to protect their imperial holdings in Africa. In 1956 the South African government closed down the Soviet Consulate because of Moscow's support for the anti-apartheid movement. The presence of an East European in Africa, especially a Soviet official, was always regarded by the South African racist regime as a threat to "democracy." According to the South African High Commissioner in Salisbury (now Harare), R. Kirsten, Africa was "the only base from which a counter attack could be launched" against the communists after the latter's victory in Europe. He cautioned the West to be "exceptionally careful and take all possible steps to prevent the Communists from becoming established even slightly in Africa."[158] The South African racists sought an alliance with European colonialists with "territories in Africa" to "drive out any Communist influence."[159] An apologist of colonialism, Henry C. Wolfe, cried out:

> Moscow is expertly manipulating its Egyptian and Syrian puppets and waging a subtle, elusive, and destructive campaign to win the Middle East and Africa. The West's most effective counter-strategy would be to close ranks. In the face of this Soviet menace the free nations can no longer afford the luxury of rivalries and conflicting policies. The stake is survival.[160]

---

[158] "Africa is last base for West," The Sunday Mail, Salisbury, Rhodesia, April 7, 1957.

[159] Johannesburg Star, April 29, 1957.

[160] Henry C. Wolfe, "The importance of Africa," New York Herald Tribune, (European Edition), May 31, 1957.

In an editorial captioned "The Red Light from the North", the Johannesburg Star of January 6, 1958, underlined the importance of the Afro-Asian Conference in Cairo by recognizing that the delegates, including the "unofficial delegates" from South Africa, had resolved to liberate Africa from colonial bondage and racist regimes. It called on "the two white races" in southern Africa to unite and "form a single nation with common ideals" to halt the African independent movement. While South African racist political leaders were arguing that the Cairo Conference had transformed Egypt into a Soviet "bridgehead in Africa" and proposed that South Africa be utilized as a counter "bridgehead of the West"[161], Mr. Erasmus, then South African Defence Minister, was appealing to the West to "exchange atomic secrets" and unite with the South African apartheid regime to curb "the latest Russian advances in Africa."[162] The concern of both the West and the South African racist regime in attempting to "curb" Soviet cooperation with Africa's anti-colonial forces represented the debility of western imperialism in the face of the new phenomenon which was helping to accelerate the tempo of political awareness among Africans.

The CIAS in Accra, April 15-22, 1958, was an important event that underscored this growing awareness.[163] As the CIAS was in progress, Roy Welensky, Prime Minister of the colonial Federation of Rhodesia and Nyasaland, pleaded with the

> Great Powers of the West, to the NATO powers and to countries with a stake in Africa to stand together and work together to reject by every possible means the threat of ultimate subjection by the dictatorship of the Kremlin.

---

[161] Johannesburg Star, January 8, 1958.

[162] Ibid., January 18, 1958.

[163] For the Declaration and Resolutions of the Accra Conference, see Nezavisimaia Afrika v dokumentakh, edited by R. A. Tusmukhamedov, Moscow, 1965, pp.13-21.

He lamented that the racist regimes in southern Africa and their Western allies "lack a Pan-African and dynamic approach . . ."[164] as the Accra conference had demonstrated. While the CIAS had caused the racists of southern Africa to panic, it did not, however, receive favourable comments in the Soviet press.

The question of establishing diplomatic relations between the Soviet Union and Ghana had not yet been resolved. Nkrumah's delay in resolving this issue was confusing to the Soviets since Nkrumah was now supposed to be building an anti-imperialist image in the international community. The bilateral talks on this issue were held in London by the Soviet Ambassador, Ia. A. Malik, and Ghana's acting High Commissioner, J. E. Jantuah. On January 14, 1958, the Ghanaian Government announced the decision of both countries to establish diplomatic relations at the ambassadorial level. It was envisaged in Moscow that the Soviet ambassador would arrive in Accra *before* the CIAS or, at the latest, well in time for the first All-African People's Conference (AAPC) which was scheduled to open in Accra in December 1958. Ghana did not display any interest over Moscow's enthusiasm to open its Accra embassy before any of the 1958 conferences. M. D. Sytenko, the first Soviet Ambassador to Ghana, only arrived in Accra in August 1959.

The Soviet Government sent a small delegation to the AAPC in December 1958. Moscow was not pleased with Nkrumah's neutralist posture at the conference. In his address to the delegates, Nkrumah declared:

> Some of us, I think, need reminding that Africa is a continent on its own. It is not an extension of Europe or any other continent. The liberation of Africa is the task of the Africans. We Africans alone can emancipate ourselves.[165]

---

[164] Roy Welensky, interview in <u>Johannesburg Star</u>, April 19, 1958.
[165] See Legvold, 55.

Nkrumah sought to emphasize, and also to protect, the independence of Africa. He did not want a *new scramble* for Africa by competing ideological powers. This was a noble ideal, but an ideal that failed to develop a clearly defined ideological position around which Africans were to attain and safeguard their independence. In concrete terms, the thesis of Nkrumah suggests a rejection of any linkage between the task of liberating Africa and the assistance of non-African anti-colonial forces in the liberation process. Can Africans *alone* emancipate themselves? Nkrumah was to contradict himself three years later in a Kremlin speech.

However, while the seemingly independent political line initiated by Nkrumah at the AAPC did not receive Moscow's endorsement[166], it was enough to upset the racist regimes of southern Africa. It appeared that, for example, both Moscow and Salisbury were disappointed over the AAPC, obviously for different reasons. In February 1959 the Nyasa African Congress (NAC) organized a demonstration demanding the dissolution of the federation and the independence of Nyasaland (now Malawi). Many demonstrators were killed in a combat with the police. Roy Welensky blamed the AAPC:

> I want to go on record as saying that the Accra Conference was attended by a number of African leaders from the Rhodesias and Nyasaland. The public ought to know that at the Accra Conference the Russians had a strong team . . . We have if from factual evidence that direct contact was made between Russian representatives and certain of the African leaders from the Federation.[167]

Following the 1958 Accra conferences Ghana began to ally with the Soviet position on major international issues, irrespective

---

[166] Ibid.,54-56, citing Ivan Potekhin who attended the Accra conference.

[167] The Guardian, March 11, 1959.

of the fact that the Israeli Ambassador in Accra, Ehud Avriel, had tremendous influence on Nkrumah and was able to establish a network of senior Ghanaian leaders in a pro-Israeli camp.[168] Nkrumah's alliance with Sekou Toure and Ghana's membership in the Casablanca bloc compelled the Soviet Union to begin to view Ghana as a serious ally in the international arena. Soviet-Ghanaian cooperation became evident in 1960-1961 as both parties condemned the West and sought to press other African states to form a counter-attack against the West in the Congo. Convinced that Nkrumah had tilted towards its side in the East-West cold war, the Soviet Government decided to invite him to Moscow in July 1961.

Nkrumah arrived in Moscow on July 10 leading a 50-man delegation. In his welcome address Nikita Khrushchev underscored a truism that had contributed to the demise of major international organizations:

> But it is perfectly obvious that the domination of this
> or that group of states in an international organization
> prevents the organization from being able to fulfil its
> functions.[169]

Khrushchev was obviously referring to the UN whose activities he and Nkrumah believed were dominated by the West and hence the debacle in the Congo. The UN was an arena of intense ideological battle between Moscow and Washington as the two power centres sought to establish and maintain their respective spheres of influence in global politics. The Soviets would have preferred to *dominate* the UN in place of the U.S. and its Western allies. Both Khrushchev and Nkrumah did not appreciate the domination of

---

[168] See Thompson, <u>Ghana's Foreign Policy</u>, 46-51; 285-287.

[169] For the full text of the speeches of Nikita Khrushchev and Kwame Nkrumah, see <u>Soviet News</u>, Embassy of the USSR, London, July 31, 1961.

western imperialism as the West sought to maintain its positions, and curtail Soviet penetration in Africa.

In his response to Khrushchev, Nkrumah referred to the Soviet Union as "a champion of the African cause and a true friend of the oppressed people of the world."[170] He opined:

> If it were not for the Soviet Union, the independence movement from colonial yoke in Africa would have experienced the full force of brutal repression.[171]

Nkrumah's declaration in the Kremlin was of immense significance for Soviet policy in Africa as it lent credence to Moscow's general political line that the national liberation movements of Africa, Asia and Latin America would not have grown to be "anti-colonial" were it not for the Soviet Union.[172] His Kremlin speech was widely publicized and published in Soviet writings on Africa. It should be recalled that at the AAPC in December 1958, Nkrumah had warned non-African states, including the Soviet Union, not to meddle in African affairs. His Kremlin speech indicated to what extent he had shifted grounds since 1958, a shift which was perhaps accelerated by the neo-colonial policies of the U.S. and its allies in Africa. Nkrumah saw in the Soviet Union a prototype of a new Africa. He commended the union of different nationalities "in one big country"—the USSR—and stated that there existed a far more "compelling necessity" for a similar union of African states.[173] Moscow and Accra had recognized a basis for cooperation, as Ghana joined Guinea in a Soviet-African alliance.

While the Soviet Union and Ghana had found a basis for comradely relations, Moscow was experiencing difficulties in pacifying Guinea over the Solod affair of December 1961. In its quest

---

[170]   Ibid.

[171]   SSSR in strany Afriki, 1946-1962 gg., vol. 2, p.360.

[172]   See Vneshniaia politika SSSR, Moscow, 1968. Note chapter 4.

[173]   See Daily Express, July 25, 1961.

for ways to ameliorate Soviet-Guinean relations Anastas Mikoyan, then Soviet first deputy Premier was despatched to Conakry, on a visit which Moscow had announced was at the "friendly invitation" of Sekou Toure. However, Sekou Toure was not at the airport to welcome him when he arrived in Conakry on January 4, 1962. He received Mikoyan on January 6 only to inform him that Guinea "refuses to be drawn into choosing sides in a power struggle between blocs." The Solod affair was discussed, and most probably Mikoyan had pleaded for Solod's return to Conakry. Mikoyan's trip did not yield the expected result: Solod did not return to Conakry. His return would have exonerated the Soviet Government from complicity in the anti-Toure demonstrations of 1961. Mikoyan was in Guinea at a time of growing public disenchantment over Soviet aid. Soviet products were considered unsuitable for the climate and said to be of an inferior quality.[174] The public disenchantment became noticeable in early 1961 and had reached its peak at about the time of Solod's expulsion. The reception accorded Mikoyan was less than friendly and he was rather an embarrassed guest of Sekou Toure, as a result of which his stay in Guinea was not reported with any enthusiasm by the Soviet press as was the case during Brezhnev's visit of February 1961.

Mikoyan's itinerary included Ghana and Mali where he hoped to achieve better results in Soviet-African cooperation. Nkrumah had emerged as a strong Soviet ally, and Soviet-Ghanaian relations had grown increasingly warmer since 1960. British advisers, whose presence in Accra constituted a major source of irritant for the Soviets, had left Ghana, and Nkrumah had reflected Soviet positions in international politics. Brezhnev's visit to Ghana in early 1961 had set the tone for friendly relations between the two countries. When Mikoyan arrived in Accra on January 10, 1962, he was accorded a warm reception befitting the head of state of a friendly nation, even though he was only a deputy premier of the Soviet Union. Mikoyan did not hesitate to publicize the gradual shifting of Soviet priorities

---

[174] See Legvold, 123-124.

from Guinea to Ghana. He upgraded Ghana and the CPP far beyond expectations, perhaps in a move to indicate to Sekou Toure Moscow's disappointment over the deterioration of Soviet-Guinean relations. In his first statement in Accra, Mikoyan declared:

> Ghana, under the leadership of the Convention People's Party, had made great progress in building socialism.[175]

While Guinea was merely pursuing a policy of *non-capitalist development*, Mikoyan's declaration implied that Ghana had already overtaken Guinea by making "great progress in building socialism." However, since the "building of socialism" in Ghana did not feature in Soviet political journals and newspapers after Mikoyan's visit to Accra, we can postulate that Soviet ideologists recognized the statement as an ideological blunder committed in order to publicly downgrade Guinea. Ghana was thereafter referred to as a *progressive anti-imperialist* state in the forefront of the African revolution. The list of African states in this avant-garde club included Guinea, Mali, Algeria, Egypt, Congo (Brazzaville), and Tanzania.

As we have demonstrated in the preceding pages of this chapter, the Khrushchevian era of Soviet policy encountered a number of problems caused by a variety of factors. Soviet response to these problems vividly illustrated a conflict in *ideology* and *policy*. The ideological construct of Soviet Marxism was very explicit in its objectives and goals, but the *policy* formulated to attain these objectives-goals ran counter to the theoretical tenets of the *ideology*. For example, before a state can be said to be *building socialism* such a state must have completely restructured its economic basis to reflect the postulates of Marxism. Nkrumah's Ghana did not reflect these, yet Mikoyan declared that Ghana was "building socialism." Though Nkrumah was a *progressive* anti-colonial leader, it must however be recognized that the CPP was not a Marxist, but a social democratic party. Secondly, Khrushchev's speech regarding the demise of

---

[175] <u>Soviet News</u>, Embassy of the USSR, London, January 15, 1962.

international organizations because of the struggle of "this and that group of states" to dominate, suggests an ambivalence in policy. It demonstrated an attempt to withdraw from the responsibilities imposed by Soviet Marxism.

The Soviets had hoped that African bourgeois nationalist parties, e.g., the ASU (Egypt) and the PDG (Guinea), could transform their respective societies into socialism via the parliamentary path. This explained Moscow's support for these parties, and also demonstrated the nature of the problems encountered with them in the 1958-1962 period when the leaders of these parties rejected Soviet overtures. The crises that ensued grew out of Moscow's over expectation. In the post 1962 period, Moscow became more cautious in its African policy, but still related to these parties on comradely and fraternal basis.

Under Khrushchev the Soviet Government took bold steps to recognize, and cooperate with African *nationalists* in their anti-colonial struggle. Ironically, this cooperation did not enhance the position of Marxism in Africa, but led to the outlawing of Marxist parties in all such countries. While cooperation with African nationalist parties was a wise tactical move, the elevation of these parties to the status of comradely and fraternal relationship with the CPSU, as witnessed by their attendance at CPSU congresses since 1956, raised a fundamental problem for Marxism in Africa. It seemed to legitimize the outlawing of Marxist parties.

ATTENDANCE OF AFRICAN POLITICAL PARTIES
AT CPSU CONGRESSES[176]

COUNTRY	PARTY	STATUS OF COM PARTY	CPSU CONGRESSES					
			1956	1959	1961	1966	1971	1976
Algeria	Comm.P	Ban'd	—	Att.	Att.	—	—	FLN.
Angola	DPF	None	—	—	—	Att.	MPLA	MPLA
Congo (B)	NLM	None	—	—	—	Att.	Att.	Att.
Egypt	ASU	Ban'd	—	—	—	Att.	Att.	—
Ghana	CPPC	None	—	—	Att.	—	—	—
Guinea	PDG	None	—	—	Att.	Att.	Att.	Att.
Guinea-Bissau		None	—	—	—	Att.	Att.	Att.
Malagasy	ICP	None	—	—	—	—	—	Att.
Mali	SU	None	—	—	Att.	Att.	—	—
Mauritania	MPP	None	—	—	—	—	Att.	—
Morocco	Comm.P	Ban'd	Att.	Att.	Att.	Att.	—	Att.
Mozambique	FRELIMO	None	—	—	—	—	Att.	Att.
Namibia	SWAPO	None	—	—	—	—	Att.	Att.
Nigeria	SWAFP	None	—	—	—	Att.	—	—
Reunion	Coom.P		—	—	—	Att.	Att.	Att.
Senegal	Comm.P	Ban'd	—	—	Att.	Att.	—	Att.
Somalia	SDU	None	—	—	—	Att.	**Att.**	**Att.**
South Africa	Comm.P	Ban'd	—	—	Att.	Att.	Att.	Att.
	ANC		—	—	—	—	Att.	Att.
Sudan	Comm.P	Ban'd	—	Att.	—	Att.	—	Att.
Tanzania	TANU	None	—	—	—	Att.	Att.	Att.
Tunisia	Comm.P	Ban'd	Att.	Att.	Att.	Att.	Att.	Att.
Zambia	UNIP	None	—	—	—	—	Att.	—
Zimbabwe	ANC	None	—	—	—	—	—	Att.

---

176 See <u>Vneocherednoi XXl sezda kommunisticheskoi partii sovetskogo</u> <u>soiuza: Stenograficheskii otchet</u>, Moscow, 2 vols., 1959; <u>XXll sezda</u> <u>kommunisticheskoi partii sovetskogo soiuza: Stenograficheskii</u> <u>otchet</u>, Moscow, 1962: <u>Privetstviia XXlll sezda KPSS, Moscow, 1966</u>; <u>Privetstviia XXlV sezda KPSS</u>, Moscow, 1971; <u>Privetstviia XXV sezda</u> <u>KPSS</u>, Moscow, 1976.

CHAPTER SEVEN

THE BREZHNEV YEARS

The overthrow of Nikita S. Khrushchev on October 15, 1964 caused grave concern among Soviet allies in Africa. Soviet African allies needed to be re-assured of continued Soviet assistance irrespective of the Kremlin coup against Khrushchev. Mr. Youkine, Soviet charge d'affaires in Algeria, had to assure President Ben Bella that the change of leadership in the Kremlin did not affect "Soviet policy of goodwill in Africa and the Arab countries."[1] Though Khrushchev's political leadership was free from the ills of Stalinism, it was however feared that his overthrow would cause a change in Soviet African policy. Apart from being blamed for failures in Soviet agriculture, he was also criticized for misdirecting Soviet foreign policy, especially Soviet setbacks in Africa between 1958 and 1962. In defending the rationality of Soviet economic and technical aid to Egypt at a time when Nasser was persecuting Egyptian Communists, Khrushchev had replied that the aid was a monument for Egyptian posterity. It should be stressed that Soviet scholars endorsed this position as they considered the monumental Aswan Dam a symbol of Communist victory over capitalism. However, there were mixed feelings in the Kremlin when Khrushchev, during his state visit to Egypt in May 1964, awarded President Nasser the title of *Hero of*

---

[1] Egyptian Mail, October 17, 1964.

the Soviet Union, and the *Order of Lenin* to vice president Amer. It was difficult to ascertain whether Khrushchev acted unilaterally in bestowing these Soviet highest awards on Nasser and Amer.

Though Soviet leaders had assured their allies that Soviet foreign policy would not change with the overthrow of Khrushchev, what became gradually noticeable in the post Khrushchevian era was the tactical change of approach in policy implementation. The Brezhnev-Kosygin leadership offered a two dimensional and more cautious approach to foreign policy. The leadership represented an attempt to balance contending views in Soviet foreign policy. While Brezhnev was considered the representative of the "hardliners" in the Politburo, Kosygin appeared to be moderate and led the "liberal" group in the Politburo. The decision to increase the membership of the Politburo from 11 to 15 during the 24th CPSU Congress in 1971, and to 16 at the 25th Congress in 1976, which was subsequently brought down to 14 at the 26th Congress in 1981, was a reflection of the struggle within the Kremlin leadership under Brezhnev.

According to Helen Desfosses Cohn, the post Khrushchevian collective leadership system afforded Soviet foreign policy analysts the opportunity for objective self-criticism that helped to increase the level of non-Soviet reliability on Soviet scholarly works.[2] While Soviet interests in Africa started to decline in 1963, as a result of Moscow's failures and disappointments in the preceding five years, Soviet Africanists began a process of self-criticism in light of their better understanding of African politics. This process became quite noticeable in the second half of the 1960s, especially after the military coups that toppled Soviet *socialist* allies in Ghana and Mali. In a 1964 article titled "Afrika na puti svobody", V. Solodovnikov, Potekhin's successor as director of Moscow's Institute of Africa, was optimistic in his assessment of the African masses. He claimed that: "Many African countries have chosen the non-capitalist path of development" while the "progressive public of Africa declares for

---

2   See Helen Desfosses Cohn, pp.5-14.

socialism."[3] This was an over simplification of Africa's political realities in 1964. The agitation for de-colonization and the demonstrations against the West over the Congo crisis were misinterpreted by Solodovnikov and his colleagues to mean a movement towards socialism. It is significant to note that Solodovnikov's evaluation of Africa's "progressive public" changed in 1965 as he criticized his 1964 article.[4]

Egypt

Notwithstanding the deterioration of Soviet-Egyptian relations between 1958 and 1961 under Khrushchev's leadership, both Nasser and the new Soviet leadership seemed resolved to strengthen their *anti-imperialist* alliance in Africa and the Middle East. By the end of 1964 China had emerged on the African scene to challenge Soviet "revisionism" and "social imperialism." In late December 1964 Soviet deputy premier Alexander Shelepin was despatched to Cairo to assure Nasser of continued Soviet aid. Speaking in the Egyptian National Assembly on December 27, 1964, he told his hosts that Moscow would honour its bilateral agreements signed with Cairo *before* October 15, 1964, and that Soviet-Egyptian friendly relations would continue. It is interesting to note that, throughout his speech, Shelepin did not mention Khrushchev by name, but merely concluded by stressing that Soviet policy "does not change with individuals."[5]

Kosygin and V. V. Kuznetsov, the first deputy foreign minister, were guests of Nasser in Cairo in 1966. They arrived in Cairo on May 10 for an eight-day visit. This was Kosygin's first trip to a foreign

---

[3] V. Solodovnikov, "Afrika na puti svobody," Pravda, December 1, 1964.

[4] See Pravda, June 4, 1965; A. Iskenderov, "Razvivaiushchiesia strany i sotsializm," Pravda, June 4, 1965.

[5] For the full text of Shelepin's speech, see Egyptian Gazette, December 28, 1964.

country outside the socialist camp since he replaced Khrushchev as premier. (His brief visit to India in January 1966 was primarily to attend the funeral of India's Prime Minister Shastri who died in Tashkent, USSR, on January 11, 1966, during the Indo-Pakistani Peace Conference. The conference was initiated by the Soviet Government following the December 1965 Kashmir war). The choice of Egypt symbolized its importance in Soviet policy in Africa and the Middle East. Nasser's role in leading most Arab-speaking countries to severe diplomatic relations with West Germany was welcomed in the Kremlin. Kosygin and Nasser found common grounds on which to continue their countries' collaboration in international politics. They condemned U.S. "imperialist war" in Vietnam and western aggression in Africa. While Nasser perceived U.S. military entanglement in Vietnam as a "horrifying aggression which shakes the conscience of the free world, including free men in the United States," Kosygin predicted that the imperialist aggressors in Vietnam "will be defeated there just as they were defeated here" in Egypt. In a dramatic reversal of Cairo's previous position, Nasser expressed Egypt's gratitude for the "moral and material support" that the Soviet Union rendered Egypt during the 1956 war.[6] It should be recalled that in 1959, during the deterioration of Soviet-Egyptian relations, Nasser had stated that the Soviet Union offered *only* "moral" but *not* "material" support during the 1956 war. Was Nasser admitting that he falsified history in 1959? Or was he only pacifying Soviet leaders in 1966? Whatever his calculations might have been, his *1966* speech was a confirmation that Egypt defeated the Anglo-Franco-Israeli aggression of 1956 thanks to Soviet "material" support during *Khrushchev's* leadership. It was Nasser's expectation, therefore, that Kosygin's visit and the pledge of continued Soviet *material* assistance would guarantee Egypt's victory in a future armed conflict with Israel. In 1956 Soviet leaders perceived the Egyptian victory as a communist victory in the Middle East:

6   <u>Soviet News</u>, Embassy of the USSR, London, May 11, 1966.

285

Imperialist monopoly on arms supply in the Near and
Middle East was destroyed. Soviet-Egyptian agreement
and its fulfilment drastically changed the traditional
situation when colonial powers would wage wars against
unarmed peoples by supplying arms to local reactionary
regimes that assist colonial robbery . . . The collapse of
imperialist aggression against Egypt and the eventual
evacuation of the aggressor's troops clearly demonstrated
the debility of imperialist powers' policy of crushing a
national liberation movement when such a movement
has at its defense the might of the socialist countries.[7]

The Soviet Government was informing the West of its intention
to compete with them in *arms supply* to its clients in regional conflicts.
In his speech at the Egyptian National Assembly on May 17, 1966,
Kosygin hailed the July 23 revolution in Egypt as a landmark in the
anti-imperialist struggle: "The Egyptian Revolution dealt a blow to
the positions of the imperialist countries not only in Egypt but also
in the Near East and Africa." He argued that while the

October Socialist Revolution was a great incentive to all
peoples interested in liquidating the colonialist regime,
and has moreover, created a suitable atmosphere for the
struggle of these peoples, the July 23, 1952 Revolution
in Egypt was one of the outstanding stages of this
struggle.[8]

The dominant aspect of Kosygin's speech was the implication
that the July 23 officers' coup in Egypt was an off-shoot of the

---

[7] Mezhdunarodnye otnosheniia posle vtoroi mirovoi voiny, vol.3,
     p.146.
[8] Alexei Kosygin, "Speech in the UAR National Assembly," Egyptian
     Gazette, May 18, 1966. See also Soviet News, Embassy of the USSR,
     London, May 19, 1966.

October 1917 Russian socialist revolution which toppled Tsarism. Obviously an off-shoot with a different ideological orientation, the strong anti-western undertone of Nasser's policies compelled Egypt to ally with the Soviet Union in international politics, irrespective of Nasser's anti-communism. The rationale for alliance maintenance made the Brezhnev-Kosygin leadership to commit the Soviet Union to the preservation of "*the might of the socialist countries*" in Africa and the Middle East. Thus, an Israeli victory over Egypt would imply Soviet defeat in the region. This was the conclusion reached by Soviet citizens in June 1967 when Egypt collapsed at Israel's first strike, as the destruction of modern Soviet weapons by "imperialist forces" was regarded as Soviet defeat. Anti-Arab sentiments reigned in Moscow. Some Soviet scholars in discussions with the author were upset over the incident and even suggested the withdrawal of Soviet military aid to Egypt.

It is significant to note that before the outbreak of war in June 1967, President De Gaulle, on June 5, had proposed a Four Power Summit—USSR, U.S., Great Britain, and France—to help ameliorate the situation in the Middle East. The Soviet Government opposed the French proposal and regarded it as a "conspiracy" to delay the defeat of western imperialism in the region. Moscow was convinced that the time was *ripe* for Egypt's victory. However, on June 7, following the capitulation of Egypt and the destruction of Soviet weapons in the war, the Soviet Government promptly requested an emergency session of the UN Security Council to discuss the armed conflict. N.T. Fedorenko, Soviet representative at the Security Council, called for a ceasefire to commence at "20:00 hours GMT June 7, 1967."

Meanwhile, Nasser, in a symbolic gesture perhaps to test his popularity in the wake of the crushing defeat, resigned from office on June 9. Public demonstrations forced him to withdraw his resignation on June 10. In a bid to comfort the Kremlin in the midst of this disaster, some Soviet political analysts interpreted the demonstrations to mean a victory for Moscow's revolutionary ally. In the views of G. Mirsky, a leading Soviet Africanist:

The vast crowds that poured into the streets of Cairo and other Arab cities at the announcement of President Nasser's resignation to urge him to remain at his post was striking proof of the viability of the revolutionary democratic system.[9]

It should be noted that Mirsky had, in an earlier writing, condemned what he referred to as Nasser's "nebulous conception of democracy."[10] The fact that he now perceived Nasser as a representative of a "revolutionary democratic system" demonstrated the fluctuations in policy analysis as both Moscow and Cairo, operating from opposite poles and pursuing conflicting goals and objectives, sought to maintain a tactical alliance to benefit competing ideological interests in their respective anti-imperialist policies. The meeting of East European Communist leaders in Moscow on June 9 that decided to severe diplomatic relations with Israel was appreciated by Nasser.

The defeat of Egypt in the 6-day war of June 1967 humiliated Soviet and Egyptian leaders. In Egypt, Marshal Amer alleged that Moscow was responsible for the defeat, and he refused to resign as the Commander-in-Chief when asked to do so by Nasser. It was alleged that he plotted to overthrow Nasser on August 27, 1967. He subsequently died on September 14, 1967 from "an overdose of sleeping pills."[11] The circumstances surrounding Amer's death did suggest that a certain level of power struggle took place between June 10 and September 14, 1967. It seemed logical to conjecturize that the basis of the struggle concerned the question of continued alliance with the Soviet Union, given Amer's claim that Moscow was responsible for Egypt's defeat in the 6-day war.

Algeria's President Houari Boumedienne was in Moscow on June 10 to discuss the 6-day war with Soviet leaders, while Soviet

---

[9]   G. Mirsky, "Israeli Aggression and Arab Unity," New Times, Moscow, no.28, 1967, p.4.

[10]   Mirsky, "The U.A.R. Reforms," p.13.

[11]   See Mirsky, "Israeli Aggression and Arab Unity,' pp.4-6.

President N. Podgornyi was in Cairo, June 21-24, to confer with President Nasser. Egypt's decision to remain a Soviet ally after the war was undoubtedly a reflection of Nasser's position regarding the ineptitude of Egyptian army under Marshal Amer's command, and his belief that U.S.-Israeli alliance, and not the Soviet Union, posed a greater threat to Egyptian survival. He had underlined this view during his August 1965 visit to Moscow when he declared that:

> Our friendship is enhanced by our identical positions
> in the struggle for the triumph of freedom, progress and
> peace, and by all over thoughts, efforts and sacrifices we
> are endeavouring to extend these positions.[12]

Kosygin had echoed the basic tenets of Nasser's Moscow speech during his visit to Cairo in May 1966:

> Relations between our two countries go beyond
> peaceful coexistence. They are relations of a new type,
> imbued with a spirit of mutual trust and based on close
> cooperation in all fields.[13]

Egypt had been the main focus of Soviet African policy under Khrushchev, and it was imperative for the post Khrushchevian Soviet leadership to retain the alliance with Nasser, irrespective of the defeat of June 1967. However, following the death of Nasser in October 1970, the new Egyptian president, Anwar Sadat, began to chart a foreign policy course which sought to undermine Soviet policy in Egypt and the Middle East. He was convinced that continued Egyptian reliance on the Soviet Union was a burden on Egypt's foreign policy. This view was clearly stated in his autobiography, where he revealed, for instance, that the Soviet Union pointedly

---

12   Nasser as cited in New Times, Moscow, no.36, 1965, p.2.
13   Kosygin as cited in I. Belyaev and E. Primakov, "Cairo May 1966," New Times, Moscow, no. 21, 1966, pp.3-4.

refused "to extend a helping hand to Egypt" during the critical days of the Suez Canal crisis when a combined force of Britain, France and Israel attacked Egypt. He declared:

> This made me believe, from that moment on, that it was always futile to depend on the Soviet Union. On November 5 Eisenhower intervened and asked Britain and France to withdraw at once. When the Soviet Union learned that Britain and France had responded to the U.S. President's request, it addressed a warning—known as the Khrushchev-Bulganin Ultimatum—to both countries. It was nothing in effect but an exercise in muscle-flexing and an attempt to appear as though the Soviet Union had saved the situation. This was not, of course, the case. It was Eisenhower who did so.[14]

With the above sentiments in mind, Sadat remained suspicious of Soviet intensions. By the summer of 1972 it was clear that Moscow and Cairo were cruising on collision course. When the Soviet Union declined Egypt's request for more sophisticated weapons systems, Sadat decided to expel Soviet military advisers from Egypt in August 1972. This was considered a major setback for Soviet diplomacy in Africa and the Middle East, given Egypt's stature in the regions' politics.

When the Middle East war broke out in October 1973, Egypt fought without Soviet assistance. The international community was surprised at Egypt's military capabilities displayed during the 1973 war. For Sadat, it was a calculated stratagem to demonstrate that Egypt could survive without the Soviets. The gradual retreat of Egypt from its pro Soviet position to rapprochement with the U.S. and Israel following the 1973 Middle East war set the Soviet Union on a nose dive it never recovered from. The Camp David Accord engineered by U.S. President Jimmy Carter in 1978, which led to

---

[14]   See Anwar el-Sadat, *In Search of Identity. An Autobiography*, p.146.

an Israeli-Egyptian Peace Treaty signed in 1979, further alienated the Soviet Union from Egyptian affairs.

East Africa

Besides Egypt, East Africa, particularly Ethiopia and Somalia, represented an important aspect of the post Khrushchevian inheritance for Brezhnev and Kosygin. Before discussing Ethiopia and Somalia, it is imperative that we briefly review the East African scene as it was in 1964 prior to the overthrow of Khrushchev in the Kremlin.

In early 1964 the volatile political situation in East Africa compelled western analysts to speculate about an alleged communist intervention in African politics. Premier Chou en-Lai of China had just completed his celebrated tour of Africa which he climaxed with a speech in Somalia that Africa was "ripe for revolution."[15] When on January 14, 1964, a People's Democracy was declared on the Island of Zanzibar, other East African states were also engulfed in political turmoil. Moscow's decision to "officially recognize the People's Republic of Zanzibar and Pemba"[16] on January 18 compelled Julius Nyerere of Tanganyika and Milton Obote of Uganda to meet with their Kenyan counterpart Jomo Kenyatta in Nairobi, where the three east African leaders discussed the impact of the revolution on their respective countries. On January 17, Nyerere despatched 100 Tanganyikan policemen to Zanzibar to help maintain "order", while British war ships remained in Zanzibar's territorial waters. This provoked the Soviet Government to issue a statement condemning Britain and "some Western powers" for attempting to subvert the People's Republic of Zanzibar.[17]

---

[15] Chou en-Lai, "Revolutionary Prospects in Africa Excellent," <u>Peking Review</u>, Vll, 7, February 14, 1964, pp.5-8.

[16] <u>Pravda</u>, January 19, 1964.

[17] See <u>Pravda</u>, January 27, 1964.

In a rather surprising coincidence the army mutinied in Tanganyika, Uganda, and Kenya. A linkage was immediately established between the Zanzibarian revolution and these mutinies. In a dramatic move that caused both concern and indignation, Nyerere, Obote and Kenyatta invited British armed intervention to quell the mutinies. It was obvious that the proximity of Zanzibar to the three east African states clouded the reasons behind the mutinies, as the leaders of these states and the West accused the communists of complicity in the incidents.[18] Addressing the Conference of the Movement for Colonial Freedom in London, Fenner Brochway, a British Member of Parliament, condemned the east African leaders and argued that:

> . . . the summoning of external troops into a territory destroys the reality of independence; it is inconsistent with the demands of those governments for the withdrawal of British forces and bases from those territories . . .[19]

Perceived as a neo-colonial machination to abort progressive political development in the region, the British Communists condemned the British government's intervention and stated that "friends of the African liberation movement will regret the requests of Premiers Kenyatta, Nyerere and Obote for British troops to be sent to their territories."[20]

However, in pro-British government circles the intervention of Britain to crush the east African mutinies was regarded as "a

---

[18] See Financial Times, London, January 27, 1964. For an account of the revolution, see Michael F. Lofchie, Zanzibar: Background to Revolution, Princeton, New Jersey, 1965.

[19] The Guardian, January 27, 1964. See also Anthony Sampson, "Evidence Discounts East African Plot," OFNS, no. 19986, January 27, 1964.

[20] The Daily Worker, January 28, 1964. For TASS Statement, see Soviet News, Embassy of the USSR, London, February 14, 1964.

triumph of Commonwealth cooperation."[21] Nigerian troops
participated in the so-called "commonwealth cooperation" to quell
the mutinies. Julius Nyerere demanded an emergency meeting of the
OAU Foreign and Defence Ministers to discuss what he perceived
as a "grave danger not only to this area but to the whole of our
continent. African unity is at stake."[22] In their joint reaction towards
the mutinies the three east African leaders, especially Nyerere,
chased the shadow and ignored the substance. For instance, African
officers in the armed forces had been agitating for salary increases
since independence, and had fruitlessly demanded promotion
of Africans to commanding positions. It was their expectations
that the attainment of *uhuru* would Africanize the leadership of
the armed forces. We witnessed this dilemma in the Congo. This
expectation was based on the true spirit of progressive nationalistic
anti neo-colonial policies as, ironically, personified by Nyerere.
Tanganyikan officers demonstrated this in Dar-es-Salamm and
Tabora when they expelled their European "superior" officers from
the army. Thus, the move by Nyerere was primarily a device to
forestall his personal rule but not to solve the problems that caused
the mutinies.

Meanwhile, a 30-man Revolutionary Council had been established
to rule the People's Republic of Zanzibar. The political struggle within
the Council was exploited by Nyerere whose main objective was
to neutralize the pro-communist policies of the People's Republic.
Besides the prompt Soviet Government recognition of Zanzibar's
revolutionary regime, the presence of Chinese representatives on the
island significantly increased Nyerere's fears. President Karume, the
leader of the Revolutionary Council, in his desire to maintain a
balance found himself sandwiched between two strong personalities
whose policies were considered crucial in determining Zanzibar's
ideological orientation. The power tussle within the Council had all
the trappings of a Sino-Soviet dispute. Zanzibar's foreign minister,

---

21   Daily Telegraph, January 27, 1964.
22   The New York Times, January 28, 1964.

Sheik Abdul Rahman Babu, led the pro-Chinese faction in the Council and he was determined to increase China's influence on the island. He was considered Zanzibar's *strong man*. The vice president, Kassim Hanga, was a Soviet educated economist and married to Liya Golden who was a former assistant of Professor Ivan Potekhin, the founding director of the USSR's Institute of Africa. Golden, who later became a renowned History professor at the Institute of Africa, was the daughter of an African American (Oliver John Golden) and an American Jewish mother of Polish origin (Bertha Black) who left the USA and settled in the Soviet Union in 1931. Hanga led the pro-Soviet faction in the Council. Babu's pronouncements and his trip to Peking (now Beijing) following the revolution seemed to suggest Zanzibar's inclination toward China.

In order to curtail Babu's influence in the Council, Hanga had to ally with Karume's nationalists. On his return from Moscow where he met with Soviet leaders, Hanga immediately proceeded to Dar-es-Salaam for talks with Nyerere. His talks with Nyerere set the stage for the latter's surprising two hour visit to President Karume. It is significant to note that Babu was visiting Indonesia and Pakistan when Nyerere arrived in Zanzibar on April 22, 1964. An article of union between Tanganyika and Zanzibar was hastingly drafted. Zanzibar's Revolutionary Council ratified the Article of Union on April 24, 1964.[23] The absence of the Foreign Minister—Babu—from the team that handled Zanzibar's *negotiation* of a union with another sovereign state—Tanganyika—, coupled with Hanga's rushed visit to Nyerere in Dar-es-Salaam immediately following his Moscow trip, undoubtedly suggested a conspiracy to outwit Babu and China in the process. Though Babu dismissed rumours of a rupture in the Revolutionary Council, the fact that not a single Zanzibarian minister was at the airport to welcome him from his Asian trip indicated the contrary. In the first government of the new state—the United Republic of Tanzania—Babu was appointed Director of

---

[23] See The Times, London, April 24, 1964; Clyde Sanger, "Zanzibar to Unite with Tanganyika," The Guardian, April 24, 1964.

Planning; but President Nyerere, in announcing the appointments, quickly added: "The new national directorate of planning will be directly under me."[24] This was meant to curb any assumption of full power by Babu. The union was a product of fear. For the Hanga-Karume alliance, Babu's strong pro-Chinese orientation had to be aborted, while the Hanga-Soviet alliance perceived the Sino-Babu alliance as a dangerous phenomenon in African politics. On the part of Nyerere, he felt threatened by the establishment of a communist state close to Tanganyika hence he quickly exploited the internal contradictions in Zanzibar's Revolutionary Council by allying Tanganyika with the Hanga-Karume-Soviet tripartite alliance. While the birth of Tanzania was a relief for Moscow, it was, in the short term, a setback for China. However, the merger was later to involve China in its major economic and technical aid in Africa,—the Tanzam Railway project.

Ethiopia: From Feudal Emperor to Socialist Comrade

Ethiopia is the oldest African state which had, over the centuries, maintained special relations with Russia *and* the USSR. Soviet interests in Ethiopia predated the socialist revolution of 1917.[25] For religious and political reasons imperial Russia cultivated Ethiopia's friendship, a friendship which was concretized in 1896 at the historic battle of Adowa where the army of Emperor Menelik ll defeated Italy. Russia contributed to Ethiopia's efforts at Adowa. The mention of Ethiopia in any public discourse in the Soviet Union always invoked a nostalgic feeling as invariably the discussants were bound to refer to Alexander S. Pushkin, the great Russian poet of the 19th century and

---

24 <u>Daily Express</u>, April 28, 1964.
25 For a detailed expose of this subject, see Edward Thomas Wilson, <u>Russia and Black Africa before World War ll</u>, New York, 1974. See also my review of ibid., in <u>Canadian Journal of African Studies</u>, 9, 2, 1975, pp.349-350.

great grandson of an Ethiopian slave, Ibrahim Petrovich Gannibal who served in the court of the Russian Emperor, Peter the Great, and later attained the rank of general in the Russian (tsarist) army. Though the oldest independent African state (Ethiopia was never colonized), Ethiopia was, prior to the overthrow and abolishment of the monarchy in 1974, predominantly a feudal and semi feudal society presided over by Emperor Haile Selassie l, the *King of Kings, Lion of Judah and the Elect of God*. Haile Selassie in the Amharic language means *Strength of the Trinity*.

As an inheritance from imperial Russia, Ethiopia was the central focus of Soviet policies in east Africa. Imbued with contradictory characteristics, Soviet policy towards Ethiopia remained a study of constancy in a rapidly changing world. To illustrate this postulate, our analysis of Soviet policy towards Ethiopia will have to draw from the pre Brezhnevian era of Soviet policy. This historical excursion is of vital significance if we must come to grips with the dialectics of Soviet foreign policy vis-a-vis the Horn of Africa, and Africa in general.

The north-eastern portion of Africa stretching from Egypt to Somalia have been of great strategic importance to the world's super powers, an importance which acquired a radical ideological connotation with the emergence of a socialist state—the Soviet Union—in the international community. In analysing Soviet foreign policy, Euro-American scholars *as a rule* mechanically treated the subject as a *continuation* of tsarist Russia's foreign policy. Such an interpretation invariably ignored the *class* nature of foreign policy, the most significant determinant of foreign policy which united tsarist Russia's foreign policy with the foreign policies of Euro-American imperialism in contradiction to the Marxist-Leninist foreign policy of the Soviet Union. Soviet interests in the north-eastern portion of Africa, as indeed in Africa generally, must be understood in class ideological terms.

In the 1930s as the Italo-German alliance began to lubricate its armament in preparation for its diplomacy of aggression, the Euro-American states did not conceive of any move to halt the aggression, but rather they aided both Italy and Germany. With references to Ethiopia, Italy sought to avenge its disastrous defeat at

Adowa in 1896. The intra-imperialist contradictions in Europe were to be *resolved* by the imperialist appeasement of colonial aggression. When on October 2, 1935, Italy, from its colonial holdings in Eritrea and Somalia invaded Ethiopia; the western nations encouraged it in its aggression. Soviet position in the League of Nations was strongly in support of Ethiopian independence. The western bloc, headed by Britain, was decisively in support of Italian occupation of Ethiopia as it rallied to defeat Soviet demand for sanctions against Italy, as provided for in Article 16 of the League of Nations. Anglo-French diplomacy to resolve the problem of Italian occupation sought to compel Ethiopia to cede portions of its territory to Italy and for a League of Nations' team to be stationed in Addis Ababa. In return, according to Britain and France, Ethiopia was to acquire the Eritrean port of Assab. These proposals were rejected by Ethiopia. It is instructive to note that when on June 30, 1936, the League of Nations considered Ethiopian request for the League not to recognize Italian occupation, it was only the Soviet Union that supported Ethiopia.[26] Ethiopia was liberated in 1941 following the quick capitulation of Italy in the war of 1939-1945, and Britain, representing the allied powers, assumed the administration of Eritrea in 1941.

From its inception in 1945 the question of independence for the colonies, particularly the Italian colonies, was tackled by the UNO. Though Italy, like Germany, was an aggressor power that was defeated in the war of 1939-1945, it was immediately re-admitted into the fold of Euro-American imperial circle as the Western powers strove to maintain their hegemony in world politics. When NATO was established on April 4, 1949, Italy was among the 12 founding nations. On the basis of this, therefore, it was expected that the Euro-American powers would pursue a pro-Italian policy vis-a-vis the decolonization of former Italian colonies. As we have argued in chapter four the politics of decolonization determines the outcome

---

[26]   See M. V. Rait, "Efiopiia," in <u>Noveishaia istoriia Afriki</u>, Moscow, 1968, pp.394-396.

of the phenomenon. Thus, decolonization and the question of the right of nations to self-determination can only be thoroughly comprehended when explained ideologically. The Ethio-Eritrean question affords us such an opportunity.

The Fourth Session of the UN General Assembly grappled with the problem of former Italian colonies in Africa—Libya, Eritrea, and Somaliland. While the U.S., Britain and France proposed a trusteeship system that was meant to sanctify their imperialist rule in those territories of strategic importance, the Soviet Union demanded for their independence. The Soviet position was explained thus:

> In the conditions when the Western powers were on the path to create aggressive blocs and unleash a new war a trusteeship system in these strategically important territories would only aid the West. Therefore the representative of the USSR opposed the American proposal.[27]

The Soviet Union proposed an immediate independence for Libya and "the withdrawal of all foreign military bases and personnel", and that "Eritrea be granted independence after a 5 year period during which it should be administered by an Administrator of the Trusteeship Council with representatives from the USSR, USA, Britain, France, China, Italy and Ethiopia, including one European and two non-European Eritrean nationals appointed by the above mentioned seven countries."[28] According to professor M.N. Rait, a Soviet expert on Ethiopia, Haile Selassie 1 raised the question of uniting Eritrea with Ethiopia during the war of 1939-1945.It is interesting that Rait referred to the decision of the Fifth Session of the UN General Assembly on the federation of Ethiopia and

---

[27] M. N. Ivanitskii, Put k nezavisimosti. Iz istorii resheniia voprosa o sudbe byvshikh italianskikh kolonii 1945-1950, Kiev, 1962, p.43.

[28] Ofitsialnye otchety chetvertoi sessii generalnoi assemblei. Pervyi komitet, New York, 1949, p.22.

Eritrea, but failed to discuss the strong Soviet pro-Eritrean independence position at the same session of the UN. She claimed that on November 14, 1962, the "Eritrean assembly decided to alter the federation status in favour of complete integration with Ethiopia"[29], whereas it was Ethiopia that abrogated the terms of the UN federal resolution by unilaterally annulling the arrangement and incorporated Eritrea into the Ethiopian empire. It is vitally important that analysts come to grips with the concrete prevailing political atmosphere in which the question of the *disposal of Eritrea* and other Italian colonies—Libya and Italian Somaliland—was discussed at the UN.

In July 1946 twenty-one countries, including the Soviet Union, USA, Britain, France, China, India, Canada, Norway, Poland, Ethiopia, and (the union of) South Africa gathered in Paris for a Peace Conference to map out the modalities of peace with the former allies of Germany in the 1939-1945 war—Italy, Rumania, Bulgaria, Hungary, and Finland. The four power conferences at Tehran, Yalta and Potsdam had taken care of Germany. The Paris Peace Conference lasted until October 15, 1946. The holding of a peace conference after a war gives the victorious parties an opportunity to dictate (humiliating) terms to the defeated parties, particularly where the latter were the aggressors. For example, the 1919 Paris Peace Conference following the 1914-1918 war completely stripped Germany of all its African colonies. But there was a fundamental difference between the Paris Peace conferences of 1919 and 1946. While an aggressor was punished in the 1919 peace conference, another aggressor was appeased in the 1946 variant. Furthermore, while the Paris Peace Conference of 1919 primarily represented an intra-imperialist struggle devoid of establishing democratic peace, the 1946 variant represented a sharp ideological struggle between the centres of socialism and capitalism. It is within this context that we propose to discuss the Eritrean question.

---

[29]   Rait, *loc.cit.*, pp.397-398.

The Council of Ministers of the Four Powers—USSR, USA, Britain, and France—had agreed to decide on the status of former Italian African colonies at the same time of concluding *peace* with Italy. However, when the Peace Treaty was signed with Italy on February 10, 1947 in Paris, the "disposal" of Italy's former colonies was left open. Article 23 of the Peace Treaty simply stated that Italy had given up all rights over its "territorial holdings in Africa—Libya, Eritrea, and Italian Somaliland."[30] The four powers agreed to refer the case of former Italian African colonies to the UN if, *within one year*, they could not resolve on how to decolonize the colonies. Since they failed to reach an agreement on the issue, it was referred to the UN.

The issue was first discussed at the UN during its Third Session in early 1949. Britain proposed a blatant imperialist plan to divide the former Italian colonies among itself, France and Italy! For example, Libya was to be fragmented into British, French and Italian spheres of influence under a trusteeship, and to attain independence within ten years; while Italian Somaliland was to be under Italian trusteeship. With regards to Eritrea, Britain proposed that Ethiopia should annex its south-eastern portion while the north-western region is given to Anglo-Egyptian Sudan. The Euro-American bloc pushed this exploitative and undemocratic proposal through the Political Committee of the UN General Assembly. However, the anti-colonial movement, especially the uprising in Libya, compelled a re-examination of the question at the UN. The nascent neo-colonial policies began to crystallize. How was the Eritrean question handled at the UN?

As a result of the failure of the Four Powers to reach an acceptable decision on Eritrea, a UN Commission was established to study the question with the following as members:

Justice Aung Khine (Burma);
Carlos Garcia Bauer (Guatemala);
Justice Erling Qvade (Norway);
Ziaud-Din (Pakistan);

---

30 See <u>Diplomaticheskii slovar</u>, vol.2, Moscow, 1961, pp.301-304.

Major General F.H. Theron (Union of South Africa); and
Petrus J. Schmidt (Principal Secretary).

The terms of reference of the Commission were to "ascertain more
fully the wishes and the best means of promoting the welfare of the
inhabitants of Eritrea, to examine the question of the disposal of
Eritrea . . . and the capacity of the people for self-government; the
interests of peace and security in East Africa; the rights and claims
of Ethiopia based on geographical, ethnic or economic reasons,
*including in particular Ethiopia's legitimate need for adequate access
to the sea*; . . ."[31] According to the Report of the Commission, the
Four Powers agreed to "dispose" of former Italian African colonies
"in the light of the wishes and welfare of the inhabitants and the
interests of peace and security, *taking into consideration the views
of other interested Governments*."[32] The position of the Four Powers
on the *disposal of Eritrea* and the Commission's terms of reference
indicated the type of report to be released.

But before examining and analysing the Report of the
Commission, and the ensuing debate and resolutions, it is pertinent
that we evaluate the contradictory proposals of the Four Powers *before*
the Report was presented to the UN. The Soviet Union proposed
that Eritrea be placed under Italian trusteeship for a "definite
acceptable term", while France argued that Eritrea be "placed under
the trusteeship of Italy" and "the territories situated between the Gulf
of Zula and French Somaliland should be assigned to Ethiopia in
full sovereignty." The British Government proposed that "Ethiopia
should be appointed to the Administering Authority in Eritrea for
a period of ten years", while the U.S. maintained that "the southern
section of Eritrea (including the Damakil Coast, and the districts of
Akkele, Guzai and Serae . . .) be ceded to Ethiopia", and that the

---

[31] Report of the United Nations Commission for Eritrea. General
Assembly Official Records. Fifth Session Supplement no.8 (A/1285),
Lake Success, New York, 1950, p.3. Italics mine.

[32] *Ibid.*, p.1. Italics mine.

Foreign Ministers of the Four Powers recommend to the General Assembly the *disposition* of "the remainder of Eritrea, that is, the northern and predominantly Moslem portion, including Asmara and Massawa, be postponed for one year."[33] The absurdity of these proposals was that Italy was being seriously considered by the Four Powers to administer its former colonies in one form or the other, instead of an outright granting or recognition of the independence of these colonies. It was a replay of the Berlin Conference on the partition of Africa.

Two conflicting memoranda were subsequently submitted by two opposing groups of the UN Commission. The first memorandum, submitted by the delegations of Burma, Norway and the Union of South Africa, argued that:

> . . . the fact cannot be escaped that at present the Eritrean people lack the capacity for the self-government of Eritrea entirely on their own . . . Moreover, the leaders of the community have no knowledge of the responsibility of government and possess no administrative or judicial experience other than in the regulation of tribal affairs and the application of customary law.[34]

Burma, Norway and South Africa further argued that: "in the absence of any rich sources of raw materials, Eritrea can have no real industrial future." Eritrea had "neither the resources nor the revenue to make her economically viable in the foreseeable future."[35] In order to give their position a universal outlook they postulated that:

> . . . the movement for union with Ethiopia has many of the characteristics of a popular movement, and it is more than likely that outright frustration of these

---

[33] Ibid., p.2.
[34] Ibid., 12.
[35] Ibid., 16.

wishes would make the position of internal security in Eritrea untenable. Nor would it in that event be unrealistic to expect assistance for the unionist groups from Ethiopia, in view of that country's own espousal of the same cause . . . in view of the acute internal political division and state of tension in Eritrea, the conclusion is ineluctable that the creation of a separate Eritrean state entirely on its own would contain all the elements necessary to prejudice the interests of peace and security in East Africa, now and in the future.[36]

Surprisingly, after presenting the above memorandum, the three countries failed to table a unanimous recommendation to the UN. Burma and South Africa recommended a "federation" of "two countries" thus:

(a) "Eritrea to be constituted a self-governing unit of a federation of which the other member shall be Ethiopia, under the sovereignty of the Ethiopian crown.

(b) Each member shall possess local legislative and executive autonomy, but full authority shall be vested in the federal government with regard to such matters as defence, external affairs, finance, inter-state commerce and communications.

(c) A customs union between the two members shall be obligatory.

(d) A common citizenship shall prevail throughout the federation."

Norway disagreed with the above recommendations, and instead proposed an outright union with Ethiopia.[37]

The second memorandum, submitted by the delegations of Guatemala and Pakistan, recommended as follows:

---

[36] Ibid., 23.
[37] Ibid., 26-28.

> We believe the best solution for the future of Eritrea to
> be independence. But, at the same time, we are of the
> opinion that independence cannot be made effective
> immediately. Therefore, the welfare of Eritrea can best
> be promoted by placing the territory under direct
> trusteeship by the United Nations for a maximum
> period of ten years, at the end of which it should become
> completely independent.[38]

The above recommendations pointedly represented the
conflicting locations of the politics of decolonization in the UN.
The Euro-American bloc dismissed Eritreans as a group of people
who only excelled "in the regulation of tribal affairs and the
application of customary law" with "no administrative and judicial
experience" and thus "lack the capacity for the self-government of
Eritrea." This has been the standard *argument* of colonial powers to
justify colonialism. What emerges from this is the unquestionable
ideological rationalization of the process of de-colonization. Placed
in time and space, the right of nations to self-determination is pure
and simple an ideological issue. Its rationalization is significantly
influenced by the concrete historical circumstances defined by the
locations of the various classes in the struggle to decolonize.

Decolonization is an ideological issue, and a section of a
colonized people of any given colony has, historically, always
demonstrated its alliance with neo-colonialism. Such an alliance,
consciously contracted, is defined by the specific class interest
of the people concerned. In most cases, however, it arises as a
product of false consciousness on the part of the given colonized
peoples coerced by the neo-colonial powers. This is the history of
colonialism, neo-colonialism and decolonization. The Eritrea case
helped to underline this dilemma, and demonstrated how Eritrea

---

[38]   Ibid., 35. For the full text of the Guatemalan and Pakistani
recommendation, see ibid., 29-35.

became a victim of UN decisions. But how did Eritreans respond to the UN Commission? Let us consult the following table.

TABLE 3: POLITICAL WISHES OF ERITREANS

PARTIES AND ORGANIZATIONS	GOAL
1. Independence Bloc. A coalition of:— (a) Moslem League (b) Liberal Progressive Party (c) New Eritrea Party (formerly the Pro-Italia Party) (d) Nationalist Party (e) Veterans' Association (f) Italo-Eritrean Association (g) Independent Eritrea Party (h) Intellectual Association of Eritreans.	Immediate independence of Eritrea.
2. Independent Moslem League of Massawa. (opted from 1 above)	Union with Ethiopia.
3. Unionist Party	Union with Ethiopia.
4. Liberal Unionist Party	Union with Ethiopia.
5. Independent Eritrea United to Ethiopia Party.	Eritrean independence before union with Ethiopia.
6. Moslem League of the Western Province.	British rule in the western province "for a period of ten years leaving the rest of the territory to decide its future for itself."[39]

[39]The above table shows that, after the defection of the Moslem League from the *Independence Bloc*, seven political parties/

[39] Ibid., 16.

305

organizations remained resolute in their demand for Eritrean independence. On the other hand, only three political parties/organizations wanted a union with Ethiopia, while the Independent Eritrea United to Ethiopia Party wanted an independent Eritrea that would be free to decide on the issue of a union with Ethiopia. It is intriguing that the UN Commission disregarded this aspect of its own findings. In reaching its majority decisions the Commission was not guided by the genuine wishes of Eritreans, but by a consideration to satisfy Euro-American interests in league with Ethiopia, whose *"legitimate need for adequate access to the sea"* became the main concern for the neo-colonialists on how to *dispose* of the Eritrean question. The divergent Leninist and Wilsonian concepts of the rights of nations to self-determination, which had polarized the question of decolonization since 1917, again manifested itself in the UN deliberations on Eritrea.

Following the presentation of the Report to the UN, the General Assembly debated the issues involved and passed a resolution on the "disposal of Eritrea." The General Assembly considered three draft resolutions on this question. First, a Soviet draft resolution "providing that Eritrea should be granted independence immediately." A Polish draft resolution demanded independence for Eritrea after 3 years. The third draft resolution was tabled by an Ad Hoc Political Committee of the General Assembly calling for the federation of Eritrea with Ethiopia. The Soviet delegate, Professor A. A. Arutiunian, in presenting Moscow's position, argued:

> The USSR has consistently supported the proposal that Eritrea should be granted independence and has continued to do so at the current session. We base our argument on the fact that all peoples have a right to self-determination and national independence . . . the USSR delegation objects to the proposal for the federation of Eritrea with another state, as such a federation would disregard the right of the Eritrean

people to self-determination by preventing the Eritreans from exercising that right.[40]

Arutiunian argued that the proposed federation of Eritrea and Ethiopia represented "a compromise among the colonial powers." Writing in 1962, Professor M. N. Ivanitskii maintained that the 1950 Soviet proposal emanated from the "principle of the right of nations to self-determination, the right on national and independent existence." In the Soviet view "the independence of Eritrea can be realized only after its territory is freed of foreign troops and the foreign interference in its domestic affairs is stopped."[41] Ivanitskii declared:

> The proposal of the Soviet Union reflected the sincere concern of a socialist state for the fundamental interests of the Eritrean people, of their economic, political and cultural development.[42]

The Soviet position as argued by Arutiunian at the UN in 1950 had elements of compromising with Euro-American imperialism on the Eritrean question. On the so-called *"Ethiopia's legitimate need for adequate access to the sea"*, the Soviet Government proposed that "Eritrean territory which is *essential* to Ethiopia for access to the sea through the port of Assab be ceded to Ethiopia."[43] This concession significantly ruptured the basic tenets of Soviet demand for Eritrean independence as it enhanced the position of those who wanted Eritrea to remain a colony of another state.

---

40 United Nations, <u>Official Records of the General Assembly Fifth Session. Plenary Meetings. Verbatim Records of Meetings. Volume 1, 19 September to 15 December 1950</u>, New York, 1950, pp.536-537. Hereinafter referred to as <u>UNGA Fifth Session</u>.

41 Ivanitskii, p.107.

42 <u>Ibid</u>.

43 <u>UNGA Fifth Session</u>, p.537. Italics mine.

O. Igho Natufe

In his contribution to the UN debate, Garcia Bauer (Guatemala), a member of the UN Commission on Eritrea, reiterated Guatemala's position for Eritrean independence after a transitional period under UN Trusteeship. Guatemala opposed the Soviet draft resolution on two grounds. First, Bauer argued that immediate independence for Eritrea will "result in chaos." Second, he perceived as unrealistic, Soviet advocacy for Eritrean independence *and* the promotion of Ethiopian territorial aggrandizement. He declared:

> We shall also vote against the part of the Soviet Union draft relating to the cession of some Eritrean territory to Ethiopia, because we are convinced that access to the sea through the port of Assab would not satisfy the requirements of Ethiopia and that the cession of that part of the territory would be contrary to the wishes of the population concerned.[44]

TABLE 4.1: UN VOTE ON AD HOC POLITICAL COMMITTEE DRAFT RESOLUTION ON ERITREA[45]

FOR	AGAINST	ABSTENTION
46 including Egypt, Ethiopia, Liberia, Union of South Africa, Yugoslavia, France, UK,USA.	10 including Cuba, Czechoslovakia, Dominican Republic, El Salvador, Guatemala, Pakistan, Poland, Ukrainian SSR, USSR, Byelorussian SSR.	4. Israel, Saudi Arabia, Sweden, and Uruguay.

---

[44] Ibid., 541.
[45] Sources for Tables 4.1 - 4.3, see ibid.

TABLE 4.2: UN VOTE ON USSR DRAFT RESOLUTION ON ERITREA

PARAGRAPH	FOR	AGAINST	ABSTENTION
First	13	32	8
Second	9	34	10
Third	5	38	14

TABLE 4.3: UN VOTE ON POLISH DRAFT RESOLUTION ON ERITREA

PARAGRAPH	FOR	AGAINST	ABSTENTION
First	10	36	14
Second	5	37	13
Third	8	34	11
Fourth	5	35	11

As the results of the above Tables indicate, the UN General Assembly in 1950 decided in favour of the ad hoc Political Committee draft resolution which called for the federation of Eritrea with Ethiopia *based* on the Burmese-South African recommendation that emanated from the Report of the United Nations Commission for Eritrea. This resolution, which came into force on September 15, 1952, also recognized that both Eritrea and Ethiopia will maintain their *separate legal identities,* as contained in the Burmese-South African recommendation, under the sovereignty of the Ethiopian crown.

However, on November 14, 1962, Ethiopia unilaterally abrogated the terms of the UN resolution and incorporated Eritrea into Ethiopia, thus destroying Eritrean autonomous status. The nationalist movement for Eritrean independence that emerged in the aftermath of November 14 was supported by the Soviet Union and some other countries that had reasons to want the pro Euro-American regime of Emperor Haile Selassie's Ethiopia overthrown.

Ethiopia had argued that historically Eritrea was part of its empire, a part which was acquired and colonized by Italy in 1890. Eritreans refuted this claim and maintained that Eritrea "had never been ruled by Ethiopian kings and emperors prior to 1952."[46] Assuming that Eritrea was actually colonized by Ethiopia prior to 1890 when Italy allegedly replaced Ethiopia as the colonial overlords in Eritrea, the key question was whether *in fact* Eritrea, like any other colonies, had a right to be independent. This was the question which the Ethiopian regime did not want to address. Imperial powers do not willingly accept the decolonization of any part of their holdings, even though they would seek the decolonization of opposing empires. The colonized peoples within the Soviet system were aware of this dilemma. In a paper titled *"Legacy of Colonialism" in Africa* Professor Ivan Potekhin denounced what he called the absurdity of Ethiopia's *historical* claim over Eritrea. Potekhin quoted Nikita Khrushchev to dismiss Ethiopia's claim on Eritrea:

> ... if we were to take as a basis for solution of a boundary problem the history of several thousand years, then, evidently, everyone will agree that in many cases we would come to no solution at all.[47]

---

[46]   See The Eritrean Review, no.11, February/March 1983, p.31.

[47]   Khrushchev as cited in I. Potekhin, "Legacy of Colonialism in Africa," International Affairs, no.3, Moscow, 1964, p.18

Moscow's support for Eritrean independence in post 1962 was motivated by the ideological imperative to fragmentize and or overthrow Haile Selassie's Ethiopia.

Notwithstanding Soviet pro-Eritrean posture, the Soviet Government maintained very cordial relationship with Haile Selassie's Ethiopia. The Ethiopian Emperor was a frequent guest in the Kremlin and he was, undoubtedly, the African leader most respected by the Soviet leadership. The traditional friendship between Moscow and Addis Ababa predates the 1917 Russian socialist revolution, and the mysticism of Haile Selassie's personality may also have contributed to cementing this relationship. Ideologically, Haile Selassie's Ethiopia was allied with Euro-American interests, while the Soviet Union aided the centrifugal forces within Ethiopia desirous to effect a pro-Marxist change. Even though this was understood in Soviet policy toward Ethiopia, the Soviet Government consistently granted economic and technical assistance to Haile Selassie's regime, thus demonstrating the dichotomy between *peaceful coexistence* as a government-to-government policy and *proletarian internationalism* as a people-to-people policy. However, it must be stressed that Soviet scholarly analysis and Soviet policy statements vis-a-vis Ethiopia were devoid of any critical reference to Haile Selassie's feudal rule. It was only after Haile Sellasie was overthrown that Soviet analysis of Haile Selassie's monarchy became more systemic.[48]

An Ethiopian economic delegation arrived in Moscow in July 1958 to seek Soviet assistance. As a result of the negotiations with the Soviet Government, two Soviet vessels—*Shakhty* and *Kamyshin*—unloaded 5,00 tonnes of wheat in Ethiopia in

---

[48] Compare, for example, the analyses in the following works: D.R.Voblikov, Efiopiia v borbe za sokhranenie nezavisimosti 1860-1960, Moscow, 1961; A. Abramov, Efiopiia: Strana ne vstavshaia na koleni, Moscow, 1961; A.N. Stepunin and I.L. Stepunina, Efiopiia, Moscow, 1965; V.S. Yagia, Efiopiia v 1941-1954 godakh. Istoriia borby za ukreplenie politicheskoi nezavisimosti, Moscow, 1969, and his Efiopiia v noveishee vremia, Moscow, 1978.

September-October 1958.[49] In 1959 Ethiopia became the first sub Saharan African country to receive Soviet economic and technical aid. Haile Selassie arrived in Moscow on June 29, 1959 to solicit for Soviet economic and technical assistance. In welcoming the Ethiopian monarch Khrushchev assured him that the "USSR is Ethiopia's reliable and disinterested friend." The visit fetched Ethiopia 400 million rubles (about US$450 million) long term loan to obtain industrial materials from the Soviet Union. A bilateral trade agreement on a most favoured nation status was also signed, while on March 25, 1960, in Addis Ababa, a Soviet-Ethiopian Protocol was signed on the basis of which Soviet specialists were despatched to assist in Ethiopia's oil refinery situated at Assab (capital of Eritrea) which was financed by the Soviet Union.[50]

It is interesting to note the divergent views of Soviet analysts on the role of Ethiopia under Haile Sellasie in the *capitalist camp*. For example, in their respective analyses D. R. Voblikov and V. S. Yagia offered contradictory assessments of Ethiopia's policy under Haile Sellasie. In Voblikov's view, while the "government of Ethiopia strived to utilize American military, economic and technical aid to strengthen the country's defence capability and to develop its national economy" U.S. "policy in Ethiopia ruined the country's economy."[51] However, according to Yagia:

> Ethiopia strived to attract foreign capital necessary for the country's economic development. Utilizing the intra-imperialist contradictions, it obtained concessions from the advanced capitalist states, thus weakening their positions in the country.[52]

---

[49] See Voblikov, Efiopiia v borbe . . . , p.178.
[50] See ibid., pp.180 and 184; and Pravda, July 12, 1959.
[51] Voblikov, op.cit., pp.151 and 154.
[52] Yagia, Efiopiia v 1941-1954 . . . , p.161.

Yagia further argued that a "positive importance for Ethiopia's path was the development of contacts with the socialist powers especially the Soviet Union", even though Haile Selassie's attempt to pursue a policy of "balancing the positions" of the ideologically opposed powers was not successful, because the "United States of America has more weight in the country."[53] Yagia did not identify the concessions Ethiopia obtained "from the advanced capitalist states" that he claimed weakened "their positions in the country", but he recognized the pre-eminence of U.S. "weight in the country." Neither Voblikov nor Yagia criticized Haile Sellasie for relying on Euro-American "military, economic and technical aid", irrespective of Voblikov's observation that U.S. "policy ruined" Ethiopia's economy. We should state, however, that the Soviets were disappointed with the abortive coup to overthrow Haile Sellasie on December 13, 1960. Yagia argued that: "After the Egyptian revolution of 1952 which had a great influence on Asia and Africa, new nationalistic and progressive tendencies emerged in the Ethiopian officers' circle . . ." But in lamenting the failure of the coup he concluded: "The Revolutionary Council was not able to broaden the social base of the coup. The inclusion of the Emperor's son and cousin in the leadership did not help either. This was done, apparently, intentionally in accordance with the social and psychological traditions of Ethiopia."[54]

This non-critical position dominated Soviet analysis of Ethiopia in the pre-1974 period. For example, at the peak of the drought that killed over 200,000 people in Wollo province, when Haile Sellasie visited the Soviet Union in October 1973, Soviet authorities prevented Ethiopian students from demonstrating against Haile Sellasie. According to Belay Girmay who was then a student in the Soviet Union:

> When we planned to demonstrate against Haile Sellasie
> and feudal Ethiopia during Haile Selassie's visit to the

---

[53] Ibid., 161-162.
[54] Yagia, *Efiopiia v noveishee vremia*, pp.208 & 211.

USSR in 1973, the Soviet authorities disallowed us on
the ground that Haile Sellasie, though a feudal Emperor,
was more progressive that a number of African presidents
and we (Soviets) respect him.[55]

Soviet cautious attitude toward Haile Selassie's Ethiopia
cannot be explained *solely* by reference to Ethiopia's close ties with
tsarist Russia which, as we have observed, laid the foundation for
Soviet-Ethiopian relations. It would be an oversimplification to
do so. Haile Sellasie was aware of Soviet support for the Eritrean
independence movement whose objective was to either dismember
or overthrow his imperial rule. He was also aware of Soviet *military*,
economic and technical assistance to Somalia with whom Ethiopia
had outstanding territorial disputes. Even though it was repeatedly
stressed in various Soviet-Somalian communiqués that inter-state
conflicts, *including territorial* should be resolved by peaceful
settlement, it was clear to all observers that Soviet weapons to
Somalia aided the latter in its attacks against Ethiopia. Thus, Haile
Sellasie was sandwiched between two hostile entities—Eritrea and
Somalia—who were both aided by a *friendly* Soviet Government.
The geo-strategic significance of the North-East African coastline
from Egypt to Somalia has long been recognized by competing
world powers, and for the Soviet Union it would be an ideological
blunder to concede the region to the Euro-American powers. It
was therefore imperative for the Soviet Government to maintain
cordial relations with a feudal pro-U.S. Ethiopia. As an emperor
of an African country that was never colonized, and whose
country is the headquarters of the OAU, Haile Sellasie enjoyed
considerable respect from a cross section of African heads of states
and governments. Soviet leaders were aware of this; a fact which
perhaps further explained the high level of cordiality and caution in
Soviet-Ethiopian relations. Moscow supported Ethiopia's economic

---

[55] Interview with Mr. Belay Girmay, First Secretary, Ethiopian Embassy,
Moscow, October 24, 1979.

and technological development while at the same time it encouraged the Eritrean independence movement in recognition of Eritrea's right of national self-government.

Meanwhile, the Soviet Government intensified its cooperation with Haile Selassie's regime. In accordance with the terms of the Soviet-Ethiopian Agreement of March 8, 1960, the Soviet Government, in June 1963, built a technical college in Ethiopia as a gift. The college was to train mechanics and technologists with an initial intake of over 1,000 students.[56] Following the Somalian-Ethiopian cease fire accord reached in Khartoum in April 1964, Nikita Khrushchev sent a congratulatory telegramme to Haile Sellasie expressing the hope that the accord would further "strengthen the solidarity of the peoples of Africa, durable peace and friendship among peoples."[57]

Haile Sellasie was a guest of the Soviet Government from February 27-March 2, 1967. His discussions with President Podgorny and Premier Kosygin took place in a "sincere, mutual understanding and friendly atmosphere." Both parties "noted with satisfaction the traditional friendship of Soviet-Ethiopian relations" which were developing well, and agreed that Soviet specialists be despatched to Ethiopia "to study the ways and means of further developing the economic cooperation and trade between the two countries." Furthermore, they reiterated in the joint communiqué their commitments to the struggle for international "peace and security" and "for the liquidation of foreign military bases in foreign countries which are utilized or could be directly or indirectly utilized for interference in the internal affairs of other states."[58] In the Soviet-Ethiopian joint communiqué, Haile Sellasie and his Soviet hosts were convinced that, in the conditions of increased

---

[56] See Ministertsvo inostannykh del SSSR, SSSR in strany Afriki, 1963-1970gg., chast 1, Moscow, 1982, p.34.

[57] Ibid., p.105.

[58] Ibid., chast 2, p.15 See also Vneshniaia politika sovetskogo soiuza 1967. Sbornik dokumentov, Moscow, 1968, pp.58 and 61.

neo-colonialist activities in Africa, "the necessity to strength the unity and solidarity of African countries, *on the basis of anti-colonialism and anti-imperialism,* acquires a specially important meaning."[59] The joint communiqué revealed the dialectical construct and tactics of Soviet policy which was anchored on the ideological advancement of Marxism. It should be recalled that a U.S.-Ethiopian defence agreement was signed on May 22, 1953, and that the U.S. maintained a military base in Ethiopia, the facilities of which were used to aid Israel during the 6-day war of 1967 barely three months after the Soviet-Ethiopian joint communiqué. Thus, Haile Selassie's preparedness to cooperate with the Soviet Union *"on the basis of anti-colonialism and anti-imperialism"* did not only betray a contradiction in his thinking but aptly demonstrated the strategic calculations of Soviet policy.

Even though Haile Selassie's Ethiopia was in the grips of the U.S. the Soviet Government continued to make its presence felt in all aspects of Ethiopia's development. In early February 1970 during the celebrations of the Ethiopian Armed Forces and Navy Day, the Soviet Union despatched its navy on board *Blestiashii* to Massawa to participate in the event. Haile Sellasie visited *Blestiashii* at Massawa and thanked the "Soviet Government and the Commander of the USSR Armed Forces" and viewed the visit of *Blestiashii* as a "manifestation of the sincere friendship between Ethiopia and the Soviet Union."[60] On the invitation of the Presidium of the USSR Supreme Soviet and the Soviet Government, Haile Sellasie visited Moscow from May 28-30, 1970. His discussions with Soviet leaders explored the avenues of broadening the scope of the bilateral relations between both countries. Haile Sellasie promised to "positively look into the question of direct air services between Moscow and Addis Ababa."[61]

---

[59]   SSSR in strany Afriki 1963-1970, chast 2, p.15. Italics mine.

[60]   Pravda, February 7, 1970.

[61]   Ibid., May 31, 1970.

Before the storm of February 1974 Haile Sellasie visited the Soviet Union for the last time in 1973 as a guest of the Soviet Government on a "business visit." His visit, which was prominently reported on the front page of Pravda, lasted just 24 hours—October 29-30, 1973. According to the report of the bilateral talks[62], Haile Selassie's discussions with Soviet leaders occurred in an "atmosphere of frankness and mutual understanding",—a diplomatic euphemism for mutual disagreement over key policy issues. It was highly probable that the Soviet Government raised the vexing problem of the drought in the Wollo province during its *frank* discussions with Haile Sellasie, an issue which had caused the latter real crisis in Ethiopia. However, President Podgorny and Haile Sellasie still managed to express satisfaction for the "current changes in the world"

> . . . and emphasized their unswerving desire to struggle together with other peace-loving peoples so that the positive changes in international relations assume an irreversible character.[63]

Little did Haile Sellasie know that part of "the positive changes in international relations" which will "assume an irreversible character" was already brewing in his feudal empire. The Soviet Union was to support these "positive changes" as Haile Selassie's monarchy gradually disintegrated. The disintegration process which started as a reaction to government increase of gasoline prices on February 13, 1974, and culminated in the overthrow and abolishment of the monarchy in September 1974, is referred to as Ethiopia's "creeping revolution."[64]

---

[62] See Pravda, November 1, 1973.

[63] Ibid.

[64] For a chronological sequence of the creeping revolution, see Raul Valdes, Ethiopia. The Unknown Revolution, Havana, Cuba, 1978, pp.129-147.

The gasoline price increase, and the spiralling inflation necessitated by the escalation in the price of essential household commodities, couple with Ethiopia's government obnoxious education policy, created a solid platform for alliance building uniting workers, taxi drivers, students and teachers. On the basis of this alliance, teachers and students demonstrated against Haile Selassie's government on February 20, 1974, a demonstration which had far reaching political undertones. It took place two days after taxi drivers had gone on strike. Sensing the social and political repercussion of these demonstrations, Haile Selassie was compelled to appeal to the nation on a national television and radio broadcast on February 24, 1974. He indicated his government would take necessary measures to normalize the situation by introducing programmes to improve the standard of living by imposing a price control on essential commodities. His government was to discard its educational reform system which was to increase the number of years in primary and secondary schools from 10 to 12 years.[65] Years of societal discontent with no organized outlet for articulating the grievances of the working class systematically began to find viable constituencies as the military gradually became involved by supporting the anti-regime forces.

The Soviet News Agency, *TASS* reported that Haile Selassie had increased the salaries of the army, police and teachers in a move to appease these sections of the population.[66] *TASS*, which was collecting news agency reports from Addis Ababa, Paris, New York, and London, was merely *reporting* the deepening crisis in Ethiopia and had not yet taken a critical stand against Haile Selassie's regime. Moscow was yet not sure of both the depth and direction of the crystallizing anti-regime forces in Ethiopia.

Towards the end of February 1974 dissent within the army began to assume a disquieting posture inimical to Haile Selassie's interests. He therefore despatched his armed forces chief of staff to try to

[65]   See Pravda, February 25, 1974.
[66]   See ibid., February 26, 1974.

mollify the striking soldiers in Asmara. The striking soldiers had declined the increase in pay. As the Asmara disturbances engulfed Massawa (both centres in Eritrea) and public disenchantment intensified, the cabinet of Aklilou Habte-Wolde resigned on February 27 and Haile Selassie appointed Endalkatchev Makonnem as prime minister on February 28, 1974. These developments compelled the OAU to terminate its 22nd session of the Council of Ministers then sitting in Addis Ababa.[67] Vital strategic institutions were occupied by members of the armed forces still loyal to Haile Selassie, while dissident soldiers in Eritrea also occupied equally strategic positions as Makonnem promised to restore "law and order" with the help of the armed forces. It was no surprise that the centre of the anti-regime forces was located in Eritrea, given the Eritrean national liberation movement that had begun since 1962.

In the first Soviet comment on the Ethiopian crisis, V. Korovikov claimed that Haile Selassie had succeeded in normalizing the situation because "representatives of the army and police declared loyalty to Emperor Haile Selassie l and the new government."[68] Reporting on March 4, *TASS* confirmed this assertion of normalized situation and that the armed forces were now off the street, and soldiers had returned to their barracks in Asmara.[69] It seemed as if the Soviets were hoping that Haile Selassie's regime would prevail, otherwise, it was difficult to understand how they could have concluded that the situation had been *normalized* simply because the soldiers *"had returned to their barracks."* They had a faulty reading of the situation. It is interesting to note that, barely forty-eight hours later, now citing U.S. news agency, *TASS* informed its readers in the Soviet Union that the situation had "worsen" as Ethiopian trade union had gone on strike demanding salary increase and better working conditions, while students demanded socio-economic reforms, coupled with a

---

[67]   See <u>Pravda</u>, February 28, and March 1, 1974.

[68]   V. Korovikov, "Obstanovka normalizuetsia," <u>Pravda</u>, March 3, 1974.

[69]   <u>Pravda</u>, March 4, 1974.

prisoners' revolt.[70] This was the first organized workers' strike in Ethiopian history involving over 85,000 workers. The government was shaken and began, rather helplessly, to seek for quick solutions. It promised to implement workers' demands, while Haile Selassie instructed Makonnem to convene a constitutional conference and report back to him within six months! As the workers' strike entered its third day threatening to halt Ethiopia's economy, representatives of the feudal-capitalist ruling class met with Haile Selassie, requesting that the government negotiate with the Ethiopian Trade Union Confederation (ETUC). Foscha Tekle, the General Secretary of ETUC, later announced that an accord had been reached with the government, and that the workers' demand had been satisfied. Accordingly, about 120,000 workers returned to work on March 11, 1974.[71]

The victory of the ETUC and the continued strike of university teachers strongly indicated the capabilities of an organized group to effect *positive changes* in Ethiopia. Ethiopia's government was compelled to establish a workers' minimum wage structure and to recognize workers' right to pension. These gains and the prospects of a systemic change undoubtedly influenced Soviet write V. Korovikov to conclude on March 12:

> The current situation in Ethiopia is conducive for progressive reforms, for a *genuine renovation* of the country.[72]

It should be recalled that, just nine days earlier, Korovikov had informed Soviet leaders that Haile Selassie had *normalized the situation*. His call for "a genuine renovation" of Ethiopia indicated

---

70 Ibid., March 6, 1974. See also V. Korovikov, "Vseobshchaia zabastovka trudiashchikhsia efiopii," Pravda, March 28, 1974.

71 See Pravda, March 9, 10, and 11, 1974

72 V. Korovikov, "Efiopiia: Pobeda trudiashchikhsia," Pravda, March 12, 1974. Italics mine.

Moscow's expectations at this stage of Ethiopia's crisis. As workers ended their strike, teachers took up the strike baton in a chaotic environment which forced the authorities to close both the Addis Ababa and Asmara airports. Teachers and workers were now demanding democratic and constitutional reforms as well as land reforms. Junior officers defied their superiors in the armed forces. Ethiopian women also demonstrated demanding equal pay with men. While the Association of Ethiopian Teachers (AET) ended its strike on March 19, the university teachers remained on strike.[73] As per the accord reached between the ETUC and government, workers were supposed to be paid for the period they were on strike. However, company executives refused to honour this understanding and instead reprisal measures were engineered against radical members of the ETUC.

Reprisals were also undertaken in the armed forces. This led to renewed army and police disturbances in Asmara due to the arrest of junior officers who had revolted against the government. The rebelling Asmara army and police command gave the government three conditions under which it was prepared to end its strike. First, the government should institute court proceedings against corrupt army and civilian leaders of previous governments. Second, arrested junior officers accused of instigating the February revolt should be released. Third, the government to guarantee it would not take any reprisal measures against the junior officers accused of taking part in the revolt.[74] The Asmara army and police command ended its strike only after the Ethiopian government had accepted the above conditions. Addis Ababa's acceptance of these conditions clearly demonstrated the weakness and the state of near collapse of Haile Selassie's regime which was forced to capitulate. The victory of the Asmara army and police command reflected the emergence of a new and powerful centre of dissent capable of seizing power from Haile Selassie's government.

---

73 See Pravda, March 19, and 20, 1974.

74 TASS, "Polozhenie v efiopii," in Pravda, March 29, 1974.

As the anti-regime sentiments gained momentum, members of Ethiopia's Lower House of Parliament also pressed their demand that corrupt elements of the regime be punished. This prompted the Minister of Internal Affairs to promise that the government will deal severely with corrupt army and civilian leaders. In its bid to remain in power at all cost, the Ethiopian government also promised to undertake land reforms in order to improve Ethiopia's "economic and social development" to "redistribute land" and "stimulate production."[75] Though the arrested junior officers were released on April 14, municipal and transport employees continued their strike amidst Haile Selassie's appeal for calm.

Haile Selassie's appeal for calm failed to yield the anticipated result as his government's request for the armed forces to "maintain law and order" seemed to further aggravate the crisis: demonstrators encountered the police on the streets.[76] Between April and September 12, 1974, when Haile Selassie 1 was dethroned, the Armed Forces Coordinating Committee (AFCC) was engaged in a power tussle with succeeding Ethiopian governments as the latter fruitlessly grappled with the crisis.[77] The inability of the government to restore normalcy, and the AFCC's involvement in governance created a dual power situation in the country. Even though the AFCC, with Lt.General Aman Andom as chairman, maintained an

---

[75] See TASS, "Trebovaniia deputatov," in <u>Pravda</u>, April 4, 1974; "Polozhenie v efiopii," <u>Pravda</u>, April 5, 1974; "Na poroge reforma," <u>Pravda</u>, April 10, 1974.

[76] V. Korovikov, "K polosheniiu v efiopii," <u>Pravda</u>, April 25, 1974.

[77] For reports on the development between April-September 1974, see Vivo, <u>Ethiopia. The Unknown Revolution</u>; "Efiopiia: Sokraniaetsia napriazhennosti," <u>Pravda</u>, April 22, 1974; V. Korovikov, "Addis Ababa. Polozhenie obostriaetsia," <u>Pravda</u>, April 28, 1974; <u>Pravda</u>, May 3, 1974; V. Korovikov, "Burnyi dni efiopii," <u>Pravda</u>, June 3, 1974; I. Doronin, "The Events in Ethiopia," <u>New Times</u>, no. 28, Moscow, 1974, p.11; "Developments in Ethiopia," <u>New Times</u>, no. 33, Moscow, 1974, pp.9&11.

anti-government posture, it however still declared the armed forces' loyalty to Emperor Haile Selassie.[78] This confusing posture of the AFCC failed to re-assure both Haile Selassie and the anti-regime forces. Former cabinet ministers and senior police officers, along with leading trade unionists, were arrested as the army occupied strategic establishments in the country.

The extra-ordinary parliamentary session of July 9, 1974 failed to map out a political arrangement to democratize Ethiopia amidst the escalating anti regime demonstrations, and the increased influence of the AFCC in the political process. Endalkachew Makonnem's cabinet was dissolved on July 22, and the AFCC's choice, Michael Imru, was appointed prime minister by Haile Selassie. Imru's appointment could not by itself resolve the crisis. It was clear that the AFCC, as a body of conflicting views contending for hegemony, had a faction that was obviously opposed to the Imru regime. This faction, which constituted the *inner circle* of the AFCC succeeded in pressuring Imru to institute measures curbing the Emperor's powers. A Draft Constitution released on August 7, 1974, limited the Emperor's powers and increased those of parliament, with the latter now possessing the jurisdiction to elect a prime minister. Voting age was lowered from 21 to 18, and the right to establish political parties was granted. Ethiopia was declared a secular state.[79] These developments reflected the degree of influence the *inner circle* of the AFCC had on Prime Minister Imru. The AFCC gradually became more consistent in its criticism of Emperor Haile Selassie by systematically propelling itself into a position of *primus inter paris* vis-a-vis the government of Prime Minister Imru. In his assessment of the revolving crisis and the government's inability to stabilize the polity, V. Korovikov noted that "the democratically inclined section of the armed forces decided once more to interfere."

[78] See <u>Pravda</u>, July 1, 4, 5, and 7, 1974.
[79] See "Developments in Ethiopia," <u>New Times</u>, no.33, Moscow, 1974, pp.9&11.

Korovikov's view underlined the intra AFCC contradictions concerning the development of the Ethiopian *creeping revolution.* Lt.General Andom, who had the characteristics of an Alexander Kerensky, presided over an AFCC which was dominated by strong anti-regime forces committed to the overthrow of the monarchy. Andom could not comprehend the forces he had to contend with in the AFCC as its attack on the monarchy took a more systemic twist. It accused Emperor Haile Selassie of anti-patriotism, declaring that the Emperor had forfeited the trust of the people.[80] The AFCC of the *Dergue* (an Amharic word meaning a *Committee*) began to demonstrate its determination to seize political power. On September 12, 1974, the *Dergue* decreed that Haile Selassie l, "King of Kings of Ethiopia, Lion of Judah, the elect of God" was now dethroned! While it decreed that Haile Selassie was to be succeeded by his eldest son, Asfa Wossen then in Switzerland, it was made categorically clear that state power now resided in the *Dergue.* Parliament was dissolved "until such time as the people elect true representatives in a true democratic manner, who will serve the interests of the people." Andom assured the foreign envoys accredited to Ethiopia that the coup would not affect Ethiopia's relations with other countries.[81]

Following the dethronement of Haile Selassie the AFCC, on September 16, transformed itself into the Provisional Military Administrative Council (PMAC) with Lt.General Andom as its chairman and Minister of Defence. The PMAC became the substantive government of Ethiopia. Andom, an Eritrean by nationality, had served Haile Selassie as Ethiopia's military attaché in both France and the U.S. He was highly respected by the Western diplomats in Ethiopia. His involvement in the dethronement of the Emperor enhanced the credibility of the *Dergue*, while he, at the same time, was able to retain the respect of the West. He had a

---

80   V. Korovikov, "Efiopiia: Vremia bolshikh peremen," <u>Pravda</u>, September 1, 1974; <u>Pravda</u>, September 12, 1974.
81   See I. Doronin, "Ethiopia without the Emperor," <u>New Times</u>, no. 38, Moscow, 1974, pp.12-13; <u>Pravda</u>, September 13, 1974.

dual function to serve, but could not articulate the dynamics of the *Dergue's inner circle* whose motive conflicted with his own perception of governance. He was not the leader of the *Dergue*; neither did he know the membership of the *Dergue*. Professor Bereket Habte Selassie claimed that Andom's "prestige and fame were resented by the young members of the Dergue inner circle"[82] as the conflict between him and the inner circle sharpened.

The resentment of Andom had more ideological undertones than one engineered by a mere jealousy of his "prestige and fame." Andom was caught in a web of contradictory tendencies between the forces of liberal reformism and socialist radicalism. Between February and November 1974 Ethiopia was passing through a phase reminiscent of Tsarist Russia in the February-October period of 1917. A period of missed opportunities for the liberal reformists and the socialists. Andom was gradually rationalized out of power by the *Dergue's* inner circle. He was among the sixty people executed by the *Dergue* on November 14, 1974. The list included former prime ministers Aklilou Abte-Wold and Endalkatchew Makonnem, the Emperor's grand-don Real Admiral Iskander Desta, and Ras Asrantie Kasia, former chairman of the Emperor's Council. Andom was accused of dictatorial powers, of conspiracy with a foreign nation, and of offering custody to a foreign military adviser whom he secretly smuggled out of the country. On November 28, 1974, the *Dergue* appointed 53 year old Brigadier General Teferi Banti as the new chairman of the PMAC.

The Ethiopian revolution began to progress along the path mapped out by the *Dergue's* inner circle. Professor Selassie, in recognition of the role played by non-military personnel in this development, opined that, due to the constant pressure of radical university students and trade unionists, the *Dergue* gradually transformed its slogan from *Ethiopia First* (1974) to *Ethiopian*

[82] Bereket Habte Selassie, "The Dergue's Dilemma: The Legacies of a Feudal Empire," <u>Monthly Review</u>, 32, 3, July-August, 1980, p.10.

Socialism (1975) and to *Marxism-Leninism* (1976).[83] It is interesting to note that this view agreed with the analysis of Raul Valdes Vivo whose work predates Professor Selassie's. Vivo had argued that the Ethiopian revolution "was not a military but a people's revolution, a mass spontaneous revolution, to which the armed forces gave direction in the absences of a revolutionary party or movement." Vivo further postulated that the process "led to more revolution, to more participation by the people, to having the proletariat set-up its dictatorship in alliance with the peasants, to *uniting military and civilian revolutionaries* within a Marxist-Leninist Party that provides the kind of general staff that all revolutions need."[84]

By December 20, 1974 the PMAC had declared its decision to form a "progressive political party conforming to Ethiopia's socialist revolution." This decision and the subsequent economic policy of the *Dergue* gravitated Ethiopia towards the Soviet Union as a comrade-in-arms. Soviet analysts began to adopt a more systemic critique of Haile Selassie's regime. A Soviet Africanist, G. Galperin accused the dethroned Emperor of creating conducive "investment climate" for western capital which he alleged was not in Ethiopia's national interest. Eritrea, whose independence the Soviet Union had championed since 1945, was now referred to by Galperin in 1975 as "the so-called Eritrean question."[85] Even though the Soviet Union was in the process of disentangling itself from its pro-Eritrean position, extreme caution was however still noticeable in Soviet assessment of the Ethiopian transformation. Writing in September 1975, on the anniversary of the Ethiopian revolution, F. Pushkov underlined Soviet support for Ethiopian government reform policy, but advised that the progressive posture of the reform should be

---

83   Ibid., p.13.

84   Vivo, *op.cit.*, p.61. See also G. Galperin, "Revoliutsia v efiopii: Osobennosti razvitiia," Aziia i Afriki segodnia, no.3, Moscow, 1978, pp.9-12.

85   G. Galperin, "Efiopiia: Revoliutsia prodolzhaetsia," Aziia i Afriki segodnia, no.7, Moscow, 1975, pp.11-13.

critically evaluated as the "exact" focus of Ethiopia was not yet certain.[86] This was two months after Brigadier General Banti, during his tour of Eritrea, had announced PMAC's decision to establish a national political party guided by "socialist ideology" that will unite the workers, farmers and all Ethiopia's progressive forces. Banti appealed to Eritrean secessionists to abandon their quest for self-determination and join the "peoples of Ethiopia in constructing a new democratic country." It was a support seeking tour to bring Eritrea into the fold of an embryonic Ethiopian *socialist* polity.[87]

As the Ethiopian revolution progressed, intra-ideological contradictions within the broad national front began to sharpen. Banti gradually became identified with a counter-revolutionary group within the leadership. The debate on the proposed *National Democratic Revolution* caused ideological disarray between the All Ethiopian Socialist Movement (MEISON) and the Ethiopian People's Revolutionary Party (EPRP)—the two political groupings contending for power to advance the Ethiopian revolution. MEISON proposed a programme for a *National Democratic Revolution* which appealed to the inner circle of the *Dergue*. While the EPRP endorsed the idea of such a programme it, according to Professor Selassie, predicated its participation on "the elimination of the Dergue from the political scene", and demanded the proclamation of a Marxist people's government. Selassie argued that the *Dergue* considered the EPRP a serious threat to its pre-eminence in Ethiopia's politics and therefore had to ally itself with MEISON "and used it to liquidate EPRP."[88] EPRP's confrontation with the *Dergue*-MEISON alliance led to a series of violence and assassinations of political opponents

---

[86] See K. Pushkov, "Ethiopia. The Programme for Restructuring Society," International Affairs, no. 9, Moscow, 1975, pp.132-133.

[87] See Pravda, July 23, 1975; and V. Korovikov, "Programma preobrazovanii," Pravda, July 25, 1975.

[88] Bereket Habte Selassie, loc.cit., p.15. See also his "Political Leadership in Crisis: The Ethiopian Case," *Horn of Africa*, 3, 1, Summit, New Jersey, 1980, p.9.

between 1976 and 1978, a situation which compelled some analysts to refer to the period as "the Red Terror." While Moscow supported the *Dergue*-MEISON alliance, it was speculated that the EPRP enjoyed Beijing's patronage.[89] Lt.Colonel Mengistu Haile Mariam emerged as the leader of the *Dergue* during this confrontation. Those accused of *counter-revolutionary* activities by the *Dergue*, which included Brigadier General Banti, were executed on February 3, 1977; and Lt.Colonel Mengistu Haile Mariam was proclaimed the president of the PMAC on February 11, 1977.

Towards the end of 1977 Moscow's assessment of the Ethiopian revolution had swung from a position of cautious endorsement to that of fraternal embracement. The PMAC had closed down the offices of the United States Information Services (USIS), and ordered its employees to quit Ethiopia, while the correspondents of *Reuter, France Press* and the *Washington Post* were given 24 hours to leave the country. When the Ogaden war broke out, and Somalia expelled Soviet diplomats from Mogadishu because of Moscow's support for Ethiopia, a base for an improved Soviet-Ethiopian *socialist* fraternization was thus established. How did Soviet scholars perceive the *new* Ethiopia in the midst of these developments? V. S. Yagia's view is representative of the Soviet position.

Writing in 1978 Yagia opined that with "Haile Selassie's consent" Ethiopian government officials systematically embezzled state funds at the expense of the poor, and argued that: "Haile Selassie utilized his personal foreign initiatives to strengthen the country's belief in his leadership and the wisdom of the monarchy, . . ."[90] It is significant to note that Yagia would not want us to conclude that, the "personal foreign initiatives" of Haile Selassie that he referred to included Haile Selassie's close political relationship with the Kremlin, which did much to enhance the status of the Emperor in

---

[89]   Selassie, "Political Leadership in Crisis: The Ethiopian Case," p.10.

[90]   Yagia, *Efiopiia v noveishee vremia*, pp.179-191; 227. For a favourable assessment of Haile Selassie before the revolution, see Yagia, *Efiopiia v 1941-1954 godakh*, pp.161-162.

international politics. Without any reference to the Soviet Union, Yagia posited that Ethiopia's inability to resolve the Eritrean question "significantly influenced Ethiopia's relations with many African and Asian countries."[91] The Eritrean Liberation Front (ELF) established in 1962 had attracted both material and political support from certain Afro-Asian and East European states, including the Soviet Union. In his rationalization of Soviet support for the ELF during the Haile Selassie regime, Yagia declared:

> The bases for the growth of separatism in Eritrea were the following: Eritrea's colonial past, its higher level of development compared to the other provinces of the Empire; ethnic discrimination of the central authorities on administrative appointments; the unwillingness of the Eritrean bourgeoisie to share its profit . . . But the stimulus for the activation of the ELF was the liquidation of the Eritrean autonomous status as defined by the V Session of the General Assembly of the UNO, *and its complete integration into the Ethiopian empire in 1962.*[92]

On the *creeping revolution*, Yagia observed that by mid-1974 "the political role of the armed forces had increased", even though power was concentrated in the "right wing" of the armed forces which was "aligned with prime minister Makonnem" attempting to "maintain the old regime."[93] On the overthrow of Haile Selassie, Yagia averred:

> First of all, an anti-feudal revolution took place in Ethiopia, for which objective and subjective factors existed in the country . . . The fundamental interest of the people demanded the destruction of the leadership

---

[91] Yagia, *Efiopiia v noveishee vremie*, 220.

[92] *Ibid.*, 220-221. Italics mine.

[93] *Ibid.*, 259.

of the landlords and the monarchy. The revolution was
effected by the army which appeared on the political
arena in the course of the spontaneous anti-feudal
movement of the masses.

In the absence of political parties, Yagia concluded, the "Ethiopian
army assumed the role of the political representative of a coalition of
social groups: petty bourgeoisie, peasantry, intelligentsia, etc."[94]

A vital issue emerges from Yagia's analysis. To put it bluntly,
the Soviet Union supported the independence of Eritrea which
implied the dismemberment of Haile Selassie's Ethiopia. We pose
the question: What happens to Eritrea's demand for independence
in post Haile Selassie's Ethiopia? But before we address this crucial
question, let us consult with Belay Girmay, a post Haile Selassie
Ethiopian diplomat educated in the Soviet Union. On Moscow's
attitude toward the Eritrean question, Belay Girmay declared:

Ethiopia was convinced that the USSR was aiding
Eritrea. It was Moscow's advantage to aid Eritrea as the
USSR was interested in the overthrow of Haile Selassie's
regime. Cuba was training Eritrean freedom fighters.
The Soviet authorities recognized both the Ethiopian
Students Union and the Eritrean Students Union in the
USSR before the revolution of 1974.[95]

Belay Girmay opined that Eritrea was Moscow's "soft spot" in Haile
Selassie's Ethiopia. In his view, if Eritrea had succeeded with Soviet
aid to break away from Haile Selassie's regime, the Emperor "would
have sought for Western aid. Progressive elements of Ethiopia
would have continued the struggle against Haile Selassie, because

---

[94] *Ibid.*, 264-265.
[95] Interview with Mr. Belay Girmay, First Secretary, Ethiopian Embassy, Moscow, October 24, 1979.

Ethiopian progressives of all nationalities were supporting the Eritrean revolt."[96]

In line with revolutionary stratagem it could be postulated that "Ethiopian progressives" that supported the Eritrean revolt under Haile Selassie's rulership did so on the assumption that the revolt would be utilized as a launching pad to overthrow Haile Selassie, in the process of establishing a *new* Ethiopia of which Eritrea would remain a constituent unit. This postulate negates the agitation of the ELF, while, in Addis Ababa's views, a post Haile Selassie Ethiopia seeks to resolve the problems that engineered the independence aspiration of Eritrea. In an Ethiopian *socialist* polity, as argued by Addis Ababa, the demand for an independent Eritrean state becomes irrelevant. As for the Eritreans, the proclamation of a *socialist* Ethiopia should not obliterate their independence agitation. When Soviet attempt to persuade Eritrea to unite with the embryonic *socialist* Ethiopia failed, the Soviet Union elected to abandon the former in favour of the latter. The independence of Eritrea which the Soviet Government had supported since 1945 suddenly became obsolete! Soviet *justification* for this position can be found in the works of Lenin, who had argued:

> There is not a single Marxist who, without making a total break with the foundations of Marxism and socialism, could deny that the interests of Socialism are above the interests of the right of nations to self-determination. Our Socialist Republic has done and is continuing to do everything possible for implementing the right of self-determination for Finland, Ukraine, etc. But if the concrete position that has arisen is such that the existence of the Socialist Republic is endangered at a given moment in respect of an infringement of the right of self-determination of a few nations (Poland, Lithuania, Courtland, etc.), then it stands to reason that

---

[96] *Ibid.*

the interests of the preservation of the socialist Republic
must take preference.[97]

The above Leninist postulate perceives the nationality question
as a manifestation of the class struggle, a position which was readily
adopted by the Ethiopian socialist regime. This presupposes the
guarantee of the rights of all constituents within a unified socialist
whole. Ethiopian Marxist-Leninists underlined this argumentation
in their debate with the ELF theoreticians, as exemplified in the
December 1982 issue of *MESKEREM*.[98] The ELF condemned
this reductionist approach of Ethiopia's socialists. In its critique of
Ethiopia over this issue, the ELF asserted:

> It claims that the desire of national self-determination,
> the right of any people, is merely a function of the class
> struggle—a typical Soviet analysis. What it does not do,
> of course, is to explain why the entire people of Eritrea,
> whatever their class backgrounds, wish to achieve
> self-determination and independence.[99]

Soviet de-recognition of Eritrean independence, explainable in
the above Leninist constructs, challenged the concept of national
independence and self-determination. It demonstrates the
expendability of a minor client, Eritrea, where a major one, Ethiopia,
unexpectedly emerges. It would be naive to ascribe much credibility
to the niceties of ideological postulates as the major determinant, as
it was obvious that the major determinant was the military might of
Ethiopia. The Maoist dictum that political power emanates from the

97 V. I. Lenin, *Sochineniia, Moscow*, 1949, 4 edition, vol. 26, p.408.
98 See "Democracy and the Question of Nationalities in the Ethiopian
    Revolution," MESKEREM, Addis Ababa, 3, 11, December 1982,
    pp.88-103.
99 "Marxist Dogma is no Solution," *The Eritrean Review*, no. 12,
    April-May, 1983, p.21.

barrel of a gun was very appropriate in this instance. Ideology thus serves as a justifier of political actions. The agitation for Eritrean independence predates the Ethiopian revolution, and, according to the ELF, the Ethiopian revolution should not negate the rights of Eritreans to self-determination. Following the October 1917 Russian socialist revolution, for example, non-Russian constituent units of the Russian empire like the Ukraine, Georgia, etc., emerged as independent states but were later *reintegrated* into the Soviet Union. Notwithstanding the various criticisms against the process of *reintegrating* these independent states into the Soviet Union in the 1919-1922 period[100], these states still existed as independent entities before the process of *reintegration* was successfully effected.

Anti-Ethiopian external support for Eritrean independence affected the chances of the ELF attaining its objectives. This support, which came mainly from anti socialist Arab states and the West, was perceived by both Addis Ababa and Moscow to have compromised the supposedly Marxist revolutionary zeal of the ELF. Arguing that "the major contradiction in class society is class contradiction", Ethiopian Marxist re-emphasized the Leninist postulate:

> Today when imperialist exploitation has not yet been done away with, Communists support all national liberation movements that contribute to the downfall of monopoly capital and the furthering of popular revolutions. On the other hand, they firmly oppose and resolutely fight against those movements which weaken the class unity and revolutionary zeal of the masses by polluting them with nationalist and chauvinistic

---

[100] See, for example, Leonard Schapiro, *The Government and Politics of the Soviet Union*, London, 1968,pp.45-46; Richard Pipes, The Formation of the Soviet Union, New York, 1964, passim.

sentiments and prevent them from struggling in unison
for their class interests.[101]

The main objective of the Soviet-Ethiopian position on *class
struggle* was to depict the Eritrean independence movement as
nationalistic and chauvinistic. It was their point of view that the
emergence of a *socialist Ethiopia* had negated the right of Eritreans
to attain national independence. Eritreans, however, refused to
subjugate their independence on the altar of Ethiopian Marxism.
The Soviet-Ethiopian interpretation of *class struggle* and *national
liberation* was considered reactionary by the ELF.[102]

Soviet policy toward Ethiopia, and in deed the Horn of Africa,
raised a fundamental problem in Soviet-African relations. A movement
or a regime was considered *"progressive"* by the Kremlin in as much
as its policies were consistently structured on anti-Westernism. The
constant breakdown of Soviet-African alliances over the questions of
nationalism, independence and sovereignty remained a major factor
that hindered any sustained Soviet alliance with an African state.
Even though the Soviets initiated policy changes at the 20th CPSU
Congress in 1956 to mollify African nationalism, the Kremlin was
not that successful in operationalizing this delicate issue. Part of the
problem seemed to be in the unpredictability of African politics and
the *personalized* nature of African radicalism. The Soviets, like the

---

[101] "Democracy and the Question of Nationalities in the Ethiopian
Revolution," MESKEREM, 3, 11, 1982, p.92. See also G. Galperin,
"Natsionalno-demokraticheskoe preobrazovaniia v efiopii," *Aziia
i Afrika segodniia*, no.8, Moscow, 1976, pp.9-12; *Natsionalno-
demokraticheskaia revoliutsia v efiopii*, Moscow, 1976.

[102] For a critique of the Soviet-Ethiopian position on class struggle and
national liberation, see Tekie Fessehatzion, "The Eritrean Struggle
for Independence and National Liberation," *Horn of Africa*, 1, 2,
April-June, 1978, pp.29-34; Bereket Habte Selassie, "The Evolution
of the Principle of Self-Determination, *Horn of Africa*, 1, 4,
October-December, 1978, pp.3-9.

U.S., did not appreciate the strong *independent* posture exhibited by African nationalist leaders whose policies seemed to check the intensity of Soviet influence. We witnessed this in Soviet-Egyptian relations, as well as in the Solod affairs in Guinea. "On a doctrinal level", according to Carol R. Saivetz and Sylvia Woodby, "the Soviets constructed a tentative formula linking nationalism with 'progressiveness' up to the point at which it contradicts proletarian internationalism, i.e., Soviet interests"[103] Saivetz and Woodby, like Brutents, a Soviet specialist on national liberation movements, recognize the limitation in any attempt to *permanently* link nationalism with progressiveness. However, unlike Saivetz and Woodby, Brutents provides a subtle philosophical distinction in the linkage when he warned:

> We should note especially that recognition of the progressive role of revolutionary democratic conceptions is of course not the same as admitting that their *entire* content is progressive.[104]

Recognition does not guarantee admittance; the focus is tactical while the latter represents a higher level of ideological compatibility. This process led to a system of constantly shifting alliances in Soviet foreign policy.

Notwithstanding this, however, Soviet preference for Ethiopia and the resultant expendability of Eritrea could only be understood as a Soviet stratagem. Soviet support for Eritrean independence was based on Moscow's conviction that Eritrea was not a part of Ethiopia, a support which enhanced the decolonization process in post 1945 Africa. A reversal of Soviet position in post 1974 undoubtedly compromised Soviet decolonization thesis on the *disposal* of Italian colonies during the Fifth Session of the UN General Assembly.

---

[103] Carol R. Saivetz and Sylvia Woodby, *Soviet-Third World Relations*, Boulder, Colorado, 1985, p.118.

[104] Brutents, 2, p.93. Italics in the original.

Moscow's support for Eritrean nationalism significantly enhanced the international status of the Eritrean question. Soviet reversal to what was essentially a U.S. view on the future of Eritrea raised a couple of vital questions. Why the emergence of a socialist-oriented Ethiopia did suddenly made irrelevant Eritrea's independence aspiration? What would have happened if an anti-socialist leader had overthrown Mengistu Haile Mariam's regime in Ethiopia? Would the Soviets have reverted to their pre-1974 position and renewed their support for the ELF? Meanwhile, a Soviet-Ethiopian 20 year Friendship Treaty was signed in 1978. In 1972 and 1977 respectively, Egypt and Somalia had unilaterally abrogated similar treaties contracted with the Soviet Union. With Egypt and Somalia out of favour in the Kremlin, the Soviet-Ethiopian treaty represented a Soviet attempt to retain its strong presence in the North-Eastern African sub-system. Cooperation between Moscow and Addis Ababa had grown to encompass all aspects of socio-political and ideological questions. Ethiopia's 1975 promise to establish a vanguard party featured prominently in Soviet-Ethiopian discourse as Ethiopian leaders visited Moscow to understudy the process of forming a socialist party. The Commission for Organizing the Party of the Working People of Ethiopia (COPWE) was established in 1980. It was the responsibility of COPWE to sensitize Ethiopians on the issue of forming a Marxist-Leninist political party.

Somalia: From Fraternal Alliance to Class Hostility

"If anyone has a case for redrawing the map of Africa along ethnic lines, it is the Somalis."[105] The Anglo-Italian Protocol of 1891 had ceded portions of Somalian territory to Kenya and Ethiopia, i.e., the present Northern Province of Kenya and the Ogaden Region of Ethiopia, respectively. In 1899 Muhammed ben Abdall Hasan led a revolt against the British and the Italians for the unification of

---

[105] Anthony J. Hughes, "Reagan and Africa": Policy Options in the Horn", *Horn of Africa*, 4, 2, 1981, p.3.

Somalians "including those in Ogaden" in a single Somalian state.[106] Thus, the concept of a *greater Somalia* has united all Somalians since European colonial powers arbitrarily partitioned Somaliland into their respective spheres of interest. Before October 1969, there were three main political parties in Somalia: Somali Youth League (SYL), which sought the unification of all Somalis (including those in Kenya and Ethiopia) into a single Somali state; Dabka; and the Somali Democratic Union which had extensive relations with the socialist countries.

When Somalia attained independence in July 1960, the emergent state inherited the concept of a *greater Somalia* which defined its foreign policy actions. This explained why it agreed to establish diplomatic relations with the Soviet Union in October 1960—three months after it achieved independence. This was a *fast track* process, considering the difficulty Moscow had encountered in establishing diplomatic relations with Ghana and Nigeria. It was obvious that the political situation in East Africa significantly influenced Somalia to quickly establish diplomatic relations with the Soviet Union. It was envisaged that closer ties with Moscow would balance the strong influence of the West, Britain and the U.S. in the region since the Western powers were supporting Kenya and Ethiopia, portions of whose territories the SYL sought to incorporate into its *greater Somalia*.

East Africa, as a region, had a strategic appeal to the Soviets as well as to the Western powers. The ports of Kenya and Somalia could serve as refuelling stations for their military and commercial vessels. The relative economic backwardness coupled with the high level of illiteracy had made the region, particularly Somalia and Ethiopia, highly vulnerable to East-West power politics. Toward the end of 1960, barely two months after it established diplomatic relations with Somalia, Soviet embassy staff in Mogadishu totalled about 300 as opposed to China which had a relatively small staff at its embassy. Beijing had a strong team of journalists in the

---

[106] D. Voblikov, <u>Somali</u>, Moscow, 1970, p.13.

China News Agency, while Moscow had no *TASS* correspondent in Mogadishu as of the end of 1960. Somalia was able, therefore, to maintain a balance between Moscow and Beijing. China's revolutionary stance and support for the *greater Somali* policy of the SYL was an encouragement to Premier A. Shermarke. While the Soviet Union did not endorse the philosophy of the SYL, it was rather contradictory to note that the weapons Somalia needed to fight the cause propagated by the SYL came from Moscow.

Irredentism seemed the only single factor that could unite all Somalis in one Somali state. In 1963 and 1964 Somali irredentist movement clashed with Kenya and Ethiopia along the Somali-Kenyan and the Somali-Ethiopian borders. In mid-1963 Kenya, which was to attain independence on December 12, 1963, signed a defence pact with Uganda and Tanzania (then Tanganyika). Somali irredentism also influenced the growth of Kenyan-Ethiopian relations. In Addis Ababa on July 13, 1963, Kenya and Ethiopia signed an agreement on economic, social and cultural cooperation. Both parties also signed a mutual *military aid pact.* These agreements in East Africa were designed to isolate Somalia.

Soviet courtship of Somalia began in earnest following the establishment of diplomatic relations between both countries. A Soviet "goodwill mission" led by M.A. Lesechko visited Somalia in April 1961. The delegation was received by President A. Osman and Prime Minister A. Shermarke. In the joint communiqué released following their discussions, both parties recognized the "prevention of a new war and the safeguarding of peaceful coexistence as the main task of all peace-loving people." They agreed to work toward a "universal and complete disarmament." It was their view that the attainment of this objective will enhance the capabilities of interested rich and more advanced countries to assist the less developed countries.[107] The Somalian government sent a note to the Soviet Government through Lesechko requesting for Soviet

---

[107] *Vnezhniaia politika sovetskogo soiuza i mezhdunarodnye otnoshenia. Sbornik dokumentov 1961g.*, Moscow, 1962, p.104.

economic and technical assistance for "the implementation of the economic development plan of Somalia, and a Soviet long-term loan on favourable terms." The Soviet Government expressed interest in importing Somalian produces—hides, cotton, bananas, etc.—in "exchange for Soviet agricultural machines and industrial equipment."[108]

As a reciprocal gesture to Lesechko's visit, Prime Minister Shermarke led a Somalian delegation that visited the Soviet Union from May 24—June 2, 1961. The delegation included the ministers of education, trade and industry, health, and the deputy minister of foreign affairs. In the Soviet-Somalian Joint Communiqué, both parties underlined their unanimity of views on major international issues, and condemned the "imperialist aggression against the Republic of Congo" while Somalia stated that it "highly values Soviet friendly and disinterested aid to independent African countries, and to the African national liberation movement."[109] The Soviet Government agreed to aid Somalia as requested by the latter in Mogadishu in April 1961 during the Soviet "goodwill mission" to Somalia. The series of bilateral agreements covered economic and technical, trade, and cultural fields. These agreements fetched Somalia a 40 million roubles long-term credit on favourable terms to develop Somalia's industries and agriculture, and also a 7 million roubles trade credit on favourable terms for 5 years.

It is interesting to note that the financial assistance that Somalia received from the Soviet Union was used to "purchase Soviet equipment and materials and also to pay for the services of Soviet specialists" in Somalia. As was the custom in Soviet trade with Africa, the trade agreement negotiated with Somalia was essentially a *barter trade* as Somalia had to repay the loan with its cotton, hides, and

---

[108]   *Ibid.*, p.105. See also Pravda, April 24, 1961.

[109]   *Vnezhniaia politika sovetskogo soiuza i mezhdunarodnye otnoshenia. Sbornik dokumentov 1961g.*, p.126.

oleaceae (oil bearing plants) products[110], and "to purchase Soviet made agricultural machines, industrial equipment, and pay for the services of Soviet specialists based in Somalia" with the trade credit it received from the Soviet Union. In a gesture motivated by "sincere friendly feelings toward the Republic of Somalia" the Soviet Government decided to present to Somalia, free of charge, two hospitals, a secondary school, a press and a radio station to be constructed by the USSR. The Soviet Government agreed to despatch a number of Soviet medical doctors and teachers to Somalia, as well as to train Somalians in Soviet medical institutions.[111] This system of trade which the Soviet Union imposed on Somalia was a classic example of how to create a dependency polity in the international economic environment. Its fundamental objective was to make Somalia completely dependent on the Soviet Union, by opening up the Soviet market to Somali products, in return for compelling Somalia to rely solely on Soviet goods and services.

The visit of Prime Minister A. Shermarke to Moscow in 1961 proved to be the catalyst in the development of subsequent relations with the Soviet Union. According to Mr. Warsane, the Somali Ambassador in Moscow: "Ever since Shermarke's visit the USSR has been very generous to Somalia." This led to the training of Somali armed forces personnel in the Soviet Union. He noted that President Aboulla Osman was "pro West", while Shermarke was "more oriented to the socialist camp for aid." This push and pull of policy articulation caused a major friction between Osman and Shermarke. This friction reached its climax in 1964 following "Shermarke's acquisition of Soviet military aid which did not satisfy President Osman who was in Rome." They quarrelled and parted

---

[110] E.S. *Sherr, Somali v borbe za sotsialnomu orientatsiiu,* Moscow, 1974, p.203.

[111] *Izvestia,* June 2, 1961.

ways, as a result of which Osman did not re-appoint Shermarke following the 1964 elections.[112]

SOMALI PRESIDENTS AND PRIME MINISTERS 1960-1976

July 1, 1960-June 10, 1967: President A.A. Osman Daar
June 10, 1967-October 15, 1969: President Abdirashid Ali Shermarke
Oct 15, 1969-Oct 21, 1969: Interim President Sheikh Muktar Muhamad Hussein
Oct 21, 1969-July 1, 1976: President Mohamed Siad Barre

July 1, 1960-July 12, 1960: Prime Minister Muhammad Egal
July 12, 1960-June 14, 1964: Prime Minister A.A. Shermarke
June 16, 1964-July 15, 1967: Prime Minister Abdirashid Hussein
July 15, 1967-Nov 1, 1969: Prime Minister Muhammad Egal
Nov 1, 1969-March 1970: Mohamed Farah Salad

E.S. Sherr, a Soviet economist who had worked and studied in Somalia, underlined the dilemma that plagued Western policy in Africa which seemed to have compelled many African states to *reluctantly* turn to the Soviet Union for economic assistance. He observed that:

> When the West declined to assist Somalia in training its national army, A.A. Shermarke approached the Soviet Union. This decisive step, not at all dictated by the leaders' revolutionary inclination, entailed serious consequences. The army began to get out of Western influence.[113]

---

[112] Author's interview with Mr. Warsane, the Somali Ambassador to the Soviet Union, Moscow, October 4, 1979.

[113] *Ibid.*, 86.

While the Somali army succeeded in getting "out of Western influence", it found itself subjugated to the political machinations of Soviet Communism. We had noticed a similar development in Guinea in 1958 when the West *pushed* Sekou Toure toward the embrace of Moscow. It could also be argued that an identical ideological paralysis in Western political thought facilitated the process for Patrice Lumumba's gradual shift toward the Kremlin. In 1960, the Western powers failed to initiate a policy that would keep Somalia out of Moscow's influence. Washington was already entrenched in Addis Ababa, economically and militarily, just as London was in bed with Nairobi. Neither Washington nor London could devise a stratagem to satisfy or neutralize the irredentism of the SYL which laid claim to Ethiopian and Kenyan territories populated by ethnic Somalis. This single factor may have compelled the U.S. and Britain to withhold any economic or military assistance to Somalia.

In August 1963 Prime Minister Shermarke visited Beijing and Moscow. He had earlier rejected U.S. offer of military aid, claiming that the U.S. Government was offering Somalia inferior weapons compared to the U.S.-equipped Ethiopian army. A much *bigger* and *superior* Soviet aid was accepted especially since the Soviets had undertaken to build a 20,000 Somali army. The Soviets were pleased to fill the vacuum in Somalia as a result of the impasse in U.S.-Somali relations. Shermarke's visit to Moscow resulted in a Somali-Soviet military aid agreement concluded in October 1963. Under the terms of the agreement the Soviet Government undertook to train Somali pilots and over 100 army officers in the Soviet Union. It was apparent that U.S. large scale military aid to Ethiopia motivated Somalia to seek Soviet military aid. Soviet gradual military build-up in Somalia caused grave political indignation in Washington. In an attempt to assure the West of Somalia's neutralism, Ahmed Mohammed Darman, Counsellor of the Somali mission to the UNO, stated that Soviet military aid did not mean the introduction of Communism in Somalia.[114] But, while referring to U.S. military aid and accusing Washington of supporting Ethiopia, Shermarke stated that "every country needs an army to protect itself."[115] The threat to national security, real or perceived, has always determined the foreign policy of states.

As Sherr pointedly observed, the decision to approach the Soviet Union was "not at all dictated by the leaders' revolutionary inclination", but by their determination to safeguard the sovereignty of Somalia. The Somali cabinet was, however, not unanimous on the issue of close ties with the Soviet Union. President A. Osman Daar did not appreciate Shermarke's seemingly pro East policies, and he subsequently replaced Shermarke as prime minister with Abdirashid Hussein in 1964. Sherr regarded Shermarke as an "active supporter for the creation of an independent economy", but concluded that as a representative of the "national bourgeoisie he could not, and did not try to get out of this class."[116] Irrespective of this ideological limitation, he was still the best ally of Moscow in Somalia. Hussein's ministry ignored the state sector developed under Shermarke.

The fact that Shermarke was no longer in power did not prevent the Soviet Union from intensifying its relations with Somalia. Moscow was aware of President Osman Daar's "pro West" policies; just as it was equally aware of Somalia's schism with Kenya and Ethiopia. It was therefore vital that this schism be exploited in order to enhance the power and influence of the Soviet Union in the Horn of Africa. At the invitation of the Soviet Government, President Osman Daar led a Somali delegation to the Soviet Union from September 20-28, 1966. He was accompanied by the ministers of foreign affairs, defense, education, planning, trade and industry. The purpose of the visit was for both parties to review the direction of Soviet-Somali relations. According to the joint communiqué published at the end of the visit, both parties expressed satisfaction

---

114   See *The New York Times*, November 17, 1963.
115   *The New York Times*, December 13, 1963.
116   *Ibid.*, 87.

with the implementation of Soviet-Somalian agreements, while the Soviet Government "positively values the policy of nonalignment and positive neutrality pursued by the government of the Somali Republic." They condemned, as usual, the "imperialist powers' arms race which creates tensions in international relations and halt economic progress." Osman Daar extended an invitation to President Podgornyi to visit Somalia.[117]

Osman Daar would not be in office to host the Soviet president, as he was defeated by Shermarke at the presidential elections in 1967. However, Shermarke's foreign policy orientation ran into conflict with that of Prime Minister Muhammed Ibrahim Egal, who Warsane depicted as "pro West."[118] At the time of Shermarke's assassination on October 16, 1969, Prime Minister Egal was in Washington negotiating for U.S. investment. He promptly returned to Mogadishu, but could not survive the ensuing power struggle. A pro U.S. millionaire Hajmoussa Bogor was endorsed by the SYL as president. The army struck at 02:00 hours on October 21, 1969 and arrested Egal and other ministers.

The Supreme Military Council (SMC) that seized power on October 21, 1969, began the process of transforming Somalia into a socialist state. On March 12, 1970, in preparation for the celebration of V.I. Lenin's 100th birthday on April 22, 1970, the Somalian government decided to rename one of Mogadishu's main streets in honour of the late founder of Soviet communism.[119]

As Somalia celebrated its tenth year of independence on June 30, 1970, Soviet analysts were scrambling to *explain* the causes of the coup of October 21, 1969. According to *TASS*: "After the attainment of independence, imperialist powers, relying on the forces of internal reaction, tried to impose on the country a course beneficial to them. That was why on October 21 of last year the

---

[117] *Izvestia*, September 29, 1966.

[118] Interview with Mr. Warsane, Somali Ambassador to the Soviet Union, Moscow, October 4, 1979.

[119] *Pravda*, March 13, 1970.

Somalian army seized state power."[120] In the view of O. Petrov, the incident of October 21, 1969 in Somalia was a "revolutionary coup" which could "liquidate the legacy of colonialism, corruption, oppression and economic dependence on the imperialist powers." In its progress toward "real independence" Somalia "will naturally need the help of its sincere friends" which are the "Soviet Union and the other socialist countries which cooperate unselfishly with the people of Somalia helping them to build a new life."[121] The concept of transferred dependency was clearly underlined in Petrov's analysis of Somalia's "revolutionary coup." While the incident of October 21 would, in the Soviet view, terminate Somalia's "economic dependence on the imperialist powers", it was envisaged that it would *transform* Somalia into a Soviet client state.

V. Ermakov, a Soviet journalist based in Mogadishu offered an explanation for the assassination of President Shermarke in October 1969. His informants differed on the circumstances surrounding the murder of Shermarke on the eve of the October revolution. Supporters of former president Osman Daar were suspected of murdering Shermarke; while others theorized that the assassination was inspired by ethnic hostility. However, the fact that his alleged assassin was from his (Shermarke's) own ethnic group rendered this version untenable. The most plausible version, according to Ermakov, was the alleged involvement of the U.S. "CIA or other Western secret services" who were "disturbed by Shermarke's nationalist slogans" and had prepared the "pro-American Prime Minister Egan" to take over the presidency. Commenting on the Somali October revolution, Ermakov opined:

> There is no working class in Somalia as the industry
> is in its embryonic stage; there is almost no settled
> peasantry, and even the bourgeoisie, as is understood in

---

[120]   *Pravda*, July 1, 1970.

[121]   O. Petrov, "Istoricheskaia vekha respubliki Somali", *Pravda*, October 22, 1970.

contemporary usage, is absent . . . The only organized
force in the country is the army in whose ranks are many
progressively inclined officers. They are the sources of
the national revolution.[122]

The absence of an organized working class in African politics was a
source of concern for the Soviets. This necessitated a shift in Soviet
ideological analysis of the *progressiveness* of Africa's military corps.
The only cases when the military lost its *progressiveness*, according to
the Soviets, were when it overthrew the *progressive* regimes of Kwame
Nkrumah and Modibo Keita in Ghana and Mali, respectively. Soviet
ideologues increasingly came to rely on Africa's military corps to
effect social change. They perceived the military as the *last hope* of
the oppressed in Africa.[123]

In his report from Mogadishu seven months after the Somalian
October revolution, Ermakov acclaimed the *revolutionary gains* of
October 21. He asserted that the post-independent national leaders
of Somalia failed to produce tangible results of independence
satisfactory to the broad masses of Somalians. "Therefore", he
concluded, "the revolution of October 21 was an attempt by the
more progressive army officers to create the conditions under which
Somalians could benefit from national independence..."[124] From his
discussions with Somalian leaders, including President Siad Barre,
Ermakov determined that Somalians regarded the Soviet Union as
their "real and sincere friend" who would assist Somalia in its chosen
non-capitalist path of development leading to socialism. In the
view of G. Viktorov: "The bourgeois parliament had degenerated
into a caricature of democracy" as Somalia was "ruled by the tribal

---

[122] V. Ermakov, "Peremeny v Mogadisho", *Pravda*, May 14, 1970.

[123] For an analysis of this phenomenon, see O. Igho Natufe, "Nigeria and
Soviet Attitudes to African Military Regimes, 1965-70", *Survey*, 22,
1(98), London, 1976, pp.93-111.

[124] V. Ermakov, "Respublika namechaet put", *Pravda*, May 16, 1970.

and feudal oligarchy."[125] Before the coup of October 21, 1969, the ruling party had nominated a millionaire, Hajmoussa Bogor, as its presidential candidate.

It was in the midst of these reviews by Soviet analysts that a Soviet government-party delegation headed by D.S. Polianskii, CPSU Politburo Member and first deputy Prime Minister, arrived in Somalia October 20-24, 1970 to attend the first anniversary celebrations of Somalia's *October socialist revolution*. Members of the delegation included I.V. Arkhipov, first deputy chairman of the State Committee of the USSR Council of Ministers; army general P.N. Lashchenko; and P.I. Manchkha, head of the International Affairs Division of the Central Committee of the CPSU. The bilateral talks were held under an atmosphere of "brotherly mutual understanding." Both parties perceived the October 21 revolution as a catalyst in effecting fruitful cooperation between the Soviet Union and Somalia. They agreed to cooperate jointly in the "struggle against imperialism, colonialism and neo-colonialism, for self-determination, national independence and social progress," Significantly, both parties endorsed

> the peaceful settlement of unresolved inter-state problems, including territorial and border questions, and to refrain from the use of force or threat in the resolution of international disputes.[126]

Speaking before Polianskii in Mogadishu at the celebration, President Barre declared: "We solemnly and resolutely proclaim: Somalia has chosen the socialist path of development."[127] The joint

---

[125] G. Viktorov, "Somalia. The Coup: Causes and Consequences", *International Affairs*, Moscow, nos.2-3, 1970, p.112.

[126] "Sovmestnoe Sovetsko-Somaliiskoe kommiunike", *Pravda*, October 30, 1970.

[127] G. Viktorov, "Somalia: Towards Progress", *International Affairs*, Moscow, no.12, 1970, pp.84-85.

declaration that recognized the "peaceful settlement of unresolved inter-state problems, including territorial and border questions", and condemned the "use of force" to resolve these issues, was an indication of Moscow's pressure on Somalia to seek peaceful coexistence with both Kenya and Ethiopia on its territorial disputes with these states. Before his return to Moscow, Polianskii extended Soviet government invitation to President Barre to visit the USSR.

Mogadishu's shift from reliance on the West to dependency on the Kremlin was welcomed by Soviet leaders. In the Soviet view, the coup of October 21, 1969 was engineered by the "progressive forces led by the army" who succeeded in "overthrowing the pro-Western regime" that had developed Somalia "along capitalist lines."[128] Moscow was no longer critical of Somalia's foreign policy, since the post October 1969 "traditional Somalian neutrality assumed a positive character"[129] and tilted toward the Soviet Union. It should be recalled that, during President Osman Daar's state visit to the Soviet Union in September 1966, the Soviet Government had declared that it "positively values the policy of nonalignment and positive neutrality pursued by the government of the Somali Republic." This declaration did not differ from Sherr's assessment in 1971, except that, in 1971, Somalia had transformed itself into a Soviet client state. The Soviets assured themselves that the socialist orientation policy of Somalia will lead the country to "socialism and social progress."[130] In 1970 Somalia established diplomatic relations with the German Democratic Republic and the People's Republic of Vietnam.

President Siad Barre arrived in Moscow on November 16, 1971 on an official state visit. According to the front page report in *Pravda*, Siad Barre "led the revolution of October 21, 1969 which

[128] E. Sherr, "Somali: vneshniaia politika strany sotsialisticheskoi orientatsii", *Aziia i Afrika segodnia*, Moscow, no.1, 1975, p.42.

[129] E. Sherr, "Veter peremen nad Somali", *Aziia i Afrika segodnia*, Moscow, no.11, 1971, p.12.

[130] See N. Kosukhin, "Novyi put Somali", *Pravda*, June 30, 1971.

was effected by the progressive forces of Somali armed forces." *Pravda* described President Barre as a "well-known political leader actively fighting for African unity, against the forces of imperialism, neo-colonialism, and racism . . ." and a "consistent advocate for the development of friendly relations and all-round cooperation with the Soviet Union."[131] The gathering of Soviet leaders that were at the airport to welcome Barre indicated Soviet enthusiasm about Barre's tilt toward Moscow. Led by President N.V. Podgornyi, the list included Foreign Minister A.A. Gromyko, Defense Minister A.A. Grechko, first deputy Prime Minister D.S. Polianskii, and the Secretary of the USSR Supreme Soviet, M.P. Georgadze.

Podgornyi's speech at a state banquet in the Kremlin underlined the importance the Soviet Union attached to Somalia. He recognized the "positive changes" in Somalia since October 21, 1969, and declared that the Soviet Union "welcome the proclamation by the Supreme Revolutionary Council to construct a socialist society in the Somalian Democratic Republic . . ." and that the Soviet Union shall render "full support in the difficult tasks facing Somalia in its chosen path of development." In his response, Barre agreed with Soviet leaders that the Soviet Union "renders disinterested aid to young independent countries to enable them strengthen their independence . . ." He declared:

> I am glad to inform you, Comrade Podgornyi, that from the moment of our October revolution, we in Somalia undertook to construct in the country the tested and proven system of scientific socialism.[132]

President Barre held separate meetings with Leonid Brezhnev and Alexei Kosygin on November 18 and 19, respectively. However, Brezhnev was absent at the signing ceremony in the Kremlin

---

[131] *Pravda*, November 16, 1971.

[132] For the full text of Podgornyi and Barre's speeches, see Pravda, November 17, 1971.

on November 19, 1971, when Barre and Podgornyi signed the Soviet-Somalian Statement in which both parties reiterated their "sincere friendship and close cooperation" in different spheres. The USSR agreed to construct a dam on the banks of the Juba river (Somalia's "Aswan"), hydroelectric stations and canals.[133] Barre and his entourage left Moscow on November 22.

Soviet and Somalian leaders continued the reciprocal exchange of visits which they had established following Shermarke's first visit to Moscow. Soviet Defense Minister Marshall A.A. Grechko left Moscow on February 13, 1972 for Somalia at the invitation of the Somalian government. Following his discussions with Somalian leaders, he left Mogadishu on February 18.[134] There was no official statement released. Somali vice president and Defense Minister, Brigadier General M. Ali Samantar arrived in Moscow on July 11, 1972 at the invitation of Marshall Grechko for bilateral discussions.[135] This meeting also produced no official statement. It was not clear why both meetings, in Mogadishu and Moscow, failed to produce official statements.

Writing in 1972, Soviet analysts V. Gorodnov and N. Kosukhin continued to rationalize Soviet assistance to Somalia. They contended that "Kismayu's port was built by the Americans, who left behind an ill memory of themselves . . . To this day rusting metal and smashed trestles stand as a mute reproach of American 'aid'." As a result of Soviet "disinterested aid", they continued, Kismayu now has a "highly-mechanized" modern meat-packing plant, the products of which, however, "are exported through the Kismayu port to Egypt and the USSR."[136] These products, which were in lieu of payment for the Soviet-built "highly-mechanized" modern meat-packing plant, were meant to subsidize the Soviet communist system.

---

[133] *Pravda*, November 23, 1971.

[134] *Pravda*, February 14, 1972.

[135] *Pravda*, July 12, 1972; Pravda, July 18, 1972.

[136] V. Gorodnov and N. Kosukhin, "In the Somali Democratic Republic", *International Affairs*, Moscow, no.5, 1972, p.105.

In the view of the Soviets, Somalia, prior to October 1969, was a land infested with corrupt practices. E. Sherr, a leading analyst on Somali observed that: "Before the events of October 1969, power was in the hands of the rich elite, and corruption among government officials was a characteristic feature of political life in that period."[137] The post October 1969 transformation of Somali polity created a welcoming atmosphere for the articulation of policies favourable to the Kremlin. "Somalia's policy of non-alignment and neutrality" continued Sherr, "became more principled and consistent after the revolution, when Somali neutrality became *truly positive.*"[138] As stated by V. Sofinsky: "The decision to take the socialist orientation logically led to the adoption of scientific socialism as the ideological basis for the practical activity of the Supreme Revolutionary Council" of Somalia . . . Somalia "has become an outpost in the struggle for national liberation and social emancipation on the African continent, and is one of the most progressive states in Africa."[139] The Soviet Union was systematically increasing its investment in Somalia. By mid-1974, Soviet-built projects in Somalia included a milk factory in Mogadishu; meat-packing plant in Kismayu; deep-sea port in Berbera; fish-canning plant in Las Khoreh; printing works; and two hospitals. These projects yielded tangible results for the Soviet Union, as its fishing trawlers, for example, had unrestricted access to fishing within the territorial waters of Somalia.

Moscow could now claim that: "The Soviet Union's political support and its assistance in the economic and defense spheres have helped the young national state to implement its programme to transform Somalia's society on socialist lines . . . to effectively resist the internal reactionary forces."[140] In the Soviet view, the goal of the

---

137 E. Sherr, "Somalia: Socialist Orientation", *International Affairs*, Moscow, no.2, 1974, p.84.

138 *Ibid.*, p.85. Italics mine.

139 V. Sofinsky, "Somalia on the Path of Progress", *International Affairs*, Moscow, no.11, 1974, p.63

140 *Ibid.*, p.64.

October socialist revolution in Somalia was "to build a society free from the exploitation of man by man."[141] In his speech at Kismayu on July 10, 1974, President Siad Barre gave credence to Soviet *assistance* when he declared:

> Ninety per cent of Somali specialists with a higher education are graduates of Soviet universities and institutes. Let me recall in this connection that some countries claimed to be our friends merely because they gave scholarships to five or six students. Thanks to the Soviet Union's assistance we now have our own highly skilled specialists in various branches of the national economy: engineers, doctors and agronomists.[142]

As of the 1974-75 academic year, there were more than 1,000 Somali students studying in Soviet institutions.

As part of Soviet strategy to develop and maintain an all-round collaboration with Somalia, a joint Soviet-Somalian scientific expedition was established in 1973. N. D. Kosukhin, a policy analyst in Moscow's Institute of Africa, led the Soviet delegation to the expedition in Somalia. In the report of the expedition entitled *Uchenye zapiski sovetsko-somaliiskoi ekspeditsii* Soviet scholars presented their research findings on the socio-economic and political development of Somalia. In his contribution, Kosukhin criticised the SYL for its failure in resolving the nation's crisis irrespective of the fact that it professed "democratic socialism." Kosukhin observed that "Islam is weak in the country" and that, unlike other Muslim countries, Somali women "do not conceal their faces, do not subject themselves to disgraceful religious customs, but actively participate

---

[141] V. Shmarov, "New stage in Soviet-Somali Relations", *New Times*, Moscow, no.29, 1974, p.6. See also V. Kudryavtsev, "Somalia Today", *New Times*, Moscow, no.27, 1974, pp.23-24.

[142] As cited in *Ibid.*, p.64.

in socially useful work."[143] Kosukhin revealed that the Somali Supreme Military Council (SMC) explained socialism to Somalians via the vehicle of Islamism. He seemed to agree with the SMC that "Islam aids the formation of a national consciousness" and stated that SMC leaders critically attacked those religious leaders opposed to "revolutionary principles."[144] In his bid to mollify religious leaders in both the Soviet Union and elsewhere, Kosukhin declared:

> Marxist-Leninist world outlook and the policy emanating from it do not exclude, but, on the other hand, supposed to draw into the struggle for social progress peoples of various religious beliefs.[145]

Kosukhin's criticism of what he described as Somalia's "disgraceful religious customs" was a demonstration of Soviet insensitivity to practices considered inimical to Soviet Marxism. His statement that Marxism-Leninism welcomed the views of "peoples of various religious beliefs" was merely designed to mollify these peoples, as his statement contradicted the position of the Soviet Union vis-à-vis "religious beliefs" and the CPSU's doctrine of scientific socialism.

President N.V. Podgornyi arrived in Mogadishu on July 8, 1974 for an official visit at the invitation of President Siad Barre. Speaking on his arrival at Mogadishu airport Podgornyi declared that Somalia was on the "path of peace and socialism" and that Soviet-Somali friendship was "based on their mutual interest in the struggle for peace and social progress . . ." and that his "visit would further cement the friendship and cooperation of both

---

[143] N.D. Kosukhin, "Revoliutsia 21 oktibria 1969g i rasprostranenie idei nauchnogo sotsializma v somali", in *Uchenye zapiski sovetsko-somaliiskoi ekspeditsii*, Moscow, 1974, p.62.

[144] *Ibid.*, 63.

[145] *Ibid.*, 65. See also his "Sotsiologicheskie obsledovaniia sredi rabochikh i molodezhi somali", in ibid., pp.237-295.

countries."[146] At a state luncheon in his honour on July 9, Barre informed his Soviet guest that Soviet-Somali relations had "attained a higher level" since "our socialist revolution of October 21, 1969", and that Somalia had adopted the "path of scientific socialism as the only path capable of achieving the socio-economic development" of Somalia. It is interesting to note that, in his response, Podgornyi referred to the "revolution of 1969" without the prefix *socialist*. He observed that: "In the short historical period, particularly beginning from the revolution of October 21, 1969, the Somalian people had taken a vast step from colonial slavery toward state independence." Referring to the nationalization of key industries by the Somalian government, Podgornyi stated that: "Today there is no Somalia where foreign monopoly prevailed which had robbed and exploited Somalians." On Soviet African policy, Podgornyi asserted that the Soviet Union wanted to see Africa "completely free from colonialism and neocolonialism."[147] On July 11, in Mogadishu, Podgornyi and Barre signed a 20-year Soviet-Somali Treaty of Friendship and Cooperation. Podgornyi and his entourage left Mogadishu for Moscow on July 12.

The Friendship Treaty, which was a replica of the ones the Soviet Government had signed with Egypt (and later with Angola and Afghanistan), contained 13 articles. In Article 2, the contracting parties agreed to broaden their trade relations "on the basis of the principles of mutual benefits . . . as contained in the agreement concluded in Moscow on June 2, 1961." It should be recalled that the 1961 Moscow agreement was a *barter system of trade* whereby Somalia was to *export* to the Soviet Union its hides, bananas, etc., in exchange for Soviet financial assistance, which Somalia was to use to pay for Soviet products and professional services. Both parties agreed to intensify the relations between their respective "working class political and social organizations. (Article 3). The

---

[146] *Pravda*, July 9, 1974.

[147] For the speeches of Siad Barre and N.V. Podgornyi, see *Pravda*, July 10, 1974.

Soviet Government agreed to provide Somalia with the necessary military assistance "in the interest of strengthening the defence capability of the Somali Democratic Republic. (Article 4). Article 10 was the key section of the Friendship Treaty. According to Article 10, each of the contracting parties agreed "not to participate in any military alliance or in any group of states, as well as partake in any actions or activities that are directed against the other contracting party."[148] This was in essence a military alliance between Moscow and Mogadishu. It was an identical clause in the Soviet-Afghanistan Friendship Treaty that Moscow eventually used to *justify* its invasion of Afghanistan in 1979.

The Friendship Treaty had elevated the status of Somalia in Soviet foreign policy calculations. It brought Somalia firmly within the Soviet orbit. In celebrating the 6th anniversary of Somalia's October *socialist* revolution, a Soviet analyst opined:

> Though the country attained independence in 1960, the genuine Somalian liberation day is now October 21, 1969 when a group of progressively inclined officers with the support of the democratic forces effected a bloodless coup and toppled the anti-people, pro-colonialist regime.[149]

The contents of the Soviet-Somali trade agreement and Friendship Treaty, phrased in anti-colonialist terms, were not materially different from the neo-colonial policies of Western powers in Africa that the Soviet Union claimed to be opposed to. Instead of providing financial assistance by erecting factories in Somalia to process the raw materials into finished products, the trade agreement required

---

[148] For the full text of the Friendship Treaty, see "Dogovor o druzhbe i sotrudnichestve mezhdu Soiuzom Sovetskikh Sotsialisticheskikh Respublik i Somaliiskoi Demokraticheskoi Respublikoi", *Pravda*, October 30, 1974.

[149] Iu. Pichygin, "Godovshchina revoliutsii", *Pravda*, October 22, 1975.

Somalia to exports its raw materials to the Soviet Union "in exchange for Soviet financial assistance, which Somalia was to use to pay for Soviet products and professional services." This form of trading relations merely moved Somalia from one orbit of foreign economic domination to the other; while the Friendship Treaty solidified Somalia as a military ally of the Soviet Union.

Before February 24, 1966, when the army struck and toppled the progressive regime of Kwame Nkrumah in Ghana, Soviet analysis of the role of African armies in politics was based on a one-track vision which perceived the army as a progressive instrument of change in Africa. Soviet perception of the progressiveness of African armies was determined by the country concerned. For example, when a group of young military officers led a coup attempt against the regime of Abubakar Tafawa Balewa in Nigeria on January 15, 1966, the Soviets hailed this as a victory against Britain's "showcase of democracy in Africa". By the late 1960s, the Soviets were now compelled to increasingly rely on the African military as its staunch ally to effect social change on the continent. It was therefore, in Moscow's interest, for the Soviet Union to assist in the civilianization and politization of Africa's progressive military regimes. Such regimes were encouraged to transform themselves into political parties. Such was the case in Somalia.

Brigadier General M. Ali Samantar, Somali vice president/Minister of Defence, and Somali Revolutionary Socialist Party (SRSP) politburo member had visited Moscow in August 1976, to arrange for functionaries of the SRSP to understudy CPSU organizational structure and functions. The formation of the SRSP was publicly hailed in the Soviet Union as a victory for the progressive forces. Leonid Brezhnev sent a congratulatory telegramme to "comrade Mohammed Siad Barre" on the occasion of the formation of the SRSP and Barre's election as the first general secretary of the central committee of the party. In his message, Brezhnev underlined the pleasure of the Soviet Government with the establishment of the SRSP:

> Soviet Communists see in the formation of the SRSP
> a new important stage in the development of Somalia's

revolution, a testimony of the steadfast decisiveness of the working class of Somalia to struggle for the ideals of national independence, freedom and socialism[150]

The inaugural congress of the SRSP, June 27-July 11, 1976, was reported on the front page of *Pravda* amidst the reports of the 25th CPSU Congress. According to the *TASS* correspondent based in Mogadishu, the programme of the SRSP was based on "scientific socialism."[151]

Samantar met with a team of Soviet leaders which was led by A.P. Kirilenko. Others in the Soviet team were Boris N. Ponomarev, Deputy Prime Minister I.V. Arkhipov, first deputy foreign minister V.V. Kuznetsov, and the first deputy minister of defence V.G. Kulikov. Samantar briefed the Soviets on the activities of the SRSP and informed them of the party's determination to pursue "revolutionary progressive socio-economic policies" in Somalia.[152] The brewing crisis in Ethiopian-Somalian relations was a priority item on their agenda. According to the Soviet-Somalian Joint Communiqué released at the end of the discussions:

> Both parties declare their intensions to ensure that all the countries in East Africa build their respective relations on the basis of peace, friendship and good-neighbourliness.[153]

The Soviet Government was still hopeful that the territorial disputes between Somalia and Ethiopia would not resort into armed conflict,

---

[150] *Pravda*, July 2, 1976.

[151] "Novyi etap razvitiia", Pravda, July 12, 1976. See also A. Shirinskii, "Narod za partoi", *Pravda*, March 10, 1976, who reported from Mogadishu that the people of Somalia were strongly in favour of the embryonic SRSP.

[152] *Pravda*, August 3, 1976.

[153] *Pravda*, August 10, 1976.

especially since both countries were now members of Moscow's socialist fraternity.

Writing in 1976, G.V. Nadezhdin acknowledged that the state sector which is the "economic base of a state of socialist orientation is developing and strengthening" in Somalia.[154] In the Soviet perspective, as articulated by G.V. Kazakov, Somalia's adoption of a "socialist path of development" compelled the country to recognize the significance of a "planned" economic system as the instrument for establishing "socialism in Somalia." Soviet assistance was considered vital in Somalia's advancement towards socialism. Kazakov claimed that Soviet aid to Somalian industrial development in 1958-1969 surpassed the combined aid of the U.S. and the Federal Republic of Germany.[155] He argued:

> After the revolution of 1969, Soviet-Somalian cooperation attained a new, high level. This became possible because the new leadership of the country, in proclaiming its aim to construct a socialist society, pursued a policy of rapprochement with the socialist states and struggles against imperialism and neo-colonialism.[156]

The Ogaden crisis dominated Soviet-Somalian relations throughout 1977. Soviet and Cuban delegations paid several visits to Mogadishu in an effort to convince Siad Barre to seek peaceful resolution of the conflict. On March 15, 1977 a Cuba-Somalian joint communiqué condemned "the conspiracy of imperialism and reaction in the Middle East and Africa." The "imperialist" powers were blamed for instigating the Ogaden crisis.[157] Two weeks after the Cubans were in Mogadishu, on April 2, 1977 Soviet President

---

[154] G.V. Nadezhdin, *Somali*, Moscow, 1976, p.22.
[155] G.V. Kazakov, *Somali na sovremennom etape razvitiia*, Moscow, 1976, p.129.
[156] *Ibid.*, p.134.
[157] *Pravda*, March 16, 1977.

Podgornyi stopped over in Mogadishu for an "unofficial meeting" with the Somali president. Both parties discussed Soviet-Somali relations and paid "particular attention to the situation" in the Horn of Africa. President Barre accepted an invitation to visit Moscow.[158] It was becoming obvious that Moscow and Mogadishu could not agree on a *general line* regarding the Ogaden crisis. The Soviets were now concerned on how to manage their support for Somalia whose main foreign policy objective had been the unification of all Somalians into a single Somali state; a policy which the Soviet Government had not endorsed, but whose goal was made attainable by Moscow's military aid to Mogadishu. Just under two weeks following Podgornyi's visit, Cuban President Fidel Castro arrived in Mogadishu on April 13, 1977 for discussions with Siad Barre. Both leaders discussed the deteriorating situation in the Horn of Africa. Castro underlined the significance of "proletarian internationalism" in the pursuit of "peace and progress" in the foreign policy of socialist states.[159] Castro was appealing to Barre to forego his territorial claim in the interest of *proletarian internationalism* which was supposed to guide the foreign policies of socialist states. The idea of a federation involving Somalia, Ethiopia, and Eden was discussed at the meeting. The establishment of such a federation would have, in the Cuban view, made irrelevant the *ownership* of Ogaden.

The Soviets were convinced that the "construction" of socialism in Somalia, coupled with the emergence of *socialist* Ethiopia and the People's Democratic Republic of Yemen would enhance the position of the *progressive forces* around the Indian Ocean. It is interesting to note that, in January 1976, while attending an OAU meeting, President Barre, in his discussion with Ethiopian Head of State Megistu Haile Mariam, proposed that Somalia and Ethiopia formed a "federation" as a practical way to resolve the territorial dispute between the two countries. The implications of this did not go unnoticed in the Kremlin, where it was recognized that, with

---

[158] *Pravda*, April 4, 1977.

[159] *Pravda*, April 14, 1977.

Somalia, Ethiopia and the People's Democratic Republic of Yemen constructing "socialism, the position of the progressive forces in this important region has been strengthen."[160]

Writing in early 1977, E. Sherr, a Soviet economist who had visited, and worked in Somalia on several occasions, stated that after Somalia adopted *scientific socialism*, Soviet-Somalian relations became an example of comradely cooperation between a "country of developed socialism" and a "state of socialist orientation led by revolutionary democrats . . . who are thoroughly studying the works of V.I. Lenin . . . while Marxism-Leninism has been designated a compulsory subject in Somalia's national university."[161] Russian had become a popular language among many Somalians trained in the Soviet Union.

Irrespective of the *Marxist-Leninist* basis of Somalia's policy, the Soviet Union found itself caught between Addis Ababa and Mogadishu as its two *socialist* client states prepared for battle in the Ogaden. Somali vice president Ali Samantar returned to Moscow for further talks with Soviet leaders in June 1977. In his meeting with Leonid Brezhnev on June 1, they discussed the Horn of Africa and deplored the attempts by "imperialist and reactionary forces" to create a dangerous situation in the region.[162] It was obvious that both parties disagreed on how to resolve the Ogaden crisis. The preferred choice of the Soviet Union was for Somalia to renounce its territorial claims on Ethiopia, given the fact that a *socialist* regime was now in power in Addis Ababa. The irredentist policy of the SYL had been adopted by the SRSP in the articulation of its *Marxist-Leninist socialist ideology*, thus posing a serious dilemma for the Soviet Government. By blaming "imperialist and reactionary

---

[160] E. Sherr, "Novye rubezhi Somali", *Aziia i Afrika segodnia*, Moscow, no.1, 1977, p.15.

[161] *Ibid.*, p.14. See also E. Denisov, "Vashnyi etap razvitiia", *Aziia i Afrika segodnia*, Moscow, no.9, 1972, pp.25-27.

[162] *Pravda*, June 2, 1977.

forces" Samantar and Brezhnev were searching for an escape hatch to avoid confronting the real issue.

In an analysis of the crisis, Pavel Demchenko called upon the warring parties to seek a peaceful resolution of the conflict arguing that: "The conflict between Ethiopia and Somalia is being used by the imperialist states and local reactionary forces whose aim is to destroy the progressive regimes of both countries."[163] Demchenko was merely re-echoing the Soviet political line on the crisis. The real culprit was not the imperialist world, but the irredentist policy of the SYL which had been adopted by *socialist* Somalia. The Soviets failed in their bid to convince Somalia to renounce irredentism, notwithstanding the fact that in several Soviet-Somalian previous declarations, both parties had condemned the use of force to resolve (territorial) disputes between states. The Soviets were aware of the dangers this could pose to a country's policy, as was exemplified in the Sino-Soviet border conflict of early 1969.

Soviet-Somalian relations began to grow sour as a result of Soviet reluctance to support Somali claim of the Ogaden. President Siad Barre found himself in Moscow once again for discussions with Soviet leaders on the Ogaden war. While *Pravda* reported that Mohammed Siad Barre was in Moscow, August 29-31, 1977, it did not refer to him as "comrade", a significant indication of the current state of relations between Moscow and Mogadishu. Barre held talks with Premier Alexei Kosygin, Soviet chief ideologist M.A. Suslov, and Foreign Minister A.A. Gromyko. The only report about his deliberations with Soviet leaders simply stated that: "During the discussions both parties exchanged views on problems of mutual interest."[164] This was an indication that there was no agreement reached between the parties. They had failed to safeguard the *socialist bloc* in East Africa. As Siad Barre's plane left Soviet territory on September 1, 1977, he sent a telegramme thanking "comrade Brezhnev" and his colleagues for the warm reception accorded him

---

[163] Pavel Demchenko, "Za mirnoe reshenie", *Pravda*, August 19, 1977.

[164] *Pravda*, September 1, 1977.

and his team[165] during his abortive attempt to secure Soviet support for Somalia's war in the Ogaden.

When the Soviet Government failed in its bid to convince Somalia and Ethiopia into forming a *socialist federation*, it did not hesitate to demonstrate its preference for Ethiopia. Moscow's obvious preference was to be able to retain its two socialist client states in the Horn of Africa, but when this did not materialize it elected to side with the *bigger* and more influential socialist Ethiopia. Somalia was thus considered expendable, just as it had been so considered by the West in 1960. It should be recalled that the U.S. and Britain had declined to aid Somalia due to the latter's *greater Somalia policy*, which sought to unite ethnic Somalians in Ethiopia and Kenya into a single Somali state. This did not bother the Soviets whose primary objective was to reduce or obliterate Western power and influence in East Africa. Notwithstanding Soviet protestation to the contrary, it was clear that Moscow's military assistance to Mogadishu encouraged subsequent Somali governments to remain steadfast vis-à-vis the concept of greater Somalia. The Soviet Union had built a modern Somalian army, while its military base in the port of Berbera provided vital strategic information to Moscow's military. The port of Berbera, built with Soviet aid in 1965-1968, was opened in April 1969. But Moscow's decision to abandon Somalia in favour of Ethiopia paved the way for U.S. entry into Somalia as both super powers armed their respective client states to fight over Ogaden. The U.S. replaced the Soviets in Somalia, and the Soviet-built port of Berbera began to serve U.S. interests.

Somalia and Ethiopia were busy soliciting for allies in their respective war policies. The report that certain Arab states were aiding Somalia provoked Ethiopia's condemnation of the "interference of reactionary Arab regimes in African problems." The Soviet News Agency, *TASS*, re-echoed Ethiopia's claim as it reported that "Saudi Arabia and other reactionary Arab regimes" were interfering in

---

[165] *Pravda*, September 2, 1977.

the conflict by aiding Somalia.[166] The Arab League meeting in Cairo, September 6, 1977, failed to attain unanimity on the issue of supporting Somalia. On its part, Ethiopia was able to reach an understanding with Kenya on how to deal with the Somali threat. In a joint communiqué following their bilateral meeting in Addis Ababa, both parties condemned "Somalian aggression against Ethiopia" and "Somalia's territorial claims toward Ethiopia and Kenya", while Kenya promised to aid Ethiopia in its war effort against "Somalian aggression."[167]

On November 15, 1977, the Somalian Government expelled all Soviet specialists and diplomats from Somalia, and renounced its Friendship Treaty with the Soviet Government. According to *TASS*, President Barre took the "unilateral decision" to abrogate the Friendship Treaty and expel Soviet diplomats and specialists "because the Soviet Union did not support Somalia's territorial pretensions" in the Horn of Africa. It declared:

> Judging by the current steps in the government of Somalia, chauvinistic and expansionistic tendencies have taken the upper hand over common sense.[168]

This was the first time that the Soviet Government admitted being solicited by Somalia to support the latter's "territorial pretensions." The expulsion of its entire diplomatic corp from Somalia was a devastating blow to Moscow unparalleled in Soviet diplomacy. It surpassed the expulsion of Soviet military advisers from Egypt in 1972. That it came from a client state the Soviet Government had carefully cultivated and nurtured further weakened Soviet prestige in Africa.

---

[166]   Pravda, September 5, and 6, 1977.

[167]   *Pravda*, September 11, 1977.

[168]   "K voprosu o sovetsko-somaliiskikh otnosheniiakh", *Pravda*, November 16, 1977.

Even in post Ogaden and the exit of the Soviet Union, the *greater Somali* concept of the SYL remained the only issue which unites Somalians. According to Mr. Warsane the "unity of all Somalis through peaceful means is still central in current Somali foreign policy." He asserted that Somalia "will seek unification through self-determination."[169] It is interesting to note that when I asked the Somali Ambassador in Moscow, on October 4, 1979, whether the Soviet Union advised Somalia to desist from the *greater Somali* policy, his response was an emphatic: "No comment." But when I asked him to forecast the future relations between Moscow and Mogadishu he pointedly stated:

> We are very optimistic regarding the future because of the similarities of our systems. Things will normalize between the USSR and Somalia. Cooperation could re-emerge, but I do not know what form it will take.[170]

---

[169] Interview with Mr. Warsane, Somali Ambassador to the Soviet Union, Moscow, October 4, 1979.

[170] *Ibid.*

CONCLUSION

My concern in the preceding chapters was to demonstrate the intricate relationship between Marxist ideological construct and national interest in the articulation of Soviet foreign policy, as well as to show the impact of the dynamics of international politics on the conduct of Soviet foreign policy. Soviet behaviour in international relations, from the October 1917 socialist revolution to the demise of the Soviet Union, strongly indicated that the Soviet Union was just like any other state in terms of the pursuit and protection of its national interest in the international scene. But, unlike non-communist states, the Soviet Union, because of the ideological basis of its policies, was always able to relate its actions to a given ideological prism: Marxism-Leninism. This, however, did not mean the supremacy of *ideology* over *national interest* in the articulation and execution of Soviet foreign policy. On the contrary, it was evident that *national interest* was the main variable of Soviet foreign policy. The Soviets employed *ideology* primarily to mollify foreign and domestic Communists. Irrespective of this, however, it would be wrong to completely discard the ideological approach. Rather it is imperative that we recognize the strong inter-relationship that existed between *national interest* and *ideology* as the two basic determinants of Soviet foreign policy. This is equally true with regards to any other state, irrespective of the colour of its ideological jacket.

Besides having to contend with the ordeal of African political realities, the Soviet Union devoted much of its time in Africa battling Chinese and Western policies. While the challenge posed by the West, as exemplified in the anti-Soviet stance of leading African allies (Kenya, South Africa, Nigeria—before 1967—, Ivory Coast, Morocco, Egypt—after 1972) compelled the Soviet Union to utilize its dwindling resources in defence of its ideology in Africa; its ideological dispute with China exposed the Soviet Union as a "social imperialist" state. The split in Africa's revolutionary movement caused by the Sino-Soviet schism was more devastating to Soviet calculations in Africa than any Western critique of its policies.

Ironically, China posed the main obstacle to Soviet overtures in Africa. When the Soviets entered Africa in the 1950s, it was on the assumption that they were leading a Communist *monolithic bloc* in a crusade to defeat Western imperialism in Africa. However, as from the early 1960s it became evident that Moscow had to fight on *two fronts* in Africa: Western imperialism and Chinese "political adventurism." Chinese anti-Soviet posture constituted a greater threat to Soviet policy than the well-known Western aggression. The Sino-Soviet conflict did not only weaken Communist design in Africa but significantly helped to expose the nagging issue of Communist "imperialism" as the Chinese sought to ally with Africa to fight Soviet "social imperialism." But in "exposing" Soviet "social imperialism", the Chinese were also seeking avenues to create their own sphere of influence that they hoped could counter Soviet sphere of influence in Africa. For example, as from 1965 China began to concentrate its efforts in East Africa. The TANZAM railway built by China was the largest Chinese economic involvement in Africa at that time. From the Chinese perspective, the TANZAM railway was Beijing's response to Moscow's Aswan Dam in Egypt.

One of the interesting revelations of the Sino-Soviet dispute was the contending burden of international politics shouldered by Moscow and Beijing, respectively. While China demanded an *immediate* conversion of major global crises into Communist gains, the Soviet Union preferred a gradual and cautious approach; while China consistently propagated armed revolutionary struggle, the Soviet Union called for restrain and demanded responsive and pragmatic actions. In the Chinese view, the revolutionary spirit had completely *withered* away in the Soviet Union. For the Soviet Union, it was merely exercising its role as a world power, the leader of the Socialist Commonwealth of Nations upon whose shoulders rested the responsibility of preserving international security and universal disarmament. The realization of this responsible role had tremendous impact on Soviet behaviour in international politics. Perhaps it was this same leadership responsibility, perceived from a different angle that prompted China to accuse the Soviet Union of ideological desertion and collaboration with U.S. imperialism for the division of the world into Soviet and U.S. spheres of influence.

While the Soviet Union was prepared, and in deed willing, to be recognized as one of the two super powers, it was at the same time propagating the demise of capitalism as a socio-economic and political system. This posed a challenge to the West, since Soviet Marxist-Leninist ideological framework did not seem to have room for peaceful cohabitation with capitalism. Arguing that its foreign policy was guided by *scientific socialist ideology*, the Soviet Union believed that it was immuned from the hazards that confronted the West in Africa. However, as was demonstrated in the preceding pages, it was obvious that the Soviet Union did not possess the foresight to escape the pitfalls its Marxist-Leninist ideology had attributed to Western imperialism.

As the founder of the Soviet state, Lenin was the only leader whose works were constantly referred to by succeeding Soviet leaders. While Joseph Stalin, Nikita Khrushchev, and Leonid Brezhnev professed their loyalty to Lenin, they differed substantially on their interpretations of Leninism. The process of ideological legitimization which each of them initiated was essentially a negation of the other. This phenomenon posed considerable problems for the Soviet Government as it had to constantly shift its policy orientation as dictated by CPSU resolutions, which in turn were determined by the changing nature of international politics. For example, Soviet fluctuating relationships with *neutralism* and *national bourgeoisie* which we analyzed in chapter four compelled Moscow to ideologically legitimize its shifting attitudes toward these phenomena. This development did not advance the position of local communists as bourgeois nationalists dominated the various liberation movements.

Soviet leaders faced a number of problems as they struggled to balance *ideology* and *national interest* in Soviet foreign policy. This was exemplified most vividly in Algeria, Egypt, Ethiopia, and Somalia. In all these cases the Soviets had to deal with nationalists inimical to communist ideology.

A comparative analysis of the Khrushchev and Brezhnev eras of Soviet policy in Africa, as evident in chapters six and seven, would, on the surface, reveal the following:

SOVIET-AFRICAN RELATIONS UNDER KHRUSHCHEV

Pro-Soviet States:
Algeria; Egypt; Ghana; Guinea; Mali.

Friendly States:
Congo (B); Ethiopia; Somalia; Sudan; Tanzania.

SOVIET-AFRICAN RELATIONS UNDER BREZHNEV

Pro-Soviet States:
Angola; Benin Republic; Congo (B); Ethiopia; Libya; Mozambique.

Friendly States:
Nigeria; Sudan; Tanzania; Zimbabwe.

The period 1957-1962 was a revolutionizing occasion in Africa as the anti-colonial movements swept away most European empires on the continent. Many of the emergent Africa states, like Algeria, Ghana, Guinea and Mali, had charismatic leaders whose maladaptive foreign policies appealed to Soviet ideological posture in Africa. In the other *moderate* states, which were considered pro-West, for example, Nigeria and Kenya, radical political thought was also aligned to Soviet posture. Thus, the Khrushchev regime in the Kremlin did not have much difficulty exploiting the profound anti-colonial sentiments across the continent. Khrushchev succeeded in establishing the basis for Soviet *penetration* into the continent. Even though he also succeeded in maintaining Soviet friendship with a number of African states, it is debatable whether he could have been able to retain these states if he had not been overthrown in October 1964. We therefore do not know how his regime would have handled the turbulence of the late 1960s and 1970s as internal revolts reigned over Africa.

Under Brezhnev, the Soviet Union *lost* Egypt, Ghana, Guinea, Mali, and Somalia. While the *loss* of Ghana and Mali could be attributed to the military coups that ousted Kwame Nkrumah and Modibo Keita on February 24, 1966 and November 19, 1968, respectively, it is safe to say that Moscow *lost* Egypt and Somalia due to the mismanagement of its relations with these states. It failed to reach an accord with Egypt at a time when President Anwar Sadat was striving to pursue an *independent* foreign policy. It is interesting to note that though the controversy between Khrushchev and President Abdel Nasser was more profound than that between Brezhnev and Sadat, yet Moscow did not *lose* Egypt under Khrushchev. While the schism between Conakry and Moscow emanated from the Solod affair under Khrushchev, Guinea and the Soviet Union did manage to re-establish their comradely relationships before the Kremlin coup that overthrew Khrushchev in October 1964. Under Brezhnev, however, we witnessed a systematic deterioration of Soviet-Guinean relations as Moscow was no longer able to provide meaningful assistance to Conakry. Thus, Sekou Toure began his courtship of Washington and Paris. With regards to Somalia, the zeal with which the Brezhnev regime courted Siad Barre's military junta and converted it into a *socialist vanguard* betrayed the opportunistic tendencies that were inherent in Soviet ideological construct. Because it wanted to oust Washington from the Horn of Africa, Moscow bank-rolled the militarization of Barre's junta and in the process created a monster that it was unable to control.

On the basis of the analyses contained in the preceding chapters it might be pertinent to ask whether the Soviets were consistent in the pursuit of Moscow's foreign policy. The author would not hesitate to state that the Soviets were remarkably consistent in their foreign policy. From Lenin to Brezhnev (and to the end of the Soviet Union in December 1991) Soviet leaders upheld the primacy of *national interest* in Soviet foreign policy. This did not prevent them from propagating the communization of the world. This propaganda technique was a lubricant for the Soviet political system, without which the CPSU could easily have lost its grip on the masses long before the collapse of Sovietism. As a non-ruling party the Bolshevik party retained the revolutionary flavour of Marxism that terrorized European democracies in the inter-war years, but as leaders of a State the Bolsheviks began to recognize the primacy of Soviet national interest over ideology. Communists outside the Soviet orbit did not appreciate this position, as was exemplified by George Padmore following the Nazi-Soviet Non-Aggression Pact. However, what was vital to Soviet leaders was the satisfaction of the basic needs of Soviet citizens. They realized that this was best achieved by promoting Soviet national interest couched in Marxist-Leninist terminology.